Human Resource Management: Ethics and Employment

Human Resource Management: Ethics and Employment

Edited by

Ashly H. Pinnington

Rob Macklin

Tom Campbell

OXFORD

UNIVERSITY PRESS

OXFORD
UNIVERSITY PRESS

Great Clarendon Street, Oxford ox2 6DP

Oxford University Press is a department of the University of Oxford.
It furthers the University's objective of excellence in research, scholarship,
and education by publishing worldwide in

Oxford New York

Auckland Cape Town Dar es Salaam Hong Kong Karachi
Kuala Lumpur Madrid Melbourne Mexico City Nairobi
New Delhi Shanghai Taipei Toronto

With offices in

Argentina Austria Brazil Chile Czech Republic France Greece
Guatemala Hungary Italy Japan Poland Portugal Singapore
South Korea Switzerland Thailand Turkey Ukraine Vietnam

Oxford is a registered trade mark of Oxford University Press
in the UK and in certain other countries

Published in the United States
by Oxford University Press Inc., New York

First published 2007

British Library Cataloguing in Publication Data
Data available

Library of Congress Cataloging in Publication Data

Human resource management: ethics and employment / edited by Ashly
Pinnington, Rob Macklin, Tom Campbell.
    p.   cm.
    Includes bibliographical references and index.
1. Personnel management–Moral and ethical aspects.   I. Pinnington,
Ashly. H.   II. Macklin, Rob.   III. Campbell, Tom, 1938–
    HF5549.H8427 2007
    174'.–dc22   2006026542

Typeset by SPI Publisher Services, Pondicherry, India
Printed in Great Britain
on acid-free paper by Biddles Ltd., King's Lynn, Norfolk

ISBN 978-0-19-920378-9 (hb)
ISBN 978-0-19-920379-6 (pb)

1 3 5 7 9 10 8 6 4 2

☐ ACKNOWLEDGEMENTS

The editors would like to thank the Centre for Applied Philosophy and Public Ethics (CAPPE), (Australian National University, Charles Sturt University, University of Melbourne), an Australian Research Council Special Research Centre, which sponsored the workshop on Ethics and Human Resource Management in Sydney, April 2004. Also, financial support was received from UQ Business School, The University of Queensland, for some of the expenses in developing this book. The workshop, from which it originated, was administered by Sheena Smith, then a Research Assistant at CAPPE, who also participated in the workshop. Our thanks to those who attended the workshop and contributed papers, commentaries, and suggestions: David Ardagh (Charles Sturt University), Lynne Bennington (La Trobe University), Breen Creighton (Corrs Chambers Westgarth, Melbourne), Michelle Greenwood (Monash University), David Guest (King's College, London), Robin Kramar (Macquarie University), Karen Legge (Warwick University), Gill Palmer (Monash University), Les Pickett (Australian Human Resource Institute), Chris Provis (University of South Australia), Sheena Smith (Australian National University), Bernadine Van Gramberg (Victoria University of Technology), and Adrian Walsh (University of New England). Thanks are also due to Karen Legge, David Guest, and Tony Watson (University of Nottingham) for reviewing some of the subsequent draft chapters for the book.

☐ CONTENTS

PART III **PROGRESSING HUMAN RESOURCE MANAGEMENT**

⬚ LIST OF FIGURES

☐ LIST OF TABLES

☐ LIST OF CONTRIBUTORS

David Ardagh, Senior Lecturer in HRM, School of Commerce, Charles Sturt University, New South Wales, Australia.

Serkan Bayraktaroglu, Associate Professor of HRM, Department of Business Studies, Sakarya University, Adapazari, Turkey.

Lynne Bennington, Professor and Head of School of Management, RMIT Business, RMIT University, Melbourne, Victoria, Australia.

Peter Boxall, Professor of Human Resource Management, Department of Management and Employment Relations, The University of Auckland Business School, Auckland, New Zealand.

Tom Campbell, Professorial Fellow, Program Manager, Business and Professional Ethics, Centre for Applied Philosophy and Public Ethics, Charles Sturt University, Canberra, Australian Capital Territory, Australia.

Breen Creighton, Professorial Fellow, Faculty of Law, University of Melbourne, Victoria, Australia.

Helen De Cieri, Professor and Director of the Australian Centre for Research in Employment and Work (ACREW), Department of Management, Monash University, Melbourne, Victoria, Australia.

Adam M. Grant, Doctoral Candidate in Organizational Psychology, University of Michigan, Ann Arbor, Michigan, USA.

Michelle Greenwood, Assistant Lecturer, Department of Management, Monash University, Melbourne, Victoria, Australia.

David E. Guest, Professor of Organizational Psychology and Human Resource Management, Department of Management, King's College, London, UK.

Ken Kamoche, Associate Professor, Department of Management, City University of Hong Kong, Hong Kong.

Karen Legge, Professor of Organisational Behaviour, Industrial Relations and Organisational Behaviour Group, Warwick Business School, University of Warwick, Coventry, UK.

Rob Macklin, Senior Lecturer, School of Business, Charles Sturt University, Albury, New South Wales, Australia.

Joshua D. Margolis, Associate Professor, Harvard Business School, Boston, Massachusetts, USA.

Andrew L. Molinsky, Assistant Professor of Organizational Behavior, Brandeis International Business School, Waltham, Massachusetts, USA.

Gill Palmer, Professor and Dean of the Faculty of Business and Economics, Monash University, Melbourne, Victoria, Australia.

Ashly H. Pinnington, Professor of Human Resource Management, Aberdeen Business School, The Robert Gordon University, Aberdeen, Scotland, UK.

John Purcell, Professor of Human Resource Management, Director of the Work and Employment Research Centre, School of Management, University of Bath, Bath, UK.

Michael I. Reed, Professor of Organisational Analysis (Human Resource Management Section) and Associate Dean (Research), Cardiff Business School, Cardiff University, Wales, UK.

Sheena Smith, Postgraduate Research Student, Department of Philosophy, Australian National University, Canberra, ACT 0200, Australia.

Tom Sorell, John Ferguson Professor of Global Ethics, University of Birmingham, Birmingham, UK.

Adrian Walsh, Senior Lecturer, School of Social Science, University of New England, Armidale, New South Wales, and Research Associate, Centre for Applied Philosophy and Public Ethics, University of Melbourne, Melbourne, Victoria, Australia.

Tony J. Watson, Professor of Organisational Behaviour, Nottingham University Business School, University of Nottingham, Nottingham, UK.

Introduction: ethical human resource management*

Ashly Pinnington, Rob Macklin, and Tom Campbell

It is a curious fact that the current surge of interest in business ethics has largely bypassed the theory and the practice of human resource management (HRM). While business as a whole is presenting itself more and more in terms of social responsibility, and employees are routinely accepted as crucial stakeholders in most business organizations, HRM practice continues to affirm its significance for corporate profitability and prefers to distance itself from its traditional welfare image. It is, therefore, timely to revisit the subject of ethics in employment with respect to HRM, and to do so in a way that brings out the complexity of articulating a conception of ethical HRM that goes beyond a shaky affirmation that 'good ethics is always good for business'.

The contemporary context

Business ethics as a field of study and as an issue with currency in the broader community has grown considerably in recent years. This interest has been increased, it can be suggested, by a series of corporate scandals that have stimulated a small explosion in academic publications on corporate governance (Zoffer and Fram 2005) and led to a greater concern to include ethics courses in business school curricula (Crane 2004; Elliott 2004; Evans and Marcal 2005; Koehn 2005).

At the regulatory level many government bodies have or are establishing mechanisms to facilitate good business practices. For example, in the USA in July 2002 the Sarbanes-Oxley Act was passed, while in Australia the Federal government has adopted an approach that focuses on providing principles that help to educate people in organizations about good corporate governance (Williamson-Noble and Haynes 2003). In the UK, the government

* The editors acknowledge the significant contribution made by Sheena Smith to this introduction and thank her for all her work on the project as a whole.

encourages adoption and reporting on corporate social responsibility (CSR) through guidance on best practice, regulation, and fiscal incentives (DTI 2004). In addition, within the corporate sector it would now appear that there is also a growing interest in the development of corporate codes of conduct or ethics (Florini 2003). In this respect the Illinois Institute of Technology, Center for the Study of Ethics in the Professions, 'Codes of Ethics Online' provides a large and growing collection of codes drawn from a wide variety of industries including communication, IT, engineering, finance, and real estate.

Given all of these initiatives in business ethics and CSR, one might expect a similar growth of interest in ethics and HRM. After all an extremely important component of making business more ethical is to take seriously the ethical aspects of managing people (Winstanley and Woodall 2000a). A review of the literature does indeed reveal a modest growth of interest in the subject. Over the last decade there have been a number of books, edited collections (Parker 1988a; Winstanley and Woodall 2000b; Woodall and Winstanley 2001), and articles published on ethics in academic journals (e.g. *Personnel Review* Vol 25, No 6 1996) and elsewhere (e.g. Schumann 2001; Shultz and Brender-Ilan 2004; Weaver 2001). Nevertheless, it has not really kept pace with developments in the broader field of business ethics.

Many business ethics textbooks contain chapters on the ethical issues that may arise in the employment relationship, including the ethics of discrimination, and employees' rights and duties (e.g. DesJardins and McCall 2005; Jennings 2006; Velasquez 2006). However, often they focus on individual practices rather than on the ethics of HRM policies and practices in organizations or on the roles of human resource (HR) practitioners. There is, therefore, a need to address these gaps in the business ethics literature to foster more debate on ethics amongst HR practitioners, commentators, and academics.

Bringing ethical awareness into the core of HRM is all the more important given the trend in Western societies towards decline of trade unionism and the emergence of more individualist approaches to employment (Deery and Mitchell 2000; Peetz 2004; and Legge Chapter 2 in this volume). The turn towards individualism in employment has arguably placed the morality of HRM increasingly in the hands of managers and HR managers in particular. In the past, the employment relations practices of employers were more open to scrutiny by other powerful parties such as trade unions and industrial tribunals. These collectivist systems of industrial relations (IR) helped to maintain some checks on employers who sought to exploit their employees. Moreover, collective agreements and especially those with clauses on the conduct of the employment relationship, acted as a guide for many employers and employees as to what constituted acceptable behaviour.

The decline of collectivist arrangements has left many employees potentially more vulnerable to opportunistic and unethical behaviour (Watson et al.

2003). Except in occupations where market conditions overwhelmingly favour the employee, employers are in an increasingly powerful position to govern and dominate the employment relationship (Smith 1997). This throws more into question the morality of contemporary HRM and increases the significance of engaging in moral evaluation of the behaviour of directors, managers, and HR practitioners. It is within this broad context that this book seeks to highlight the ethical and moral dimensions of HRM.

There are many different ways of defining HRM (e.g. for a more detailed discussion Legge 1995; Storey 2001). 'HRM' may be seen as one amongst many possible labels, such as 'personnel management', that denote the *generic* practices pertaining to certain functions such as recruitment, selection, training, remuneration, promotion, and separation. Alternatively, HRM may be seen as identifying a particular approach to such functions of employment rather than as a generic name for the management of employees within a public or private service organization. Its common conception of 'people management' is one that focuses on the creation and sustainment of a committed, loyal, and capable workforce required to deliver significant competitive benefits for the organization (Legge 1995: 64–7). According to Storey (1995), HRM in this more *specific* sense involves line and top management in pursuing the belief that a committed and capable workforce will give the organization a competitive advantage. It offers a theory of HR decisions as being of strategic and commercial importance and promotes development of an organizational culture of consensus, commitment, and flexibility. Within this specific conception of HRM, Storey helpfully distinguishes a 'soft' and a 'hard' version of HRM. Emphasis on culture is associated with soft HRM (although even soft HRM sees itself as promoting long-term profitability) in which employees are regarded as a source of creative energy and participants in workplace decision-making, while an emphasis on alignment of HRM with the strategy and structure is more characteristic of a hard version of HRM that is more explicitly focused on organizational rationality, control, and profitability (Pinnington and Lafferty 2003).

It is often argued that the stereotypes of hard and soft HRM are both inimical to ethics because they attend to the profit motive without giving enough consideration to other morally relevant concerns such as social justice and human development. It remains a matter for empirical research whether the hard and soft stereotypes of HRM in some circumstances offer the most effective means of maximizing corporate profitability. Even so, it is an important ethical issue whether the moral issues outweigh pragmatic concerns for organizational profitability. Clearly, these clusters of empirical, normative, and substantive questions cannot be resolved solely by terminological definition or even through a singular mode of conceptual analysis (Graham 2004). Therefore, we determine in this book to assume a generic and open-ended definition of HRM as denoting a bundle of functions relating to the management of employees, thus encouraging a certain open-mindedness on the ethical and moral questions that arise. Most of the contributors to this book work with such a generic conception of HRM. Nevertheless it is important to keep in mind that the context of this work is one in which the more instrumental connotations of HRM as a contemporary form of strategic employee management for enhancing corporate profitability is frequently assumed to be the dominant paradigm.

Business ethics and HRM

'Business ethics' we understand in this book as referring to the moral evaluation of the goals, policies, practices, and decisions taken within business organizations as they impact on human well-being, fairness, justice, humanity, and decency. Here, the term 'ethics' is synonymous with 'morality' which are in general equivalent terms, the former stemming from Greek and the latter from Latin roots. Both refer to that aspect of human experience which involves making what purport to be impartial judgements as to the ultimate rightness and wrongness of conduct and the values to which priority ought to be given in personal, social, and political decision-making (Maclagan 1998). In so far as the usage of the two terms does diverge, ethics is more commonly deployed to refer to what we call 'role performance' which applies to the conduct of persons fulfilling a particular social role, such as parent, or employer, while morality has a more general connotation, ranging from personal behaviour to the assessment of laws and social organizations (see, e.g. Baier 1958; Beauchamp and Bowie 2004; Solomon 1997).

Often business ethics is presented in terms of the decisions facing individuals as board members, managers, or employees and the dilemmas (i.e. choices between competing moral considerations), or temptations (as in conflicts of interest) facing them. However, these individual choices have to be seen in the context of the roles that people are expected to play within a specific organization operating in a particular type of political, economic, and social system. This means that business ethics has to consider the moral critique of business and management practice as a whole and not just address the behaviour of individual managers and others. It is individuals who must ultimately make moral choices, either on their own or collectively, but identifying what choices exist and decisions they ought to make requires analysis of the morality of the existing and potential system and its constituent roles (Bowie and Werhane 2005: 1–20; MacIntyre 1981, 1988).

This broad approach to business ethics does not entail that ethics in business is something that comes into business ready made from the wider world as an external imposition of standards that have been developed and refined elsewhere. Rather, business has its own ethics, a specific ethics that draws on general moral principles but refines and develops these in the light of its own particular goals, requirements, institutions, and objectives. Consequently, business ethics is not a compartmentalized add-on to business, but a *dimension* of business and specifically one that is inescapably present in all management decisions.

In making this point we nevertheless recognize that in recent times some writers have sought to critique the foundations of ethics. Writers commonly associated with postmodernist ways of thinking have been strongly critical of the assumption that our actions and pursuit of an ethical existence can be justified by returning to the essence of the matter or by explaining exemplars and relating master narratives (Lyotard 1984). Many postmodernists eschew such descriptions purporting to demonstrate how the world and societies operate, and caution against giving general prescriptions on how it should operate (Bauman 1989, 1994, 1995).

Bauman's questioning (1993) of attempts to ground ethics in foundations or essences has been especially influential on some of the recent academic debates within business and management and organizational theory (Jones, Parker, and Bos 2005; Parker 1998a, 1998b). He draws attention to the immoralities apparent within modernist and totalitarian government rule suggesting that they are nurtured by a bureaucratization of the ethical. Many of the technical procedures and rule-following behaviours characteristic of modern societies, he argues, often promote an emotional distance and lack of respect for others, and particularly for those who are relatively more disadvantaged (Munro 1998). To avoid a descent into nihilism, Bauman proposes that the way out of the dilemma is through encouraging development in others of what he calls the 'moral impulse'. His post-foundationalist approach to ethics endeavours to overcome some of the inevitable confusion created by empirical relativism and moral uncertainty by inviting individuals to transcend their egoistic moral understandings of the social self and consequently, act more caringly and responsibly towards others (Benhabib 1992; Legge 1998a, 1998b; Letiche 1998; Willmott 1998).

In general, the chapters within this book are not 'against ethics' as such although all are to varying degrees critical of ethical codes or moral recipes that oversimplify the realities of making moral decisions. All of the contributors to this book are interested in understanding the many duties, responsibilities, and issues of care and concern for others that arise within employment and in HRM. This means that in some cases norms, principles, and codes are raised and discussed, but we suggest this is largely done with an awareness of the deleterious effect that creating rules can have on the autonomy of others. The chapters address both the more recent and other long-standing debates on ethics and moral problems through adopting a wide variety of perspectives on business, ethics, HRM, and employment. The summaries in the remainder of this Introduction, bring out the common thread of a concern for the role of HRM in the structure and dynamics of both (business) utility and moral decency in modern employment relations.

The chapter contents

Part I (Situating Human Resource Management) deals with the economic, political, and legal contexts within which ethical issues in contemporary HRM arise, including employment relations, theories of management, economic philosophy, strategic management, innovation, and the productive use of physical and human resources. Part II (Analysing Human Resource Management) looks at the emerging practices and institutional settings of HRM in ways that bring to the fore their ethical dimensions. Here, the prospect of HRM as an emerging profession with distinctive ethical commitments and responsibilities for workplace business ethics, justice, and human rights is considered critically in the light of existing and potential cultural, legal, and economic frameworks. Part III (Progressing Human Resource Management) explores the avenues for reforming HRM in the light of different managerial futures, moral philosophies, and institutional arrangements.

All of the six chapters in Part I concentrate on the contemporary macroenvironment, albeit from very different perspectives.

Chapter 1 by Gill Palmer (Socio-political theory and ethics in HRM) seeks to contextualize the comparatively new discipline of specific HRM in older debates on the management of people at work (generic HRM). Generic HRM is related to socio-political frameworks that have been used to understand the nature of authority, government, and consent within society. Three types of political theory are discussed: unitarist, radical, and pluralist. Palmer charts the historical changes of focus and content of the debates ranging from unitary theories with their use of organic analogies and emphasis upon the managerial prerogative to radical theories seeking to end the exploitation they believe to be inherent in capitalist employment relations. In more recent times, the debates have tended to focus less on arbitrating between the oppositions of unitary and radical theories and more upon how to deal with an inevitable plurality of interests at work. Three major theoretical approaches throughout the twentieth century are compared and contrasted: liberal-individual pluralism, liberal-collective pluralism, and coordinated, neo-corporatist pluralism.

Liberalism, it is argued, remains the basis of our modern economic and political democratic thought, although it has been suffused by concepts from corporatism emphasizing the roles of the nation state for regulating or influencing the economy and labour markets. Using illustrations from central Europe and China, Palmer notes that whereas there are common and ingrained social and political values evident in many Western economies they have not been sufficiently influential to erase substantial differences occurring across the globe in the normative organization of work.

Chapter 2 by Karen Legge (The ethics of HRM in dealing with individual employees without collective representation) examines the slow death of collectivism and the distinctions between the respective ethics of individualism and collectivism. In the context of autonomy at work, the privileges and benefits pertaining to knowledge workers are contrasted with the much tighter constraints and more limited benefits faced by routine service sector workers. Legge asks what would constitute the most ethical employment relations system for employees without collective representation. Her conclusion is that collective representation is essential for establishing and preserving a just and reasonable level of equality of relationship between employer and employee.

Legge considers what forms such representation might take and proposes that the most realistic role for trade unions will be to work within the pressures and restrictions of individualistic, consumer-oriented culture. Essentially this requires playing the instrumental collectivist role whereby unions are first and foremost a means of redressing individual employees' vulnerabilities when dealing with employers. This position is arrived at through the examination of recent developments in HRM and employee relations applying Isaiah Berlin's 'positive' and 'negative' conceptions of liberty as the means of analysis. The overall picture presented is one in which groups of employees without collective representation are not enjoying the good life at work as a result of explicit or implicit HRM policies. Furthermore, there is little evidence that what is ethically desirable for employees is emerging out of the contemporary roles and responsibilities of HRM.

Chapter 3 by David Guest (HRM and performance: can partnership address the ethical dilemmas?) reflects on the idea that HRM has been built on two main propositions that: (a) people are a source of competitive advantage, and (b) effective management of HR should lead to superior performance. In this context, Guest addresses four issues in HRM which raise potential ethical questions. The first is that while HRM claims to be primarily concerned with the management of people, in practice it largely ignores them, and second, that HRM is a subtle way of exploiting people. The third is the research on HRM and performance is far more provisional than some of its proponents and followers claim, and the fourth is the challenges and problems that are created when attempting to apply an integrated HR system in these circumstances.

Guest draws the reader's attention to the significance of research work on HRM and performance conducted during the 1990s which found strong evidence for a relationship between the two. However, he criticizes the discipline both in terms of research endeavour and as a management practice for sometimes paying no more than lip service to the tenet that 'people are our most important asset'. Evidence from research studies of recent implementations of HR practices designed to achieve a 'high-commitment' workforce suggests that first most people prefer soft HRM to the other available approaches and second, moral safeguards, nevertheless, need to be established. These would include HR systems focused on employee well-being, such as in establishing and maintaining channels for independent employee voice. Ethical problems, he argues, also arise from institutions making inflated pronouncements on the extent of causal linkage existing between implementing HR practices and achieving improved performance. This is a particular consideration for governments, consultancies, and professional bodies where the temptation to exaggerate the efficacy of HR practices can be greater than within the academic research context. Since the early 1990s there has been growing talk of partnerships between employers and trade unions, but the evidence is that they have not really taken root, in part due to mistrust remaining on both sides. Guest concludes that partnership still has the potential to address a number of ethical concerns in HRM practice, but cautions his reader to be sanguine about the limited adoption and efficacy of HRM to date.

Chapter 4 by Peter Boxall and John Purcell (Strategic management and human resources: the pursuit of productivity, flexibility, and legitimacy) is concerned with the nature of strategic HRM (SHRM), its role and influence on business performance and the ethical issues involved in this relationship. It commences by defining strategy and reviewing common strategic problems facing firms, inquiring how HRM contributes to a firm's viability and the achievement of competitive advantage. The central ethical question addressed is the way that managers pursue their goals for labour productivity and organizational flexibility whilst also meeting the requirements for social legitimacy. These goals are often in tension.

Boxall and Purcell's chapter adopts a broad view of business performance and presents an innovative conceptual framework for a socially responsible and sustainable model of generic HRM. While many business analysts accept the goal domains of labour productivity and organizational flexibility, the authors argue that the pursuit of legitimacy is also vital because firms are always 'embedded in structures of social relations' (Granovetter 1985). In summary, legitimacy is a contested area wherein employers and employees must observe the ethicality of their actions in the eyes of others.

Chapter 5 by Breen Creighton (Ethical employment practices and the law) commences by noting that ideas about what constitutes ethical behaviour tend to reflect the moral values of society at a particular point in time. This chapter focuses specifically on the extent to which the law can be seen to mandate and/or facilitate ethical employment practices in Australia in the early-twenty-first century. On the one hand, current legislative provision retains a distinctive 'IR' character. On the other hand, as in other countries such as the UK,

New Zealand, and the USA, it has also clearly been influenced by HRM and ER practices and assumptions.

Ethical behaviour in this context comprises four key elements: respect for individual employees' dignity and personal integrity, protecting their physical and mental integrity, providing access to 'decent work', and moderating the detrimental effects of power imbalances between buyers and sellers of labour. The historical role and contribution of the law as a facilitator of ethical behaviour is examined, first in the law of master and servant and family law and then in modern statute law. Creighton concludes that for over 200 years there has been legislative recognition that it would be unacceptable from an ethical perspective to leave the well-being of working people entirely at the mercy of market forces.

This is reflected in the fact that after federation in 1901, a process of compulsory conciliation and arbitration became established and remained in place until a fundamental reorientation of the system occurred in the early 1990s. The recent changes are characterized by a move away from centralized regulation of terms and conditions by awards of tribunals in favour of direct negotiation at the level of the enterprise. Since 1996 there has been a further shift in favour of individualization and 'de-collectivization' of work relations. This process was given further impetus by major legislative changes that were adopted in late 2005. Despite these shifts in emphasis, the law continues to make some attempt to encourage ethical employment practices. Reflecting on the achievement of the Australian system in this context Creighton concludes: 'The collectivist character of the provisions relating to awards and agreements may strike a discordant note for some observers, and for some participants in the system. But the contribution is none the less real for that.'

Chapter 6 by Adrian Walsh (HRM and the ethics of commodified work in a market economy) examines HRM from the perspectives of political and economic philosophy. It argues that work in a market economy can be exploitative and lead to commodification but not to such an extent that renders an ethical HRM impossible. Walsh argues that the market presents employers with certain 'moral hazards' especially in areas where employers and employees do not have shared interests. The chapter focuses on three areas of concern: attitudes towards wealth, economic exploitation, and the content of work. Its central assumption is that regarding employees solely and ultimately as *mere* commodities is unethical. In essence, market institutions such as price corrode our capacity to value goods intrinsically.

Contemporary HRM is commonly declared to have more of a focus on the profit motive than had previous forms of personnel management, but ethical problems arise whenever the profit motive leads to exploitative wage–labour contracts. Moreover, market economies often place systematic pressure on participants to increase the level of exploitation of available labour, for example, by aggressively reducing labour costs to meet falling prices for goods and services, although this is not to say that pursuing profit is inherently unethical. Walsh distinguishes 'lucrepathic action' (profit-making is an all-encompassing motive) from 'accumulative action' (profit-making is moderated by moral constraints) and 'stipendiary action' (profit-making is not a central goal). He reasons that the responsibility of employers is to desist from acting lucrepathically, and following Amartya Sen's capabilities approach, advises that both employers and employees should regard work as more than just a way of gaining an income. Work, as Sen and others have argued, ought to function primarily as a meaningful context for the further development of our capabilities.

The next six chapters in Part II (Analysing HRM) concentrate on the contemporary organization but still situated within its broader environment, particularly ethical theories and perspectives on HRM such as stakeholder theory, moral advocacy, moral decency, cultural leadership, appropriation, and contemporary collectivist and individualist moralities. All of the chapters within this section concentrate on difficult questions of ethics facing employers, managers, and people working specifically in the HR function.

Chapter 7 by Michelle Greenwood and Helen De Cieri (Stakeholder theory and the ethics of HRM) analyses the potential of stakeholder theory as an approach to formulating and enacting ethical HRM. The authors note that stakeholder theory focuses on the relationship between organizations and constituent groups, which they suggest offers a fruitful and alternative way of conceptualizing ethics in contrast to existing debates on rights and procedural justice in employment relations. The stakeholder concept narrowly defined refers to groups that the organization depends on, typically shareowners, employees, customers, lenders, and society (Freeman 1984). A claimant definition of stakeholders however is preferred by the authors whereby: 'A stakeholder is an individual or group that has a moral claim, by virtue of a sacrifice or contribution and therefore is owed a moral duty by the organization.'

Greenwood and De Cieri note that the ethical debates in HRM adopt either a macro-level environmental analysis or a micro-level focus on individual practices. At the macro end of the scale, the central subject for ethical scrutiny is HRM as a system. This analysis corresponds to some extent with the SHRM literature's focus on multiple practices at the organizational level of analysis (Wright and Boswell 2002). Macro-level research has the potential to reach beyond the limitations of these methodologies by conceptualizing the totality of HRM within the contexts of both corporate and societal levels of analysis. Greenwood and De Cieri review the contribution of stakeholder theory in managerial discourses and the moral duty of management to act in the interests of stakeholders and engage them in decision-making. Stakeholder engagement places specific moral demands on managers through understanding employees as moral claimant stakeholders rather than simply 'strategic stakeholders'. The authors observe that the economic costs of this scenario can be especially high and may not always be justified, but other approaches present opportunity for moral hazard and expose the vulnerability of employees to unethical treatment.

Chapter 8 by Lynne Bennington (HR managers as ethics agents of the state) focuses on the ethical duty of legal compliance in equal employment opportunity (EEO) and affirmative action (AA). It observes that the amount of common and statute law has increased over the last thirty years imposing greater responsibilities and duties on employers and their respective HRM teams. The situation is an especially challenging one for HR managers when, at least in the USA, they have been excluded from legislated whistle-blowing protection and are only advocates of EEO within strict boundaries. Bennington argues that the state can expect little improvement in employer conduct in areas such as EEO and AA until better protection is offered to employees working within HRM aiming to ensure legal compliance.

With the onset of private sector styles of operation in the new public management, the public sector has lost its premier position as a role model for sector adherence to EEO legislation. Consequently, controls over consistency, fairness, and equity in personnel systems have become weakened. Employers adopt different perspectives ranging from hostility to support; external recruitment consultants do not always adhere to EEO laws; and applicants for jobs more often than not are in a weak position to identify or counteract recruitment and selection practices that are unfairly discriminating. This has tipped the balance towards a corporatist focus rather than, for example, an employee-centred approach. A broad survey of legal protection of HRM managers who seek to go down this path demonstrates little effective protection.

Chapter 9 by David Ardagh (The ethical basis for HRM professionalism and codes of conduct) searches for an invigorated profession of HRM by investigating the potential of combining Aristotelian ideas of virtue ethics with current criteria for assessment of what constitutes an exemplary profession. His purpose is to empower practitioners to uphold high ethical standards. Members of an HRM profession, he argues, should be supported to the point where they can be relied on to espouse strong moral values, possess integrity, and demonstrate independence in the exercise of their professional responsibilities and duties.

Ardagh contends that the Aristotelian idea of basing ethics on the development of capacities and perfection through virtue continues to hold relevance for people, including employees working in HRM. In this neo-Aristotelian system of ethics, the ideal object is 'well-being', abstractly understood as living and acting well—known as eudaimonia. Influenced by the neo-Aristotelian conceptualization of ethics, Ardagh recommends professionalization of HRM and granting it greater authority as steps towards forming a much stronger corporate conscience. He discusses how a number of criteria for forming a profession are missing in contemporary HRM systems—mandatory training process, self-licensing, exams/induction, monopoly control, a tradition of practice, and an enforced code of ethics. In addition, there are a number of other criteria which he outlines as necessary and desirable for creating a rigorous HRM profession. These include a code of conduct specifying altruistic duty to clients, a de-registering mechanism, mandatory continuing education, fiduciary relationships, professional-like detachment, strong public ethics relevance, the right to advocate within an institutionalized system, and the expectation of potential clashes with as organizational policy.

Inevitably, such changes would require substantial change in social policy and corporate law reform. Ardagh argues in favour of a social concessional model of corporations and for increased corporate moral responsibility. To educate HR professionals, he recommends an interdisciplinary social policy and social economics curriculum, adopting an overt critical, justice-oriented approach.

Chapter 10 by Michael Reed (Engineers of human souls, faceless technocrats or merchants of morality?) examines changing professional forms and identities in Western countries following from more than ten years of neo-liberal government policies. It seeks to draw attention to three possible ethical futures for professionalism. The first phrase (engineers of human souls) refers to a simplistic vision of return to the traditional professional values of autonomy and ethical service. The second phrase (faceless technocrats) evokes a managerialist and technological determinist future for the profession-exhorting professionals to become thoroughly reconciled to serving the goals of corporate capital, whereas the third (merchants of morality) is intended to indicate an emergent role for the professions and professionals as purveyors of trust during an age of public suspicion and corporate uncertainty.

Reed reflects on the fact that professionalization of the expert division of labour was the dominant strategy for occupational closure over much of the previous century. During the last three decades, however, a number of crises have occurred within the Western traditional liberal professions and the political economies of welfare states resulting in a somewhat more fragmented collection of competing occupations.

Under such circumstances, he asks, 'How is institutionalized trust, as the structural cornerstone and cultural lodestone of professionalism, to be generated and sustained in an economic, social, and political environment dominated by unregulated market competition, unrestrained consumerism, and rampant individualism?' His answer is a somewhat pessimistic one since he sees little prospect of reestablishing the autonomy of professions, of their public acceptance of skilled social engineers. Nevertheless, he sees a continuing role for professions in providing theories, programmes, and control technologies operating simultaneously at the macro level of institutional governance and at the micro-level of individual choice and subjectivity. In summary, the politics of expertise in advanced capitalist societies is becoming increasingly complex, contested, and uncertain as to its longer-term implications for professional jurisdiction, power, and values. This means that professional contexts can only offer increasingly undecided contexts for formulating ethical frameworks, discussing, and making moral decisions.

Chapter 11 by Ashly Pinnington and Serkan Bayraktaroglu (Ethical leadership in employee development) challenges people working within HRM to pursue employee development more vigorously than has occurred in the previous century. The chapter identifies ways that HRM can become more capable of ensuring joint fulfilment of organizational goals and employees' interests. Its central contention is that HRM has in the past had a tendency to overplay the significance of the organization's part of the bargain and has failed to exercise leadership through somewhat blatantly ignoring employees' development.

The problem of one-sided managerial prescription is examined and it is proposed that it fails to serve employees both ethically and economically. Then research conducted on HRM and performance during the 1990s is considered and its preference for operationalizing narrow and somewhat naive conceptualizations of strategy is critiqued. The predominance of simplistic quantitative criteria for measuring performance outcomes in research studies is noted and the suggestion made that HRM should be considered applying both economic and cultural frames of reference. The term 'cultural capital' is introduced defined broadly as subsuming a variety of types of capital that are irreducible purely to economic relations. As a way of thinking more insightfully about leadership and employee development, the concepts of economic and cultural capital developed by the late sociologist Pierre Bourdieu are proposed. The cultural aspect of Bourdieu's theory of practice is applied to two case studies on HRM leadership in employee development. The cases illustrating employee-centred and business-dominated leadership styles are discussed and finally recommendations are made for establishing more ethical practice in HRM.

Chapter 12 by Tom Sorell (Ethics and work in emergencies: the UK fire service strike 2002–3) addresses contemporary Western economies' IR and collective bargaining processes in the specific context of emergency services work analysing the case of industrial action carried out in 2002–3 by the UK fire services. Collective action by trade unions operating in emergency services, Sorell notes, has traditionally been regarded as morally sensitive and it has taken new significance throughout Western countries since September 11 2001.

The morality of the strike first declared by the Fire Brigades Union (FBU) in November 2002 is discussed, and so is the justification of various governmental and management attempts to reorganize work so that emergency and disaster services workers deal more proactively with terrorist problems than has been expected of them hitherto. The new terrorism duties allocated to the

UK fire service in contrast significantly strengthen its claims for exceptional treatment in pay negotiations. Not only are these duties often burdensome when discharged, they are likely to involve dangerous tasks. Tom Sorell concludes that the UK fire service strike demonstrates the need to disaggregate the general category of emergency service work and occupations and the importance of analysing more carefully the fairness of allocation of tasks and responsibilities within occupations such as the fire brigade or the police. Perhaps most significant, it asserts that politicians, public service officials, employers, and employees have opportunities to make their policies and actions morally defensible, namely by attending rigorously to the distributive and procedural justice of the reorganization of work.

The four chapters in Part III (Progressing HRM) concentrate on proposed courses of action taken by organizations and by individuals to attain a more ethically sound HRM. The first two chapters concentrate on moral dilemmas, formulating moral intentions and problems arising from having to deal with the intended and unintended consequences of our actions. The last two chapters address institutional and individual ethics encouraging mutual respect and moral decency.

Chapter 13 by Tony Watson (HRM, ethical irrationality, and the limits of ethical action) begins with the words of an HR director who is reflecting on his naivety when, as a young personnel officer, he accepted a view of the personnel function as the moral conscience of the organization. He is now much more realistic and takes a view consistent with Watson's contention that opportunities for individual initiative and 'ethical' intervention are rare and tightly circumscribed by management's business goals. Several lines of argument are advanced to help explain the dilemma of ethics in human societies in general and, more specifically, in the institution of HRM within industrial capitalist societies.

Drawing from work by Max Weber, Watson proposes that ethical irrationality is pervasive. This means that no set of values can ever be entirely consistent. Additionally, no set of particular actions will inevitably lead to the intended ethical outcomes. He observes that in practice in HRM personal ethical criteria are invariably enmeshed with business-oriented criteria. Then, further complicating matters for ethicists and moralists is the existence of the paradox of consequences. In essence, institutions and procedures established to achieve certain social goals paradoxically, once in operation, tend to become disconnected from those goals. Chosen means come to undermine the desired ends for which they were chosen. To illustrate this dilemma, Watson describes, from his research, the experience of a personnel officer who, by her own account, found her presence and interventions to be working against her own intent and her assigned personnel objectives.

Watson concentrates on giving a sociological explanation for HR managers' behaviour and influence in workplaces. As agents of industrial capitalist organizations, HR managers are governed by the institutional setting and its required role performances. They are not free to introduce ethical criteria exclusively in or on their own terms. Their primary role is to manage the employment relationship with the purpose of sustaining the viability of the organization. Thus, HR managers operate within social, structural, political, and economic limitations and are unable to make entirely free ethical choices. Even so, they still have the opportunity to make some difference, but only so far as moral choice and ethical actions are seen by the management to coexist with business interests.

Chapter 14 by Joshua Margolis, Adam Grant, and Andrew Molinsky (Expanding ethical standards of HRM: necessary evils and the multiple dimensions of impact) examines moral problems which appear when wrestling with necessary evils. They discuss the distinctive ethical challenges that arise in organizations and investigate how managers can navigate such challenges with practical effectiveness and moral integrity. It is argued that professionals often must perform 'necessary evils', difficult and often unsettling tasks that require harming other human beings in order to advance a worthy purpose. Consequently, this chapter seeks to provide practical guidance on the age-old moral problem of minimizing harm to others when serving the greater good.

The authors commence by acknowledging the unpleasant fact of organizational life that managers engage in acts that harm people. Understanding how managers perform ethically challenging tasks, and providing advice for handling these tasks, are therefore significant responsibilities for organizational researchers. The relatively large volume of research conducted on procedural justice identifies a number of guidelines for treating people consistently and equitably: granting voice to individuals, providing justifiable explanations for decisions and actions, and expressing compassion to those affected. Interestingly, studies show that people are then more willing to accept negative outcomes and less likely to respond in a destructive manner when outcomes are delivered with procedural justice.

Margolis, Grant, and Molinsky draw on two streams of research to examine how in ethically challenging situations, managers can improve their conduct and ameliorate the responses they receive from the affected employees. The first stream focuses on how necessary evils are performed, and the second focuses on HR managers' attainment of positive impact by developing their awareness and skills in dealing with others. The authors then proceed by presenting and explaining three ethical standards for governing HR practice: Standard # 1, advance the organization's objective; Standard # 2, enhance the dignity of those harmed by the action; and Standard # 3, sustain the moral sensibility of those executing morally ambiguous tasks.

The three standards proposed are intended to stimulate greater awareness of ethical challenges in HRM and present principles for guiding action. The authors propose that structuring jobs and tasks to foster interpersonal interaction can have a positive impact on managers' perceptions, feelings, and behaviours. In addition, enabling managers to identify themselves as helpers rather than just messengers or dispensers of tasks may facilitate prosocial behaviour directed towards the parties affected. In essence, the aim of the ethical standards is to promote due consideration of organizational objectives, increase the dignity of harmed parties, and develop the managers performing the tasks of HRM.

Chapter 15 by Ken Kamoche (Strategy, knowledge, appropriation, and ethics in HRM) seeks to extend existing debates within HRM by engaging in a more thorough inquiry into the management of innovation and appropriation of value generated by HR. The chapter investigates the problematic nature of the appropriation of knowledge by organizations and questions the adequacy and ethicality of recent formulations of the resource-based view (RBV). The RBV portrays HR as one of several assets contributing to the achievement of competitive strategies. It has played its part in raising the status of the HR function as a significant player in nurturing and delivering economic value from HR. However, one of the limitations of the RBV is that it reaffirms an exclusive view of labour as a factor of production at the disposal of the organization.

Kamoche discusses the utilization and appropriation of valuable resources explaining how they have been central questions in studies on human capital and knowledge management. Close attention has been paid by researchers to the difficulties surrounding tacit knowledge and some have recommended the articulation and codification of tacit knowledge to reduce organizations' dependency on particular individuals and select groups, although this often creates problems arising from the involuntary transfer of knowledge. In general, managers recognize the need to protect valuable knowledge resources and have often sought to retain them to the primary benefit of the organization through protective mechanisms such as patents, copyrights, secrecy, and isolationism.

Kamoche proposes that while governance structures and protective mechanisms can help organizations to minimize unwanted occurrences of inter-firm transfer of knowledge, they remain insufficient for understanding the roles individuals play in knowledge creation and diffusion, and also offer inadequate support for the ethical treatment of productive employees. He reflects that appropriation regimes influence individuals in a wide variety of ways extending beyond the significance of organization structure and hierarchy into areas of personal identity, individual motivation, and work commitment. For employees engaging in the creation and utilization of knowledge the asymmetric power relations favour the organization's side of the bargain and thus remain unresolved. This, therefore, presents a challenge for management to reconsider the appropriation process and offer stronger incentives for people willing to share and develop their knowledge.

Chapter 16 by Rob Macklin (The morally decent HR manager) is addressed to HR managers who wish to promote ethical decision-making. Macklin distinguishes: (*a*) the moral dimensions of the HR manager's role, (*b*) principles and advice on HR decision-making, and (*c*) influences and constraints on HR managers intending to be ethical in their work. His research shows that HR managers report that moral conflicts are frequent and they find it hard to ensure just and moral processes in their organizations. HR managers often say they lack formal influence and position in their organizations, although they still can wield a positive influence. Four frequently mentioned ways that HR managers gain influence, found in Macklin's interview research are: capitalizing on their acknowledged expert role in people management decisions, packaging agendas and messages in acceptable language, applying effective interpersonal skills, and maintaining a high level of credibility.

Drawing on the work of Agnes Heller, the overall line of argument of this chapter is that morality is grounded in the existence of 'decent' people. Macklin summarizes their condition as follows: 'Thus, morality exists because decent people exist and decent people exist because they have made an existential choice to suffer wrong if faced with the alternative of committing wrong.' Building on writers, such as Habermas, interested in the role of discourse and communicative competence, Heller emphasizes the role of discussion in making moral decisions since modern societies are characterized by a pluralist diversity of norms and values. In Heller's opinion, our freedom for moral choice is to an extent constrained by the moral norms of our contemporary community but it is not so determined that we are unable to reflect, resist, and change them. Macklin proposes that calls for ethically based action are more likely to be perceived positively by managers when they appeal to a normative concept of a decent person acting within the community rather than those generated by more abstract principles of moral philosophy such as transcendental reason, an ideal speech act, or hypothetical discussion behind a veil of ignorance.

More ethical HRM?

These brief synopses indicate the basic themes of the chapters but not the rich substance of their analyses and recommendations. Each makes an important and distinctive contribution. However, the reader will become aware of certain recurrent themes that appear in different guises throughout the book, some of which are taken up again and discussed in the concluding chapter. These themes tend to take the form of unresolved tensions which reflect the conflicting interests at play in the workplace, the moral disagreements to which these give rise, and conflicting, sometimes incompatible, views as to how ethical policies are best implemented.

In Part I (Situating Human Resource Management) all of the contributors discuss in their different ways the potential for conflict in the means–end relationships between, on the one side, the moral treatment of employees and, on the other side, the achievement of demanding political and economic goals. Walsh argues that ethical behaviour is possible when individuals pursue economic interests, but he cautions readers that this means ensuring moral intent and behaviour remain integral to human behaviour in economic activities. Palmer's and Creighton's chapters emphasize the many different ways that ethical behaviour has been understood during the historical evolution of socio-political and legal systems in Western capitalist countries. In general, Guest, and Boxall and Purcell present an optimistic message in favour of a grounded consideration of the strategies of businesses combined with a more enlightened but realistic implementation of HRM. Although they draw attention to the significance of the social infrastructure for encouraging ethical behaviour, Legge contradicts their position arguing that without collective representation the prospect of a more ethical HRM treatment of employees is limited.

In Part II (Analysing Human Resource Management) the contributors consider how the implementation of HRM in organizations may increase the moral awareness, behaviours, and outcomes of employers and employees. The theoretical perspectives adopted on ethics and HRM vary greatly within this section. Greenwood and De Cieri discuss the merits of a stakeholder approach which has been known to emphasize the utilitarian *consequences* of various actions and stakeholder arrangements. They reveal the inevitable tension between maximizing employers' economic interests and focusing on moral outcomes for various stakeholders. Bennington continues in a similar vein to Creighton's discussion in Part I of ethics and legal systems, observing that individuals' *intentions* to promote equal opportunity must be backed by an appropriate legal system; one which provides employees with the freedom to make moral decisions that may conflict with their loyalty to their employer by questioning moral intentions or economic interests. Pinnington and Bayraktaroglu endeavour to take this line of argument a step further by proposing that people employed in HRM should ensure that instrumental economic goals in organizations do not exclude other ethical and cultural aims. Such ambition must be tempered by an acknowledgement that employees' collective and individual interests will sometimes conflict with the general interests of organizations and societies, as indeed Sorell admirably demonstrates in his discussion of a strike in emergency services.

Ardagh outlining a framework for professionalization directly considers how to encourage HRM to be more ethical in pursuit of political and economic objectives. We further consider the professional project he recommends, based on a *virtue* ethics approach to living and acting well, in the concluding chapter where we discuss ways that HRM as an ethical institution may be established in society. Reed's chapter however offers a very thorough and sceptical critique of this project examining how professional work historically has been differently valued and organized.

In Part III (Progressing Human Resource Management) we focus more on the opportunities for promoting collective ethics in HRM and for encouraging high standards of individual moral behaviour. Watson's opening chapter contends that it is unrealistic to conceptualize HRM as having principal authority for ethics in organizations. His argument, informed by sociological theories, focuses on the general intended and unintended consequences of our actions. Margolis, Grant, and Molinsky also consider our actions' consequences but concentrate more on how a deontology comprising specific HRM standards can improve matters. The next two chapters address ways that HRM might become more ethical. Kamoche's innovative contribution examines the contemporary context of knowledge work explaining how employers' and employees' moral behaviour is underpinned by regimes and individual expectations of economic appropriation. Macklin draws this section to a conclusion by examining in detail how individuals working in HRM can reflect on moral dilemmas and on their own moral decisions. His message is an uplifting one recommending individuals have the courage to reflect on the morality of their practices in HRM. Inspired by Heller's work, Macklin's ontology offers a number of ideas for discussing moral behaviour in the workplace: our intentions, our actions, and their various consequences.

Overall, one of the most highly evident themes in this book is the ideological tension between individualism and collectivism and especially the increasing vulnerability of many employees when trade union protection is reduced while the collective power of the corporation is enhanced. While this may benefit economic performance and may be justified in terms of the general well-being, it has some stark and, for some, unacceptable consequences for those whose economic security is at the mercy of market imperatives. Can and should HRM simply seek to mitigate these consequences in individual cases, or could there be a more positive and systematic approach to the CSR of companies to their employee stakeholders?

Another recurring tension is between those who, self-consciously or not, identify 'ethics' with respecting the autonomy and well-being of those individuals with whom we daily interact and working to protect their interests against the threats posed by the social and economic system within which we operate, and those who take a broader, more utilitarian view, focusing on how to improve social and economic systems so as to achieve outcomes that have overall social benefits. While HRM can be presented as an ethical movement that presents new ideas on how employee management can better contribute to the advancement of particular companies and hence to general economic prosperity, there are those who see HRM more as a repudiation of an ethical approach to employees than as a competing or supplementary moral viewpoint, and wish to rehabilitate a more kindly generic form of HRM in which the HRM specialist strives to promote employee interests.

A similar tension appears in the different approaches that are taken towards HRM reform. Many of the current theories of HRM point towards management as a whole taking HRM more seriously and recommend ethical advance by demonstrating to companies the importance, for instance, of employee training and development, for the sustainable prosperity of the companies. This is usually associated with calls for leadership on the part of senior management as a prerequisite of moral progress. A number of our contributors are sceptical of the potential of such HRM reform and argue that more substantial changes have to be made to societal institutions, legislation, government, and corporate policies to support more ethical practice in HRM. Several of them implicitly and explicitly recommend a further professionalization of HRM practitioners to counterbalance the impersonal forces of market economies and the decline of legal and trade union protection. The compatibility, feasibility, and desirability of such developments are underlying subthemes of the book to which further attention is given in the concluding chapter.

Part I

Situating Human Resource Management

1 Socio-political theory and ethics in HRM

Gill Palmer

Human resource management is a relatively new 'discipline' in management, but debates about appropriate ethical approaches to the management of people at work have a much longer history. This chapter comments on the history of socio-political and economic ideologies, in order to provide a broad context relevant to current debates about ethics and HRM.

Many theorists, from different backgrounds, have pondered the ethical basis of employment relations. The academic disciplines of industrial and organizational sociology, political theory, and IR shared a concern to analyse employment relationships, and these can be used to enrich the current studies of HRM. This widespread interest is not surprising because the types of employment relationships that develop in society are important, not only for the success of organizations and for the life experience of individual employees, but for the wider political and social culture of society as a whole.

Clearly, the nature of relationships between employees and employers can vary greatly. At one extreme are casual, short-term, and probably strictly instrumental exchanges of small amounts of time and labour for limited rewards (e.g. a student paid an hourly rate for evening or Saturday work at the local shop/garage/restaurant or bar). At another extreme is the employment relationship that consumes the majority of an employee's time and emotional energy, with the expectation of a lifelong career within one organization, determining not only financial rewards and immediate lifestyle, but a person's lifetime opportunities for personal development, organizational influence, and social prestige.

For most employees, in most countries, and for much of recent history, the rewards and job satisfaction associated with their employment relationship will have a determining influence on their standard of living and life experience. For breadwinners with dependent family, the standard of living of loved ones will also be involved.

For most employers the relationship is also of critical importance. The cost of labour, and the effective use of the HR, is often a major influence on the success of an organization. The employee body as a whole will be important, although the economic importance of individual employees will depend on the employers' dependence on their skills, and ability to replace them if necessary on the labour market. In the same way, the employee's dependence on a particular employer will rest on whether there are employment opportunities elsewhere. Nevertheless the employment relationship is important for both sides. It is therefore not surprising that it has attracted much attention and that ethical dilemmas associated with the relationship have for long been the subject of analysis.

Several recent debates about ethics and HRM are summarized in the Winstanley and Woodall (2000b) edited compilation of papers originally given at conferences in the UK. They briefly note how various management theories might be seen to approach ethics and HRM, and then explore some ethical dilemmas associated with particular HRM practices, for example recruitment and selection, training and development, work practices, remuneration, and employee participation. They conclude that there are significant constraints facing ethical HRM. Rather than continue this form of analysis, this chapter comments on the underlying social and political theories that have influenced ideas about work and society, and have a relevance in the more specific field of employment and work.

The analysis of ethics and HRM can be related to the socio-political frameworks that have been used for many years to explore the nature of authority, government, and consent within society. Ethical dilemmas within work organizations often reflect ethical dilemmas about society as a whole and the role and organization of government in society. The theoretical frameworks for one can contribute to the analysis of the other.

In most classifications of political theory one finds unitarist, radical, and pluralist theories. Unitary theory has been developed to explain the view, still sometimes expressed, that the authority structures within social organizations are uncontentious. Under unitary theories, no significant ethical dilemmas will emerge if everyone submits willingly to the rule of the given authority. Authority figures can and should be trusted to take decisions and resolve issues in the best interests of the 'unitary' organizational whole. Ancient concepts such as 'the divine right of kings' are unitarist. In more modern times, 'managerial prerogative' has been seen as a moral claim to authority within the unitary frame. Perspectives that see human organizations as akin to organic, biological constructions have a similar view. They embody and support the argument that all interpersonal conflicts and ethical dilemmas can and should be resolved by trusting that those in positions of social power will invariably act in the overall, long-term interests of the community as a whole.

There are few advocates of a totally unitary perspective towards HRM in the advanced economies of our globalized world. However, unitary ideas are seductive, and are often assumed.

Totally unitary theories on employment at work are rarely expressed, because it is ingrained in modern economic theory that we understand that the employment relationship is constructed as an exchange between people who have interests which are quite legitimately different and distinct. The employee in the labour market has the interest of selling their labour for the best possible price and conditions. The employer in the labour market has the interest of buying labour on the best terms, and on conditions that will enable the labour time which has been bought to be turned into productive output, in terms of the employer's organizational goals. Modern economic theory recognizes that there are quite distinct and varying interests at work and in the labour market. There will inevitably be pluralism in the interests of different people within the work organization, and therefore there will not be a unitary, common interest that can be expected to totally eliminate all moral dilemmas arising from interpersonal conflicts of interest at work.

Modern economic (and democratic, political) theories start with an acceptance that there are plural interests in social organizations which will make interpersonal conflict inevitable. Conflicts of interest in the workplace, and ethical dilemmas on how to handle them, should be expected, they may even be constructive in terms of making people consider complex issues, adjust to market realities and work through mutually acceptable accommodations.

Given the existence of plural interests between employers and employees in work organizations, how should they be managed? In the nineteenth century, when industrialization was sweeping through Great Britain and the new economy was taking hold, the unitary claims of management prerogative were attacked by people who were unwilling to legitimize the new mill-owners' right to employ child labour or set pay rates or hours of work in their own interests. To counter the unitarist arguments of employer rights, radical theories were developed by those who believed the growing economic power of the new capitalist entrepreneurs was unethical, and rested on their illegitimate exploitation of human labour. Theoretical debates abounded, and Marxists developed the most powerful ideological attacks, arguing that the new employment relationships were unethical because they involved the exploitation of human labour and that there was a wide discrepancy in the power relationship between the owner of capital and the owner of labour. Workers lost human dignity as their skills became commodities in the capitalist's accumulation of personal wealth. The radicals' proposed solutions still had a unitarist slant. They argued for revolutionary political action to eliminate private property rights. If private property was forbidden, and workers owned the organizations that used their labour, then it was argued, there could be no exploitation. The major conflict of interest between sellers and buyers of labour would be eliminated, and organizations could be managed in the interests of all, in a visionary return to a unitarist utopia.

Many European early trade union movements mobilized around these ideas, and of course the Russian Revolution of 1917, and the spread of Communism in the early twentieth century were based on theories that ethical relationships at work required, and could be guaranteed by, transferring the ownership of the means of production from the capitalists to the workers. Marx's notion that a revolutionary transfer of ownership from capital to labour would lead to the demise of politics and the power of the state proved unfounded, and modified radical theories developed, arguing for the transfer of ownership, not to an amorphous 'people' but to the government or nation state, which was seen to be 'neutral' between the different economic interests. Socialist and state socialist theories developed. They sought to end the exploitation they believed was inherent in private property rights and capitalist employment relationships. Their solution to the major discrepancies in social power caused by private ownership was nationalization, and the transfer of the employer role from private entrepreneurs to governments and the state.

Modern HRM is now practised in both privately owned and government-owned organizations, and experience has taught that state ownership does not significantly alter employment relationships, or guarantee radically different employment conditions. The question of ownership is no longer placed at the centre of debates about the development of fair and ethical working relationships in a society. However, the history of these nineteenth and early twentieth century concerns have had their influence on different legal systems. It is the history and power of these ideas that explains the more managed economies of central Europe, compared with the more liberal economy of the USA (Whitley 1999). And although the ownership of resources is no longer given the same theoretical significance (except perhaps for Russian oil and gas), the role of government in a plural economy and state is still a significant issue.

Most recent debates about relationships in employment have rested, not so much on unitary or radical theories, as on notions of how to deal with an inevitable and unavoidable plurality of interests at work.

Before turning to pluralist theories, it is worth noting that at the turn of the nineteenth and twentieth centuries, moral concerns about the nature of emerging capitalism were raised by religious as well as communist and socialist thinkers. In a classic article, Child (1964) notes that the Quaker businessmen who developed the confectionery industry in the UK came under moral attack from their colleagues in the Society of Friends, because the role of employer was seen to contradict four fundamental Quaker moral prescriptions. These Quaker values were: (a) a prohibition of exploitation and profit at the expense of others; (b) the importance of service, stressing hard work, and renunciation in the service of others; (c) egalitarianism and the need for democratic relations between people; and (d) abhorrence of social conflict. From 1902 to 1922 Quaker employers came under considerable pressure from the Society of Friends to renounce property rights and the profit motive and establish democratically run businesses, based on moral rather than material objectives. Child describes the Quaker employers' response to this pressure. They developed an ideology which could be accommodated with commercial activities and which emphasized the Quaker ideals of service and the abhorrence of conflict. The ideas of the socialists, or the growing cooperative movement were not endorsed, and the Quaker egalitarian and democratic values were downplayed. As Child notes, faced with their ethical challengers, the Quaker employers were spurred to produce an articulate defence of management in social terms. They argued that employers had the moral and social responsibility to lead their organizations effectively. They had a duty to use the most efficient managerial techniques in order to promote the greater good of the community. Faced with considerable attack from within the Society of Friends, they took the lead in the development of welfare measures for employees, introducing paid holidays, sick pay, good working conditions, and pensions. An example of their response to their ethical dilemma can be seen at Bourneville, a village in the Midlands in the UK built to provide an ideal living environment for the workforce at Cadbury's. Cadbury's employees were provided with employer-built housing, schools, and churches and, of course, there were no pubs. These employee benefits might have been seen as harming the employer interest by raising labour costs, but the Quakers provided economic as well as moral justifications for their strategy. They argued that these policies had economic as well as moral advantages, serving to reduce labour turnover and increase productivity.

The Quaker welfare provisions did not alter the basic authority relationships at work, but they did provide arguments for the ethical, utilitarian value of capitalist employment relationships. As Child notes, these arguments were adopted by others and were to have an influence well beyond the Quaker community. Quaker employers therefore led the way on welfare benefits, and in promoting arguments about the value of industrial development for employees and society as a whole. However, their abhorrence of social conflict led them to reject employee demands for representation and the right to a voice in negotiations on pay and conditions. They were not at the forefront of employer acceptance of pluralism in the management of employment relations.

From the mid-twentieth century, ethically based calls for the avoidance of exploitation and the development of fair or just relationships at work have often rested on pluralist assumptions about the nature of conflicts at work. Pluralism characterizes the political theory that came to dominate thought in Western economies at the end of the Second World War. Pluralism assumes that there will inevitably be a complex web of different interests between people in any complex social organization or society. These interests cannot and should not be denigrated or ignored. They cannot be eliminated by the revolutionary elimination of private property or the transfer of ownership to the state. Instead, pluralist theory advocates democratic, participative decision-making process as the way to ensure that justice prevails, that people's differences can be debated and agreements reached acceptable to all. At the political level, pluralist theory underlies democracy, and the right of different interest groups to seek support in the ballot box for their various policies.

In the workplace and in the employment relationship, the existence of different, pluralist interests between employer and employee is understood and accepted as a fundamental aspect of modern economic theory. However, there are different ideas about how the plurality of economic interests should be managed. Different ideas about the appropriate management of pluralism at work lie behind the major political and legislative conflicts of the twentieth century, and are still relevant today to the analysis of ethical behaviour at work.

The great policy debates in Western IR through the twentieth century can be summarized in terms of the differences between different variants of pluralist theory, in particular between various liberal and corporatist ideas. To summarize these great debates, and relate them to the question of ethics and HRM, this chapter contrasts theoretical approaches of: (*a*) liberal-individual pluralism, (*b*) liberal-collective pluralism, and (*c*) coordinated, neo-corporatist pluralism. Each of these three social theories provide different analyses of conflict at work, and have advocated different solutions to the question of achieving fair and ethical relationships at work.

Liberalism and the Western tradition of liberal thought developed in the UK and USA from the seventeenth century and still flourishes as the dominant political theory of the USA, even though in current use, the term is being used by US conservatives to attack what Thatcher in the UK would have called 'the wets'. Classical liberal theory rests on the importance of individual freedom to express and act in support of human needs. It puts faith in the power of freedom of choice, the balancing impact of markets, and the ability of democratic political processes to ensure that social outcomes will be fair and equitable. In the work environment, liberalism accepts the inevitability of conflicting interests between sellers and buyers of labour. It sees labour markets and contracts of employment as the mechanisms through which these conflicts of interest can be resolved in a fair, equitable, and ethical manner. Provided labour markets are competitive, and workers have freedom of choice, then Adam Smith's concept (1999 [1776]) of the market's 'guiding hand' can be expected to move people and resources around the labour market in ways that enable employees to improve their position, while encouraging employers to avoid the worst employment practices or forms of exploitation.

Classical liberalism is still the basis of our modern economic and political democratic thought. However, the faith in the market's ability to ensure fair outcomes is rarely absolute and, faced with difficulties in implementing the liberal ideal, people have developed various interpretations of liberalism, advocating different solutions in the name of achieving greater social justice. Two pluralist variants have had considerable impact on employment relationships, and the conflicting solutions of liberal individualism and liberal collectivism need to be explained.

Liberal individualism represents the classic 'laissez-faire' economics of the eighteenth century. This is the 'pure' unmodified acceptance of liberal theory, which argues that individual contracts of employment are the main or only social mechanism needed to ensure social and economic justice at work. A legal framework will be necessary to support contractual rights, but other forms of interventionist legislation should be minimal, and are not required to regulate relationships between adults at work. Any collusion in the marketplace must not be tolerated. Therefore employees forming trade unions, or employers forming employer associations to agree terms of employment in an industry, must be prevented, as these will prevent the free and individual working of the market. Liberal individualism is still used to justify the strong anti-unionism of many companies in the USA, and to support calls for greater labour market deregulation.

Opposition to, or modification of, the basic Western belief in liberal individualism has come from those arguing for collective representation in the workforce, or for a more interventionist state through legislation. The first challenges to the pure laissez-faire individualism arose from the early ethical concerns about the exploitation of child labour (well represented in the writings of Charles Dickens). Faced with evidence of the exploitation of children and of health and safety abuses, the nineteenth century Britain saw the first legislation to prevent child labour and the slow development of government regulation to enforce some basic safety practices at work. Pressure to regulate the employer's use of labour in these ways came from the collective mobilization of groups lobbying to represent employee interests. Unions developed the argument that the individual contract of employment could not represent a balanced bargain between two equal parties. Only collective representation on the labour side of the equation would go some way to ensure that the liberal market was liberal in a social and political sense. Slowly labour movements gained support in Europe, building alliances and political power to press for some government regulation of employment conditions. In the UK associations of employers began to establish pay rates, and eventually accept the participation of trade unions in their regulation of standard hours, wages, and conditions for their industry or region. As some employers' associations and trade unions began to establish collectively agreed terms of employment, legislation slowly developed to recognize the right of employees to form trade unions and employers to form associations, and both to act collectively in the negotiation of collective bargains to establish contracts of employment. This variant of liberalism has been labelled 'liberal collectivism'. This was the social theory that emerged after the Second World War as the solution to the need to establish fair and equitable employment relationships. After the War, the allied powers of the USA and UK introduced legislation into the defeated nations of Germany and Japan to create free trade unions and collective bargaining. This key element of liberal collectivism was introduced, not only to support collective bargaining at work, but also because it was seen as the way to support the growth of democracy in the political sphere. Encouraging the growth of independent trade unions was seen as an essential step to the introduction of plural political parties, in particular labour parties, able to balance the power of the militarist, business-related regimes that had supported the German and Japanese axis in the Second World War. The German Nazi regime represented the next political ideology to be discussed, that of corporatism.

Corporatism is a variant of pluralism that puts great emphasis on the role of national government. In contrast to the liberal preference for as little state intervention as possible in economic issues, the corporatist view sees that it is a prime duty of the nation state, through its government, to play an active role in regulating the economy and its related employment relations. State intervention is seen as the way to ensure that the plural interests in society are brought into accommodation for the benefit of all. Separate interests in the economy must be recognized and, indeed encouraged to organize, so that these interests can be represented and conflicts resolved in a mutual partnership under the guiding hand of government, which represents a higher order of social interest. The role of the state is therefore key, and instead of the neutral 'umpire' role envisaged under liberal collectivism, it is given centre stage. However there are variants of corporatist intervention. In extreme corporatist cases, the state prescribes the nature of the collective trade union or employer bodies allowed, and the type of accommodation permitted. In the German and Italian Nazi and Mussolini state socialist regimes, the incorporated trade unions were required to be active partners in supporting the political party agendas, operating under strict controls, like the trade unions allowed under communist regimes—the main difference between communism and corporatism in this context being whether the state had taken ownership control of the production units in the economy.

Pure corporatist or communist ideologies have not survived to remain as relevant to the discussion of the ethics of HRM in modern economies. However neo-corporatism is still important. It can be defined as a milder form of state intervention, in which governments work with employee and employer representatives in the regulation of such issues as health and safety, and training. Where a liberal collectivist state will seek to limit state intervention to providing a 'safety net' for the most vulnerable members of the workforce, or acting as a neutral umpire in the context of collective negotiations, or individual grievances at work, a neo-corporatist state will play a more active role. Under neo-corporatism, government acts to regulate economic and employment issues, with the involvement and assistance of representatives of the conflicting economic parties, usually unions and employer associations. Neo-corporatist policies can be seen in the legislation establishing the works councils and employee representation on company boards of mainland Europe. Early government attempts to encourage the development of enterprise bargaining in the UK in the 1960s and 1970s can also be seen as neo-corporatist (Palmer 1986), as can the origins of the traditional Australian compulsory arbitration system (Palmer 1989). Current health and safety debates in Australia about the value of government regulation, as opposed to the value of education, to promote health and safety consciousness at work, continues the debate on the value of state intervention in support of morally valued practices (Cook 2003; Nash 2000; Australian Government 2002).

In what ways can this history of Western socio-political ideas enrich modern concerns about the ethics of HRM? Harley and Hardy (2004) have argued the need for more critical analysis surrounding HRM topics. As the HRM discipline developed, it has been subjected to criticism from writers drawing on earlier fields of study (e.g. political sociology or IR) on the grounds that HRM prescriptions too often assumed an oversimplistic, unitarist approach. Many prescriptions of good HRM practice appeared to be based on the assumption that managerial prerogative would be accepted as legitimate, or that no ingrained or underlying ethical difficulties would emerge, or none that could not be resolved by the simple application of good management and goodwill. Harley and Hardy note the need for a more critical approach, to confront the complexity and importance of the field. An analysis of the varying impact of broad social and political ideologies on ideas about working relationships can open up new angles for critical analysis and questioning.

Conflicting arguments using either unitary or pluralist assumptions of social organization are still heard in the debates about how various stakeholders can or should participate in decisions about employment and work. Economic theories clearly assume conflicting interests between employees and shareholders as groups. In recent years there have been growing voices arguing the need to accept the legitimacy of different interests among social identity groups, based on ethnicity, age, gender, occupation, or organizational role. Can these social and economic conflicts of interest be resolved in ways which will satisfy organizational and individual needs? For example, can 'good' HRM and individual contracts of employment resolve these pluralist conflicts? If collective group interests are still important, what is the current role of the old pluralist solutions, in terms of processes and procedures to recognize and represent collectivities? Are regulations or policies which ensure that different interests have a voice, enough? Or do work organizations need different stakeholder interests to be protected by some system of voting or veto in a participative decision-making process (perhaps supported by works-council type regulations and legislation)? Does interest group representation need to be supported by sanctions (like the right to withdraw labour, or the right to appeal certain decisions through conciliation or tribunal support)? These issues are still contested, often on the basis of assumptions and beliefs that have their origins in the earlier debates on pluralism in social organization.

The responsibility, authority, and appropriate role of government remains as relevant to debates about employment now, as it was in the nineteenth century. There have been radical changes in the arguments about public ownership and control, however, there is broad recognition of the need for some governmental regulation to constrain the unethical use of economic power by managers or employers. Despite this broad agreement, there is room for much debate on the form this should take, for example, on the role of government regulation over health and safety, remuneration, training and development, equal opportunity or EO, and job security.

The shrinking world and the extraordinary growth of multinational corporations have introduced new complications. Whereas the need for publicly focused regulation in these areas was once discussed in terms of an analysis of different ideas about the 'role of the state', globalization challenges the solutions which relied on the power of the nation state to establish regulations. International Labour Organization (ILO) and international 'governmental' regulation is not well developed, but this form of government intervention must be seen as of increasing importance to HRM, as the sovereign power of the nation state is eroded by the increasing cross-national mobility of capital and labour. The importance of cross-national debates about economic regulation, including the regulation of employment relations, should provide an increasing angle of interest for teaching and research in HRM.

Globalization has also brought a recognition of the diversity of the socio-political traditions that have importance for modern HRM. The Western traditions discussed in this chapter are not the only ones that will influence employment policies in the twenty-first century. The very different socio-political theories of the newly developing nations can confront or challenge ideas once taken for granted in studies of the management of humans in a modern economy.

This is clearly illustrated by the work of Whitley (1999). His study of *Divergent Capitalisms* provides a picture of the different types of social, political, and managerial arrangements that are constructing very different capitalist systems. He illustrates the power of different traditions in social and political thought in his analysis of the attempts by the USA and its allied powers to restructure the economies and politics of West Germany and Japan after the Second World War. They adopted a strategic policy to introduce liberalism, in the form of liberal economic, IR, and management practices, in order to create the social structures and processes believed to be necessary to support democracy and prevent the re-emergence of totalitarian military regimes. However the allied strategies of social reform did not have the results expected. The different systems altered, but there was no general convergence towards the expected American-style liberalism. A strong element of neo-corporatism remained in West Germany, while Japan continued its dual labour market practices with privileged and lifetime employment for the male, regular workers in large corporations in the primary labour market, supported by strong social norms on gender inequality and close government–industry collaboration regulating economic affairs. Changes were made, but it did not prove easy to change the fundamental nature of established economic and social systems, based as they were on traditional beliefs about the nature of authority and the appropriate social roles for government, employers, and employees. Whitley went on to compare the current systems in East Asia and Eastern Europe, contrasting South Korea with Taiwan, and Hungary with Slovenia. Again his study demonstrates the complexity and continuing diversity of management and employment systems. Humans are capable of creating and maintaining an extraordinary range of social and economic organizational forms to structure work and employment. There is no simple logic in the solutions that people find to the many dilemmas associated with organizing work, and certainly no evidence of a simple convergence to traditional, developed-economy, or Western, norms.

Some fascinating issues for the analysis of HRM in the twenty-first century are likely to arise from the development of the Chinese economy. After the 1950s, the rise of the Japanese economy stimulated important academic debates about differences in the organization of work and practices in HRM. The early arguments confidently predicted that Japan's traditional HRM policies could not survive economic development and would inevitably transform to the familiar, more liberal, occupational rather than organizational, labour markets of Western Europe and the USA. Such arguments were then replaced by suggestions that Japan's HRM might represent a 'late-development' effect and that Japanese policymakers did not need to follow the path of the early industrializers, indeed there would be a 'reverse-convergence' as large European and US firms adopted Japanese HRM practices and used dual labour markets to drive the success of their large-scale work organizations. Finally, comparative analysis has led to work like that of Whitley, which recognizes the continuing diversity in work practices that is fuelled by the interaction between ideological traditions and long-established social and political structures, and the pressure of economic development. In Japan, the influence of the USA after the Second World War helped explain the strength of the early assumptions about the relevance of liberal labour markets, and pluralist employee representation and participation in the newly developing economy. In China and the newly industrializing countries in its region, Western influences do not have this type of support. In a society where dominant ideas derive from Confucius, Mencius, and Mao, the developments in HRM are not likely to be liberally based. Government control and political concerns about tensions between the peasantry and city will continue to play major roles.

Broad traditions in socio-political thought impact on the policies and solutions created to manage the inevitable ethical dilemmas at work. Many of the legislative and managerial policies that have been developed to help regulate the workplace have their roots in broad ideas about the nature of social organization, the legitimacy of different types of social conflict, and the roots of social justice. An analysis of socio-political theories and ideas can provide a useful bridge between the more abstract philosophical theories about ethics, and the concrete policy prescriptions that are found within HRM. An understanding of the impact of these broad sociological and political theories can also throw light on the contextual limits of particular HRM prescriptions.

2 The ethics of HRM in dealing with individual employees without collective representation

Karen Legge

Introduction

In this chapter I wish to do four things. First, to establish the degree to which collective representation has declined in neo-liberal Anglo-American economies (with particular reference to Britain) and to consider why this has occurred. Second, using Berlin's ideas (1958/2002) about the two conceptions of liberty as a heuristic, to explore the case for and against the ethicality of both collectivism and individualism (see also Gray 1995). Third, on the basis of this, to consider whether and to what extent particular groups without collective representation enjoy the good life at work in the light of the explicit or implicit HRM policies deemed appropriate to their occupational group. Finally, I consider how the role and responsibilities of HRM might develop in relation to these employees, noting that what might be ethically desirable shows little evidence of emerging.

The slow death of collectivism?

First, let me make clear that in this chapter I am focusing on the so-called 'Anglo-American', neo-liberal, shareholder-oriented business systems of the Western world, which arguably would include Canada and New Zealand as well as the UK and the USA. A very different picture might be painted if the focus was on the corporatist, stakeholder business systems of northern Europe, where collectivism, although increasingly under attack from the proponents of labour market flexibility, resists the rampant individualism of neo-liberal economies.

'Collectivist representation' rests on the assumption that employees have a right to have their independent voice heard and to exercise legitimate power in the negotiation of their terms and conditions of employment. In its full manifestation this is reflected in trade union(s) recognition at local level for the purposes of collective bargaining over a wide agenda of issues, along with formal grievance and consultation procedures. In a climate favourable to trade unions, whether as a result of an adversarial (but only in the context of full employment) or a collaborative relationship with the employer, one might look for high levels of union density, reinforcing the institutionalization of unionized collective representation. Such collective representation reached its zenith in the heyday of the twentieth century post-Second World War Fordist/Keynesian settlement, where the growth of mass production and public sector services, along with a commitment to social justice, provided fertile ground for union recognition and the centrality of collective bargaining in establishing the individual and social wage (Jessop 1994). Nostalgia for this lost world is the *leitmotiv* of Sennett's (1998) polemic, *The Corrosion of Character.*

The statistics illustrate the parlous state of collectivism in private sector industry outside of Continental Europe and, arguably, Australia (Morehead et al. 1997). In the US private sector, by 2000, only 9 per cent of the workforce was unionized (Reinhold 2000). In Canada union density in the private sector has declined since the end of the 1990s, from almost 22 per cent in 1997 to just over 18 per cent in 1999 (Akyeampong 1997, 1999). China, India, Japan, Korea, Singapore, Taiwan, and the Philippines, in spite of variation between countries, all suffered a steady decline in union density in the 1990s (Kuruvilla et al. 2002). Even in Australia where, according to the Australian Workplace Industrial Relations Survey (AWIRS), only 29 per cent of locations lacked a union presence that figure had almost doubled in the last five years (Morehead et al. 1997: 467). Following the dramatic labour market reforms and lurch to a neo-liberal economic policy in New Zealand in the early 1990s, union density fell from almost 45 per cent in 1989 to under 20 per cent in 1996 (Wailes, Ramia, and Lansbury 2003).

I will look in more detail at this phenomenon in relation to Britain. The Workplace Employee Relations Survey 1998 (WERS 98) (Cully et al. 1999) shows the extent of the retreat from the traditional forms of collectivism over the past two decades. Guest (2001) provides a good summary of the findings. In workplaces employing 25 people or more, according to management estimates, about 30 per cent belong to a trade union. This varies with size of establishment, averaging 23 per cent in workplaces with 25–49 employees but rising to 48 per cent in those employing over 500—a significant statistic as the trend is towards smaller workplaces. While 47 per cent of workplaces have no union members, only 2 per cent have 100 per cent union membership. Whereas in 1980, 64 per cent of workplaces recognized a trade union for collective bargaining purposes, in 1998, this figure had fallen to 42 per cent. Whereas in 1984, 71 per cent of employees were covered by collective bargaining, in 1998 the figure had declined to 41 per cent. What emerges clearly from WERS 98 is that collective representation in Britain is now largely a public sector phenomenon, with 56 per cent of employees in the public sector belonging to a union as compared to only 26 per cent in the private sector. Further, where union members exist in a workplace, but where there is no recognition, the non-recognition rate is much higher in the private sector at 30 per cent than in the public sector at 3 per cent.

According to WERS 98, 60 per cent of workplaces have no worker representatives including 25 per cent where unions are actually recognized. Nevertheless, in workplaces where there are no union members, management report that 11 per cent have non-union representatives, a figure which rises to 19 per cent of workplaces in which union members are present but where unions are not recognized for collective bargaining. This is not very reassuring if we look at the findings on consultation. Only 34 per cent of the public sector and 20 per cent of private sector workplaces had a consultative committee and, as Guest (2001: 100) argues, there is evidence to suggest a high degree of management control of such committees. For example, although 51 per cent of managers in the public sector and 29 per cent in the private sector rated their committees as highly influential, they were more likely to receive this rating if there were non-union representatives and particularly where they were appointed by management rather than elected by workers. Although they were rated as more influential when they met more often, it is notable that the committees composed of union representatives in unionized settings tended to meet less frequently. As Guest (2001: 100) succinctly puts it:

In short, managers appear to rate committees as influential where they are able to exercise control over them. In other settings, the committees are more likely to be marginalized in the decision-making process.

The general marginalization of any expressions of collectivism in British workplaces is summed up not only by the retreat from union membership and recognition, but by the impoverished agenda for collective bargaining and consultation where it still exists. Of the WERS's list of nine conventional items for bargaining (pay or conditions of employment, payment systems, recruitment and selection, training, grievance handling, staff/manpower planning, equal opportunities, health and safety, and performance appraisals), there was no negotiation with union representatives over *any* of these issues in half the workplaces where unions were recognized. On average, union representatives negotiated on only 1.1 of the nine issues, while non-union representatives negotiated over even less, 0.9 issues. Nor were these issues covered much better by consultation: the average number covered by consultative committees was

2.9 where union representatives and 3.7 where non-union representatives were involved.

What we have here is a picture of collective representation surviving in the organizations that epitomized the Fordist/Keynesian settlement—the public sector and large manufacturing plants. For the rest of the private sector, and particularly in the flourishing service sector, the norm is non-unionization and without worker representation.

The reasons for this decline are not hard to find. There are what might be termed the structural reasons. Central is the shift to sectors and workforces that traditionally have not been unionized—the service sector, part-time, and female labour. WERS 98 reflects these trends. Since 1984, the proportion of workplaces where women comprised a low percentage (less than 25 per cent) of employees has fallen from around a third in 1984 to a quarter in 1998. Correspondingly, the proportion of workplaces with a high percentage of female workers (75 per cent or more) has risen from 22 per cent in 1984 to 29 per cent in 1998. Further, the proportion of workplaces in which at least a quarter of employees work part-time has grown from 32 per cent in 1990 to 44 per cent in 1998. Cully et al. (1999: 223–4) reckon that much of this can be accounted for by the changing survey population. Thus, while around two-fifths of the difference were accounted for by the growth in private service industries, where part-time work is more common than in manufacturing, three-fifths were accounted for by greater use of part-time work among service sector workplaces which had joined the survey population in 1998. A further structural issue is the failure to organize new private manufacturing and service workplaces, set up since 1980 (Machin 2000). Another dismal statistic for trade unions is the declining number of young people joining unions. Comparing figures from the 1983 General Household Survey with those from the 1999 Labour Force Survey, only 17 per cent of individuals aged 18–29 years were union members in 1999, compared with 44 per cent in 1983 (Machin 2000).

To some extent these are structural manifestations of cultural changes in society, epitomized in the last two decades by the advocacy of neo-liberal economics, individualism, and an enterprise culture in Britain (Keat and Abercrombie 1991). This has been reflected not only in the anti-union policies of the Conservative governments in the 1980s and 1990s, but in the so-called 'Third Way' espoused by 'New Labour' (Howell 2004). In spite of some gestures towards the unions embodied in the Employment Relations Act, 1999, New Labour not only failed to repeal much of the Conservative legislation, but, according to Waddington (2003: 336), through the reversal of the opt-out from the Social Protocol of the EU and the introduction of a National Minimum Wage 'supports the provision of a wider range of individual rights, while restricting the extension of collective rights enabling trade unionists to enforce their individual rights'. As Howell (2004: 19) neatly summarizes:

It is now individual legal rights at work, provided and enforced by the state, that are the primary motors of industrial relations, with collective bargaining relegated to the public sector and those areas of the private sector where, for the most part, employment is declining.

Individualism has been fostered through the notion of the 'sovereign customer' and the primacy of individual choice and enterprise responsiveness to that choice (Korczynski 2002; Sturdy, Grugelis, and Willmott 2001). This is embodied in New Labour's proposed reforms of public sector services, which unions view as likely to undermine collective organization in its last bastion. The 'enterprising individual', with its connotations of personal initiative, independence, self-reliance and the willingness to take risks, and accept responsibility for one's actions, celebrates individualism at the expense of collectivist solidarity. In a world enamoured of the virtues of free markets, supply-side economics, privatization and deregulation, collectivism is distinctly out of fashion. It conjures up 'past-their-sell-by-date' images of blue-collar workers, in dying industries, resisting the tide of progress or 'feather-bedded' public sector workers selfishly putting the rest of the public, working flexibly and in a 'disciplined' fashion in 'leaner', 'fitter', 'new' sectors of the economy, to unnecessary inconvenience. It is significant that New Labour's mantra with regard to trade unions is the call for 'modernization', which seems to embrace the idea that the way forward is 'to extend individual rights, rather than rights acquired through union membership' (Waddington 2003: 338). From this perspective, collectivism may be seen as a passing phase, redolent of Fordism and the Keynesian settlement that privileged producers—a phenomenon completely at odds with a post-Fordist, post-modern world where individual choice, expressed through consumption, is privileged. Collective bargaining's only justification from this perspective is in its 'contribution to the construction of partnership in the workplace in the quest for global competitiveness' (Howell 2004: 19).

Against this background of declining collectivism, what ethical justifications might be made in support of individualism and collectivism respectively?

The ethics of individualism and collectivism

Ethics is about the identification of the good and its just or fair distribution. Just as trade unionism, as an expression of collectivism, may be seen as an essentially modernist project, so the modernist ethics of the Enlightenment and beyond (Kant, Mills, Rawls), are in a sense collectivist, as they depict ethics as comprising collective codes of conduct that exist over and above the individual and which can be used to legitimate independent action. This contrasts with the individualism of a post-modern perspective, where ethics are seen as a matter of personal choice in the project of the creation and care of an aesthetic personal identity (Bauman 1993; Cummings 2000).

A useful heuristic in thinking about the ethics of individualism and collectivism is Berlin's idea about 'two concepts of liberty'. Berlin suggests that there are two ways of thinking about liberty, the positive and negative conceptions. The positive conception views liberty in terms of rational self-determination or autonomy:

I wish my life and decisions to depend on myself, not on external forces of whatever kind. I wish to be the instrument of my own, not other men's [sic], acts of will. I wish to be a subject, not an object; to be moved by reasons, by conscious purposes, which are my own, not by causes which affect me, as it were, from outside. I wish to be...a doer—deciding, not being decided for, self-directed and not acted upon by external nature or by other men [sic]...(Berlin 2002: 178)

Such rational autonomy is often seen as the essence of the individualism lauded in the enterprise culture. It is also consistent with a modernist view of ethics.

The negative conception of liberty, in contrast, is purely the absence of constraints imposed by others that allows for choice among alternatives. 'By being free in this sense I mean not being interfered with by others' (Berlin 2002: 170). This resonates with a post-modern conception of ethics.

Berlin sees negative liberty as preferable to positive liberty (Gray 1995). This is because he sees negative liberty as an enabling condition where people, through self-chosen and plural lifestyles, constitute themselves as human beings. Berlin sees the individual as defined by her self-transforming nature. Along with the postmodernists, human nature, he argues, is not something that awaits discovery and realization, but something invented and reinvented through choices that are inherently plural and diverse, not common or universal. Contrast this with the rationalist view of the Enlightenment ethicists that saw the individual as a natural object in a natural order, subject to natural laws and understandable in behaviour and nature by reference to these laws. Berlin rejects this monist perspective on ethics, arguing that, rather than freedom, positive liberty is nothing more than obedience to the rational will. Whereas choice presupposes rivalry among conflicting goods, rationality points to just one course of action for the individual. From Aristotle to Kant, from the good life to the 'categorical imperative', the rational will once oriented towards the order of nature or the 'form of the good' cannot contain conflicting goals, desires, and rivalries among cherished goods as this betokens unreason. Freedom, from this perspective, lies in pursuing the rational will, an opportunity to pursue the good, the rational adoption of worthwhile ends. If all true goods are compatible with one another, then a community of truly free persons will be one without significant conflict of ideals or interests, but rather a harmonious dovetailing of identical rational wills (such as Rousseau's vision of the General Will). Berlin saw this monist view as inherently liable to abuse because, if there is a natural identity of wills among rational people, then conflict may be seen as a symptom of immorality, unreason, or error and inherently pathological. In Berlin's eyes, viewing conflict as pathological underpins all forms of totalitarianism. For Berlin, the negative view of liberty allows for people in their acts of self-creation to make choices that, in the eyes of a rationalist or Aristotelian, would count as bad or worthless—engaging in 'immoral' activities, choosing self-harming lifestyles.

The two concepts of liberty enable us to pose questions about the desirability of collectivism per se. Collective representation may constitute a form of positive freedom as an expression of harmonious *collective* self-determination in the pursuit of the rational ends of want satisfaction, through the institution of collective bargaining. The route to being 'the instrument of my own, not of other men's, acts of will', may be through collective organization and action, in the spirit of 'united we stand, divided we fall'. Collectivism may seek the rational goal of securing for employees the 'good life at work'. From the position of positive liberty, what counts as good work and employment is not subjective, but constituted by the securing of ends that rational people might agree are good. There might be a fair measure of agreement, for example, that good work might comprise Hackman and Oldham's requisite task (1976) attributes (optimizing skill variety, task identity, task significance, autonomy, and feedback) combined with developmental opportunities for self-actualization and a collegial organizational climate. This would roughly satisfy both Kantian and Aristotelian principles. Good employment conditions might be defined as a 'fair' relationship between employee inputs (skill, effort, and time) and material outcomes in relation to comparison others (including other employees in the same or comparable organizations and other stakeholders) reached by negotiation and agreement, with the organization additionally committed to a duty of care towards the employee. This would comply with Adam's equity theory of satisfaction and stakeholder theory and would not be incompatible with Rawls' theory of justice. Hodson's ideas (2001: 264) about what constitutes 'dignity at work' make very similar 'rational' points, in identifying the creation and enforcement of norms which provide both protection from mismanagement and abuse *and* the creation of bilateral structures of participation that provide opportunities for workers to realize their human potential through creative, meaningful, and productive work.

Collectivism may also protect negative freedom, in so far as it protects union members from the constraints imposed by employers' unilateral imposition of exploitative and arbitrary terms and conditions of employment. For example, an employee's choice and ability to live her chosen good life may be constrained by the working of very long hours for subsistence pay (echoes of the old union cry: 'Not a minute on the day, not a penny off the pay!').

'Ability' raises two further issues. Negative freedom may be undermined by acts of omission as well as commission, when situations that constrain choice and which, it is believed, could be altered, are left unchanged. So, following critical theory, leaving unquestioned and unchanged the deep structures of a capitalist society that promote inequality and, hence, constrain the choices of the resultant disadvantaged people, diminishes negative freedom. A union's role in challenging deep structures of inequality, conversely, promotes negative freedom. Similarly, because negative freedom is defined as choice among alternatives that is unimpeded by others, it is further diminished if people have been so conditioned to take for granted structures of inequality and exploitation that choices that might be available to them are not perceived as available choices (Lukes 1974). Unions, as instruments of political consciousness-raising, may again promote negative freedom.

However, it could be argued that institutional collectivism may also undermine negative freedom. Weber was clear that, in a pluralist society, the only protection against the all-encompassing, constraining 'iron cage' of bureaucracy was the development of competing, counterbalancing institutions, such as unions. But, as Michels pointed out, even institutions that were anti-bureaucratic and democratic in intention, tend to become bureaucratic and undemocratic. This is because, being avenues of social advancement for energetic and talented members of the working class, the latter tend to abandon any revolutionary aims for their class once their own social advancement is achieved and the 'iron law of oligarchy' prevails, supported by collusion with the bosses. As Beetham (1987: 63) puts it, 'institutions created by the working class to secure their emancipation [can], through processes of bureaucratization, turn into agencies to perpetuate their own subordination'. Put differently, this is the classic tension trade unions experience between the 'administrative rationality' of bureaucracy and the 'representative rationality' of a voluntary organization (Child, Loveridge, and Warner 1973). Furthermore, in pursuing positive freedom through *collective* self-determination, the individual employee may find both his or her *individual* positive and negative freedoms restricted in two ways. First, although collective self-determination may be chosen by the individual as the rational path towards some valued outcomes (e.g. a higher rate of pay for the job than that offered to equivalently skilled non-union labour) (Freeman and Medoff 1984), his or her positive freedom at the same time may be restricted by union opposition to differential payment via performance appraisal and performance-related pay within a job category. Second, an individual's negative freedom may be restricted by the 'tyranny of the majority', in that the individual trade union member has to abide by decisions of the majority of the membership, with which he or she may disagree, or risk expulsion or opprobrium (e.g. in exercising the choice to cross picket lines of a strike). It may be argued, of course, that in joining a union, an individual makes a choice to accept such constraints to individual autonomy and, if the choice is fully informed and freely made, this implies no loss of negative freedom. However, such an argument would be undermined by the most extreme manifestations of collectivism, namely the closed shop and lack of secret balloting.

The ethics of individualism are evident from Berlin's arguments. Positive and negative freedoms are about the values of rational individual autonomy (a value in itself, quite apart from being a route to want satisfaction) and of self-creation through unimpeded choice. A collectivist critique might argue that rampant individualism, unimpeded by any notion of a collective good derived through social contract, results, not in the good life, but one that is 'solitary, poor, nasty, brutish, and short', to use Hobbes' famous words. The Rawlsian 'egalitarian theory of justice' (Rawls 1971), that each person should have an equal right to the most extensive basic liberty compatible with like liberty for others and that social and economic inequalities should exist only where they are reasonably expected to be to everyone's advantage and attached to positions open to all, preserves the notions of individual autonomy and choice but within the bounds of social justice.

This is an abstract discussion of the ethics of collectivism and individualism. In the next section, I will apply Berlin's ideas to two groups of employees which, in the private sector at least, tend not to be unionized: knowledge workers and routine service sector workers. Do they enjoy positive and negative liberty at work without collective representation?

Rational autonomy and unimpeded choice at work?

THE KNOWLEDGE WORKER

Knowledge workers are those who possess either job or organizational knowledge that are recognized as essential to organizational effectiveness. In terms of the resource-based value perspective, these are the employees that are core in developing an organization's unique, valuable, scarce, and inimitable competencies (Barney 1991). Some of these workers, for example, the liberal professions and those professionals working in public sector bureaucracies, are likely to be collectively represented, either through professional associations or unions. Those that are professionals or managers in the private sector, such as Reich's 'symbolic analysts' (1991) or Ohmae's 'transnational man' (sic) (1989) are more likely to be on individualized, personally negotiated, contracts. Where such employees are considered to be the core asset of an organization, their individual bargaining power is likely to be high.

For such knowledge workers, the positive freedom of rational self-determination, is achieved, at least in part, through choice of employer, the enjoyment of a high discretion job, which may carry with it elements that rational people might agree constitute the good life: work that is high on Hackman and Oldham's requisite task attributes, offering genuine empowerment, high material rewards, and a reasonable degree of job security. If this implies respect for the employee's skills and knowledge in their own right, then the criterion of Kantian ethics is fulfilled; if recognition and career development leads to self-actualization and the achievement of a coherent narrative that renders life meaningful, then such work and employment conditions score highly in Aristotelian terms. If such knowledge workers receive very high material rewards, then this might be considered ethical under Rawls' rule, if one believes in a 'trickle down effect' (high pay is necessary to retain high skills, which are necessary for organizational success, which is necessary for economic growth, which contributes to everyone's advantage). Even if it is recognized that knowledge workers are not respected as ends in themselves, but only instrumentally, as the means to organizational sustained competitive advantage, this can still be considered ethical if, in terms of utilitarianism, a case can be made (however difficult to demonstrate) that their work and employment results in the greatest happiness to the greatest number.

However, can it be said that such employees enjoy negative freedom of unimpeded choice? Strictly speaking, probably not. The choices presented to knowledge workers in high discretion jobs, in terms of how they do their jobs and in terms of work–life balance may be constrained by the demands of other more powerful organizational stakeholders, promoting values that may conflict with their own (short termism, shareholder value, long hours culture). The pressure of an auditing society culture may give rise to processes that may be highly constraining on their choices about what work they do and the manner in which they do it (Power 1997). Nevertheless, in so far as they freely chose to join the organization in the knowledge of the likely terms and conditions of employment and with alternative choices available, the spirit of negative liberty is fulfilled. This is especially true if the nature of their knowledge and skill development, combined with the material benefits they can command, extend the choices they can make in other life roles.

This argument is consistent with what, at first sight, might appear to be a surprising finding by Guest and colleagues (2000): that working on a fixed term contract correlated with perceptions of fairness on the part of their Chartered Institute of Personnel and Development (CIPD) survey respondents. Guest and colleagues explained this finding in terms of both positive and negative freedom (Guest et al. 2000 cited in Guest 2000: 109–10). The workers' negative freedom was protected in so far as a transactional contract protects them from open-ended commitments 'expected' by an overly demanding organizational culture.

In particular, they are able to escape from the potential tyranny of 'organizational citizenship', the kind of cultural requirement to work long hours, to help out colleagues in difficulty and to promote the organization at all times.

In the case of knowledge workers, in particular, given their high employability, the resultant ability to negotiate a contract on their own terms enacts their positive freedom. As Guest (2001: 110) puts it:

They are taking control of their careers and their working lives by negotiating contracts which offer a much better balance between work and the rest of their lives and which free them from day-to-day aspects of exploitation by the organizational culture.

ROUTINE SERVICE SECTOR WORKERS

The sorts of workers I have in mind here are those working at unskilled or semi-skilled, mainly customer or client-facing jobs, such as in retailing, catering, call centres, and care homes. The amount of liberty such jobs afford is heavily dependent on whether the 'high' or 'low' road to work design and employment conditions is adopted (Batt 2000; Holman 2003; Korczynski 2002). Where the high road is adopted, in theory at least, quality of service is prioritized and, with it, some degree of job discretion is afforded, often expressed in terms of empowerment. In such cases, erstwhile 'routine' work begins to take on some of the characteristics of knowledge working and the arguments developed above apply, particularly in relation to positive freedom. However, this only holds if 'empowerment' really does involve an extension of employees' autonomy, choices, and development, not, as Sisson (1994: 15) has it, 'making someone else take the risk and responsibility', or, as Kaler (1996) puts it, 'what is happening is that management is being relieved of some of its "responsibilities of command" by employees converting them into "responsibilities of subordination"'. Interestingly, in the service sector, much employee empowerment focuses on the 'service recovery' of resolving customers' complaints, an activity likely to be stressful and involving emotional labour, rather than on the proactive taking of initiative in the original service offer (Korczynski 2002: 133). Certainly, the so-called 'empowerment paradox' (Ganz and Bird 1996), whereby empowerment is used to disempower people through their co-optation into a group that represses dissent, would be highly damaging to both positive and negative liberty.

Where the low road is adopted in the service sector, the outcome appears to be Tayloristic task design, aimed at cost minimization, along with a stress on surveillance and control (Korczynski 2002; Taylor and Bain 1999). The stress associated with labour intensification may be exacerbated by the strains of surface acting associated with emotional labour (Hochschild 1983; Rafaeli and Sutton 1987). Thus, Taylor and Bain, from a labour process perspective, describe operative work in a call centre as comprising

…an uninterrupted and endless sequence of similar conversations with customers she never meets. She has to concentrate hard on what is being said, jump from page to page on screen, making sure that the details entered are accurate and that she has said the right things in a pleasant manner. The conversation ends and as she tidies up the loose ends there is another voice in her headset. The pressure is intense because she knows her work is being measured, her speech monitored, and it often leaves her mentally, physically and emotionally exhausted. (Taylor and Bain 1999: 115)

Clearly such work design violates the ideas of rational self-determination and of unimpeded choice which underlie both forms of freedom. Further, Kantian ethics would deplore the instrumental, not to say exploitative, use of human labour; Aristotelianism would criticize the failure to provide opportunities for the development of human potentiality and stakeholder theory might question whether there was mutuality in the treatment of employee vis-à-vis either customer or shareholder. This is particularly the case when such work design is complemented by the use of non-standard contracts (e.g. zero-hours contracts, subcontracting ['outsourcing'], agency working ['insourcing'], temporary, and casual working), which may involve the organization loosing its bonds of obligation to its workers when their presence is no longer perceived to be continuously indispensable and, hence, no longer a necessary fixed cost. Such contracts, particularly prevalent for support staff in the growth areas of the service sector, are marked by temporal discontinuity and the treatment of labour as a commodity. Outsourcing and insourcing exacerbates this commodification of labour because the workers are not directly employed by the organization whose policies and decision-making directly affects the quality of their employment. Thus Purcell (1997) cites some overhead transparencies used in a presentation by a major employment agency, suggesting the key advantages to employers of using agency labour, which encapsulates the commodification of labour contractually outside the boundaries of the organization:

1) Enhances flexibility (turn on and off like a tap)
2) No legal or psychological contract with the individual
3) You outsource the management problems associated with non-core staff
4) Greater cost efficiency (on average 15 to 20 per cent).

The commodification of labour suggests the exact opposite to Berlin's conception of positive freedom: people have been turned into objects rather than subjects and are the instruments of other people's acts of will rather than their own.

Yet some work in the service sector, while it enables the rational self-determination of positive liberty, is damaging of other stakeholders' negative freedoms to make unconstrained choices. For example, Korczynski (2002) identifies 'extreme' forms of sales work, characterized by the active stimulation of demand, rather than responding to customers requests—such as in selling financial products—as particularly vulnerable to ethically questionable practices. Korczynski argues that the practice of paying such salespersons largely by commission, induces an instrumental orientation, whereby customers are perceived purely as a means to an end: profit for the organization and high reward to the salesperson. This results in salespersons, in defiance of Kantian, Rawlsian and stakeholder ethics, developing an ideology which legitimizes techniques of customer manipulation, either by viewing the customer paternalistically, as someone who needs help to see the true benefits of the product, or by internalizing an image of the customer as dishonest that enables them to justify and rationalize their own manipulation of the customer. To survive, it is suggested, salespersons need to develop a 'will to ignorance' about the tensions between a paternalistic image of customers and their instrumental manipulation (Oakes 1990: 87). However, as Korczynski argues, this will to ignorance, combined with a managerial vacuum, consequent on the culture of selling promoting values of entrepreneurial self reliance among the (largely male) workforce, led directly to the massive and systematic mis-selling of financial products in the UK in the late 1980s and early 1990s.

The instrumentality of capitalism in the pursuit of profit is also at the heart of the colonization and commodification of the emotional labour of service workers (Sturdy and Fineman 2001). As 'quality of service' becomes increasingly the differentiator in achieving competitive advantage, so front-line service workers are required to both manage their own emotions and provide behavioural displays associated with feelings in their interactions with customers (Hochschild 1983; Korczynski 2002). Hochschild argues that this leads to alienation on the part of the service worker as a result of the commodification of emotion, structured inequality in relation to customers and managerial imposition of feeling rules, thereby restricting the employee's positive and negative liberty. Employees are required not only to act inauthentically through 'surface acting', in contravention of Aristotelian ethics, but to internalize the feelings they are meant to display ('deep acting'). If this involves internalizing an ethic of care towards abusive customers, in order to create profit for the organization, the employee is being abused by management as much as by the customer. If the employee genuinely feels caring towards the abusive customer, perhaps he or she (usually she) (Tyler and Taylor 2001) might be simultaneously applauded for altruism (caring for someone with a 'problem', as flight attendants are encouraged to redefine a troublesome passenger) or pitied for their false consciousness and eroded autonomy.

However Korczynski (2002) argues that Hochschild's identification of the conditions for *objective* alienation ignores the possibility that emotional labour may be a source of fulfilment, as the natural and spontaneous enactment of an altruistic ethic of care, of respect for others, an expression of positive liberty. When employees have some autonomy in their expression of emotional labour, and have socially embedded relationships with customers, as in many of the traditional 'caring' jobs associated with the 'naturally' caring female labour (or rather socially constructed through patriarchy) (Tyler and Taylor 2001), real satisfactions for both parties may result. Indeed, Korczynski points out that tensions may arise in what he terms the 'customer-oriented bureaucracy' when employees are constrained by its instrumental rationality from delivering the degree of individual care and attention that they consider to be appropriate—an erosion of their negative liberty.

Nevertheless, a case *can* be made for the ethicality of routine semi-skilled or unskilled work in the private service sector, albeit a weak one. That is, that the worker as a rational, autonomous person (positive liberty) freely chooses to engage in that activity and freely enters a contract with the employer that specifies an 'acceptable' effort-reward bargain. While the work may lack Hackman and Oldham's requisite task attributes and be characterized by fragmentation and repetition, or by manipulative, inauthentic behaviour, whether on the part of the employee or agents of capital, it may be justified in utilitarian terms by the production of products and services of high use value and low cost to consumer, by the generation of wages to the employee-producer and of dividends to shareholders. Although the work may lack the characteristics to provide for self-actualization, it may deliver some satisfactions to the worker through the rhythms of the activity itself (Baldamus 1961), through social interaction (Roy 1958), and through the collusive game playing that 'manufactures consent' (Burawoy 1979). Further, in Aristotelian terms, by providing the opportunity for the worker to endure such work in exchange for a wage that may support dependents, it enables the expression of altruism, even at the cost to her negative liberty. It could also be argued that it is patronizing to portray such workers as downtrodden automata, as much evidence exists of their resistance to surveillance and control in order to protect their autonomy and negative liberty (e.g. Bain and Taylor 2000; Knights and McCabe 1998). There again, is it ethical to restrict autonomy beyond the extent that Kantian and Rawlsian rules apply?

A major critique of such a justification is the questionable nature of the assumption that the employee 'freely' enters such an effort-reward bargain, as an enactment of positive liberty. For many people, choice of what work they do and what employment contract they can command is limited by the structural inequalities of their society, by the fact that it does *not* adhere to Rawlsian principles of a just society and thereby erodes many employees' negative liberty. Further, the mantra of 'global competitiveness' encourages First World governments to cut back on employee rights and welfare, as these may be perceived as costs eroding a country's ability to compete in tradables and as encouraging portfolio and foreign direct investment to shift to where such costs are lower. Similarly, even where firms do not outsource jobs to developing countries, the threat of relocation may be used to put a downward pressure on wages (Standing 1999). This has a knock-on effect too. For those entering the labour market without much education, the jobs in manufacturing no longer exist in such plentiful supply and they have to look for temporary or part-time work in low paying service sectors, which are no longer under pressure to raise wages more in line with the (erstwhile better paying) manufacturing sector, owing to the depression of wages and lack of employment in that sector. Hence the income gap, under these conditions and assumptions, inevitably rises between such routine, *disposable* production or in-person service workers (to use Reich's terminology)—generally the young, the old, women, ethnic minorities, and the unskilled—and the *core, indispensable,* knowledge working professional and managerial elites and skilled, often unionized workers—generally, white, educated, prime age males (if with increasing numbers of women and ethnic minorities). Given that life choices can be constrained by low income, negative liberty is further undermined for routine workers in the largely non-unionized private sector.

The ethics of HRM for employees without collective representation

So what is the most ethical employment relations system for employees without collective representation? In line with Berlin's privileging of choice in his conceptions of liberty, one might suggest that it is a system which employees themselves might choose. Clearly, in relation to the UK and elsewhere, the majority of employees are *not* choosing to join a union (to put this choice at its weakest—some may be actively *choosing* not to join a union). Guest and Conway's data (1999) from their 1998 CIPD survey found that workers' attitudes towards unions were lukewarm to say the least. For example, around 70 per cent of unionized as well as non-unionized respondents felt that union membership either made or would make no difference to fairness in the workplace.

So what employee relations system might employees choose? If they sought the rational self-determination embodied in the idea of positive liberty, logically they might choose a system which they believed would deliver the good (want satisfaction) in the 'right' way (the just distribution of the good). These two ideas, as Guest (1998, 2001) and Guest and Conway (1998) persuasively argue, come together in the idea of a psychological contract resting on workers' perceptions of the fairness, trust and 'delivery of the deal' in employment relationships. On the basis of their CIPD surveys (Guest 1999;

Guest and Conway 1998, 2000; Guest et al. 1997), Guest and colleagues argue that such a contract is most likely to come into being in good workplaces, where high-commitment HRM policies are implemented as part of a RBV business strategy, or even in 'lucky' workplaces where they are implemented because they are fashionable (Guest and Hoque 1994). In such workplaces, the respondents who report the existence of more HR practices also report a more positive psychological contract and greater job satisfaction, job security and motivation and lower levels of work pressure (Guest 1999: 22). The more HRM practices are implemented and the more there is scope for direct participation, perhaps through schemes of employee involvement (EI), the more likely it is that workers will experience positive liberty in the sense that they feel they have more opportunities to participate in and exercise some influence over relevant company decisions (Guest 2001). The unitarism of HRM would not be problematic from the perspective of positive liberty as rational self-determination on the part of all stakeholders would imply the compatibility of the different ends they might seek. From the perspective of negative liberty, though, with its assumption of plural, rivalrous, and conflicting ends, this could be a problem.

The real problem with this suggestion, though, is not one of principle, but one of pragmatics. The fact is that only a small minority of workplaces (14 per cent), at least in Britain, have high-commitment HRM in place (defined as eight plus out of fifteen high-commitment management practices) and these tend to be *unionized* workplaces (being present in 25 per cent of workplaces that recognize a trade union and in only 5 per cent of those that do not) (WERS 98). As EI is generally considered to be part of a high-commitment HRM strategy, by definition, it is unlikely to be widely implemented in workplaces failing to adopt such a strategy. Further, Marchington (2001: 250) concludes that, even where EI *is* implemented,

It is also clear that the impact of EI upon employees has not been great... but perhaps little more [than employees' 'mildly favourable' response] could be expected given the minor impact which EI has on most employees' lives.

What role does this leave for trade unions? The finding from WERS 98, that workplaces which were unionized tended to have a higher incidence of HRM practices than those that were not, points to an important function that they serve. As Brown et al. (2000: 627) aptly put it in a clear statement of unions' role in protecting positive and negative liberty, 'collective procedures are the custodians of individual rights'—a conclusion that is amply supported by Terry's research (1999) on the effectiveness—or lack of it—of collective employee representation in non-union firms. The CIPD survey data suggest that those employees who thought belonging to a union might increase fairness at work were more likely to work in the services sector, traditionally of low union density, and to report fewer HR practices at work (Guest 2001).

But, again, there is the practical issue. Workplaces practising the 'New Realism' of high unionization combined with a high level of HR practices are few and far between in the private sector, accounting for only 1 per cent of such workplaces, according to WERS 98.

Perhaps the most realistic role for trade unions in the private sector today is to go with the flow of the individualistic, consumer-oriented culture of the twenty-first century and become what has been termed the 'AA of the workplace' (Bassett and Cave 1993). The possible danger of union marginalization is less relevant in those circumstances where unionism, at this time, has no presence at all (Boxall and Haynes 1997). Most employees in the affluent West exercise their most conscious lifestyle choices in acts of consumption. (At the same time, of course, large firms may impede consumers' negative liberty through the manipulation of such choices via the media.) One role for unions is to provide individual services for member-consumers, ranging from financial, legal, training, and education services, to the expanding area of individual representation in discipline, discrimination, and grievance cases (Williams 1997). The latter area, in particular, is likely to grow given the increased emphasis on individuals' statutory legal rights in the employment relationship. Research suggests that 'support if I had a problem at work' is far and away *the* most cited reason for joining a trade union (Waddington and Whitston 1997). This form of 'collective individualism' or, as Fox (1985) put it, 'instrumental collectivism' is central to the role of trade unions as 'a means of redressing the vulnerability of the individual employee in his or her dealings with the employer' (Hyman 1997: 321). When this takes the form of protecting individuals from the arbitrary actions of management, unions are acting to protect employees' negative freedom.

Ironically, such a role recalls the pre-Fordist days of unions' birth, when 'the Webbs identified "mutual insurance" as a trade union method even more firmly established than collective bargaining' (Hyman 1997: 321). Plus ca change, plus c'est la meme chose?

3 HRM and performance: can partnership address the ethical dilemmas?

David E. Guest

Introduction

Human resource management has become established as a focus of study largely on the basis of two core propositions. The first is that people are a key source of competitive advantage for organizations (Barney 1991; Barney and Wright 1998; Wright, Dunford, and Snell 2001*a*) and, as such, should be properly managed. The second is that effective management of HR should result in demonstrably superior performance. These combined propositions have led to an interest in HRM among specialists in business strategy, concerned with the analysis of strategic choices about the most effective deployment of HR (Boxall and Purcell 2003). It has also begun to interest accountants and national policymakers, reflected in consideration of the management of human assets or human capital. The Kingsmill Report (2003) in the UK, titled *Accounting For People*, is one illustration of this. The government-sponsored Task Force that led to this report started from the assumption that if human assets are so important, the state of these assets should be systematically presented and explained in annual company reports.

From a rather different perspective, HRM has also attracted the attention of many academics from an IR background who have been interested in the question of whether HRM either supersedes or obviates any need for independent trade union representation; or, indeed, whether it is overtly anti-union. Building on this general interest in the management of HR, there has been a renewed interest in the role of HR managers and whether they have used the opportunity offered by HRM to become what Ulrich (1997) described as 'Human Resource Champions' (Guest and King 2004).

Behind each of these perspectives is a concern for human resources as key assets that are there to be managed, utilized, or possibly exploited to improve organizational performance. In many respects, therefore, these issues cohere around the question of the relationship between HRM and performance, which can serve as a focal point for analysis. Indeed, I have argued elsewhere (Guest 1997) that this has become *the* key research issue in HRM. Behind this issue are a set of familiar ethical questions about managing with the consent of the managed and how that consent is obtained.

There is already quite an extensive literature on ethical aspects of HRM (see, e.g. Legge 1995; Winstanley and Woodall 2000*b*) that debate different ethical positions. These are covered in other chapters and will not be raised here. Instead, this chapter will explore aspects of the theory and research about HRM and performance by addressing four core issues that raise potential ethical questions. The first concerns the criticism that while HRM claims to be primarily concerned with the management of people, in practice it largely ignores workers. In contrast, a second criticism sometimes levelled at HRM is that far from ignoring them, it reflects a rather subtle approach to the exploitation of workers. A third issue concerns the status of the evidence base of research on HRM and performance and the temptations and dangers of presenting as fact research that is at best provisional. Finally, there are some largely ignored issues around the application of HRM and in particular the challenges of applying in organizations an approach that emphasizes the importance of an integrated HR system. These are ethical issues that potentially affect academics who write about and research HRM, policymakers, professional bodies, and some academics who are part of the advocacy of HRM and those such as consultants, managers, and again some academics who are interested in the application of HRM. A later section of the chapter will take these themes a little further by exploring how far the pursuit of high performance and employee well-being can be a feasible ethical goal, more particularly in the context of a pluralist, or what will be defined as a partnership perspective.

Human resource management ignores workers

This rather paradoxical assertion can be traced back to the roots of contemporary interest in HRM and performance. Some of the earlier work on HRM and performance had its roots either in business schools where there was a particular interest in strategy rather than employment and employees; or in labour economics where the starting point was often assumptions of rational behaviour and a focus on productivity. The lack of concern for workers was reflected in the initial models of HRM and performance. Essentially, these models were concerned with the relationship between aspects of strategy, including HR strategy, HR practices and outcomes. This was the case in early studies by Arthur (1994) and Ichniowski, Shaw, and Prennushi (1997) in strip steel mills, by MacDuffie (1995) in the auto industry, and by Huselid

(1995) in his industrywide studies. The problem, now well recognized, was that in each case there was a concern to demonstrate a relationship between the effective strategic management of HR and firm performance. In doing so, researchers ignored the 'black box' in which workers were located and, by failing to consider either worker reactions to HRM or the consequences for the deployment and utilization of workers, were neglecting the core point about the process whereby HRM is presumed to have an impact. As a result, they might be able to demonstrate an association between HRM and performance but they could not explain how it came about. Issues about whether workers responded to HRM strategy and practices with enthusiasm, indifference, or as 'willing slaves' (Scott 1994) were not considered.

Despite the neglect of workers, in many ways these early studies of HRM and performance are impressive. In most cases, they measured intermediate outcomes such as labour turnover and productivity, which, it might be argued, serve as proxies for employee behaviour. They also serve an important role as landmark studies by showing that there is evidence of a relationship between HRM and performance. In contexts such as business schools and in the wider business community, this is a crucial message in seeking to persuade sceptics to take HR seriously. If, following the arguments of Beer et al. (1985) and Skinner (1981), HRM is too important to be left to HR specialists, then the case needs to be forcibly made for why chief executives and others should be taking it seriously. What has followed in the academic community has been a necessary and inevitable corrective but subsequent research has not undermined the core argument that 'good' HRM is associated with superior performance. Given its roots in business strategy, one of the ironies of much of this and subsequent research on HRM and performance is that the strategic approach has proved less successful in explaining outcomes than a more universalist approach (Becker and Huselid 1998).

The stream of research that emphasizes strategy and performance and largely neglects workers and their roles and concerns has been described as 'hard' HRM (Storey 1987). It has evolved, notably in the USA, into a concern for what are currently described as 'high performance work systems' which require 'high performance HR practices'. The language reflects the intended focus and purpose behind the interest in HRM. Increasingly, this stream of analysis has begun to focus more directly on workers, but in doing so, the core question is about the practices most likely to result in improved performance. Typically, the answer centres around the idea of 'performance management'. This approach advocates use of HR practices to ensure that workers who have the necessary capabilities and competencies are motivated and, through the design of jobs and teams, able to contribute fully. It can be achieved through the distinctive application of practices such as selection and training, financial incentives, and goal-setting and team-working (Becker et al. 1997). At all times, the focus is first and foremost on fully utilizing the key asset, the human resources, without much consideration for their views and without paying more than lip service to the possibility that workers are active participants within a complex system. Questions about possible exploitation of workers and concerns about providing them with an independent voice are rarely considered to be a relevant part of the agenda. Herein lies the by-now-familiar ethical dilemma of an approach that claims success by recognizing that people are the most important asset and resource and then seeking to treat them almost like any other inanimate resource. In a sense, therefore, human resources are not treated as human. By neglecting the 'good' of the worker, it is possible to question whether this approach can be considered ethical.

HRM exploits workers

To those unfamiliar with HRM, the preceding analysis might be viewed as being concerned with the exploitation of workers; and of course in some respects this is the case. However, the aim here is to draw a distinction between arguments about ignoring workers and an approach that explicitly recognizes the role of workers as active participants in organizational life and therefore recognizes the challenge of managing with the consent of the managed. Rather than being neglected, workers move centre stage with a vital part to play in the relationship between HRM and performance.

The roots of this approach lie less in the strategic and economic perspective of the business schools and more in the fields of organizational behaviour and employment relations. The key early work is perhaps that of Walton (1985) and Lawler (1987). The core point they make is that the best way to manage workers is by involving and engaging them in the workplace. In short, what is needed is 'high involvement' or high-commitment management. Where this is implemented, it is argued, workers will respond positively by displaying the flexibility, extra-role behaviour, and motivation that is seen as increasingly important for the effective utilization of their knowledge and skills. This will result in superior performance at both the individual and organizational levels. While not denying the importance of the practices associated with high-performance work systems, there is a rather different emphasis, for example with respect to the practices likely to ensure motivation. This approach is also likely to add a further set of HR practices designed to generate commitment and involvement. These may include job security, fairness of treatment, and extensive communication and consultation. By recognizing the importance of workers and their reactions, it opens up the black box with a more complex model of the relationship between HRM and performance. This has now been widely recognized and various models incorporating this perspective have been presented (e.g. Guest 1987, 1997; Purcell et al. 2003; and, to some extent, Becker et al. 1997).

This approach has led to a growing body of research exploring the relationship between HR practices and employee attitudes and behaviour (Appelbaum et al. 2000; Cully et al. 1999; Guest 1999, 2002; Ramsay et al. 2000). These results generally show that the greater application of a distinctive set of HR practices is associated with higher worker satisfaction and commitment. A dissenting voice comes from Ramsay et al. (2000) who point out that HR practices may also be associated with greater stress. Reflecting this concern, there has been a wider critique of this perspective from, among others, Legge (1995) and Keenoy (1990a; 1997). Their argument is that this approach to HRM can take the form of a new and more insidious form of control in which management achieves the control, compliance, and possibly the commitment of workers through the management of organizational culture. This implies a unitarist model in contrast to a more traditional form of control based on the notion of an exchange in the effort–reward bargain that lies at the heart of the employment relationship. In this respect, so the argument goes, this soft (Storey 1987) approach to HRM takes over the mantle of human relations and represents a subtle form of manipulation. If this is the case, it raises another set of ethical issues.

One counterargument is that if workers say they prefer this approach and report satisfaction, then we should accept what they say at face value (Guest 1999). Indeed, there is some evidence to suggest that high-commitment HRM is generally preferred to any of the alternatives (Guest and Conway 1999). An extension of this argument, and one that is open to empirical investigation is whether it meets acceptable ethical standards if it is applied in contexts where there are safeguards. One way in which such an approach is being addressed in the UK is through the concept of partnership, an issue we return to later in this chapter.

While this soft, high-commitment approach has attracted interest because of its focus and implications for workers, there has been rather less exploration of its impact on performance. One reason for this is that high quality research incorporating each step in the model is extremely difficult to do. However, we do have some evidence. In the UK, Patterson et al. (1998) conducted a longitudinal study in a sizeable sample of manufacturing companies and reported an association between HR practices and commitment at one point and subsequent changes in performance. Moreover, they reported that HR practices were associated with greater change than other management activities such as R & D expenditure. Analysis of WERS 98, based on subjective management accounts of workplace performance and cross-sectional data, also points to a positive association between HRM and performance, partially mediated by employee satisfaction and commitment (Guest and Conway 2000). However, at least one American study has challenged these findings, albeit using a rather restricted range of HR practices (Cappelli and Neumark 2001). Furthermore, Guest (2002) has suggested that the practices associated with high worker satisfaction and well-being only overlap to a limited extent with those associated with higher performance. Therefore, while workers appear to prefer the soft HRM approach to the available alternatives, the context in which they are experienced, the range of additional practices in place and the safeguards reflected in an independent voice, are all likely to be important for employee well-being. By implication, there is the potential for an ethical approach, since workers' interests and goals may be taken into account but also the risk that without safeguards this may be exploitative.

Overstating the evidence on HRM and performance

The third ethical issue associated with HRM and performance concerns the way in which the evidence about HRM and performance is presented and used. To understand why this is an issue, we need first to review some of the evidence. As a starting point, it is important to emphasize that the bulk of the published research evidence shows an association between HRM and performance. However, the evidence is open to criticism and therefore to challenge for a number of reasons. These can be briefly listed. One concern is that the evidence is not cumulative because there are no agreed measures of HRM. Indeed, there is a lack of agreement about what practices to include, what level of detail and specificity is required, and how to measure practices. Another concern is the tendency to use a single source, often near the apex of a large multi-unit organization, to describe HR practices for all parts of the organization. A further concern is that most of the emphasis has been placed on measures of HR practices to the neglect of the effectiveness of these practices, despite the logic of the argument that their presence is less important than the way they are applied.

There has also been much disagreement about what measures of performance to include in research studies and about how they should be measured. Some studies have placed the main emphasis on intermediate outcomes such as productivity and indicators of quality or materials waste. However, the main focus has often been on some sort of financial measure, ranging in sophistication from Tobin's Q (Huselid 1995) to subjective ratings of comparative performance (Cully et al. 1999). Some critics have raised the question of whether it is reasonable to expect any sizeable link between HRM and financial performance given the 'distance' between them. Instead, it may be more sensible to look for a series of intermediate links. In addition, there are a number of more general concerns. One, offered mainly by European researchers (see, e.g. Boselie, Paauwe, and Jansen 2001) is that the institutional context is largely ignored. A related concern is that the bulk of the research is American and the pattern of results may be different in Europe and elsewhere. One reason for this might be the legislative framework which requires organizations to apply many of the HR practices about which firms in the USA and to a lesser extent the UK and possibly also Australia have choice.

A final concern is that much of the evidence is cross sectional. There may be an association but it is not possible on the basis of such evidence to assert causality. The usual critique is that successful organizations may be more likely to introduce HR practices. In one recently reported study, where longitudinal data were available, there was even some evidence to support this direction of causality (Guest et al. 2003). The complexity of the causal links has been explored by Schneider et al. (2003) with data on aspects of job satisfaction and performance in twenty-five large US firms over an eight-year period. They found more evidence to support the view that successful organizational performance leads to job satisfaction than vice versa. At the same time, they did not find a consistent unidirectional causal link. Therefore, while firm success seems to lead to more satisfied workers, it is also possible, at least to some extent, that happy workers lead to firm success. Since there are continuing doubts in the research on HRM and performance about conceptualizing and operationalizing the independent variable, the dependent variable and the relationship between them, there is considerable scope for error. Given all this built-in error, it is perhaps surprising that the great majority of published findings are so robustly positive.

While there are a number of academics who would argue that the growing body of evidence does support a link, possibly even a causal link, between HRM and various measures of performance, others are more cautious and would argue that the case for a link between HRM and performance remains unproven, due to the lack of the reliability and validity of the accumulated studies. Behind the body of evidence, there are also questions about the temptation to publish positive rather than negative findings. Certainly, articles tend to emphasize significant positive results that explain a very small proportion of the variance and to ignore negative or insignificant associations. This emphasis on positive results may give a misleading impression about the scale and significance of such results. The concern is that some groups of policymakers may be less cautious than many academics in interpreting and generalizing from positive results.

There is a large body of 'grey research', undertaken by consultants, who typically highlight and market any positive links between HRM and performance. Organizations such as the Chartered Institute of Personnel and Development (CIPD) in the UK and their parallel organizations in other countries have an understandable interest in identifying and promoting a link between HRM and performance. The CIPD in particular has been a sponsor of research (including my own) and has widely marketed the existence of a clear link (see, e.g. the Foreword to Purcell et al. 2003). In the UK, government departments, notably the Department of Trade and Industry (DTI 2002), have also become enthusiastic advocates of HRM, allied to an interest in enhancing national productivity. This is reflected in their policy documents, in their support for the Kingsmill Task Force discussed at the start of this chapter, and in setting the promotion of the link between HRM and performance as one of their strategic priorities. An attraction of HRM as an approach to enhancing productivity and performance is that it is potentially largely cost free. While there will always be scope to invest in HR, perhaps through training, the main focus is on productivity enhancement through greater utilization of the existing HR.

Academics may believe there is a link between HRM and performance but many will be aware of the limitations of the research and exercise appropriate caution about advocating action on the basis of the research evidence. Governments, consultancies, and professional bodies have a different agenda and, in most cases, a different perspective on academic evidence. Allied to this, HRM may appeal partly because it offers a route to high performance that may obviate the need for collective representation as a mechanism for EI. Furthermore, our own research (Guest and King 2004) indicates that most senior managers, when challenged, believe there probably is a link between HRM, or at least good 'people management', and performance; to them it appears intuitively plausible.

The ethical issues concern over claiming the case for a link, more particularly a causal link, between HRM and performance when the evidence base remains weak. However, for academics, the ethical problems are more complex. If they are reluctant to advocate HRM based on the evidence about its link to performance, there may be other reasons to advocate it, based on some of the evidence cited above about its association with workers' satisfaction and well-being. Set against this, there is also the difficult question of how to respond if asked about the alternatives to HRM. One way of resolving this is to focus on the process and context under which decisions about HRM are made.

HRM may be advocated but there are few guidelines for its application

The feasibility of application of HRM has rarely been considered as an ethical issue; indeed, it is possible to question whether it does raise ethical considerations. It is often argued that a distinctive feature of HRM is its focus on the system of HR practices rather than on a particular practice. It implies that it is no longer enough to do selection or training or communication very well. A whole system or set of HR practices has to be implemented effectively. This raises two issues. The first is what is meant by good HRM. The second is where any practitioner should start. Discussion of an HR system is often linked to the idea of a 'bundle' of HR practices. These are typically defined as key combinations of practices. However, there remains an ambiguity in the literature about whether bundles should be considered at the level of specific practices, combinations of practices, or a broadly based approach reflecting a philosophy of HRM (Delery 1998). Without some clarification, there remains uncertainty about the level at which to consider application of HRM. More specifically, if researchers are advocating the need to apply a 'system' how does anyone introduce a system? It is conceivable that this can be done in the context of greenfield sites; but for a manager who has heeded the message and wants to get going, where does he/she start? Put another way, to what extent is it ethical to advocate an approach that many may find impractical to introduce?

A pragmatic way to address this issue is through some form of statistical analysis to identify which combination of practices is most likely to be consistently associated with outcomes. This might be achieved through regressions taking each HR practice rather than some combination of practices as the independent variables. A variant on this that has been applied to HRM is the use of sequential tree analysis (Guest, Conway, and Dewe 2004). This builds a 'tree' by identifying the key practices and then seeking the best combination of practices. Studies of this sort, as well as the more qualitative work of Purcell et al. (2003) point to the importance of job design and of providing scope for autonomy and discretion as a key practice associated with both superior performance and job satisfaction. Yet it is not clear that job design typically falls within the domain of HR managers. For example, it is relatively infrequently cited as one of the practices being implemented by them and their organization. There is a risk, therefore, that recommending that priority be given to job design as a starting point may serve to disempower HR managers.

Does partnership resolve the ethical issues?

The body of research evidence does show some sort of association, some of the time, between HRM and some aspects of performance as well as with job satisfaction and commitment. Put another way, there is evidence that whatever its shortcomings, many workers prefer to work in an organization that practices a form of high-commitment HRM to the alternatives. Furthermore, since managers will continue to seek competitive advantage, it may be better, from a worker's perspective, if they do so by pursuing HRM rather than some of the less palatable approaches that were in vogue during the 1990s such as process re-engineering or some of the current features of outsourcing. The challenge lies in putting in place mechanisms to ensure that when and if HRM is applied it occurs within a framework that provides workers with some oversight, safeguards against the more exploitative elements of HRM, and independent voice. If this can be achieved, some of the ethical concerns might lose their salience. In the UK, one approach that has been hailed as a means of achieving this is partnership.

Partnership at work is an old idea that has found fashion as a contemporary vehicle for managing the 'new deal' between government, employers, and unions. It has been endorsed by the UK Trades Union Congress (TUC) which has proposed six core principles for partnership. These are employment security; commitment to the success of the enterprise; openness and transparency; recognition that partners have overlapping but distinct interests; enhancing quality of working life; and tapping the motivation, commitment, and innovative capacity of employees to make work more interesting and to add value to the firm.

The TUC principles echo the definition presented by the Involvement and Participation Association (IPA), a long-established pressure group for greater involvement in work to which a range of organizations belong, including a number of companies and trade unions with a long-standing interest in the subject. They suggest that there are four key building blocks of the partnership principle, namely security and flexibility, sharing financial success, developing good communication and consultation, and representative employee voice (IPA 1997). In both the TUC and IPA definitions, it might be noted that there is more emphasis on principles than specific practices.

One reason offered for the interest in partnership among trade unions in the UK is that after what Undy (1999) termed 'the final settlement' between the Labour government and trade unions, including legislation to ensure that union claims for recognition would more easily be addressed through ballots and the promotion of individual rights at work, partnership was the 'only game in town'. This also reflected the pro-European stance of some senior members of the TUC who supported the notion of social partnership, reflected in legislated systems of works councils embracing consultation and communication. This has recently been introduced in the UK in a somewhat modified form through legislation to implement the European Directive on Information and Consultation. In the meantime, the government set up a 'Partnership Fund', overseen by the TUC, to encourage experimentation and development of partnership activities, a key criterion for support being that any initiatives included a commitment from both union and employer representatives to develop partnership practices.

There has been a certain amount of research that seeks to address the question of whether partnership can achieve the kind of goals set for it and therefore by implication can address the ethical issues. Those who have reviewed the literature and the rhetoric about partnership are understandably sceptical (Ackers and Payne 1998) while those with a stake in its success, argue that it has much to offer (Coupar and Stevens 1998). One of the main research studies to date explored the nature and impact of partnership, as well as the philosophy informing it, among organizations belonging to the IPA (Guest and Peccei 2001). Several findings are relevant. First, definitions of partnership endorsed by representatives of employers and employees embraced traditional forms of direct and representative participation and also various aspects of HRM including both 'soft' elements such as job redesign and communication and 'hard' elements such as performance management. Second, in so far as benefits were identified in terms of performance and employee satisfaction, they tended to be more strongly associated with the softer elements of HRM and with direct participation than with representative participation and hard HRM. An interesting exception was the positive role of the use of employee share ownership schemes. Third, most organizations felt that they had only taken some of the steps towards partnership and still had further to travel. Indeed, there were only a few formal partnership deals where, on the basis of some of the criteria listed above as principles of partnership, some partnership is actually in place. Finally, in the limited number of cases where high trust existed, reflected most strongly in management's willingness to share strategic issues with workers' representatives, there appeared to be a wider range of significant benefits as judged by both management and worker representatives. Crucially, in these contexts, there was a high level of application of HRM, particularly high-commitment HRM, as well as a high level of direct and representative participation over a range of issues. These issues are likely to include those associated with the introduction or extension and application of HRM.

A key conclusion from this analysis, and an issue picked up in the subsequent work by Peccei and Guest (2002) is that the role of trust and the process whereby trust is developed, is a key to successful partnership. Trust is also the focus of three detailed case studies of partnership reported by Dietz (2004). His conclusions about the impact of partnership are positive. An important question, and one that is addressed by other researchers (see, e.g. Oxenbridge and Brown 2002), is whether trust works best within a formal or informal setting. Dietz notes that the evidence from other research is inconclusive; his own view is that a modest amount of structure can enhance and protect partnership. Like other researchers, he notes that partnership is often developed by key individuals on the employer and employee sides who have built a high level of interpersonal trust. This needs to be formalized to ensure it spreads and survives beyond them.

While Dietz concludes from his three cases that partnership can work, Guest and Peccei (2001) are rather less sanguine about whether it will work across a swathe of organizations. There are two reasons for this. One is that management has often been in the driving seat and can determine how far partnership is developed; the second is that management, more than employee representatives, generally displays low trust. As a result, the balance of advantage, in terms of the issues that are addressed through partnership, generally lies with the employer rather than the employees.

Further evidence that the employer is in a position to take the initiative comes from the analysis of WERS 98 (Cully et al. 1999). Among other things, this reveals that managers are likely to consult in the workplace about a wider range of issues with non-union than with union representatives. In other words, the safeguard of an independent voice does not mean that the voice will be heard in partnership-related contexts. It is therefore not surprising that the newer generation of trade union leaders in the UK, although not yet the TUC (1999), are expressing growing scepticism about partnership. For them it is not the only game in town and they favour a return to a more adversarial form of IR. Whether this is more likely to result in benefits to the workforce remains to be seen. What this implies is that partnership has the potential to answer to some of the ethical issues surrounding HRM and performance; but it requires high trust from both parties and probably, as Dietz implies, the constant delivery of mutual benefits. While there is impressive case study evidence of what can be achieved with goodwill on both sides, that high trust is too often lacking. Furthermore, while it is easy to espouse partnership, the evidence suggests that it has not taken root in industry.

Discussion and conclusions

This chapter has argued that the relationship between HRM and performance is one of the key reasons for the interest in HRM and is one, if not *the* key research issue. Four ethical issues have been identified. They concern the criticism that some HRM theory, writing and research purporting to be about workers as key resources in practice ignores workers; other research goes to the opposite extreme but in so doing risks developing systems to exploit workers. A third concern is that advocacy of HRM by a range of interested parties has run ahead of the research evidence. A final concern is that HRM can be advocated as a systems approach without recognizing the problems of systems change, resulting in a risk that HR managers will feel disempowered or incompetent.

Despite a range of critiques, there is evidence that workers are more positive about working in organizations where high-commitment HRM is practised than in many other settings. However, this may also leave them potentially vulnerable unless there are safeguards. This argument must be seen in the context of the decline in trade union membership and workplace influence, a decline which authoritative sources expect to continue in the future (*Financial Times* 29 March 2004). Partnership, a distinctive approach advocated by government, unions, and some employers, has been considered as one means of addressing the ethical issues. It was found to have the potential to do so, but in practice, without high trust on the part of employers, may often fail to do so in practice.

Implicit in this chapter are assumptions about the possibilities of an ethical HRM that still offers prospects of high performance. It appears most likely to take the form of what is sometimes termed 'the high road' approach, based on an explicit pursuit of mutual gains within the context of pluralist oversight. The manager will seek high performance, but not only high performance. The model of HRM may recognize that high performance is achieved by successfully engaging workers and by ensuring their competence, motivation, and commitment. In addition, an explicit goal of HRM will be to ensure good employment and the well-being of the workforce. The evidence indicates that in the UK this is unlikely to be achieved without a change in the institutional context. The evidence cited, for example by Boselie, Paauwe, and Jansen (2001) in the case of the Netherlands, suggests that a European Social Partnership system offers the best realistic prospects of mutual gains.

Throughout this chapter, prominence has been given to the range of academic research and debate on HRM and performance. It is easy to assume from this that some form of high-performance or high-commitment management has become the dominant mode of people management in Western organizations, or at least in the USA and UK.

While any organization has to undertake some sort of people management, the evidence indicates that in the UK at least, the application of a distinctive HRM approach, let alone one embedded in a pluralist approach, is very limited. There is evidence for this at both workplace and company levels. Perhaps surprisingly, across the public and private sectors, more practices are likely to be in place where trade unions are recognized. In WERS 98, it was found that based on a list of fifteen high-commitment HR practices, more than half were in place in 25 per cent of workplaces where a trade union was recognized but in only 5 per cent of workplaces where unions were not. Focusing only on the private sector, the authors of WERS note:

only 4 per cent of recognised workplaces had a majority unionised workforce, where local representatives negotiated with management over some issues and where at least half of these high commitment management practices were in place. (Cully et al. 1999: 111)

By implication, in most private sector workplaces, only limited HRM is applied; and where HRM is applied, there are rarely realistic safeguards for workers reflected in an effective independent voice.

A final point to note is that the ethical issues highlighted in this chapter involve researchers, policymakers, and practitioners. Partnership has the potential to address the issues at a practitioner level. There are a separate set of issues for academic writers and researchers about the way they present their research. In most cases, authors are suitably cautious; or, where they go through a refereeing process, are required to display caution. There are ongoing debates about the value of positivist research, and this chapter has been written within a positivist framework. The key requirement among academics is to be aware of the ethical issues and to make them explicit in the presentation of findings. Critics may fail to understand how difficult it is to obtain high-quality data. In a still young but expanding field, it may be reasonable to develop a body of knowledge even with less than ideal data-sets. The risk lies less in the academic discourses than in the overenthusiasm of those who are unwilling, for understandable reasons, to wait for academics to develop a coherent body of knowledge; or who remain sceptical about whether academics can ever develop this in a contentious area of research such as the relation between HRM and performance. The seemingly inevitable rush to application of a less than fully formulated and researched approach to an issue as important as the management of people is a danger about which both academics and practitioners should be fully aware. Ironically, perhaps, we might therefore be more sanguine about the evidence concerning the limited take-up of contemporary HRM and about the difficulties of applying it.

4 Strategic management and human resources: the pursuit of productivity, flexibility, and legitimacy

Peter Boxall and John Purcell

Introduction

This chapter is concerned with the role that human resources play in strategic management and the ethical issues involved in this relationship. It begins by defining what we mean by strategy and then sets up our model of the strategic goals of HRM. Our contention is that three broad goal domains are important in the strategic management of people in firms: labour productivity, organizational flexibility, and social legitimacy (Boxall and Purcell 2003). While many business analysts would readily accept that the first two of these are fundamental to organizational effectiveness, we argue that the pursuit of legitimacy is also vital because firms are always 'embedded in structures of social relations' (Granovetter 1985: 481).

Like Gospel (1992), we use the notion of HRM to refer to all those activities associated with the management of work systems and employment regimes in the firm (Boxall and Purcell 2003). HRM is always part of the management of the firm—irrespective of the existence of HR specialists—and includes a variety of managerial styles. While it is quite appropriate to define HRM as one particular management style, as Guest (1987) and Storey (1995) have done, we find that a broad, inclusive definition of HRM is more appropriate for the purposes of analysing the links between strategic management and HRM. The strategy literature requires this kind of openness because it recognizes variety in business strategy across varying contexts (see, e.g. Miles and Snow 1984; Porter 1985). It rightly implies that there is no 'one best way' to compete in markets and organize the internal operations of the firm.

Strategic problems and the strategies of firms

What, then, do we mean by strategy? In our view, strategy is best defined by making a distinction between the 'strategic problems' firms face in their environment and the strategies they adopt to cope with them (Boxall 1998; Boxall and Purcell 2003).

THE PROBLEM OF VIABILITY

The fundamental problem that the firm faces is that of becoming and remaining viable in its chosen market. Another way of putting this is to say that all firms require 'table stakes': a set of goals, resources, and capable people that are appropriate to the industry context or sector concerned (Boxall 2003; Boxall and Steeneveld 1999; Hamel and Prahalad 1994: 226). Decisions about these table stakes are strategic. They are make-or-break factors. Get the system of these choices right—or right enough—and the firm will be viable. Miss a key piece out and the firm will fail. In other words, when we use the word 'strategic' to describe something, we are saying it is critical to survival, it is seriously consequential. We embrace the common sense view that the word strategic should indicate something of genuine significance for the future of the firm (Johnson 1987; Purcell and Ahlstrand 1994: 51–2).

Take the case of a company launching a new 'High Street' or 'Main Street' bank (Freeman 1995: 221). To be credible at all, it must have the same kinds of technology as other banks, a similar profile of products or services, the necessary levels of funding, systems of internal control, skilled staff who can make it happen 'with the gear' on the day, and a management team who can assemble these resources and focus the firm's energies on objectives that will satisfy its investors. While there may well be differences between banks in terms of the reliance on telephony systems and branch networks, and some may focus on niche areas serving distinctive populations of customers, the fundamentals of banking, and the strict requirements of regulatory authorities, have to be met. The same applies to new entrants to banking: for example, major supermarket chains. They may well be able to leverage their existing customer base, as Tesco have done in the UK, but banking operations still require certain capabilities. Without an effective cluster of goals, resources, and human capabilities, it is over before it starts (Figure 4.1). As Freeman (1995: 221) emphasizes, much

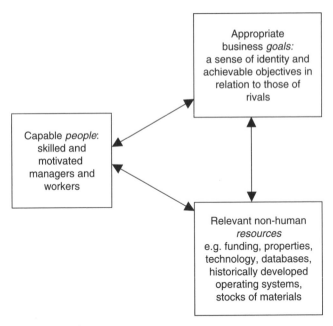

Figure 4.1 Three critical elements for the viability of the firm
Source: Boxall and Purcell (2003: 31).

of the firm's strategy is formed in a 'package' when the original choice of competitive sector is made.

The problem of viability is *the* fundamental strategic problem. While Figure 4.1 summarizes the critical elements involved in it, it naturally oversimplifies the ambiguities, tensions, and complexities involved. It is not necessarily straightforward to decide on the right mix of goals for the firm. Nor does a simple diagram like Figure 4.1 highlight the difficult relationships *among* resources that have to be managed. What Figure 4.1 does highlight, however, is that there is no solution to the problem of viability *without* capable and motivated people. Appropriate human capabilities are strategic to the success of every firm.

THE PROBLEM OF SUSTAINED ADVANTAGE

While the problem of viability is the fundamental strategic problem, and can never be completely resolved (note the decline and even disappearance of some major companies in the last decade), there is a 'second-order' problem that lies beyond it: the contest among leaders of sound businesses to see which firm can secure the best rate of return. In effect, this is not so much a problem as an opportunity, an opportunity to move beyond the pack and gain industry leadership (Boxall and Steeneveld 1999).

A firm which builds a relatively consistent pattern of superior returns for its shareholders has developed some form of 'competitive advantage' (Porter 1985). How long such superior performance can be sustained is, of course, variable. We should not think that superior performance can be maintained indefinitely. Imitative forces come into play when rivals detect that someone has achieved an unusual level of profitability and seek to compete it away. It is helpful to think of 'barriers to imitation' as having different heights and different rates of decay or erosion (Reed and DeFillippi 1990). And, as Barney (1991) reminds us, there is always the possibility of 'Schumpeterian shocks'. This refers to the view that capitalism involves 'gales of creative destruction' (Schumpeter 1950: 84). These are major innovations in products or processes which can destroy whole firms and the sectors they inhabit.

Following theorists like Porter (1985, 1991), strategy textbooks in the last twenty years have typically assumed that competitive advantage is the dependent variable of interest in the whole subject. In our view, this emphasis is somewhat unbalanced. It focuses too much on how firms might make themselves different. Firms are inevitably different—in good, bad, and ugly ways—but we think it is more balanced to use the notion of two strategic problems or dependent variables—viability and sustained advantage. In other words, firms must meet certain baseline conditions that make them similar to other firms and must continue to do so as markets and means of serving them change while also having the opportunity to make gains from being positively different.

Our emphasis on the problem of viability is broadly consistent with the arguments of 'organizational ecologists' (such as Carroll and Hannan 1995) and 'institutionalists' (such as DiMaggio and Powell 1983) who examine the processes that account for similarity among organizations. Recognition that firms face pressures to conform in order to gain social approval—or 'legitimacy' (one of the three key goals for HRM we discuss below)—and have economic reasons to adopt successful strategies in their sector is growing in the strategic management literature (see, e.g. Deephouse 1999; Oliver 1997; Peteraf and Shanley 1997).

In saying, then, that competitive advantage is a desirable end, we do not want to convey the impression that firms which pursue it will become completely different from their rivals. They will not. Rather, they will retain many similarities. If successful in securing competitive advantage, however, they will possess some distinctive traits that deliver superior profitability.

A large part of any firm's distinctiveness stems from the calibre of the people employed and the quality of their working relationships. In the hugely popular, resource-based view (RBV) of the firm, taxonomies of valuable resources always incorporate an important category for 'human capital' (Barney 1991) or 'employee know-how' (Hall 1993). Resource-based theorists stress the value of the complex interrelationships between the firm's human resources and its other resources: physical, financial, legal, informational and so on (see, e.g. Grant 1991; Mueller 1996; Penrose 1959).

Identifying what is really valuable and protecting it with barriers to imitation is at the heart of resource-based thinking. In terms of this question, it helps to make a distinction between 'human capital advantage' and 'organizational process advantage' (Boxall 1996, 1998). Since employment relationships are generally 'relational' rather than 'spot contracts' (Kay 1993: 278–9), firms have the possibility of generating human capital advantage by recruiting and retaining outstanding people: through 'capturing' a stock of exceptional human talent that is latent with powerful forms of 'tacit' knowledge. Organizational process advantage, on the other hand, may be understood as a function of historically evolved, socially complex, causally ambiguous *processes* such as team-based learning and cross-functional cooperation—processes which are very difficult to imitate. This is often referred to as 'social capital' (Nahapiet and Ghoshal 1998) to distinguish it from human capital while noting the symbiotic relationship between each of these two forms of capital.

Both human capital and organizational process (or social capital) can generate exceptional value but are likely to do so much more powerfully when they reinforce each other (Boxall 1996). Human resource strategy, then, supported by other sympathetic elements, can enable a firm to build sources of sustained competitive advantage.

Before developing this line of argument further, we should note that there is a problem with thinking about resources only at the level of the firm or even at the level of the industry. Nation states affect the resources available to firms and the HR strategies they can pursue. Consequently, some firms and industries have a 'head start' in international competition because they are located in societies which have much better educational and technical infrastructure than others (Boxall 1995; Porter 1990). American, British, German, and French firms, for example, are all assisted by the existence of long-established traditions of excellence in higher education which enhance the knowledge-creating capacities of business organizations. German firms tend to enjoy major advantages in manufacturing arising from superior technical training systems to those typically found in English-speaking countries (Steedman and Wagner 1989; Wever 1995). In short, the potential to develop HR advantage does not lie solely in the hands of managers within firms.

Just as there is competition between firms, there is, in effect, competition between nations (Porter 1990). Countries with embedded excellence in their universal education system tend to have higher wage costs, and more institutional rigidity (as seen, e.g. in Europe). This has led to the 'flight' of jobs in manufacturing, and increasingly in the service sector too, to China and other far eastern countries. This points to a wider paradox in strategy that a firm's, or a country's, competitive strength will often simultaneously be a source of weakness (in much the same way as heavyweight boxers may be poor at the

100 metre dash), and socio-economic and regulatory conditions can alter the balance between strength and weakness.

THE STRATEGIES OF FIRMS

In this context, the *strategies* of firms are their particular attempts to deal with the strategic problems they face. They are the characteristic ways in which the managers of firms understand their goals and develop resources—both human and non-human—to reach them. Some strategies are better than others in the context concerned: some address the problem of viability extremely well and others are simply disastrous—with every shade of effectiveness in between. The very best strategies are those which reach beyond the problem of viability to master the 'second order' problem of sustained advantage.

In saying this, we should not make the mistake of equating the strategies of firms with formal strategic plans. Following the 'strategic choice' perspective (Child 1972), it is better if we understand the strategies of firms as *sets of strategic choices*, some of which might stem from planning exercises and set-piece debates in senior management (in large firms), and some of which emerge in a stream of action. The latter, called 'emergent strategy' by Mintzberg (1978), is an inevitable feature of strategy. Once a firm commits to a particular strategy, it is inevitable that the process of carrying it out involves learning which itself will shape the strategy over time.

In defining a firm's strategy as a set of strategic choices we are saying that it includes critical choices about ends *and* means. A firm's strategy contains 'outward' and 'inward' elements (Figure 4.1). Firms face the problem of choosing suitable goals and choosing and organizing appropriate resources to meet them. In effect, our strategic choice definition draws on a 'configurational' or 'gestalt' perspective (Meyer, Tsui, and Hinings 1993; Miller 1981; Veliyath and Srinavasan 1995). To be successful, firms need an effective configuration of choices involving all the key dimensions of the business. At a minimum, these include choices about competitive strategy (which markets to enter and how to compete in them), financial strategy (how to fund the business over time), operational strategy (what supplies, technology, and methods to use in producing the goods or services), and HR strategy (how to recruit, organize, and motivate the people needed now and over time).

A key issue associated with the strategic choice perspective is the question of what we are implying about the *extent of choice* available to firms. It is widely accepted in the strategy literature that firms in some sectors enjoy greater 'degrees of freedom' than others (Nelson 1991; Porter 1985). Some environments are more benign—more 'munificent'—than others (Pfeffer and Salancik 1978). Some firms are heavily constrained by competitive forces pushing them towards intense, margin-based competition (something suppliers of supermarkets regularly complain about) while others enjoy a much more dominant position (companies like Microsoft come readily to mind). Consistent with John Child's re-formulation (1997) of the strategic choice perspective, we believe it is important to steer a path between 'hyperdeterminism', on the one hand, and 'hypervoluntarism', on the other. That is, firms are neither fully constrained by their environment nor fully able to create it. Adopting a strategic choice perspective means that we portray firms as experiencing a varying blend of constraint and choice positioned somewhere in between these two extremes. The 'choice' in strategic choice is real but its extent is variable.

Before moving on, we should note that this definition of strategy is based at the business unit level. This level is, in fact, the most logical one at which to define strategy because different business units are organized around markets or segments of markets which require different goals and clusters of resources (Ghemawat and Costa 1993). Strategic analysis and theory relates, nearly always, to the business unit (Kaplan and Norton 1996; Porter 1985). However, more complex frameworks are needed to encompass corporate strategy in multidivisional firms (Boxall and Purcell 2003, ch. 10; Purcell and Ahlstrand 1994). Questions about 'parenting'—about which businesses to buy and sell, which to grow organically, and so on—are vital in multidivisional firms. While recognizing this complexity, these choices are not essential to the argument in this chapter, and we will put them aside.

Strategic goals and tensions in HRM

How HRM contributes to management's efforts to deal with the problems of viability and sustained advantage is the central question in the field of Strategic HRM (SHRM). SHRM academics are interested in models and studies which link HRM to business performance or organizational effectiveness. However, identifying strategic goals in labour management has long been a troublesome project (Legge 1978). The framework we have developed (see Figure 4.2) argues that HRM is concerned with three aspects of performance that are critical to the firm's viability and that may lay a basis for sustained advantage—labour productivity, organizational flexibility, and social legitimacy (Boxall and Purcell 2003). This is not a simple matter because it is inevitable that a firm's attempts to attain its particular HR goals will be accompanied by various kinds of 'strategic tension' (Boxall 1999; Cameron 1986; Evans and Genadry 1999), as we explain in what follows.

LABOUR PRODUCTIVITY OR COST-EFFECTIVENESS

Profitability is inevitably critical in shareholder-owned firms. However, it can be affected by financial factors not connected to workforce management (such

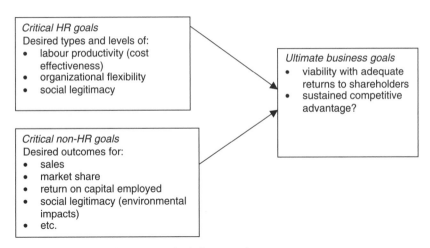

Figure 4.2 Critical goals in HRM: a basic framework
Source: Boxall and Purcell (2003: 7).

as movements in exchange rates), so several authors have argued that labour productivity—the value of labour outputs in relation to the cost of labour inputs—ought to be seen as the primary goal of a firm's labour management (see, e.g. Geare 1977; Heneman 1969; Osterman 1987). In effect, firms need to make labour productive at an economic cost.

In 'macro' or SHRM, the question becomes: is the overall combination of HR philosophy, processes, policies, programmes, and practices creating the human performance desired and is it doing so at reasonable cost (Godard 2001)? Very expensive, high-skill models of labour management, incorporating rigorous selection, high pay, and extensive internal development, are unlikely among small firms in the retail sector, for example. While firms in this sector should try to find ways of making competitive pay offers and of keeping their most effective staff, this does not imply that they should adopt the kind of HRM system needed to compete with international consultancy firms or automobile manufacturers. Another example of the principle of cost-effectiveness is given by Godard and Delaney (2000: 488):

...in a nuclear power plant employing many workers, the costs of poor morale, (labour) turnover, and strikes can be high, so the benefits of HRM innovations will tend to be high. Firm size may also introduce important economies of scale, reducing the costs of HRM innovations per worker. Thus, in this plant, the benefits of new practices can be expected to exceed the costs. In a small, low-technology garment factory employing unskilled labour, the opposite may be true.

As Godard and Delaney (2000) imply, expensive HR practices are often justified where the production system is capital intensive or where high technology is involved. The actual level of labour cost could be quite low (say, 10 per cent or less of total cost) but workers have a major effect on how well the technology is utilized or exploited. It thus pays to remunerate and train them very well, making better use of their skills and ensuring their motivation is kept high. As they find ways of making the equipment meet or even exceed its specifications, the unit costs of labour fall and productivity rises. Thus, in this kind of context, the firm can easily sustain high wage levels. It is more important *not* to alienate this kind of labour, because of the productivity impacts of disrupted production, than it is to worry about wage levels. As Osterman (1987: 55) explains:

The concept of cost must be broadened to include potential as well as actual costs. Employees can impose costs on the firm through errors of various kinds. For example, a particular kind of capital equipment may be simple to operate and require little skill but yet be very expensive and subject to damage through employee error. Many firms will choose to employ higher-skill labour and create stable employment systems...because of potential downside costs.

Clearly, then, the problem of securing cost-effective labour, of making labour productive at reasonable cost, invites some careful thinking about likely costs and benefits. This is far from easy. In reaching a suitable 'solution' or a relatively stable, cost-effective model of labour management, firms are always confronted to some degree by the *strategic* tensions associated with labour scarcity and motivation. In all countries where forced labour has been eliminated, firms need to compete in labour markets to secure talented staff (Coff 1997; Windolf 1986), a problem that was severe in the global market for IT workers in the 1990s. Even where there are high levels of unemployment (as in much of continental Europe), labour shortages can continue in particular sectors.

Well-resourced organizations that have the ability to pay the going rate or better, and are able to offer good development opportunities, tend to dominate in this contest. As a result, many small firms remain fragile, tenuous organizations with ongoing recruitment problems (Hendry, Arthur, and Jones 1995; Storey 1985). The goal of securing reasonable productivity in the firm is seriously compromised if the firm cannot make competitive job offers. It then struggles to build the capabilities it needs to meet its business objectives or respond to its clients' demands. In the extreme, the tension associated with labour scarcity can become a full-blown 'capability crisis', compromising productivity and profitability and threatening the firm's reputation and viability.

A second major tension—associated with the *motivation* of workers once they are actually hired—stems from the nature of the employment contract as an exchange relationship which, unlike the sale and purchase of commodities, involves an ongoing and unpredictable interaction between the parties. Future behaviour matters to the parties but neither party can accurately predict it when they sign up. Both are taking risks. As the pioneering IR writers, Sidney and Beatrice Webb (1902: 658) put it, the labour contract is 'indeterminate'. Or, as Cartier (1994: 182) puts it, 'the contract of employment is inherently incomplete'. As a result, the law gives employers the right to issue what are commonly known as 'lawful and reasonable orders', something that sets up an ongoing problem of motivation for the firm because control of the behaviour of other human beings is always limited. When individuals are instructed to carry out work tasks, their discretion is never fully taken away from them (Bendix 1956). The employer, like the employee, must exercise some trust. As Keenoy (1992: 95) argues, 'no matter how extensive the controls, in the final analysis, management is reliant on employee cooperation'.

There is a huge body of literature examining the relationships between employer and employee interests in the workplace and their implications for motivation and cooperation. While there is a fundamental set of common interests in healthy, sustainable enterprise, managers and academics in the 'pluralist' tradition accept that there are important conflicts of interest in the workplace (Fox 1974). These include the trade-off between employee income and the profit of the firm, the trade-off between firm survival and employee security, and the tension between employee control of work decisions and conditions and control by the employer (Keenoy 1992). These tensions are serious for the firm irrespective of the fact that workers do not typically have 'equal power' with management (Clegg 1975). In the most severe cases of conflict over these tensions, firms experience 'motivational crises' which depress productivity and profitability, and can threaten their viability.

ORGANIZATIONAL FLEXIBILITY

Labour productivity is something that is aimed for in a *given* context. In other words, given a particular market and a certain type of technology (among other things), it is about making the firm's labour resources productive at competitive cost. However, it is frequently observed that business environments are becoming more turbulent and that sources of competitive advantage are more ephemeral than they were in the three decades after the Second World War. There are many explanations for this from the introduction of more assertive regimes of free trade under the World Trade Organization, the end of monopolies in the trading sectors, including state monopolies, and rapid technological change (seen, e.g. in information technology). Markets are less dominated by long-established big players as barriers to entry have lowered and firms have been less able to protect themselves from new entrants whether at home or abroad. All this means that change is inevitable and suggests we need another goal domain in HRM: capacity to change or 'organizational flexibility' (Osterman 1987). The word 'organizational' is used here because employers typically seek forms of flexibility which extend beyond, but encompass, their employee relations (Streeck 1987).

In thinking about goals for organizational flexibility, it is useful to distinguish between *short-run* responsiveness and *long-run* agility (Boxall and Purcell 2003). Short-run responsiveness includes financial flexibility (attempts to adjust the price of labour services) and numerical (or 'headcount') flexibility (which also has financial objectives). Thus, firms engaged in very cyclical activities often relate their permanent staff numbers to their calculation of the troughs in business demand rather than the relatively unpredictable peaks, seeking to offer overtime and bring in temporary staff if, and when, the workload surges. In other cases, firms seek to pay workers a mix of wages and profit-related bonuses, with the latter fluctuating in line with company fortunes. Long-run agility, however, is a much more powerful, but rather ambiguous, concept (Dyer and Shafer 1999). It is concerned with the firm's ability to learn in an environment that can change radically. Does the firm have the capacity to create, or at least cope with, long-run changes in products, markets, and technologies? Can it learn as fast or faster than its major rivals?

Like the productivity arena, the problem of creating desirable types and levels of organizational flexibility involves the management of strategic tensions (Adler, Goldoftas, and Levine 1999; Brown and Reich 1997; Osterman 1987). There is often a major tension between actions taken to support short-run flexibility and attempts to build long-run agility. To illustrate the difficult choices involved, suppose a firm's management decides (and manages) to place most of its operating staff on temporary employment contracts providing short-term flexibility in payroll costs. This reduces the level of fixed cost but is likely to create problems with employee turnover as skilled workers, who are generally capable of attracting a range of employment offers, move to more secure jobs elsewhere. Over time, the firm is likely to find that it fails to build the kind of learning process that underpins long-term growth and makes it more adaptable to radical change in technology. Too much emphasis on short-term flexibility may mean the firm is eliminated by competitors who learn faster and capture its market share. A firm, on the other hand, which employs all labour on secure permanent contracts to build a stable, long-term labour supply (traditionally called 'labour hoarding') may find that it faces a cash crisis in a short-term recession that actually threatens its viability. The firm may have excellent long-term prospects but greater flexibility is needed in its staffing structure to ensure it can weather short-term variations in demand for its products or services. A firm with excellent long-term prospects may fail in the short-run for want of financial prudence.

The most resilient firms, then, are those which evolve a clever balance between short- and long-run requirements for flexibility. But, as we have illustrated, this is much easier said than done. In Hyman's memorable phrase

(1987: 43), 'employers require workers to be *both* dependable *and* disposable'. Change involves tensions that pose major dilemmas for management strategy and include trade-offs with the security interests of workers. To achieve organizational flexibility, one of the most important strategic choices organizations must make is to decide on the fundamental structure and processes to build in order to achieve some degree of agility. Short-run responsiveness inevitably focuses attention on the decision-making ability of the top management team since it is only they who can decide which resources to cut or develop. As noted many years ago in groundbreaking research by Burns and Stalker, business environments with 'changing conditions, which give rise constantly to fresh problems and unforeseen requirements' (1961: 121) require firms to adopt an 'organic' structure of decentralization and a more open management style. In such conditions, top management do not have a monopoly on knowledge and have to rely on the wider pool of skills and abilities of their employees to read environmental signals and adapt to them. Here, 'knowledge is assumed to be widely dispersed throughout the organization, and broadened task roles and employee commitment to the entire organization are emphasized. Communication patterns tend to be lateral rather than vertical' (Datta, Guthrie, and Wright 2005: 136). This is a fundamentally different way of managing employees than that found in sectors noted for their stability and bureaucratic order. Here, suggest Burns and Stalker, a 'mechanistic' style is more appropriate. An HR management style more based on principles of command and control is likely to be more appropriate. While Burns and Stalker tend to see the choice between styles as 'either-or' (a not unreasonable assumption in the 1950s), we would argue that in the much more turbulent environment of the first decade of the twenty-first century many organizations have to find some measure of long-run agility and manage for stable productivity simultaneously.

SOCIAL LEGITIMACY

It should by now be obvious that tensions and trade-offs are endemic to labour management. Consciously or unconsciously, management is trying to build an order within the firm which garners sufficient worker support—or sufficient perceptions of legitimacy 'from below'—to be viable (see, e.g. Burawoy 1979; Lees 1997). The social order within the firm inevitably connects to the wider society. Firms make use of human capacities that citizens and the state have nurtured and generated (e.g. through public education). In this light, governments often exercise their right to regulate employment practices. Workers may also exercise sanctions against firms that offend social norms (either as individuals who decide not to work for certain kinds of firms or to work for them only with very limited commitment, or as unions which campaign against certain kinds of employment practice). Increasingly, and especially in the more agile firms noted above, the need to adopt more decentralized and organic systems of people management and high-performance work practices means that employers are more reliant on their employees for the achievement of business goals. Employees themselves have more choices on how well they undertake their jobs. 'Discretionary behaviour' is something that employees can give and can withdraw (Appelbaum et al. 2000; Purcell et al. 2003).

This idea of employee choice has spawned a veritable host of studies with roots back to the human relations school of the 1930s and onwards, looking at the psychological contract (e.g. Coyle-Shapiro and Kessler 2000; Robinson, Kraatz, and Rousseau 1994), organizational citizenship behaviour (e.g. Organ and Moorman 1993; Podsakoff, Ahearne, and MacKenzie 1997), and organizational justice (Folger and Cropanzano 1998). A common thread is that employees' responses to management decisions and actions will be mediated and judged through a lens of legitimacy. Has the employer broken implicit promises that make up one side of the psychological contract? Has the management met the tenets of justice in the way decisions are made that affect employees, in the equity of the distribution of resources, rewards, and punishments, and in the way employees are told about them and how much say they have? Why should an employee decide to 'go the extra mile' if basic rules of legitimacy are not met?

If firms wish to grow and make greater use of a society's resources, they must generally comply with prevailing social norms (Lees 1997). Individual firms rarely have opportunities to influence social standards although they may try to locate in societies with lower labour costs, providing this will help them achieve viability in their business sector (and it may not if labour of the right type and quality is simply not available). Individual firms generally need to take the established ethical framework in relation to labour management as a given and these can vary between nations and societies. Multinational firms find they cannot behave the same way in each location. Over time, however, the picture is not so simple: business typically has a major voice in the wider political-economy of societies and can, if other forces co-align, foster significant changes in notions of legitimacy.

For example, management played a major role in reshaping institutions for employee voice in Anglo-American societies as unions and collective bargaining lost workforce support in the 1980s and 1990s. Voice practices have not disappeared in the Anglo-American world but have become more diverse and more direct (Boxall and Purcell 2003, ch. 8). The 'transformation' of IR (Kochan, Katz, and McKersie 1986) was strongly influenced by shifts in the underlying beliefs and values of executives in large firms and in the withdrawal of state support legitimizing the union role. The latter was most obvious in Britain with Mrs Thatcher's attack on collectivism in all its guises but was also seen in the USA under President Reagan and in the marketization of economies and the public services in countries like New Zealand (Boxall and Haynes 1997). Within this broad political context, and given substantial worker support for direct, non-union forms of participation, management in the Anglo-American world has clearly made an impact over the last twenty years on notions of how to structure employee voice.

Legitimacy, then, is a 'contested arena'. Our argument is that all legitimate firms must pay at least some regard to how their actions are perceived in ethical terms. This is an important part of sustaining stakeholder support and organizational effectiveness, broadly understood (Lees 1997). For most firms, certain standards of behaviour are simply a given based on the society or societies in which the firm operates. However, business interests, writ large, are not just passive vessels and are capable of playing a major role in the evolution of ethical standards over time.

Conclusions

We have defined strategy by distinguishing between 'strategic problems' the firm faces in its environment, and the characteristic ways it tries to cope with them (its 'strategy'). As common sense tells us, the word strategic implies something that is seriously consequential for the future of the firm.

The fundamental strategic problem is the problem of viability. To be viable, a firm needs an appropriate set of goals and a relevant set of HR and non-HR, a configuration or system of ends and means consistent with survival in its competitive sector and the society (or societies) in which it operates. This obviously means that without certain kinds of human capability, firms are simply not viable. Firms which deal adequately with the viability problem have the chance to play in a higher level 'tournament': the contest among leaders of sound businesses to achieve some form of sustained competitive advantage. In certain contexts, there are opportunities to pursue this goal through (somewhat) distinctive HR and HR strategies.

Identifying strategic goals in labour management has always been difficult. The framework we have developed argues that HRM is concerned with three aspects of performance that are critical to the firm's viability and that may lay a basis for sustained advantage—labour productivity, organizational flexibility, and social legitimacy (Boxall and Purcell 2003). While the first two aspects of performance—productivity and flexibility—very much reflect a business-oriented agenda, firms inevitably confront issues of legitimacy, both within their 'skins' and within the wider societies in which they operate. Tensions and trade-offs with employee goals and with broader societal expectations mean that ethical issues are inescapable. As a result, conceptions of business performance or organizational effectiveness—in theory and in practice—cannot be restricted to a narrow, profit-dominated 'bottom line'.

Here we have merely sketched a broad framework which recognizes this reality. In our model, individual firms are generally reactive to social norms: firms that want to grow need to work with existing norms. However, business interests are powerful in the wider political-economy of societies and, when other forces are compatible, have opportunities to reshape legitimacy notions over time. How they do so—and the extent to which this serves the greater social good—is an important question for the state and society.

5 Ethical employment practices and the law

Breen Creighton

Introduction

Notions of what constitutes ethical behaviour must inevitably reflect the moral values to which any given society aspires at any given point in time. Considerations of time and space preclude detailed consideration of what constitutes, or ought to constitute, ethical employment practice in Australia in the early twenty-first century. However, for purposes of exposition, ethical behaviour in employment will be taken to encompass four key elements: respect for the dignity and personal integrity of individual employees and potential employees; respect for, and protection of, the physical and mental integrity of employees; access to 'decent work' in the sense of access to an appropriate range of different forms of work, proper conditions of work, security of employment, and 'feelings of value and satisfaction' (ILO 1999: 7; 2001); and moderating the practical effects of the imbalance in economic power between individuals who sell their labour in the marketplace and those who purchase it.

No legal regime could ever effectively and comprehensively enforce ethical behaviour thus defined. However, the law can and should provide a framework that can encourage participants in the labour market to behave in an ethical manner. This can be done by, amongst other things, providing meaningful incentives for those participants to observe the norms of that framework, and a means of redress for those who have been subjected to treatment that is not consistent with the prescribed standards of behaviour.

This chapter begins by examining the role of the law as a facilitator of ethical behaviour in the workplace from an historical perspective. It does this by first looking at the law of master and servant and at its subsequent transformation into the modern law of employment. This is followed by a consideration of the increasing role of legislative intervention from the early 1800s onwards. This historical overview provides a basis for a brief description and analysis of the role of the law as facilitator and guarantor of ethical behaviour in employment in contemporary Australia, and for some thoughts as to where the law could or should go in the future.

The emergence of the modern law of employment

The common law of employment has traditionally had little concern for ethical issues. On the conventional view, the parties to the wage–work bargain strike their bargain through a process of negotiation and agreement. Provided the resultant agreement met certain minimal requirements as to form and substance, the law had no further interest in the manner in which the contract was formed, or in its content (Creighton, Ford, and Mitchell 1993: ch. 3; Creighton and Stewart 2005: 277–9; Macken et al. 2002: ch. 3).

Consistent with this view, it was of no concern to the common law that, other than in highly exceptional circumstances, the parties to the employment relationship stood in profoundly unequal bargaining positions relative to one another, or that their agreement bore more heavily upon one party rather than the other. So long as the agreement was not induced by fraud, duress, or misrepresentation, the common law proceeded on the basis that the parties must live by their bargain. Furthermore, the imperative of working or starving was never seen as vitiating the bargain between an employer and a would-be employee (Kahn-Freund 1954: 45–6):

> ...the common law has in general ignored the social and economic inequality of contracting parties, eg of the individual employer and the individual employee. It has acted on the principle that an adult person is bound by his contractual promises, however much his legal freedom to contract or not to contract may have been fictitious as a result of pressing economic necessity. Those principles of law which protect the economically weaker side against exploitation had to be grafted upon the common law by legislation.

The situation described by Kahn-Freund is a logical consequence of the application of the principles of laissez-faire contractualism to work relationships—whether between master and servant, employer and employee, or principal and independent contractor (Brooks 1988; Collins 1990; Deakin 1998, 2000; Freedland 1995, 2003: 13–26). However, it is important to appreciate that matters were not always thus.

Work relationships in pre-industrial society were governed by legal rules and assumptions that owed more to family law than to what modern observers would recognize as the law of employment. The 'servant' was under the domination and control of the 'master' in much the same way as Roman slaves were under the domination and control of the paterfamilias, and as female and non-adult members of families in pre-industrial society were under the domination and control of the family head. This meant that the servant was subject to the discipline—physical and moral—of the head of family. They often lived with, and as a member of, the family. They were entitled to certain of the benefits of family membership—including the right to be looked after in times of sickness and ill health (see *M'Keating v. Frame* 1921 SC 382). The rights and duties of the parties owed more to 'status' than to 'contract'. Often, the only significant contractual element in the relationship was the initial decision to create the relationship, and the payment of wages and/or the provision of benefit in kind as a quid pro quo for the rendering of service. The incidents of the relationship were the product of the general principles of the law of master and servant, with its strong ties to family law (Kahn-Freund 1977: 508), rather than the agreement—express or implied—of the parties (Kahn-Freund 1967, 1977). The ethical underpinning of such relationships was one of high trust, but little individual autonomy. The rights and interests of the individual were subordinated to those of the family unit, which were in turn the domain of the head of the family. However, as indicated, the traffic was not all one way. The servant, as quasi-family member, enjoyed at least some of the rights of a full family member, as well as the responsibilities (Creighton, Ford, and Mitchell 1993: 18–24, 28–32; Fox 1974: ch. 4; Selznick 1969: ch. 4).

Whatever its virtues in a pre-industrial context, this model was not well-suited to the needs of early industrial society. The traditional model was premised on geographical and social stability. Industrialization required geographical mobility, and both required and engendered social instability. The new processes of mass production in factories required large numbers of workers of varying degrees of skill. Labour needed to be dispensable, both in response to market fluctuations and to the pace of technological change. The high levels of mutual commitment that characterized the traditional master–servant relationship could not readily accommodate these imperatives. Nor were they suited—at least from the perspective of the manufacturer—to the high levels of work-related injury and disease that characterized the early stages of industrialization. In bald terms, there was a strong perception in Britain in the late eighteenth and early nineteenth centuries that if mill owners had to bear the cost of injuring and maiming workers in the same way as the master in the traditional 'family model' had to bear the cost of sick and injured servants, then profitability, competitiveness, and innovation would be significantly impaired. Sensitivity to this issue is clearly evident in the emergence of the doctrine of common employment, which had the effect that an individual worker who had been injured as a consequence of the negligent act of a fellow worker (common employee) could not recover damages from their employer either in tort or in contract—see *Priestly* v. *Fowler* (1837) 3 M&W 1; *Hutchinson* v. *York, Newcastle and Berwick Railway Co* (1850) 5 Exch 343 (see further Johnstone 2004a: 48–52, and the sources cited therein).

These considerations help explain the fact that, in the course of the late eighteenth and the nineteenth centuries, the traditional law of master and servant was infused with principles derived from the newly emergent law of contract to create the modern Anglo-Australian model of the contract of employment. Ethical considerations had little part in all of this. The market reigned supreme. Would-be employees wanted/needed work. Employers wanted/needed employees. The two came together. They negotiated. They freely entered into a contract. As noted earlier, the fact that the would-be employee was almost invariably in a vastly inferior bargaining position vis-à-vis the employer was no concern of the law. Nor was the law concerned with the manner in which the parties performed the contract, or brought it to an end: so long as they acted in accordance with the terms of their agreement. Considerations of fairness and ethical behaviour simply did not enter the equation.

This account of the law of master and servant and of the emergence of the modern law of employment is, necessarily, greatly oversimplified (Creighton and Mitchell 1995: 132):

> ... it is, for example, inherently unlikely that the judges who fashioned the emergent common law of employment consciously decided to 'infuse' the principles of contractualism with the law of master and servant. It is much more probable that they developed and applied the law in the light of their perceptions of the principles which ought to apply as between what were commonly referred to as 'masters' and 'servants'.

Furthermore, some commentators have suggested that the fusion of the old law of master and servant and the contract of employment was not completed until around the middle of the twentieth century—by which time its relevance had already been significantly eroded by social, economic, and technological change, and by the adoption of a broad range of legislative measures that were intended to ameliorate some of the harsher effects of the application of common law contractual principles to the work relationship (see Deakin 1998, 2000, 2005; Howe and Mitchell 1999).

It must also be recognized that the principle of mutuality, which characterized the law of master and servant, but which appears irrelevant to a truly contractual relationship, never entirely disappeared from employment law in either Britain or Australia. For example, the employee's duty of obedience to the orders of the master/employer has always been qualified by the fact that the duty extends only to orders that are *lawful* and *reasonable* (*R* v. *Darling Island Stevedoring & Lighterage Co Ltd: Ex parte Halliday and Sullivan* (1938) 60 CLR 601; *Laws* v. *London Chronicle (Indicator Newspapers) Ltd* [1959] 1 WLR 698. For comment see Creighton, Ford, and Mitchell 1993: 181–6; Creighton and Stewart 2005: 352–3—cf. McCarry 1984). On the other hand, until comparatively recently, the capacity of employees to stand on their rights in all but extreme circumstances was highly attenuated by reason of the fact that a refusal to obey an instruction would in many instances result in termination of employment. It would be small comfort to the dismissed employee subsequently to be found to have been entitled to refuse to obey the employer's instruction on the grounds that it was unlawful or unreasonable—especially in the light of the fact that for many years the common law has set its sights firmly against reinstatement of employees whose employment has unlawfully been terminated (see Creighton, Ford, and Mitchell 1993: ch. 12; Creighton and Stewart 2005: 442–6; Macken et al. 2002: 257–77; Pittard and Naughton 2003: 237–47).

It is also interesting to note that the notion of mutuality of obligation in the employment relationship has recently assumed an added significance in the guise of a mutual duty of trust and confidence, which requires the parties to the contract of employment not to act in a manner that is inconsistent with the mutual trust and confidence that is said to be of the essence of the employment relationship (e.g. *Bliss* v. *South East Thames Regional Health Authority* [1987] ICR 700; *Malik* v. *Bank of Credit and Commerce International SA* [1998] AC 20; *Burazin* v. *Blacktown City Guardian Pty Ltd* (1996) 142 ALR 144, 151—cf. *Johnson* v. *Unisys Ltd* [2003] 1 AC 518. For comment see Brodie 1996, 2001; Creighton and Stewart 2005: 366–8; Lindsay 2001; McCarry 1998; Naughton 1997; Riley 2003, 2005: 66–95; Spry 1997). This clearly has the potential to provide at least some incentive for the adoption and implementation of ethical employment practices.

Even though it is somewhat stylized, this account does help provide a context for an understanding of the evolution of employment law, with its characteristic lack of concern for ethical considerations. This in turn serves to explain why, from the 1830s onwards, the legislature was increasingly prepared to intervene to try to mandate acceptable levels of ethical behaviour in relation to at least some aspects of the employment relationship.

Early legislative intervention

Even in the heyday of laissez-faire contractualism, the law intervened in the privity of the employment relationship to enforce, or at least to facilitate, ethical treatment of employees. Three areas of legislative activity merit particular consideration in this context: the enactment of 'truck' legislation; the emergence of occupational health and safety legislation; and the adoption of legislative measures to facilitate and indeed encourage collective regulation of terms and conditions of employment.

Before moving on to look at these issues in more detail, it is interesting to note that as early as 1862 there were attempts in Britain to legislate to mitigate one of the harsher manifestations of contractualism, the doctrine of common employment. These attempts were unsuccessful, and it was not until 1948 that the doctrine was finally abolished in that country, whilst in Australia it was abolished in all jurisdictions between 1926 (New South Wales and Victoria) and 1956 (Northern Territory) (Johnstone 2004*a*: 51). Meanwhile, the emergence of statutory workers' compensation schemes in the late nineteenth and early twentieth centuries did much to mitigate the harshness of the common law in relation to compensation for work-related injuries. This also made some contribution towards ethical treatment in employment—for example by helping ensure that financial pressures did not force injured employees to return to work sooner than was in their best interests, and that such employees were able to maintain a reasonable standard of living (bearing in mind that the various workers' compensation systems predated modern social security legislation) (Johnstone 2004a: 55–63, and the sources cited therein). It is, however a telling indictment of judicial attitudes to employment relationships that over the course of 100 years the courts were unwilling or unable to undo what they had done in deciding *Priestly* v. *Fowler* in 1837, and that in the end it was left to the legislature to redress the imbalance between employer and employee in this area.

TRUCK LEGISLATION

The term truck 'connotes a large number of types of exploitation, including such different things as payment in kind, the "tommy shop", and the arbitrary imposition of fines' (Kahn-Freund 1949: 2). According to the *Shorter Oxford Dictionary* a tommy shop is 'a store (especially one run by an employer) at which vouchers given to employees instead of money wages may be exchanged for goods'. These practices often had the effect that workers were deprived of the true value of their work—whether through the provision of substandard goods, the charging of exorbitant 'prices' to a captive market, or simply hold-ing back wages due on account of defective workmanship or some (real or imagined) infraction of the employer's disciplinary rules.

The first comprehensive attempt to regulate these practices was the Truck Act 1831 (Webb and Webb 1920: 50). In broad terms, this measure, together with later amendments made by the Truck Amendment Act 1887 and the Truck Act 1896, required that wages be paid in the coin of the realm and forbade the making of unauthorized deductions from wages. These measures were repealed and partially replaced by the Wages Act 1986. The relevant provision is now to be found in Part II of the Employment Rights Act 1996.

New South Wales (1900), Queensland (1918), and Western Australia (1899) all introduced their own versions of the imperial truck legislation in the late nineteenth and early twentieth centuries, and all three repealed them in the 1990s. The other colonies/States did not adopt truck legislation as such. How-ever, they all made, and with the exception of Victoria, retain, legislative pro-vision which regulates unauthorized deductions from wages. The Workplace Relations Act 1996 (Cth) also limits the capacity of employers to withhold wages due, at least to the extent that they cannot be reduced below the level enshrined in the Australian Fair Pay and Conditions Standard or any relevant

Australian Workplace Agreement or collective agreement (other than on the terms set out in those agreements).

It may seem somewhat counter-intuitive that the British parliament should have been prepared to introduce legislative provision regulating the content and/or performance of what were, ostensibly at least, freely negotiated contracts between employers and workers at a time when the principle of freedom of contract was regarded as sacrosanct. As against that, the introduction of legislation to deal with the abuses targeted by the Truck Acts can be seen to be not entirely inconsistent with the rhetoric of contractualism (Kahn-Freund 1949: 2):

All of these abuses have one thing in common: the discrepancy between promise and performance. The worker is deprived of the full value of his wages, either because of the method of performance chosen by the employer, or by the assertion of counterclaims which were not contemplated by the worker at the time of the making of the contract.

Viewed in this way, legislative intervention constituted an attempt to preserve the integrity of the contract model by ensuring that workers received the wages for which they had 'bargained', so long as they had performed their side of the wages–work bargain. This reasoning is attractive, but not entirely persuasive. In particular, it does not take proper account of the fact that the legislation proscribed certain practices—for example, the payment of wages in the form of tokens that could be redeemed only in tommy shops—even if those practices were expressly contemplated by the parties to the contract of employment. This suggests that the introduction of the Truck Acts was at least in part motivated by a desire to regulate certain forms of unethical behaviour in the labour market, even where that behaviour was endorsed by what was, theoretically, a freely negotiated contract between two parties equally protected by law.

OCCUPATIONAL HEALTH AND SAFETY LEGISLATION

Starting in the late eighteenth century, the British parliament enacted a range of measures that were intended to regulate the hours and conditions of employment of children, young persons, and women in factories and in mines. On one reading, this can be seen as an attempt to protect the integrity of the contract model of employment relations by virtue of the fact that the protected classes consisted largely of persons who lacked full contractual capacity. For example, legal infants (i.e. persons under 21 years old) had only limited capacity to enter into contracts for the performance of work, whilst parish apprentices (see below) were seen to be in a particularly vulnerable position in the labour market and at the same time to be persons for whom the public had special responsibility.

It is not necessary to examine the emergence of this legislation in detail in the present context. (For detailed treatment, see Carson 1974, 1979, 1980;

Creighton 1979: 19–26; Gunningham 1984: ch. 4; Henriques 1979: chs. 4 and 5; Hutchins and Harrison 1926; Johnstone 2004*a*: 34–7; Thomas 1948.) Instead, it is sufficient to note that early measures such as the Regulation of Chimney Sweepers Act 1788 and the Health and Morals of Apprentices Act 1802 were adopted in response to concerns about the working and living conditions of 'pauper apprentices'—that is, children and young people who were in the care of the public authorities, and who, like Dickens' *Oliver Twist*, were apprenticed to private sector operators who often neglected their physical and moral well-being. In other words, these early measures can properly be seen as an extension of the Poor Law, rather than legislation that was directed to the regulation of the employment relationship as such. Nevertheless, they can also be seen as the forerunners of nineteenth century factory legislation, and, at a further remove, of modern occupational health and safety legislation.

As the nineteenth century progressed, there was a growing acceptance that it was appropriate for the legislature to intervene to regulate the working conditions not just of those workers (such as pauper apprentices or children) in relation to whom the public could be seen to have special responsibility, but also other categories of employees who appeared to be in need of protection from the operation of market forces. For example, Victorian middle-class sensibilities were particularly offended by the publication in 1842 of a report from a Committee on the Employment of Women and Children in Mines and Collieries which showed (with appropriately salacious lithographic prints) that scantily clad women and children were required to work for long hours in dark, hot, and humid conditions in underground coal mines (Parl Papers 1842: vols. XV, XVI, and XXXV). This led to the legislative prohibition of all underground working for women and children, and to the imposition of severe restrictions on the employment of juveniles (Creighton 1979: 20–1).

Less noble motives also played a part. For example, some of the larger manufacturers saw legislative regulation of hours and conditions of work of children, juveniles, and women who performed critical ancillary tasks in cotton and woollen mills, as a way of blunting the competitive edge of smaller operators who utilized cheap sources of power and highly exploitative labour practices as compared to their more established and reputable competitors. Meanwhile, Carson (1974) has suggested that certain members of the traditional landed interest saw support for factory legislation as a way of striking back at the nouveaux riches of the emerging manufacturing class.

Whatever the motives of those who supported the adoption of the early factory legislation, the fact is that by the middle of the 1840s, the principle of legislative intervention to regulate the working conditions of workers in British textile factories had become firmly entrenched. From 1844 onwards there was an increasing emphasis upon the prevention of work-related injury—especially through the guarding of machinery. There was also an increasing acceptance that the principle of legislative protection should apply to all workers, irrespective of age or gender—except those engaged in agriculture and in domestic service. These latter were, of course, the areas where the 'familial' model of master/servant law evolved, and most closely reflected reality. British occupational health and safety legislation did not extend to workers in agriculture until 1956, and does not extend to workers in domestic service to the present day—see Health and Safety at Work Act 1974 (UK), section 51.

By 1878, British factory legislation had assumed a form that is recognizably the forerunner of the regulatory regime that remains in place in the first decade of the twenty-first century. The same is true for an enforcement philosophy that accords chief priority to persuasion and education rather than prosecution and punishment. Admirable as this approach may be in principle, carried to extremes, it can severely compromise the credibility of the entire regulatory regime (Carson 1970*a*, 1970*b*, 1979, 1980; Henriques 1979; Johnstone 2004*a*: 37–41).

Starting with the Supervision of Workrooms and Factories Statute in Victoria in 1873, all of the Australian colonies/States adopted their own versions of then-current British factory legislation in the period prior to the First World War (Gunningham 1984: 65–71; Hagan 1964; Johnstone 2004*a*: 41–3). They also adopted, and by and large have maintained, the British approach to enforcement—with all of its virtues and all of its vices (Johnstone 2000, 2003*a*, 2003*b*, 2004*b*; La Trobe/Melbourne Occupational Health and Safety Project 1989; Prior 1985). The various Australian jurisdictions have also adopted essentially the same solutions to the perceived inadequacies of the traditional system as were advocated by the Robens Committee in Britain in 1972 (Creighton and Stewart 2005: 589–601; Gunningham 1984: ch. 6; Howells 1972; Johnstone 2004*a*: 63–76; Robens 1972; Woolf 1973). It is also interesting to note that the industrializing countries of Western Europe all adopted the British model of occupational health and safety regulation in the nineteenth and early twentieth centuries (Ramm 1986).

As with the Truck Acts, the adoption of factory legislation during what is generally supposed to have been the heyday of laissez-faire contractualism may seem somewhat counter-intuitive. However, it is also possible to see the emergence of this legislation, and especially the increased emphasis upon the health and safety of workers of all ages and genders from the 1840s onwards, in terms of protection of the integrity of the contract model. In particular, it can be seen to have lent legislative support to the implied contractual obligation to provide and maintain a safe and healthy workplace that is assumed to be part of all contracts of employment—see *Mathews* v. *Kuwait Bechtel Corporation* [1959] 2 QB 57; *Toth* v. *Yellow Express Carriers Ltd* (1969) 90 WN (Pt 1) (NSW) 378; *Tai Hing Cotton Mill Ltd* v. *Liu Chong Hing Bank* [1986] AC 80. This contractual duty of care is largely coterminous with the common law duty of care, breach of which will constitute the tort of negligence. Employees are under a reciprocal duty of care towards their employer: see *Lister* v. *Romford Ice & Cold Storage Co* [1957] AC 555. (For comment see Creighton and Stewart 2005: 604; Freedland 2003: 141–6; Macken et al. 2002: 118–27.)

The nineteenth century British factory legislation stands as the most conspicuous early attempt to enforce ethical behaviour in the workplace by legislative prescription. It is true that many of those who supported its introduction were impelled by motives other than a desire to enforce such standards. It is also true that from the earliest times, the state adopted a highly ambivalent approach to the enforcement of the legislatively prescribed standards of behaviour. Nevertheless, the fact remains that there has been legislative recognition for more than 200 years that the health, safety, and welfare of working people cannot simply be left to the operation of market forces and to the arid and capricious dictates of the law of contract and the law of tort.

SELF-HELP: COLLECTIVE BARGAINING

As noted earlier, the common law paid little heed to the power imbalance between the parties to the wage–work bargain. That being the case, it is hardly surprising that workers should seek to combine together, and through their collective strength to bargain for more advantageous terms and conditions of employment than they could realistically be expected to achieve as individuals. At first, the law did not take kindly to this. In the late eighteenth and early nineteenth centuries the British parliament adopted various measures, such as the Combination Act 1799, that were intended to outlaw trade union activity. These laws were, in due course, translated to the Australian colonies by force of the Australian Courts Act 1828 (UK) (Portus 1958: 88; Quinlan and Gardner 1990: 80, 82). Master and servant legislation, the origins of which could be traced to the Black Death of the twelfth century, was also deployed to try to suppress trade union activity both in the UK and in Australia. Interestingly, it survived as an impediment to trade union activity in this country long after its repeal in Britain (Creighton and Stewart 2005: 35–43; Davidson 1975; Portus 1958: 90–3; Quinlan and Gardner 1990; Simon 1954).

As if legislative proscription, express or implied, was not sufficient to make life difficult for attempts at collective organization, the law of contract was applied in a manner which in effect denied trade unions the right to exist, let alone to agitate for better terms and conditions for their members—for example, in *Hornby* v. *Close* (1867) LR 2 QB 153 the Court of Queens Bench determined that a trade union could not sue to recover funds which had been misappropriated by an absconding official on the grounds that the rules of the union were in unlawful restraint of trade with the consequence that it did not have legal standing to enforce its own rules.

Furthermore, both the criminal law and the law of torts were deployed to outlaw various forms of industrial action, and to fix unions with liability for any damage they might inflict on an employer in situations where they took industrial action to protect or to promote the industrial interests of their members—for example in *R* v. *Bunn* (1872) 12 Cox CC 316 Brett J suggested that the very fact of combination in the course of industrial action could constitute the crime of conspiracy. Tort liability in respect of industrial action was established in a series of cases starting with *Bowen* v. *Hall* (1881) 6 QBD 333 and culminating in *Quinn* v. *Leathem* [1901] AC 495 and *Taff Vale Railway Company* v. *Amalgamated Society of Railway Servants* [1901] AC 426. These principles were adopted as part of the law of Australia in cases such as *Martell* v. *Victorian Coal Miners Association* (1903) 9 ALR 231; *Slattery* v. *Keirs* (1903) 20 WN (NSW) 45; *Brisbane Shipwrights' Provident Union* v. *Heggie* (1906) 3 CLR 686; *Southan* v. *Grounds* (1916) 16 SR (NSW) 274; *Coffey* v. *Geraldton Lumpers' Union* (1928) 31 WALR 33 (Creighton, Ford, and Mitchell 1993: chs. 34–5; Creighton and Stewart 2005: 561–72; Pittard and Naughton 2003: ch. 17; Sykes 1982: ch. 8).

From the 1820s onwards attempts at blanket suppression of trade union activity were replaced by a form of reluctant tolerance, both in the UK and in Australia. This tolerance found expression in measures such as Combination of Workmen Act 1824 (UK); Combination Laws Repeal Amendment Act 1825 (UK); Molestation of Workmen Act 1859 (UK); Trade Union Act 1871 (UK); Conspiracy and Protection of Property Act 1875 (UK), and Trade Disputes Act 1906 (UK) (Creighton and Stewart 2005: 38–45). Some, but not all, of these measures were adopted in the various Australian jurisdictions—although, as indicated the master and servant legislation was still deployed in Australia many years after it had been repealed in the UK.

The increasing tolerance of trade union activity in the Australian context was reflected in the fact that unions became firmly established from the 1850s onwards, especially on the Eastern seaboard. Furthermore, these unions enjoyed a significant measure of success in terms of protecting and promoting the interests of their members. This included the achievement of the 8-hour day following a strike by Melbourne stonemasons in April 1856—one of the first groups of workers in the world to achieve this objective (Clark 1978: 93–4). Then disaster struck the unions in the form of a series of crushing defeats in the first half of the 1890s, which resulted in the decimation of union membership and significant erosion of the gains that had been made in the previous decades (Bennett 1994: 10–13; Hutson 1983: 43–6).

Significantly, the employers had fought the great disputes of the 1890s under the banner of 'freedom of contract'—that is, their purported right to negotiate terms and conditions of employment directly with workers as individuals, without the interference of third parties such as trade unions. This was, of course, the anthesis of collective bargaining and is eerily reminiscent of the rhetoric of some of the advocates of labour market deregulation in our own time (HR Nicholls Society 1986), and with the notions of individual autonomy espoused by many of the exponents of 'postmodernist' HRM (Bauman 1993 and Cummings 2000, cited by Legge in her contribution to this book). As will appear presently, this rhetoric also finds expression in the radical changes to Australia's system of workplace regulation which were introduced by the Howard government in late 2005.

The disputes of the 1890s were protracted and bitter. In many instances they involved violence and destruction of property. They had a profound effect on liberal opinion in the Australian colonies, and led a number of the leading advocates of federation to promote the inclusion in the Constitution of the nascent Commonwealth a power (section 51 (xxxv)) to make laws for the prevention and settlement by conciliation and arbitration of industrial disputes extending beyond the limits of more than one State (Macintyre 1989; Macintyre and Mitchell 1989; Markey 1989).

Many of the founding fathers considered that the conciliation and arbitration power might never be used, or be used only sparingly in order to prevent a recurrence of the events of the early 1890s. This was based on the premise that following the establishment of a form of compulsory conciliation and arbitration, employers would no longer have any incentive to refuse to negotiate with trade unions because if they refused to do so the unions could refer the matter to an impartial tribunal which could impose an arbitrated settlement upon parties who were unwilling or unable to reach a negotiated outcome for themselves.

The reality proved to be rather different. At an early stage in the history of federation, section 51(xxxv) was used as the basis for the enactment of the Conciliation and Arbitration Act 1904 (Cth). This was intended to usher in what one of its proponents (Higgins 1915) termed a 'new province for law and order', and in due course formed the basis for the system of industrial regulation which was such an important feature of the Australian polity for most of the twentieth century (Creighton 2000; Kirby and Creighton 2004). The processes established under the 1904 Act, and its State counterparts (Creighton and Stewart 2005: 138–45, 188–90, 197–203), accorded a major role to trade unions, and provided the basis for a significant degree of external regulation of the terms and conditions of employment of the greater part of the Australian workforce. It did this through an elaborate system of industrial awards which were made by the tribunal in settlement of an interstate industrial dispute between one or more unions on one side and one or more employers and/or employer organizations on the other. Often, the 'dispute' which gave rise to the making of these awards existed only on paper, and was created for the principal purpose of investing the tribunal with jurisdiction (Creighton and Stewart 2005: ch. 6; Pittard and Naughton 2003: ch. 11).

In practice, by the 1980s, the content of most awards was the product of negotiation between the parties, but within a framework which required that the outcomes of the negotiating process be moderated by reference to the public interest as interpreted by the industrial tribunal. In addition, a practice developed whereby the tribunal dealt with major issues, such as the minimum wage, parental leave and termination, change and redundancy, through a series of test cases which then 'flowed on' into all federal awards and into the State systems—see, for example, *Miscellaneous Workers' Union of Australia* v. *ACT Employers Federation* (1979) 21 AILR 88, 199 (unpaid maternity leave); *Termination, Change and Redundancy Case* (1984) 8 IR 34, 9 IR 115 (notice of termination, protection against unfair dismissal, consultation in relation to technological change and redundancy, and severance pay); *Redundancy Test Case* (2004) 129 IR 155; *Supplementary Redundancy Test Case* (2004) 134 IR 57; *Parental Leave Test Case* (2005) 143 IR 245; *Safety Net Review—Wages, June 2005* (2005) 142 IR I.

This system of industrial regulation came in for a great deal of criticism over the years from (at various times) employers, unions, business organizations, politicians, newspaper columnists, academic observers, and economists (Creighton and Stewart 2005: 23–4, and the sources cited therein). In the course of the 1990s, these criticisms led to a fundamental reorientation of the system away from centralized regulation of terms and conditions by awards of a tribunal in favour of direct negotiation of terms and conditions at the level of the enterprise. In consequence of changes effected by the Industrial Relations Reform Act 1993 and the Workplace Relations and Other Legislation Amendment Act 1996, these negotiations need no longer involve a trade union, and following the introduction of Australian Workplace Agreements (AWAs) in 1996, they need no longer be collective in character (Coulthard 1997, 1999; Creighton 2003; Creighton and Stewart 2005: 25–9, 55–63; Pittard and Naughton 2003: 776–86; Stewart 1999).

Despite these changes, up until 2006, the traditional industrial award remained at the heart of the federal system of industrial regulation. In part, that was because the award system still operated as a safety net for all employees whose terms and conditions of employment were regulated under, or by reference to, the federal system. However, it was of particular relevance to that part of the workforce for whom collective bargaining was not a meaningful proposition—for example, because they were engaged in small, scattered workplaces where union organization or collective bargaining is difficult if not impossible. For such workers, the periodic 'safety net increases' which were handed down by the Australian Industrial Relations Commission (AIRC) were of great practical significance by reason of the fact that they constituted the only means by which they had any realistic prospect of obtaining pay increases that bore a meaningful relationship to the cost of living.

The award system also played a critical role in helping ensure ethical treatment of those who engaged in collective or individualized bargaining within the framework provided by the WR Act. It did this by reason of the fact that all forms of collective agreement that were certified under the WR Act, and all AWAs, had to satisfy a 'no-disadvantage test' which required that the agreement must not, on balance disadvantage the employee(s) to whom it applied relative to any otherwise applicable award, or where there was no such award, an award that was designated for that purpose.

In November 2005 the Howard government introduced legislation which became operative in the early part of 2006, and over the next four or five years will profoundly change the character of the system of workplace regulation in Australia.

First, the new regime, entitled Work Choices, marks an historic shift away from reliance on the conciliation and an arbitration power in section 51 (xxxv) of the Constitution as the basis for federal industrial regulation. Instead, the system now derives its constitutional validity almost entirely from the power to make laws with respect to 'trading or financial corporations formed within the limits of the Commonwealth' as set out in section 51(xx) of the Constitution.

Amongst other things, this has severely curtailed the sphere of operation of the five State systems of industrial regulation (Victoria does not have a State system, having referred most of its legislative powers in this area to the Commonwealth in 1996) by reason of the fact that the great majority of employees in Australia are employed by corporations, and consequently now fall within the reach of the federal system. This is in marked contrast to the traditional system which reached only those non-Victorian employers (incorporated or otherwise) who were (directly or indirectly) involved in an industrial dispute extending beyond the limits of more than one State. Assuming (as is likely) that the legislation survives the challenge that is presently before the High Court of Australia, it will effectively mark the demise of the State systems, if for no better reason than that they now lack a sufficient 'client base' to remain viable. The Howard government has openly expressed the hope that the various States will then follow the lead of Victoria and refer their legislative powers in this area to the Commonwealth.

Second, the role of the AIRC has been severely curtailed in a number of important respects. Notably, it no longer has the capacity to set safety net terms and conditions through the traditional test case mechanism; its awards no longer form the reference point for individual and collective agreements under the legislation; and it no longer has responsibility for approving collective agreements. Furthermore, the award system, of which the AIRC has traditionally been the guardian, has been marginalized in a number of ways: first, the range of matters that can be dealt with in awards has been reduced from twenty to sixteen; second, the number of awards will be drastically reduced over time on the basis of the recommendations of an Award Review Taskforce; third the AIRC no longer has the capacity to make new awards, other than as part of the award review process and has only limited capacity to vary those that remain; and finally, it is now much easier to displace awards through agreements (individual or collective) than in the past.

A newly established Australian Fair Pay Commission (AFPC) has responsibility for setting and reviewing minimum wages at intervals to be determined by itself. These wage rates, together with legislated minimum standards relating to annual leave, personal leave, parental leave, and maximum hours of work constitute the Australian Fair Pay and Conditions Standard (AFPCS). This, rather than the otherwise applicable award, is the reference point for new agreements. Certain other award standards (e.g. relating to public holidays, rest breaks, and penalty rates) are ostensibly 'protected' by law, but can be bargained away so long as this is done in express terms in an individual or collective agreement.

Third, the new legislation contains a number of measures that must inevitably constrain the capacity of trade unions effectively to promote and to protect the interests of their members. These include: making it more difficult to initiate protected (i.e. lawful) industrial action; investing the executive government with power to terminate or suspend industrial action in a broad range of situations and to make regulations that exclude issues such as trade union training leave, paid union meetings, restrictions on the use of contract labour, and unfair dismissal from the range of matters that can be dealt with in agreements; making it easier for employers to enter into individual agreements with their employees that have the effect of excluding the operation of collective agreements and awards; introducing the somewhat bizarre concept of agreements, between employers and themselves in situations where they are about to engage in a new business, project, or undertaking but have not yet engaged any employees to work in that business, project, or undertaking; and further restricting the capacity of union officials to enter workplaces for purposes of investigating breaches of awards or agreements or communicating with members or potential members.

Taken together, these changes are the most far-reaching since the enactment of the original Conciliation and Arbitration Act in 1904. Cumulatively, they will significantly compromise the role of the law as a guarantor of ethical behaviour in Australian workplaces. Indeed, in some respects they positively entrench unethical behaviour—for example by severely limiting the capacity of employees, through their chosen representatives, collectively to negotiate terms and conditions of employment. As will appear presently, they also deny many of the most vulnerable participants in the labour market protection against arbitrary termination of employment.

Enforcing ethical employment practices in the early twenty-first century

The continued operation of the safety net afforded by the traditional award system clearly was not consistent with the dictates of certain forms of economic orthodoxy, or with the rhetoric of some advocates of HRM. For the free market purist, the continued centrality of the award system involved an unacceptable distortion of the market. For the postmodernist individualist it was suspect by reason of the fact that it tended to subvert individual autonomy in the workplace. But for those who recognize that, with rare exceptions, employers and employees do not come to the market on equal terms, it constituted an important contribution to the adoption and maintenance of ethical employment practices by limiting employers' capacity to exploit their superior market position to the disadvantage of employees and potential employees. It follows that the emasculation of the award system by the Work Choices legislation, and the preferencing of individual agreement-making over collective bargaining, must inevitably compromise the role of the law as a means of promoting ethical employment practices.

That said, the legislation does continue to recognize, and to a degree, facilitate the regulation of terms and conditions of employment through collective bargaining. It recognizes the role of trade unions as representatives of their members and potential members in negotiating agreements, and representing individuals before courts and tribunals. It provides continuing access to an independent tribunal that has the capacity to facilitate collective bargaining, albeit one that has only very limited capacity to impose arbitrated outcomes where facilitation fails. Significantly, the legislation also recognizes, and indeed encourages, employers collectively to 'negotiate' terms and conditions of employment with their employees without the involvement of a trade union or other organization. Critics of Work Choices would suggest that in many instances employer–employee agreements consist of little more than the rubber-stamping of terms and conditions unilaterally determined by the employer. Nevertheless, even the pretence of collective negotiation may serve to moderate abuse of market power by employers in some instances.

Furthermore, it is important to appreciate that the legal contribution to ethical behaviour in employment is not limited to the facilitation of collective determination of terms and conditions of employment. On the contrary, the law makes an important contribution to the encouragement and maintenance of ethical employment practices in a number of areas where the principal focus is on the rights of the individual—bearing in mind that in some instances there is a collective flavour to the enforcement of those rights, and that individuals are sometimes placed under reciprocal obligations to their employer, to themselves, and to other parties.

One of the most important of these areas is in relation to occupational health and safety. Employers, and other duty holders, are now placed under a broad range of obligations that can be seen to be intended to protect the health, safety, and welfare of employees and other persons to whom they can properly be seen to owe a duty of care. This forms part of a continuum from the nineteenth century British factory legislation which was discussed earlier in this chapter, but with a much greater emphasis on the establishment and maintenance of safe systems of work, rather than the observance of detailed rules which characterized the traditional system.

Employer obligations under occupational health and safety legislation also interact with their obligations under legislation which has been adopted at State and federal level that is intended to promote equal opportunity in employment, and to protect employees against discriminatory treatment on grounds such as race, gender, ethnicity, sexual preference, disability, age, etc. (Bourke and Ronalds 2002). Such provision clearly proceeds from the assumption that discriminatory treatment on the basis of arbitrary criteria is unethical, and that employers should be encouraged to afford equality of opportunity to all employees or potential employees. It interfaces with occupational health and safety legislation in relation to issues such as sexual harassment and workplace bullying. For example, sexual harassment, whether by a member of management or a fellow-worker can clearly constitute a threat to the health and safety of the person to whom the harassment is directed, and equally clearly can constitute a breach of the employer's obligations under equal opportunity and anti-discrimination legislation. The same is true for workplace bullying, where the victim is often selected because they possess a particular attribute that makes them stand out from their fellows and/or that makes them particularly vulnerable to physical or mental abuse.

One of the harshest effects of the application of laissez-faire contractualism to the work relationship was in relation to termination of that relationship. On the basis of contract principle, all an employer had to do in order lawfully to terminate an employment relationship was to adhere to those terms of the contract which dealt with termination, and that was the end of the matter. Procedural or substantive fairness were entirely beside the point—unless relevant standards were in some way incorporated in the contract. This meant, for example, that if a contract provided for termination on one week's notice on either side then the employer could lawfully terminate the employment of an employee who had rendered many years' loyal service on nothing more than the whim that the employer disliked the colour of the employee's tie on a particular morning, provided the employee was given the requisite notice or payment in lieu thereof.

Not surprisingly, arbitrary termination of employment was a frequent source of industrial disruption over the years. More surprising, perhaps, it was not until the 1980s that it became clearly established that the forerunner of the AIRC had the capacity under the Constitution and under the (then) Conciliation and Arbitration Act to deal with such disputes by conciliation and arbitration (*Re Ranger Uranium Mines Pty Ltd; Ex parte Federated Miscellaneous Workers Union of Australia* (1987) 163 CLR 656; *Re Boyne Smelters; Ex parte Federation of Industrial Manufacturing and Engineering Employees of Australia* (1993) 177 CLR 446). Even after the High Court appeared to have opened the way for the Commission to deal with arbitrary termination by conciliation and arbitration, there were many 'grey' areas, and enforcement of the right not to be unfairly dismissed which was inserted in most federal awards in consequence of the *Termination, Change and Redundancy Case* in 1984 (1984) 8 IR 34, 9 IR 115 was seriously flawed by reason of the fact that it could not provide the basis for reinstatement of, or the payment of compensation to, arbitrarily dismissed employees. These shortcomings and uncertainties led the Keating Government in 1993 to introduce statutory protection against unfair dismissal for the first time at federal level (Pittard 1994; Stewart 1995).

The statutory protections have subsequently been modified on a number of occasions. For example, in 1994 they were amended to exclude non-award employees earning more than a prescribed (indexed) amount from accessing the system, whilst in 2001 employees of less than three months standing were denied access to statutory protection. Most dramatically, the 2005 amendments entirely exclude employers who engage fewer than 101 employees from the unfair dismissal jurisdiction and stipulate that it is not possible for any employee to maintain an unfair dismissal claim where they were dismissed due to the operational requirements of the undertaking (including that their position is redundant). These changes mean that for many employees the only recourse available in the face of arbitrary termination of employment would be a (potentially costly) claim for unlawful termination on grounds such as gender, age, race, disability, religion, or political opinion—assuming they could establish the necessary element of unlawfulness. It must be recognized that the pre-2005 provisions were sometimes (mis)used by disaffected former employees, and unscrupulous advisers and agents, as a basis for unmeritorious claims in the hope/expectation that the employer concerned would be prepared to reach a financial settlement in order to avoid the costs of defending the claim, however lacking in substance or merit it might be. These abuses could and should have been addressed. But this could and should have been done in a manner that took proper account of the fact that, for all its faults, the earlier legislation did serve as an important incentive to ethical treatment of employees in terms of the grounds for, and methods of, termination of employment. The evisceration of that provision can only provide comfort to the unscrupulous and the unethical.

Whilst the federal legislation does continue to provide some limited protection against unfair and unlawful termination, it has never provided any real protection against unfair contracting. It is true that equal opportunity legislation provides some measure of protection against unethical contracting practices where the employer discriminates on the basis of a prescribed attribute, but by its nature this protection is of only limited scope. Similarly, sections 52 and 53B of the Trade Practices Act 1974 provide a limited measure of protection against misleading and deceptive conduct by employers in relation to the creation of contracts of employment, but do not extend to the actual content of the contract if that content was not the product of the misleading and deceptive conduct.

It also remains the case that the system of awards and agreements established under the WR Act provides a measure of protection against abusive employment practices—for example through the operation of awards and through the AFPCS. However, it is clear from the earlier discussion that the level of protection provided by this means is severely limited.

The question then arises as to whether there is a need for some mechanism whereby the content of individual contracts can be moderated by reference to some general criterion of fairness. To some extent, the WR Act does this in the case of independent contractors who are natural persons—although this provision is somewhat circumscribed in character, and little relied on in practice. More pertinently perhaps, section 106 of the Industrial Relations Act 1990 (NSW) gives the Industrial Relations Commission of New South Wales a very broad power to review the 'fairness' of contracts, including contracts of employment and independent contractor arrangements, whereby work is performed. This provision has generated a great deal of litigation, and controversy. In many respects, it has operated more as a means of shoring up the notice and redundancy entitlements of executive employees than as a means of restraining unethical employment practices in any broader sense (Macken et al. 2002: ch. 13; Phillips and Tooma 2004). The sphere of operation of section 106 has been significantly narrowed by the 2005 federal legislation in that it no longer applies to employees of corporations. Assuming that this federal override is valid in Constitutional terms, this means that section 106 is now of only limited practical relevance. Nevertheless, the popularity of section 106 with litigants (and their advisers) suggests that there is a proper role for legislative provision that affords some meaningful level of protection against unethical employment practices—especially for those employees whose terms and conditions are not regulated by awards or agreements under the WR Act. Regrettably, Work Choices evinces little sympathy for this assessment.

It can be seen from the foregoing that even in the absence of a broad-based unfair contracts jurisdiction, and despite the depredations of the 2005 legislation, the law does impose a number of significant constraints on unethical employment practices. These include the continued operation of the award system under the WR Act. It also includes statutory provision relating to unfair dismissal (for employees of larger companies), discrimination in employment, and occupational health and safety. There are even signs that the common law of employment is becoming less value-neutral—notably through the emerging concept of a mutual duty of trust and confidence.

That said, it must also be recognized that some of the existing protections do not extend to the people who might be thought to be in greatest need of protection. For example, individuals who are technically regarded as 'independent contractors', but who are in reality in a profoundly dependent relationship with their 'principal', are denied access to protection against unfair dismissal. By and large, they are also denied the protection against unfair contracting practices that is afforded to employees by the award system and the bargaining regime established under the WR Act. To take another example, protection against unfair dismissal under the WR Act is denied to a number of particularly vulnerable groups, including casual and probationary employees. Above all, as a consequence of recent legislative changes, the employees of small and medium-sized businesses are now denied protection, even though it seems reasonable to assume that these are the areas where there is greatest risk of abusive treatment of employees due to the frequent lack of any effective union presence in such workplaces, and the general lack of access to sophisticated HR advice and assistance which characterizes much of the small and medium business sector.

There are other areas where it might reasonably be supposed that the law could provide a measure of protection against unethical employment practices and where it does not in fact do so, or where it makes only very partial provision. These would include the fact that the 'National Privacy Principles' that have been put in place under the Privacy Act 1988 (Cth) do not extend to 'employee records' (section 7b(3)(a),(b)). They would also include the failure of the WR Act to make any meaningful contribution to the establishment and maintenance of an appropriate work–life balance—despite some rather pious aspirational statements of principle that might seem to suggest otherwise (e.g. WR Act, section 3(l)).

Conclusions

It is clear from the foregoing that until recently the law has made at least some contribution to the encouragement of ethical employment practices in Australian workplaces. Perhaps its most important element of this consisted of the safety net provided by the traditional award system, both in its own right and as the underpinning of both collective and individual agreement-making under the WR Act. The agreement-making procedures themselves could also make a significant contribution to the development and implementation of ethical employment practices by helping ensure that employees receive a greater share of the economic cake than might be the case if they were forced to negotiate terms and conditions on an individualized basis, and by placing procedural and substantive constraints on unethical behaviour by employers.

Recent legislative changes have seriously compromised the nature and extent of this contribution. The changes are based on assumptions about the capacity of individuals adequately to represent their interests in negotiations with employers or potential employers that simply do not bear critical examination. Not only do these changes diminish the direct contribution of the law to the encouragement of ethical employment practices, they also limit the capacity of employees and their representatives to encourage the adoption of ethical employment practices by employers—for example by denying them the right to negotiate for certified agreements dealing with unfair dismissal.

It is also important to appreciate that many of these recent changes are inconsistent with Australia's obligations in international law. They are, for example, not compatible with the obligations assumed by ratification of the key ILO Conventions dealing with Freedom of Association (Nos 87 and 98) or the Termination of Employment Convention 1982 (No 158). This has been the case for some years (Creighton 1997, 1998; ILO 2005: 34–8), but the 2005 amendments take the nature and extent of non-compliance to new levels (Fenwick and Landau 2006).

For all that, legislative provisions concerning occupational health and safety, EEO, prevention of discriminatory treatment in or in relation to employment, and remedies for unfair dismissal can still be seen to play a positive role in promoting ethical employment practices. By the same token, there are several areas where the law might be expected to make a positive contribution, and where it makes little or none. These include the regulation of unfair contracting practices and helping nurture more effective work–life balances. Even more disturbing is the fact that Australian labour law and employment law have made little attempt to address the profound changes that have taken place in the labour market as reflected in the explosion in casual employment and in other forms of non-traditional work relationships. Worse, in several critical areas, individuals who could be expected to be most vulnerable to unethical treatment by their employers (or potential employers) are expressly denied legislative protection that is afforded to their better-placed colleagues.

It must also be recognized that many of the protections against unethical behaviour that are in place have developed in an ad hoc manner over a long period of time. They do not proceed from any clearly articulated sense of what constitutes ethical behaviour in employment, or of what the law can or should do to encourage, and enforce, such behaviour. Given the fractious character of the Australian polity, this is hardly surprising. But it does seem to bear out the proposition articulated at the outset: the law cannot realistically be expected to ensure ethical treatment of employees and potential employees. However, it can and should help. Recent legislative developments provide little cause for optimism that that potential will be realized in the foreseeable future.

6 HRM and the ethics of commodified work in a market economy

Adrian J. Walsh

The very idea of ethics in marketized workplaces

Work is a central feature of our lives and an area of human activity that provides genuine possibilities for individual development and flourishing. At the same time it is a site of great economic and political conflict and, moreover, for many workers is nothing but drudge, the 'toad god work' as the English poet Philip Larkin once called it.

In the contemporary world, HRM is at the heart of many of the issues that affect the capacity of work to provide for individual development. Human resource managers are responsible *inter alia* for recruitment, selection, orientation, performance evaluation, training and development, IR and health, and safety issues (Boxall and Purcell 2003). As should be patently clear from this list, HRM is a sphere of activity where many of the central ethical issues pertaining to employers and employees arise. What kinds of issues are relevant for HR managers in determining the ethics of work undertaken in the market context?

The first question that one might legitimately ask here is whether it is even possible to talk of ethics in a context where market relations are predominant. One might argue, for instance, that market relations involve an unconscionable commodification of human relations. Things have either a price or a dignity and in so far as work (and workers) becomes commodified, it is stripped of all dignity. Alternatively, one might argue—perhaps along Marxist lines—that profit is necessarily exploitative and therefore the pursuit of profit can never be morally justified. The upshot of these lines of reasoning is that ethics at work within capitalism is impossible and if this is true, then a fortiori an ethical HRM is also an impossibility.

Herein I suggest that such objections, although containing important insights, are too strong. In defence of the *very idea of ethics* in the workplace I argue that, although work in a market economy can be exploitative and can lead to commodifying modes of regard, it need not necessarily be so. In making such claims this is not to deny that the capitalist workplace is free from moral concern. To the contrary. Below, I argue that the market, as a central organizing principle of work, presents human agents, and especially employers, with certain *moral hazards* that must be avoided if work is to be conducted in an ethically acceptable manner (Walsh and Lynch 2002). Such moral hazards in this context involve circumstances where the interests of employees and employers separate, a possibility that so-called unitarists—who do not believe that there are any legitimate conflicts of interests at work—would deny (Boxall and Purcell 2003: 15–16).

If we accept that an ethics of the capitalist workplace is possible, the second question to ask concerns how we might ground such an ethics. What rights and responsibilities do employees and employers have? From where do we derive our list of rights and responsibilities? In this chapter I do not attempt to provide a list of concrete rights and responsibilities, rather I consider some general or abstract guidelines for such an ethics. These general guidelines are grounded in, or based on, the moral hazards with which the market, by virtue of its commercial character, presents us. The moral hazards of the capitalist workplace provide the general contours, as it were, for the formation of such an ethic. There are, of course, points where the interests of employees and employers correspond and thus where the mere pursuit of self-interest leads harmoniously to the furtherance of the interests of all. However, such 'invisible hand' components of the workplace in a market economy need not concern us here in developing an ethics of work, since the interests of all are served without conscious ethical action or ethical motivations. Ethics is redundant in such circumstances. Accordingly, I focus solely on those circumstances where the interests of employees and employers might come apart.

I turn now to those moral hazards that arise for work in a commodity context; my three areas of primary concern being our attitudes towards sources of wealth, economic exploitation, and the content of work.

Regarding as *mere* commodities

Let us now consider the view that as a consequence of the inherent commodification of labour, there is some considerable tension between the treatment of employees in the marketplace and the proper ways in which we should treat human beings.

Moral concerns with the commodification of labour are of course the traditional domain of Marxists and similarly inclined socialists. Marx, for instance, discusses the way in which capitalism drags the worker and his family beneath the wheels of the juggernaut of capital (Marx 1954: 604). Marx's objection here is primarily with the attitude of the capitalist to the proletarian worker and the subsequent treatment that the worker receives. Moreover, such objections are not only to be found within the radical tradition of Marxism; concerns with the treatment of workers under capitalism were also part and parcel of various amelioration projects which were designed to take the 'claws out of capitalism'. Most famously, the Quakers of Cadbury attempted to develop model factories in which workers were not treated as mere resources but as fellow members of a cooperative enterprise (Child 1964: 293–315).

Perhaps, the clearest expression of this concern with the relationship between market and moral attitude originates with the writings of Immanuel Kant. Although Kant was not concerned with markets as we now understand them, and it would be odd to think of Kant as having a fully developed account of the market, his work on the evacuation of value by money has been tremendously influential in our understanding of how the commercial realm might generate inappropriate modes of regard. In the *Groundwork of the Metaphysics of Morals* the distinction between price and dignity appears amidst Kant's discussion of the radical difference between 'things' and 'persons' (Kant 1956: 98). According to Kant, 'things' have only *relative* value; they are valuable in so far as someone happens to desire them, in so far as they are useful for some other ends. Persons, on the other hand, are ends-in-themselves and possess a worthiness or dignity: to treat a person with dignity is synonymous with treating him or her as an end. For Kant, the value of a person, unlike that of a thing, is unconditional (in that its value is not dependent on other ends and has priority over contingent goals), incomparable (in that its value is absolute and not to be compared with other beings or things) and incalculable. According to Kant, persons cannot have a price—that is, a value in exchange—for things with a price are *substitutable*. Thus, price violates the incomparability of persons since price admits of equivalence.

Kant's apparent antagonism towards some market exchanges is certainly not an idiosyncratic feature of the *Groundwork*. In the *Metaphysics of Morals* he suggests that selling a tooth to be transplanted into another mouth or having oneself castrated in order to get an easier livelihood as a singer are ways of potentially murdering oneself (Kant 1996: 177). He does not rule out the amputation of a dead or diseased organ when that organ endangers the amputee's life nor is he concerned with cutting off parts of oneself, such as one's hair, that are not organs, although he notes that cutting one's hair in order to sell it is 'not entirely free from blame' (Kant 1991: 177). In his *Lectures on Ethics*, Kant (1963) also condemns the sale of organs (in this case fingers and teeth), a discussion in which his concern lies not with murdering oneself, but with the wrongful nature of disposing of things that have a free will.

We can view Kant's price–dignity dictum as a version of the more general 'Value Evacuation Thesis' (Walsh 2001: 528). The Value Evacuation Thesis consists of the claim that incorporating a thing into the market evacuates its non-instrumental value. According to the strong version of it (the Entailment

Thesis), it does so necessarily: value and the institutions of the market are *mutually exclusive*. Here the ascription of price entails the evacuation of value.

There is also a weaker version of the thesis in which the evacuation is understood as a causal rather than a logical phenomenon. Two features of this strong Entailment Thesis are worth noting. First, the Entailment Thesis is not fundamentally set against markets, unless one assumes—quite implausibly I would add—that everything is intrinsically valuable. The thesis merely rules out the ascription of price for those things that should be treated with dignity or respect. Second, the Entailment Thesis is routinely employed in a deductive manner to derive unconditional conclusions about the absolute immorality of certain forms of commodification. A good portion of the practical significance of the Value Evacuation Thesis resides in the role that it plays in such public policy oriented arguments.

It should be clear also what relevance this discussion has to the commodification of work that occurs in a market economy. Although Kant does not talk directly about work, a Kantian style objection would focus on the instrumentality of the wage–labour contract. The objection would be that employers regard employees as a means to profit and that this is morally objectionable since the profit motive involves regarding the surplus-value producing worker as a mere means. Equally, employees have what Antony Flew (1976) once called a 'wages motive' and in so far as they regard the employers as a means to a wage then they treat them as a means that from a Kantian point of view one might view as morally objectionable.

This has some considerable implications for the ethics of HRM and for questions concerning the ethics of work in a market economy more generally. If the claim about mutual exclusivity of price and intrinsic valuation is true then we should either reject all work for remuneration as morally pernicious or alternatively forget about ethical attitudes on the part of employers since they must regard their employees as commodities and employees regard their employers as means to wages.

However, things are not as bleak as the thesis of mutual exclusivity might suggest. First, there are extant counterexamples to the thesis that intrinsic modes of regard and price are mutually exclusive. Think, for instance, of a case where I produce art works for sale. The mere fact that I produce them for sale does not mean that I do not regard each work as intrinsically valuable. Indeed, this is not only a matter of logic but also a fact of much aesthetic production in the world. Alternatively, to choose an example more close to home, think of attitudes to certain forms of work that have a vocational aspect. Imagine that one works as a nurse and that one is committed to assisting the sick and needy. The mere fact that one is paid for what one does neither impugns my commitment to the sick and needy nor evacuates the intrinsic value one accords to one's work. This point about the possibility of price and intrinsic value co-existing in certain forms of work is one which Margaret Jane

Radin discusses in some detail in her book *Contested Commodities*. She argues that in cases where monetary values exist alongside intrinsic motivations then the good in question, be it work or some object of value, is *incompletely commodified* (Radin 1996: 102–4). She then proceeds (most usefully given our purposes herein) to employ work itself as an example of a good that is capable of such compatibility and hence often incompletely commodified (Radin 1996: 104–9). In many cases then price and dignity coexist and this would seem to indicate that claims of their mutual exclusivity are false.

Second, there are independent reasons for thinking that the moral objection which underpins the price/dignity dictum is inadequate. It cannot be the case that we are forbidden to treat others as means or instruments, since such treatment is a necessary element of human social life. It would seem that the moral underpinnings need to be reformulated. Somewhat ironically, the basis for such a reformulation is to be found in the works of Kant himself. In a passage that occurs shortly after his discussion of the mutual exclusivity of price and dignity, Kant says that we should not treat persons as *mere* means, but rather as ends in themselves. This is the famous 'Respect for Persons' formulation of the Categorical Imperative and it involves a 'compatibilist' reading of the relationship between instrumental regard and treating as an end. The sin here is not to treat someone as a means but to treat him or her as a *mere* means. Kant, not often recognized as a worldly philosopher, here is acknowledging the necessity of using others as means. Every time I catch a bus I use my bus-driver as a means to get to and from university. We necessarily treat each other as means and in doing so we do not *ipso facto* act immorally. Treating someone as a means is not incompatible with treating him or her as an end. What is morally pernicious is treating them as a *mere* means.

The import of this for the relationship between price and treating with dignity should be apparent. In order to respect others, in order to treat them with dignity, in order to treat them as intrinsically valuable, we must not treat them as mere commodities. One might well legitimately regard another being as a means to financial reward, but one must not treat them as a mere commodity.

It is, on this line of reasoning, possible to treat another as a source of profit and not to be *ipso facto* treating them in a morally objectionable manner. There is a *space* for moral modes of regard within the wage–labour contract. Accordingly, one need not think that an ethics that considers the rights and responsibilities of agents in the workplace is an impossibility.

However to concede this much is not to abandon all concerns with the connection between price and a loss of intrinsic value. Instead I endorse a weaker version of the Value Evacuation Thesis according to which subordination to the market corrodes rather than logically evacuates. In contrast to the Entailment Thesis, let us call the weaker version the 'Corrosion Thesis'. While the Entailment Thesis says that if one incorporates a thing into the market, intrinsic valuation of that thing will, *as a matter of necessity*, be evacuated, according to the Corrosion Thesis if one incorporates a thing into the market there will be a strong *tendency* for that thing no longer to be valued intrinsically. The Corrosion Thesis says that there is a tension between market institutions and intrinsic valuation such that intrinsic valuation tends to be evacuated when the two encounter one another. Market institutions, such as price, corrode our capacity to value goods intrinsically.

In illustrating the difference it is useful to think of the Corrosion Thesis analogously in terms of the medical model of diseases such as cancer, wherein alleged causal factors like smoking are understood not as fully determining but rather as providing predisposing factors towards the disease. Equally, market institutions provide predisposing factors towards evacuation. Moreover, as in the medical model, a *single* counterexample will not disprove the case. Thus, with regards to the putative relationship between smoking and cancer, a single counterexample—such as a healthy octogenarian who has smoked heavily for all of his adult life—does not prove no causal relationship exists. In a similar vein, the presentation of a single counterexample where market institutions and intrinsic valuation coexist will not prove the falsity of the Corrosion Thesis. Nor do logically possible, but physically impossible, counterexamples disprove the Corrosion Thesis any more than they would in the medical case. Hence, rather than being a sufficient condition, incorporation into the market is best thought of as a *predisposing factor* for the evacuation of value.

Perhaps even more controversially, I propose that market institutions *tend to corrode* intrinsic valuation. It would, of course, be possible to have predisposing factors for outcomes that rarely or typically did not eventuate. But the norms associated with market institutions are not like that. When we commodify goods—and in turn adopt market norms—commodities tend to become mere commodities. If this is true, and if market institutions do provide predisposing factors, then we should be particularly wary of buying and selling anything we regard as intrinsically valuable.

What we have here then is a shift from *necessity* to *contingency*. Applied to work undertaken for remuneration, the claim becomes that there is a strong tendency for those operating in this context to take a purely instrumental attitude towards their counterparts on either side of the wage–labour contract. For employers the tendency is to regard their workers as mere means to profit. For employees it is to regard their employers as mere means to wages. So while the compatibilist option is available to both sides of the workplace, there is a strong tendency for such relationships to be understood in purely instrumentalist terms.

We might say then that the economic structure of the workplace provides a *moral hazard*; that is, it provides a set of circumstances in which occasions for the performance of morally pernicious attitudes and behaviour are placed before agents. In this case the moral hazard involves the temptation to regard one's employer or employee as a mere means. And here the moral hazard is more significant for those on the side of the employers since the consequences of regarding one's employees as mere commodities can have far more reaching effects than such a mode of regard on the part of the employee.

If we translate these musings into the language of rights and responsibilities, then we may conclude that employees and employers have a responsibility not to allow the environment of the market to lead them to regard their opposite numbers as mere opportunities for the acquisition of reward or wages.

The import of all of this for our more general discussion is that it makes an ethics of the workplace possible at the same time as recognizing the inherent moral hazards associated with work undertaken in the environment of the market.

Exploitation and just profit

A second moral concern that might lead one to doubt the very possibility of an ethics of the workplace involves the idea of exploitation. One might be worried about the pursuit of profit by employers and the consequences that such pursuit might have for their relations with employees. It might be argued that pursuit of the profit motive is immoral because *ex hypothesi* profit can only be achieved through the exploitation of wage–labour. If this is true then it would seem that an ethics of work is indeed impossible in the market elements of a market economy. Furthermore, the analytic orientation of HRM is towards profit, as has been noted by many HRM theorists. Take John Ivancevich, for instance, who says that one of the distinctive features of HRM is that it analyses and solves problems 'from a profit-oriented, not just a service-oriented, point of view' (Ivancevich 1992: 9). Given such an analytic orientation then the foregoing criticism, if it holds true, would be highly damning of the discipline of HRM.

The *locus classicus* of this claim of exploitation is to be found in the works of Marx. Marx argues that profit (or surplus value) is simply the difference between the cost of production, including the cost of labour of a good and the price the capitalist obtains at the market for it. Thus, although the commodity is produced by the worker (or proletarian), that worker is not paid the full worth of his work. At the heart of the wage–labour contract is a fraud that systematically exploits the worker. One can, according to the Marxist, provide a precise and systematic account of exploitation following this analysis; exploitation is simply the difference between what the worker is paid and what the commodity he or she produces sells for (once other costs are taken out). Profit is necessarily exploitative given that it is achieved through a failure to pay the worker a just price for his or her work.

Furthermore, not only is the wage–labour contract exploitative, but market economies are so constructed as to place a systematic pressure on each capitalist to increase the level of exploitation. This is a consequence of the powerful competitive spirit of the capitalist or market economy that places each capitalist in a quasi-Darwinian struggle for survival against each and every other capitalist. Competition for markets leads to downward pressures on prices—a capitalist can gain a competitive advantage if he or she undercuts the prices of his or her competitors. This downward pressure on prices leads to a fall in surplus value. There is pressure on the capitalist to reduce his or her costs, most notably the cost of labour. Hence the competitive pressures of the market lead to downward pressures on wages and the increased exploitation of the proletariat. This is Marx's famous 'immiseration thesis' (Marx 1954: 579–82). The continued immiseration of the working class was to provide the material conditions for the eventual revolt of the working classes and the overthrow of capitalism.

The significant point for our purposes, however, is that according to Marx the exploitation that is an essential part of the wage–labour contract means that the pursuit of profit must necessarily in turn be an exploitative practice.

In addition, there are other criticisms of the profit motive within the socialist canon, especially in the writings of philosophers Marx derisively labelled 'utopian socialists', which do not rely on this idea of a true price of labour. For instance, the French socialist, Charles Fourier, believed that commerce generally rested on deceit and that the profit could only be pursued through lies and calumny. Fourier tells how although he was taught in catechism and at school that one must never lie, once he worked in his parents' business he realized he was being trained 'at an early age in the occupation of lying, *the art of selling*'. Because of his taste for truth he vowed at age 7 an eternal hatred of commerce (Fourier 1971: 150). On this view an ethics of work in a market economy is impossible since business is grounded in what is a fundamentally morally flawed relationship.

Is the pursuit of profit *necessarily* exploitative? I think there are good reasons for rejecting this claim, at least interpreted in the absolute sweeping manner we find above. On the Marxist story profit is necessarily exploitative since it is only gained by failing to pay workers the true worth of their labour. Any financial difference (i.e. the profit) between the price of a commodity and the cost of production is entirely unearned. This assumes that the capitalist does absolutely nothing whatsoever. However, there are good reasons for thinking that this is false. Consider two things a capitalist might legitimately be thought to do that are worthy of reward. First, there is the organization of both factors of production and labour. Organizing labour and other factors of production involves considerable work, as does selling outputs and ensuring the continuation of future markets. Second, there is entrepreneurial risk. The establishment of a business requires that the capitalist risk his capital.

It would seem that at least some proportion of the difference between the cost of production (including the labour) and the price that the capitalist obtains for the produced commodity is deserved by the capitalist. (It remains an open question what that proportion might be.) Interestingly reasons such as the ones given above were to be found amongst the writings of the medieval schoolmen. Aquinas, for instance, in justifying a moderate profit for merchants insisted on the essential utility of merchants to society, since they distributed goods from areas of abundance to regions of deficiency. Aquinas thought of profit as a stipend for labour (Baldwin 1959: 67). In Aquinas' work, factors of transportation, care, and risk were connected with the fundamental factors of labour and expenses as economic sources that morally justified the profit of a merchant. What underpinned Aquinas' acceptance of the idea of a moderate profit was his focus on the *motives* of the commercial agent. Moderate commercial behaviour, when oriented towards the maintenance of house and home, was morally permissible and even 'praiseworthy' (Aquinas 1963: 2a–2ae, q. 77, a. 4). The pursuit of profit becomes morally objectionable when it is pursued as an end in itself. The important point though is that Aquinas allowed that the difference between the cost of production and the price charged for a commodity could be justified as a reward for the businessman. It is somewhat ironic then that Tawney (famously) labelled Marx the last of the schoolmen since in this regard at least he does not follow their 'motivationalist' approach that allows for the idea of morally legitimate profit.

What might then be concluded? First, on the arguments presented here not all profit can be condemned as exploitative and, if this is true, it follows that an ethics of HRM becomes at the very least possible. However, that said, we should not thereby conclude that questions of exploitation and immoral pursuit of profit are entirely redundant. The socialist and Marxist canon picks up on a structural feature of work in the marketplace that presents moral hazards for employers. To be more specific, employers are in a situation where they can increase their profit by radically forcing down wages (or related conditions) and in so doing trampling on the well-being of their employees. In focusing on the different interests of the employer and the employee here the socialist isolates a morally salient feature of work in a market economy, that is, the temptation for employers to exploit employees.

Given that we do not reject profit altogether as morally inadmissible, then the pivotal intellectual task is to determine what would count as a fair or just profit. How might we do so? One approach would be to determine an actual proportion or rate of profit that is fair. One might model the approach on the ancient Roman practice of lending at interest which designated 12 per cent per annum as the fair rate of return.

I want to adopt an alternative approach that focuses on the motivations which underpin the pursuit of profit. Significantly, I think that we can distinguish between three distinct ways of pursuing profit. Consider the following three distinct types of commercial activity, all of which involve the *profit-seeking motive*.

Lucrepathic action: here seeking profit is the sole or dominant consideration in an agent's all-things-considered judgements.

Accumulative action: here whilst the profit motive is the (or a) primary aim of action, its pursuit is moderated either by moral goals that have weight or by moral side-constraints.

Stipendiary action: here the profit motive is not a goal, but rather functions as a side-constraint on action directed by other non-commercial goals.

Here, I focus on actual profit motives where the agent is a commercial agent engaging in standard commercial practices of buying and selling. (It would be possible to broaden the analysis to encompass monetary motives more generally, which would include such things as, for instance, being motivated by a monetary wage, but for purposes of simplicity, I do not do so here.) Exploitative and unjust work relations are underpinned by lucrepathic action. In cases where exploitation occurs, it is not so much that a specific rate of profit is overstepped, but rather that employers place financial ends ahead of the morally significant needs of their employees. What is objectionable is pure profit-seeking.

The responsibility of employers then is not to act lucrepathically. In so far as their aim is the pursuit of profit as an end in itself, then employers should act as 'accumulators'. In their pursuit of profit they should not ignore or override the significant other-regarding needs of their employees. Of course this is vague. What counts as a significant other-regarding concern and how we might balance various other-regarding concerns with those of the employee are issues which are not addressed here. But this is to be expected since the aim is not so much to provide the concrete details of such responsibilities, but rather to provide the general contours of such an ethic. The concrete details would need to be filled out *in situ*.

There is one final point worth mentioning. It is sometimes thought that endorsing self-interest as a legitimate motivation—to argue that self-interest is not necessarily immoral—commits one to laissez-faire liberalism. This is part of an unfortunate division commonly encountered between self-interest and other-regarding action. *Ex hypothesi*, to be self-interested is to lack other-regarding motives altogether whilst to be altruistic is to lack any self-interested motives. Accordingly, if one accepts self-interest as morally permissible, one must be opposed to any moral constraints on what self-interested activities people undertake within the sphere of the market. But this is a *non sequitur* and the mistake is a consequence of identifying self-interest with selfishness. The upshot is that we should not think that we must choose between the Scylla and Carybdis of, on the one hand, laissez-faire liberalism which rules out other-regarding constraint on actions and, on the other hand, forms of socialism which deem any taint of self-interest in one's motives a sign of moral vice. If the model I have developed is correct, then we do not need to choose.

The toad god work: Sen's capabilities approach and the idea of meaningful work

In the previous sections I focused on two structural features of work in a market economy that generate *specifically moral* hazards for those involved in these institutional settings. I turn now to what we might think of as an intellectual hazard—although it has important normative consequences—and that is the treating of human well-being purely in economic terms.

Contemporary theories of well-being are dominated by utilitarianism—and this is especially true in the philosophical discourses surrounding economics and HRM. Within this literature, 'well-being' is typically understood as involving the maximization of utility where utility is understood in purely economic terms. Such an approach has recently—and powerfully—been challenged by Amartya Sen and his so-called 'capabilities approach'. Sen introduces what we might think of as quasi-Aristotelian element into utilitarian thinking. Instead of rejecting utilitarianism he attempts to reformulate some of its central ethical orientations; most importantly, for our purposes, he argues that the normative assessment of utilitarianism needs to be grounded in what he labels 'capabilities'. He argues that the focus of social policy should be the development of human capabilities rather than utility, at least as utility is typically understood (Sen 1992, 1995, 1999).

Sen distinguishes capabilities from functionings. Capabilities refer to an agent's potential functionings. Sen's examples of functionings include taking part in community activities, being well sheltered, living in a healthy manner, being well-fed. One might think of the difference between a functioning and a capability in terms of the difference between some concrete achievement and the freedom to achieve that particular outcome. G.A. Cohen refers to Sen's approach as involving what he calls 'midfare'; '[M]idfare is constituted of states of the person produced by goods, states in virtue of which utility levels take the values they do. It is posterior to "having goods" and "prior" to "having utility"' (Cohen 1993).

By focusing on capabilities, Sen moves away from the traditional utilitarian focus on satisfaction and in so doing rules out of court the possibility of a person habituating themselves to poor conditions. On Sen's model one cannot equate the utility of a poorly sheltered person who has a poor diet, but who has become inured to her circumstances, with that of a person who is well-fed and well-sheltered, even if her satisfaction levels are identical. Sen deliberately refuses to provide a concrete specification of what capabilities are to be pursued, for he believes that what counts as a relevant capability will depend on the context in question and needs to be determined by dialogue on the part of those on whom such accounts of the good affects. He is concerned to rebut any suggestion that the capabilities approach is overly prescriptive (Alkire 2002: 54–6).

One obvious area where such an approach could be applied is to the benefits of work. By thinking of work as a site for the development of capabilities rather than merely as a means to the end of acquiring income, one is in effect developing an account of meaningful work. Meaningful work, or at least one form of it, would, following Sen's model, become that work in which one was able to develop capabilities.

If Sen is correct about the importance of the development of capabilities— which broadly speaking I think he is—and his framework is applicable to the context of work, then it follows that we should think of work as a site for the development of capabilities. On this model, then, it is a mistake to conceive of work as merely a means to the acquisition of wealth. Instead, the correct approach recognizes work as a non-instrumental source of well-being.

From all of this we might conclude that one responsibility of both employers and employees is to eschew regarding work as merely a means to income, but rather to view it as a site for the development of capabilities. How this might play out in terms of actual social policy is another matter, but for the moment it is enough to note that considerations of the meaningfulness of work occupy a central role in any legitimate ethics of work.

Commercial moral hazards and HRM

What implications do the findings in the previous sections have specifically for HRM? What I have outlined is a set of three moral hazards that arise directly as a result of the commercial framework within which work is set in modern market economies. By 'moral hazards' I mean any circumstance in which agents have an incentive, by virtue of those circumstances and in conjunction with their own desire to pursue their advantage, to undertake some course of action that is morally harmful to someone else involved in that domain. Obviously, to pursue this approach is to adopt a pluralist as opposed to a 'unitarist' approach to IR. While unitarists do not accept that there is any legitimate conflict of interest between employers and employees, pluralists accept such conflicts (Boxall and Purcell 2003: 15–16). For reasons of space I provide no sustained arguments for such an approach here in this chapter, although I should point out that if I am correct about the potential effects of the profit motive on work relations then the pluralists must be vindicated.

According to my approach, avoiding the pitfalls of moral hazards outlined is a necessary (if not a sufficient) condition for such work to be conducted in an ethically appropriate manner. HRM, by virtue of being a sphere of employment in a market economy, also faces such moral hazards and, hence, if HR managers are to act in an ethically appropriate manner, it is incumbent on them, as it is for all managers in the modern workforce, to avoid these moral hazards.

But HRM is not just another area of the workforce. To the contrary, it is a central coordinating area where many of the aims and ideals of organizations are discussed, reviewed, and put into place. If we consider each of the moral hazards listed above, we find that they have special import for the discipline of HRM.

First, consider the relationship between the concern with treating as a mere commodity and the explicit resource orientation of HRM. Many might feel that to regard members of the workforce as commercial resources is to treat them instrumentally, as mere means. Indeed, the very name of the discipline raises alarm for some critics; many such critics felt that the very shift from 'personnel' to 'HR' reflected a deeper instrumentalist shift on the part of managers in their attitudes towards their workforces. If we put the charge in Kantian terms, the change in title was part of a move to regard the workforce as mere commercial resources rather than as ends in themselves.

Beyond the issue of disciplinary nomenclature—which may well in the end be morally insignificant—there is a serious concern that within a commercial environment HRM will become a process by which people are systematically treated as mere commercial resources. Here one might point to the so-called RBV of the firm, according to which competitive advantage arises from the heterogeneous human and technical resources at a firm's disposal (Boxall and Purcell 2003: 72–5). RBV is based on the idea, contra much orthodox economic theory, that competition never entirely eliminates differences among firms and it is these very differences which provide the basis of competitive advantages (Kamoche 2001: 43–50). The aim of RBV is to identify those differences in resource base which provide a competitive advantage over other firms. Clearly, given the foregoing and applying the RBV, humans are treated as key economic resources and within such a framework it is possible for the workforce to be treated as mere means.

But that such dangers are clear and present does not mean that if HR managers are to act in an ethically appropriate manner, they must abandon their commercial orientations. This was the very point of the earlier discussion of the Value Evacuation Thesis. It is not that it is impossible to treat something as both intrinsically valuable and as a commercial resource, but rather that the two are potentially compatible. One can treat another as a means and as an end at the same time. Thus, it is permissible to treat another person as a commercial means so long as one does not treat him or her as a mere means. But the achievement of such compatibility requires vigilance on the part of HRM practitioners to ensure that when treating their workforce as commercial resources, they do not allow their attitudes to be corroded, such that the workforce becomes mere commercial resources.

Similar points can be made *mutatis mutandis* with respect to the second moral hazard regarding just profits. As we noted earlier, the orientation of HRM is towards profits. Traditional radical critiques of profit and the profit motive would have it that the commercial ends are necessarily exploitative. Following this line of reasoning, the aim of HRM would be condemned on the grounds that it is exploitative. However, the view outlined here, whilst critical of exploitation, is not unsympathetic to the pursuit of profit in general nor to it as a fundamental aim of HRM. Thus, it is morally permissible for HRM to be oriented towards profit so long as it does not do so 'lucrepathically'. Profit can be a legitimate goal of HRM, so long that it is pursued with appropriate moral side-constraints on such endeavours. To be sure, this requires further elaboration to provide concrete details of the content of the side-constraints; nonetheless it provides some general guidelines which endorse the permissibility of a profit-orientation without making it a 'morally free fire zone'.

Third, with respect to meaningful work the hazards outlined previously (the toad god work: Sen's capabilities approach and the idea of meaningful work) are of direct relevance to HRM. HR managers are involved in many activities that affect the extent to which work provides for a development of our capacities. This has not gone unnoticed. In recent years many in the HRM have explored the notion of 'competency' at work as a means of improving competitiveness (Boxall and Purcell 2003: 78–82). Such an orientation in HRM follows directly from the RBV. For instance, Hamel and Prahalad provide a list of core competencies that are required for a firm to out compete its rivals (Hamel and Prahalad 1994: 217–28). Here the orientation is towards the financial advantages that might accrue from developing competencies, rather than, as was the case in the work of Sen, the idea that the development of our capabilities is a fundamental right. However, these different orientations need not be at odds. What is most important is that HRM takes seriously the view that human progress not only involves an increase in material welfare, but also involves the flourishing of our potential for sophisticated and challenging work or, as Sen would have it, the development of our capabilities.

These three moral hazards then provide the contours against which an ethical HRM must align itself. In urging that HRM take these considerations into account, we are providing a *structural* response to problems that business ethics often lays at the feet of individuals. If it is the responsibility of HR managers to ensure that work relations are undertaken in an ethically appropriate manner, then this means that some of the issues raised in business ethics discussions are not just matters for the individual concerned but for the organization as a whole. This does not eliminate the need for business ethics, or for individual ethical action, but simply shifts the focus somewhat.

Conclusion

Milton Friedman once (in)famously suggested that the responsibility of business is to its shareholders and thus consists of nothing more than the obligation to return a profit (Friedman 1970). But business manifestly has many responsibilities beyond Friedman's minimalist characterization. One of its most important areas of responsibility is towards its employees. Conversely (although to a lesser extent given the diminished capacity for harm), there are responsibilities incumbent on employees themselves towards their employers.

What are these responsibilities? I have not tried to provide the precise details in concrete form. Instead I have explored the morally salient features of work in a market economy that give rise to what I have labelled moral hazards. On my approach, the market is not—to avail myself of a scholastic distinction— a *cause* of immorality, but may well be an *occasion* of such. This allows for an ethics of work in a market whilst not leading to laissez-faire liberalism. Further, I have focused on the morally hazardous conditions rather than on those circumstances where an invisible hand is in play since one typically need not provide lists of responsibilities where self-interest will provide an agent with sufficient motivation. Subsequently, I noted in each case where a moral hazard arose what responsibilities were entailed by such a hazard. The three general responsibilities outlined were as follows:

1. neither employers nor employees should treat each other as mere commodities;
2. the pursuit of profit or wages should always be constrained where appropriate by other regarding moral considerations;
3. the well-being of individuals in a work environment should not be understood solely in economic terms (narrowly understood).

It is around these more general responsibilities that our more concrete rights and responsibilities will coalesce. While the list of general responsibilities might not be an exhaustive one, certainly it captures the main candidates. They provide the general contours for any more detailed work that attempts to develop an ethics of the workplace in the modern market economy and it is within these contours that HRM must confine itself if it is to be a discipline that is oriented in an ethically appropriate manner.

Part II

Analysing Human Resource Management

7 Stakeholder theory and the ethics of HRM

Michelle Greenwood and Helen De Cieri

Interest in the ethical implications of HRM is fairly recent but appears to be increasing (Winstanley and Woodall 2000a, 2000b). There are many possible explanations for this growing interest: the rise of the size and power of the corporate form, the decrease in regulation in the workplace and demise of unionization in industrialized countries, the growing use of employment in Third World countries, the increasing interest and power by advocacy groups in curtailing corporate excess and holding corporations accountable for their actions.

Scholars in the field of business ethics have considered employees and the employment relationship a high priority for some time, though little consideration has been given to HRM. The focus of debate tends towards the rights of employees and the procedural justice of employment practices, rather than on the relationship between the organization and its employees. To suggest that there is a relationship between the organization per se and its stakeholders is to assume that, to some extent, the organization is a moral actor. Stakeholder theory, in contrast to emphasizing employee rights and procedural justice, attends to the relationship between the organization and its constituent groups, of which employees are considered a prime group (Freeman 1984). Hence, the purpose of this chapter is to explore the extent to which stakeholder theory can assist in understanding the ethics of managing the employment relationship.

This chapter is divided into four sections. The first will review the development of the ethical perspective of HRM and, consequently, note the absence of any substantial debate of stakeholder theory. The second section will introduce stakeholder theory, by outlining its emergence as an important force in managerial theory and providing an overview of its fundamental principles. Stakeholder theory will be identified as being based on pluralist ideology. Next, the debate about the identification and classification of stakeholders and nature of the stakeholder relationship will be outlined with particular reference to employees as 'claimant' stakeholders. The nature of the 'stake' will be considered. Criticisms of stakeholder theory, particularly the limitations of its pluralist foundations, will be identified.

The third section will focus on the nature of stakeholder relationships, particularly stakeholder engagement. The notion that the relationship with claimant stakeholders (such as employees) places specific moral demands on managers will be posited. Further, it will be argued that managing or engaging with employees is not an inherently moral practice and, as such, should be understood as separate from responsible or moral treatment of employees. Building on this, the possible relationship/s between employee engagement and the moral treatment of employees will be deliberated. Finally, the implications of this for our understanding of ethical HRM will be explored.

The development of an ethical perspective of HRM

The debate on ethical issues in the employment relationship can be linked to extant debates in employment. Critical writers have exposed HRM practices as objectifying individuals (Townley 1993), as suppressing resistance and confrontation (Sennett 1999), as creating a new reality through its rhetoric (Keenoy and Anthony 1992), in short, as manipulating employees. These writers tend to eschew adoption of normative stances. Exceptions include Legge (1995, 1996) who introduced ethical analysis to debate on the *gestalt* of HRM and Winstanley and Woodall (2000*a*, 2000*b*) have considered ethical implications in areas such as performance management, HR development, and employee remuneration. The fact that the way employees are managed may invite ethical scrutiny appears to have been overlooked (Winstanley and Woodall 2000*b*). Provis (2001) suggests a number of reasons for resistance of ethics as a form of enquiry: positivists are likely to see ethical statements as meaningless on the grounds that they are not matters of definition nor can be empirically verified; postmodernists would be unconvinced about an absolutist stance or the possibility of insight into 'reality'; and Marxists oppose both morality and religion on the grounds that they represent bourgeois interests.

The ethical debate in HRM has followed the mainstream HRM debate in that it tends to two extremes: macro-level and micro-level. Research in the area has focused on the dissection of individual practices or debating the totality of HRM as 'ethical' (Winstanley and Woodall 2000*b*). At the micro-end of the scale, the ethical assessment of individual practices mirrors the traditional functional approach (Wright and Boswell 2002) of single practice research at the individual level. In the HRM arena, policies and practices ranging from recruitment to retrenchment are grist for the equity and justice mill (see, e.g. Miller 1996; Vallance 1995). From the perspective of business ethics, individual employee rights and responsibilities are common areas of concern (Beauchamp and Bowie 2004). However, we are cautioned that reductionist research may suffer from losing sight of the end goal as the research becomes more and more focused on a narrowly defined phenomenon (Wright and

Boswell 2002). For instance, lists of employees' rights can be ambiguous and, as such, open to a variety of interpretations and applications (Rowan 2000).

At the macro end of the scale, the main subject of ethical scrutiny is HRM as a system. This analysis corresponds with the SHRM focus on multiple practices at an organizational level (Wright and Boswell 2002). The two prime areas of research in the subfield—the link between HRM practice and performance (Wright, Gardner, and Moynihan 2003) and the classification of HRM practices (Wright and Boswell 2002)—open themselves readily to the ethical debate. In the first instance, corporate performance may be interpreted in the broader sense by those interested in the social and environmental outcomes of HRM practice. Similarly, the classification of HRM practices may be conceptualized differently by those concerned with ensuring the rights of an employee to autonomy and the determination of their future. It also has the potential to go beyond the limitations of these methodologies to 'identify' and 'fix' HRM (Keenoy 1999) by consideration of the totality of HRM, within the context of the corporate form and at the societal level.

Stakeholder theory is conspicuously absent from discussions within the ethical HRM literature (see, e.g. Winstanley and Woodall 2000*b*). The notion that the 'stakeholder' status of employees is of significance to the ethical debate has been raised only recently and briefly (Matten and Crane 2003; Winstanley and Woodall 2000*a*). Some might argue that the absence of stakeholder theory from the ethical HRM literature is a reflection of deficiencies in the theory. Yet, at the very least, the stakeholder framework has become a powerful and pervasive heuristic for the understanding of organizational relationships. Indeed, the view that employees are legitimate stakeholders in the organization is often taken for granted in both fields of HRM and business ethics (see Freeman 1984; Legge 1998*a*), by practitioners (Effron, Gandossy, and Goldsmith 2003), and by organizations (Westpac 2002). In this chapter, we seek to further the ethical debate of HRM at the macro-level through the introduction of stakeholder theory.

Stakeholder theory

THE RISE OF THE STAKEHOLDER CONCEPT

'If the word "stakeholder" were a person, it would be just coming into its prime. Born in 1963, it has accumulated experience in influential position and ought to be prepared for some serious responsibility' (Slinger 2000: 31). The term stakeholder was first used with the intention of generalizing the notion of stockholders as the only group to whom management needs to be responsive. According to Slinger (2000), the term first appeared in 1963 in a research report produced by the Stanford Research Institute's Long Range Planning Service. More recently Freeman has admitted that the word stakeholder is 'an obvious literary device meant to call into question the emphasis on "stockholders"' (Freeman 1999: 234). The concept was defined as 'those groups without whose support the organization would cease to exist' and originally included shareowners, employees, customers, lenders, and society (Freeman 1984: 31–2).

The stakeholder concept has grown in prominence over recent years due to increased coverage in the media, public interest and concern about corporate governance, and its adoption by 'third-way' politics (Metcalfe 1998). The popular use of the term culminated in a speech given by Tony Blair whilst he was leader of the UK opposition Labour Party in January 1996. The stakeholder term has become an 'idea of currency' (Freeman and Phillips 2002: 332) and is now used as everyday terminology in business (examples include Australian Stock Exchange (ASX 2001; BCA 2003; Westpac 2002)). The elevation of the concept has been somewhat less dramatic in the academic literature. This represents a rare case where philosophical terminology has become part of the popular lexicon (Bowie 2002: 2). It is suggested that the examination of practices at the level of social transactions and interactions between organizational members (managers, employees, and other stakeholders) could help bridge the gap between academic theory and practice (Cornelius and Gagnon 1999).

The appeal of stakeholder theory for management theorists is both empirical and normative (Cragg 2002: 115). Empirically, stakeholder theory 'rests on an observation or what we might call a fact' (Cragg 2002: 115). Organizations have stakeholders that have the potential to influence them both positively and negatively. Likewise, the activities of organizations impact on individuals and collectives whose interests may be affected either favourably or adversely. According to Freeman (1999) stakeholder management is fundamentally a pragmatic concept. Regardless of the content of the purpose of a firm, the effective firm will manage the relationships that are important. Stakeholder theory is 'inherently prescriptive' in the sense that it 'prescribes action for organizational managers in a rational sense' (Freeman 1984: 47–8). Stakeholder theory may also be considered to be normative, if it conveys the notion that fundamental moral principles may influence corporate activities (Cragg 2002: 115). This holds the universal appeal of the attribution of morality to both actors and subjects in that it requires that we respect others as human beings and account for our actions towards them.

PRINCIPLES OF STAKEHOLDER THEORY

Stakeholder theory is based on two principles that balance the rights of the claimants on the corporation with the consequences of the corporate form.

The first, the principle of corporate effects, states that 'the corporation and its managers are responsible for the effects of their actions on others' (Evan and Freeman 2004: 79). This principle is consciously drawn from the modern moral theory of utilitarianism. Utilitarian theories hold that moral worth of actions or practices is determined solely by their consequences. Utilitarianism is committed to the maximization of the good and the minimization of harm and evil (Beauchamp and Bowie 2004). Therefore, a corporation is seen as responsible for its impact in all areas that would necessarily include its social impact.

The second principle, namely the principle of corporate rights, states that 'the corporation and its managers may not violate the legitimate rights of others to determine their own future' (Evan and Freeman 2004: 79). This principle is drawn from the deontological ethical theory of Kant (1724–1804) based on the respect-for-persons principle that persons should be treated as ends and never only as means. This implies that the corporation must treat its stakeholders as rational beings with a right to pursue their own interests without undue interference.

Significantly, stakeholder theory is underpinned by an assumption of diversity in the interests of the stakeholder groups. Interests refer to the needs and desires of individuals or parties and should be distinguished from the broader normative concept of values that 'conceptualise needs and desires … as valid claims' (Provis 1996: 474). In order for employees and management to work together, it is necessary for them to have at least some significant interest in common. It is necessary for individuals to have shared values to construct a group identity, but it is not necessary for them to do so in order for them to interact in the process of production.

Stakeholder theory assumes that stakeholders are distinct groups with their own valid needs and interests with respect to the organization. Hence, stakeholder theory is fundamentally based on pluralist ideology. Traditionally, the field of IR distinguishes between unitarist, pluralist, and radical ideologies. The principles of stakeholder theory are in keeping with pluralist assumptions that labour is more than a commodity or factor of production, that there exists inequality of bargaining power between employers and employees in imperfect labour markets, that employers and employees are likely to have differing goal and as such there is likely to be conflict between parties, and that employee voice is important in a democratic society (Budd 2004).

WHAT IS A STAKE AND WHO IS A STAKEHOLDER?

The issue of which groups or individuals are identified as organizational stakeholders is of much greater significance than may be apparent. This question is vital because of its implied assumptions about the moral relationship, or lack thereof, between an organization and its stakeholders. From a theoretical point of view, stakeholder identification is fundamental to any debate about the nature of the relationships between organizations and stakeholders. From a practical point of view, it is an immediate and observable way of ascertaining the broader posture of an organization towards its stakeholder relationships (see Miles and Friedman 2003).

Stakeholder theory offers a 'maddening list of signals' on how the questions of stakeholder identification can be answered (Mitchell, Agle, and Wood 1997). These include stakeholders identified as primary or secondary; as owners and non-owners of the firm; owners of capital or owners of less tangible assets; actors or those acted upon; those existing in a voluntary or an involuntary relationship with the firm; right-holders, contractors, or moral claimants; resource providers to or dependents of the firm; risk-takers or influencers; and legal principles to whom agent-managers bear a fiduciary duty (Mitchell, Agle, and Wood 1997). The methods by which stakeholders are defined reflect particular views of the stakeholder conception. For example, a classic definition of a stakeholder as 'having something at risk on the firm' is both derived from, and forms the basis of, Clarkson's risk-based stakeholder model (Phillips 1999: 33).

In a bid to make sense of this assortment of ideas regarding stakeholder identification, Freeman (1984) suggested that definitions of stakeholders could be categorized as 'narrow' or 'broad'. The narrow definitions included groups who are vital to the survival and success of the organization (Freeman 1984). The broad definition included any group or individual that can affect or is affected by the corporation (Freeman 1984). It is tempting to see the broad definition of stakeholders as the more moral or responsible definition. The inclusion of the category of stakeholders who are affected (as opposed to those who merely affect) the organization suggests a moral relationship absent in the narrow definition. However, Phillips (1999: 32) holds that 'stakeholder theory is meaningless unless it is usefully delineated'. Demarcation of stakeholders is necessary to allow for a moral relationship between the organization and its stakeholders by excluding those stakeholders without a moral stake.

According to Phillips (1997), acceptance of the benefit of another party's sacrifice or contribution generates an obligation to that party that in turn generates a right of that party to the fulfilment of the obligation (see Figure 7.1). It follows that if a contribution is made or risk taken, and this contribution or risk is accepted by the other party, then the party is obliged to return a benefit (or protection from harm) to the risk-taker. Thus, the act of contributing a stake (if accepted) confers rights to the stakeholder. Correspondingly, the act of accepting the contribution from the stakeholder imparts responsibilities on the organization.

Figure 7.1 The relationship between stake, rights, and responsibility

Rather than conceive of stakeholders in either a narrow or broad sense, it may be more useful to consider definitions as depicting the stakeholder as either moral or strategic. Kaler (2003) argues that, by dividing definitions of stakeholders into claimant definitions and 'influencer' definitions, the moral duties of the organization can be greatly clarified. Claimants can of course be influencers/influenced. Indeed, it can be argued that claimants must affect or be affected. Kaler (2003) notes that there seems no point in having a claim against anyone or anything which cannot affect you in any way.

Definitions of stakeholders as claimants imply that the business owes perfect or imperfect duties to stakeholders and, as such, are seen as 'moral' definitions. In contrast, definitions of stakeholders as having an influence on the organization, as being influenced by the organization, or as mutually influential, hold only strategic considerations and thus are seen as morally neutral. It should be noted that according to this classification, Freeman's original definition of stakeholders as being 'any group or individual who can affect or is affected by the achievement of organization objectives' (Freeman 1984: 46) is clearly an influencer definition. Slinger (2000: 68) asserts that this definition 'does not say all he (Freeman) would like to say' and is 'simply not strong enough'.

EMPLOYEES AS STAKEHOLDERS

Employees are identified as stakeholders in the organization from almost all stakeholder perspectives. Employees are closely integrated with the firm and this gives them a 'peculiar role among stakeholders' (Matten and Crane 2003: 224). They contribute to the firm in fundamental ways. Employees actually 'constitute' the firm: they are in many cases the most important factor or 'resource' of the corporation, represent the company towards other stakeholders, and act in the name of the corporation (Matten and Crane 2003). In addition, they are greatly affected by the success or failure of the firm. Employees often make a considerable commitment of investment in taking a job that may include a geographical move, a change in relationships, or investment in training. Employees may become financial dependent on organizations overtime. The company is likely to form the basis of their economic livelihood through their income or share ownership. Given the investment in time and effort individuals often place in their jobs and careers, they may also depend on their work for social relationships, self-identity, and self-actualization (Matten and Crane 2003). Hence, even according to the narrowest of definitions, employees can be identified as moral claimant stakeholders (Kaler 2002).

From the organization's perspective, employees have significant influence on the firm and are considered highly salient. It is noted that individuals and groups often belong to more than one stakeholder category (Greenwood 2001). An employee also may be an owner, a member of the local community, a manager in the organization, active in a union, or a combination of these. In addition, stakeholder groups are rarely homogeneous (Greenwood 2001). In any organization there are likely to be individuals from different racial and cultural backgrounds, with family circumstances, with different physical abilities and limitations, or employed under different work arrangements. Such individuals may have markedly different interests in the workplace. They must, however, share a number of elemental interests in order to be considered a stakeholder group.

CRITICISMS OF STAKEHOLDER THEORY

The stakeholder concept has attracted attention in recent years. At a minimum the stakeholder concept has provided a new depiction of the firm, a powerful heuristic by which to reconstruct our understanding of the corporate form. According to some, however, stakeholder theory 'has been advanced and justified in the management literature on the basis of its descriptive accuracy, instrumental power, and normative validity' (Donaldson and Preston 1995: 67). Stakeholder theory has acquired opponents from various sides of the ideological divide, critiques from right and left (Stoney and Winstanley 2001), from friend and foe (Phillips 2003).

The loudest critiques of stakeholder theory have come from the right, those associated with neoclassical economics, unitarist IR, and managerialism. Derived from classical Friedman principles, writers such as Sternberg (1997) have argued that the principles of stakeholder theory undermine the property rights of the owners of the company, compromise the mechanisms of the free market, destabilize the operations of government, thus, in short, subvert the very nature of capitalism. These arguments have been well documented elsewhere (Phillips 2003). They also have been resoundingly refuted on a number of fronts (Freeman and Phillips 2002).

More significant to this debate, however, are the critiques of stakeholder theory from the left, those associated with radical or Marxist philosophies. These criticisms focus on the potential for stakeholders, primarily employees, to be co-opted and controlled by stakeholder management. These arguments are not new, and echo similar criticisms of previous employee engagement practices such as total quality management, employee participation, and team building. Stoney and Winstanley (2001) note that established Marxist criticisms of pluralism are applicable to stakeholder theory: that stakeholder theory is limited in its explanation of how the different interests of stakeholder groups arise and are generated in society, that stakeholder theory provides an overly simplistic conceptualization of power as a commodity that can be negotiated between the organization and stakeholder groups, and that stakeholder theory assumes the separation of economic and political processes. Particular emphasis is given to the 'utopian and naive' treatment of power as a 'positive sum commodity over which management can arbitrate in order to manufacture a win-win compromise between competing stakeholders' (Stoney and Winstanley 2001: 611).

Indeed, stakeholder theory tends to sidestep the issue of power, making few overt references to the concept of power, as is the case for many theories of collaboration (Everett and Jamal 2004). An exception to this is the work by Mitchell, Agle, and Wood (1997) who conceive of power in a very narrow sense as an attribute held (or not held) by particular stakeholder groups. Power is an important concept for the understanding of organizations and organizational leadership (Pfeffer 1992) and organizational collaboration (Everett and Jamal 2004). Pfeffer (1992) warns that, despite the ambivalence and disdain exhibited towards the debate of power in organizations, power exists and will be used and abused. The importance of power within a stakeholder depiction of a moral employment relationship is addressed in the following section.

Stakeholder relationships and moral responsibility

If it is accepted that claimant stakeholders have a moral relationship with the organization then the nature of this relationship must be explicated. The principles of stakeholder theory, when applied to the activities of investor-owned companies, require that 'managers acknowledge that all corporate stakeholders have equal moral status and acknowledge their status in all their activities' (Cragg 2002: 115). Stakeholder theory does not give primacy to one stakeholder over another, though it is acknowledged that at times one group may benefit at the expense of another. The role of management is to balance multiple claims of conflicting stakeholders. Thus, a guiding principle for stakeholder management is that, as the corporation is managed for the benefits of its stakeholders, the 'rights of stakeholders must be ensured through their participation in decisions that substantially affect their welfare'

(Evan and Freeman 2004: 82). A second principle is that, as the managers bear a fiduciary duty to the stakeholders as well as the corporation, 'management must act in the interests of the stakeholders as their agents' (Evan and Freeman 2004: 82). In short, managers must act in the interests of stakeholders and management must engage stakeholders in decision-making.

EMPLOYEE ENGAGEMENT

Employee engagement practices are a significant feature of many organizational approaches to HRM (Effron, Gandossy, and Goldsmith 2003). For example, Luthans and Peterson (2002) report the example of the Gallup Organization's research in over 2,500 units, using the Gallup Workplace Audit to measure employee engagement. It is often implied that these practices are of benefit, indeed in the best interests of, employees (Effron, Gandossy, and Goldsmith 2003; cf. Rothschild 2000). Employee engagement is taken to mean the intention and actions on behalf of the organization to include employees in various aspects of the workplace whereby the employees respond by becoming involved. Hence, employee engagement as seen as a reciprocal activity, albeit one that is, to a large extent, initiated and controlled to the organization. This definition follows that of stakeholder engagement (Beckett and Jonker 2002) and is somewhat different to the employee-centred definition derived from HRM, whereby employee engagement is seen as the extent to which employees are cognitively and psychologically connected with others and how this affects their involvement in task performances in the organization (Kahn 1990).

Employee engagement practices can include a range of activities which vary as to the amount of employee control (Blyton and Turnbull 1998), from employee participation (low control) to employee empowerment (high control). Generally, these practices imply an increased employee input into decision-making, employee control over resources, employee self-regulation and authority—in short, increased discretionary power (Claydon and Doyle 1996). There is, however, scepticism as to the amount of true 'power' afforded employees, even at the 'empowerment' end of the spectrum (Wilkinson 1998).

There is an apparent soundness of logic to the supposition that the more an organization engages with its employees, the more responsible and accountable that organization is likely to be towards these employees. Indeed, there is a 'moralistic theme' in the employee empowerment literature (Claydon and Doyle 1996: 13). The suggestion, however, that engaging with employees is an inherently responsible action on the part of the firm is fallacious. Just because an organization attends to employees does not mean it is responsible towards them. Likewise, just because an organization does not engage with employees does not mean that the organization is not responsible towards them. Such assumptions do not account for the propensity of the organization to act in self-interest, particularly where there is a large power imbalance in favour of the organization. Claydon and Doyle (1996: 16) note that: 'The language of empowerment, like the HRM discourse more widely, slides between deontology and ethical egoism.' Hence, it is posited that employee engagement does not equate with moral responsibility.

To suggest, however, that employee engagement is amoral is somewhat simplistic. There are some moral elements to employee engagement, predominately the attribution of some free will and respect to the workers and existence of some element of procedural justice of the process (Rothschild 2000). Clearly, unless employees are to some extent voluntary and active in the process, and the process is seen as fair and just by them, then engagement cannot be said to occur (the process would be more akin to manipulation or indoctrination). However, there are other moral elements that may be assumed or implied as part of engagement process (employee involvement as being necessarily 'good' for employees) which is not necessarily present. The intent of the actors may be taken for granted erroneously. Just because someone communicates or consults with another does not mean that they have any interest in fulfilling the other's desires or wants. In the organizational setting, employee participation in decision-making is rarely undertaken to achieve the goals of employees, but rather done to further the objectives of the organization. Likewise the virtue of the actors may be incorrectly assumed. Just because managers act in a fair and respectful manner in an engagement process does not mean that these are virtues that they value or nurture. Finally, it is often incorrectly assumed that the outcome sought is that which will provide the best utility for all parties involved. A conflation between the justness of the process (procedural justice) and the justness of the outcome (distributive justice) may occur. Once more, the power differential between the parties, and the potential for abuse of power under such circumstances, has not been taken into account. Thus, it is claimed that the engagement process per se should be considered as independent of the intentions of the actors, the virtue of the actors, and the fairness of the outcomes and, as such (with the qualification identified earlier), can be depicted as largely morally neutral or unaligned (as opposed to amoral or value free).

If employee engagement is considered as independent of the moral treatment of employees then the questions arises: how are the engagement of employees and the moral treatment of employees related, and what is the influence of power on the relationship? The issue of what constitutes moral treatment of employees is of course central to ethical HRM and will be addressed at some length in the following section.

EMPLOYEE ENGAGEMENT AND 'ETHICAL' HRM

By separating engagement from moral treatment we allow for a number of diverse relationships between the organization and its employees. There is the possibility that an organization has no concern in either engaging with its employees or acting in the interests of its employees. Next, there is the possibility that an organization may act in what it believes to be the interests of the employees without consulting its employees. Also, there is the possibility that an organization may engage with its employees with the intent of acting in these employees' interests, and the counterpossibility that the organization may engage with its employees without the intention of acting in the employees' interests.

Employment at will

First, there is the scenario of neither engagement nor moral treatment. This is in keeping with the narrow conceptualization of the firm as a nexus of economic exchanges and is consistent with unitarist ideology. Duska (2004) suggests that the company should not be seen as an object of loyalty or having any moral status. Given that the goal of profit is the reason that the company is brought into existence, loyalty to a corporation is not only required, but likely to be misguided. The company's only concern is to manage its assets to obtain the goals of its owners and the workers' only concern is to get the best working conditions they can. An employer will release an employee and an employee will walk away from an employer when it is profitable for either one to do so (Duska 2004). Under these conditions hard HRM would seem ideal; this follows the classic 'ideal types' of hard and soft HRM as depicted by Storey (1987). Hard HRM would involve a clear and voluntary contract involving exchange of labour for payment and minimal work conditions. The implications of such a 'contract' are that the organization would have no moral obligation distinct from its legal obligations to the employee. Likewise the employee would have no moral obligation to the employer, for example, in a case of breaking confidentiality or whistle-blowing (Bennington 2003). Clearly, in this situation, HRM practice and policy would be entirely strategic in nature. The possibility of an entirely voluntary exchange, however, makes a number of assumptions about the employee's free will. It has previously been noted that employees tend to have significant investments in their employment relationship. Freedom to enter and exit from an employment contract would be dependent upon a number of personal and environmental contingencies, such as the marketability of the employee's skills, the rate of unemployment, and the employee's financial circumstances. Employees who take care of themselves by having a diverse set of skills that are tradable in the open market are the atypical elite (Jacoby 1998). Likewise, the company may face encumbrances that would limit its freedom in such an 'economic' exchange. Given the resource differential between the parties, however, it is far less likely for employees to be acting in a truly voluntary manner.

Paternalism

Next, we allow for the possibility for a company to act in the interests of employees without necessarily engaging with them. This traditional version of social responsibility may take the form of paternalistic management practices towards employees or philanthropic donations to the community. Paternalism in the employment relationship is hardly a new or radical concept. Its roots lie deep in the past when employers provided for the welfare of their employees (Jacoby 1998). Whilst HRM may be seen in part as a replacement of traditional paternalism, we are cautioned that employer paternalism is not dead; it is just changing in nature (Jacoby 1998). Sennett (1999) encourages us to see virtue in the dependency of the employee on the employer, and suggests that moves away from social inclusion in the workplace are detrimental to employees. Reliance on a paternalistic style of employee management has significant risks. According to Purcell (1987), such paternalism restricts the freedom of individuals by imposing well-intended regulation and is midway between treating an employee as a commodity and treating an employee as a resource. Whether the company can know or will respond to the interests of employees without the employees' involvement is highly questionable. If the employer can choose to be benevolent, they may also choose not to be, as has been suggested to be often the case in times of economic downturn (Jacoby 1998). There are, of course, scores of temporary and casual workers whose work is typically beyond the reach of paternalist management. Thus, it is contended that ethical management practices must go beyond acts of benevolence.

Ethical human resource management

When employee engagement combines with moral treatment of employees, we have a scenario of ethical HRM. According to stakeholder theory it is incumbent on the organization to treat its employees as an end in their own right and to bear the consequences of its behaviour towards employees. This stance is consistent with pluralist assumptions of the employment relationship. The parties have entered into a contract with consent and voluntary action. The organization has positive obligations by virtue of its acceptance of the benefits of employees' contribution (and vice versa).

Employees have the fundamental rights to liberty and safety within the workplace including: freedom of association, the right to organize, collective bargaining, abolition of forced labour, equality of opportunity and treatment, and other standards regulating conditions across the entire spectrum of work-related issues (ILO 2004). Bowie (1998) argues beyond this, suggesting that employees also have the right to meaningful work. In addition, Rowan (2000) argues the employee has the right to 'respect', in which he includes the rights to freedom, well-being, and equality. This view of ethical HRM implies that the organization will not only act in the interests of its employees and do so with the intent of furthering those interests, but also involve employees in decisions regarding those interests. In the light of these claims it is clear that demands on the organization of ethical HRM are very high. Essential questions of why the company would undertake such morally demanding and economically costly practices and, indeed, whether a company should undertake such practices remain unanswered. The question arises as to whether or not these are correct demands to make of a corporation? This raises the issue of whether or not ethical HRM is in fact an appropriate responsibility of business. Comprehensive debate over the purpose of the organization is beyond the scope of this chapter; however, for comprehensive coverage of the 'no' argument, see Sternberg (1997).

'Unethical' human resource management

Finally there is the likelihood that organizations will engage employees not with the purpose of furthering the interests of the employee group but rather with the intention of furthering the interests of another group, that of the shareholders. Similar to employment at will scenario of no engagement/no responsibility, employees would be treated entirely strategically. However, unlike the earlier instance, this would not be necessarily clear and unambiguous. Similar to the ethical scenario of engagement/moral treatment may be the suggestion of moral treatment. The employee empowerment literature abounds with apparent moral rightness for both organization and employees (Claydon and Doyle 1996). However, unlike the earlier instance, the consent of the employee and voluntary nature of the contract cannot be assumed. Claydon and Doyle (1996: 23) found that: ' "empowerment is voluntary but not optional", meaning that it demands the voluntary exercise of employees' capacities, but there is no option to refuse this demand'. Grave doubts are thrown on the purported nature of such practices with Wilkinson suggesting that 'management have defined the redistribution of power in very narrow terms... strictly within an agenda set by management' (Wilkinson 1998: 49). Thus, there is an apparent conflict between the pluralist overtones of employee engagement practices and the unitarist reality of powerful corporations acting in self-interest. This 'double edged sword' of 'soft' HRM practices has been noted (Greenwood 2002). In the words of Claydon and Doyle (1996: 15), 'Labour is required more than ever to be both committed as a productive subject and disposable as a commodified object.'

The gap between the rhetoric and reality of HRM has been well documented and explored (see Legge 1995). The possibility that this gap is an indication of manipulation misleading deceptive behaviour is raised. Decades ago, Friedman (1970) noted what he saw as potential fraud on behalf of the company:

There is a strong temptation to rationalize actions as an exercise of 'social responsibility'... for a corporation to generate good-will as a by-product of expenditures that are entirely justified in its own self-interest.... I can express admiration for those (corporations) who disdain such tactics as approaching fraud.

In purporting to care for the interests of employees, with the true intent of furthering the interests of the shareholders, the organization risks acting in a deceitful and manipulative manner. Such action would violate the basic principles on which stakeholder theory has been developed: the right of the stakeholder to pursue their own interests, and the responsibility of the corporation to ensure that the outcomes of corporate action benefit the stakeholders.

There is, within the business ethics literature, a tendency to attribute unethical behaviour to failure or absence of moral perception or reasoning (Seabright and Schminke 2002), that is, a passive act of omission. Seabright and Schminke (2002) argue the antithetical view that malevolence can be an active, creative, or resourceful act. They posit that unethical behaviour could be based on an 'immoral imagination' reasoning process that includes sensitivity, judgement, intention, and implementation and as such be an action of commission. Given the power base of most organizations, and the sophisticated resources available to them, the likelihood that stakeholder engagement practices are actively employed to control and manipulate stakeholders must exist. Hence this form of HRM would not necessarily be amoral but may well be considered immoral or unethical. Thus, there is a concern that employee engagement, rather than reflecting moral treatment of employees, may signify *unethical* management of employees.

Implications of stakeholder theory for ethical HRM

Stakeholder theory offers the potential to conceptualize the organization–employee relationship as a moral relationship and the employee as a moral claimant of the organization. As moral claimants, employees have the right to pursue their own interest, and to be engaged in decisions that affect these interests. It has been established, however, that engaging with, or attending to, the need of employees is not a sufficient condition for the relationship between the organization and its employees to be considered moral. The organization, in fact the managers, have too much discretionary power for any such assurance. The reason or reasons why the organization engages employees, that is, the intent of the managers, may well be a mitigating factor in the existence of a moral relationship. Is the company engaging with the employee to further the interests of the employee or to further its own interests? Alternatively, the relationship may be mediated by trust (Peccei and Guest 2002) or trustworthiness as a virtue of the organization or managers. Are they likely to be good or 'bad' people who do good or bad things, who use or abuse the power at their disposal (Pfeffer 1992)? In order for stakeholder theory to fully explicate the ethicality of the management of HR it will need to account for the power imbalance in the employment relationship and, therefore, potential immoralities.

Limitations and conclusion

Our discussion has been founded on two organizational constructs: stakeholder engagement and organizational moral treatment of stakeholders. Although we briefly described these constructs, they are worthy of much greater attention. In particular the construct of moral treatment requires development. In defining organizational moral treatment as acting in the interest of the employees a number of fundamental problems have been overlooked. First, how is the organization to determine the interests of the employees? Second, why should one employee's interests be the same as another employee's interests or be the same as the employee's interest next year? The assumption of homogeneity of the employee group is a problem facing research in both the HRM (Wright and Boswell 2002) and stakeholder areas.

Furthermore, there is the issue of whether the organization is a moral actor. We have used interchangeably the terms managers and organizations in discussions of responsibilities and moral actions. In doing so we have, to some degree, attributed the characteristics of a moral person to the organization. It has been variously argued that the moral status of organizations is absolute, secondary, limited, or absent (McKenna and Tsahuridu 2001). At one extreme it is claimed that organizations have moral personhood and as such their moral responsibility is absolute. At the other extreme organizations may be seen as amoral structures that are incapable of exercising either moral rights or responsibilities. We adopt the limited or restricted position that the organization has moral status but it is not equivalent to a person. In taking this stance the behaviours and responsibilities of the organization have not necessarily been differentiated from the behaviours and responsibilities of the managers in their role as agents of the organization. Yet, managers are stakeholders of the organization in their own right. Indeed, stakes held by managers in the organization can be very influential and complex. This is further emphasized by the fact that managers are often constituents of other stakeholder groups such as employees, owners, customers, and the community. Thus, by equating managers and 'the organization', we risk overlooking some vital features in the debate.

Finally, the development of the constructs as 'one-way' is restrictive. This inquiry has focused on the organizational engagement of employees, and the responsibility of the organization towards its employees, with no mention of the reverse. This is despite the fact that the notion of employee engagement has an inherent two-way connotation. Also, the significant debate on the moral responsibility of employees towards their employers has been neglected. Setting the discussion in this manner may be justified by its descriptive validity. It is the organization that sets the agenda. It cannot be assumed that engagement involves an equal dialogue between partners. The ground rules for engagement are more likely to be set by the dominant player (in the absence of an independent referee). It is the behaviour of the organization that is, in general, the focus of the organization and its stakeholders. The development of the constructs as descriptive, however, has obvious limitations. In addition, we are cautioned against putting the organization at the centre of analysis as it discourages consideration of the stakeholders in their own right (Miles and Friedman 2003) and thus can be accused of colluding in the misdeed we are attempting to expose. The need for research that gives weight to stakeholder voice is manifested.

Stakeholder theory is gaining prominence in many aspects of business and organizational studies. To date, little consideration has been given to the depiction of HRM as stakeholder management, the employment relationship as a stakeholder relationship, and employees as stakeholders. The theoretical debate in HRM is by no means complete. Many calls for theorizing with 'multiple lenses' have been made. It appears timely that stakeholder theory should be drawn into the theoretical debate of HRM, particularly in the light of the growing interest in the ethical dimensions of HRM.

The stakeholder concept takes a variety of different forms and has been applied in numerous ways. This chapter has argued that a distinction must be made between the moral treatment of stakeholders and the strategic treatment of stakeholders. Such a distinction has significant implications for HRM. Employees can be viewed 'morally' as individuals with their own rights and interests or they can be viewed 'strategically' as a resource to be maximized by the firm. This notion is not dissimilar to existing models in the HRM literature, such as soft and hard HRM (Storey 1987; also see Guest 1987, 1999). There are, however, several advantages of depicting employees as moral stakeholders. First, it provides both a practical and normative model for ethical HRM. Rather than automatically inferring 'caring' or soft HRM practices as being ethical (or more ethical than the hard counterparts), ethical HRM has been explicated. In doing so, it is apparent that the demands of ethical HRM are very high in that they include both the moral treatment of employees and the engagement of employees in matters affecting their interests. This raises the important question of whether ethical HRM can or should belong as part of the investor-owned corporation.

Second, by depicting the employment relationship as either moral or amoral (strategic), the possibility of 'immoral' arises. It has been argued that where employee engagement exists in the absence of a moral relationship, the possibility of the immoral treatment of employees exists. Whilst criticism of the rhetoric and practice of HRM exists in many forms, the idea of it being potentially immoral or 'irresponsible' has not been developed. One of the central tasks of business ethics is to explain the 'darker side of organizational life' (Seabright and Schminke 2002: 19). Stakeholder theory has the potential to provide a framework to consider the 'dark' side of HRM and, as such, further the theoretical understanding of this area.

In conclusion, we have explored questions of how our understanding of the ethical management of employees as HR can be informed and developed by stakeholder theory. We suggest that stakeholder theory holds the potential to contribute to understanding of the ethical nature of the organization–employee relationship in several ways.

8 HR managers as ethics agents of the state

Lynne Bennington

Introduction

Corporate governance and ethics are hot topics in both the popular press and in the academic management literature. Codes of conduct are burgeoning yet we still hear about amazing corporate collapses in which senior management not only failed to comply with various laws but has even failed to comply with, or enforce, its own code of conduct (Meisinger 2002). These codes are often developed and maintained in HR departments, and HR practitioners are often responsible for management-level ethics awareness programmes (Wiley 2000). In general, though, HRM is rarely mentioned in any of the reports on ethical failures. Similarly, HR textbooks have tended to omit any serious discussion of ethics (Marchington and Wilkinson 1996; Payne and Wayland 1999; Winstanley and Woodall 2000*a*). Notwithstanding these points, ethical conflicts are potentially of serious concern to employee HR managers.

At the professional level, most HR associations have ethical behaviour as one of their key policies and some even include promotion of ethical behaviour in their objectives. In fact, the president of the Society for Human Resource Management in the USA, the largest American HR association with well over 100,000 members (Wiley 2000), argues that it is the professional duty of HR managers to promote ethical business practices and to contribute to the 'ethical success of . . . organizations' (Meisinger 2002: 8). This core principle of the Society has associated guidelines on professional responsibility that include 'adhering to the highest standards of ethical and professional behaviour; complying with the law; striving to achieve the highest levels of service, performance, and social responsibility; advocating for the appropriate use and appreciation of human beings as employees; and advocating openly and within the established forums for debate in order to influence decision-making and results' (SHRM 2004).

Fisher, Schoenfeldt, and Shaw (1999: 19) provide more precise behavioural guidance for HR practitioners and specify the following duties for employees and job applicants: 'respecting persons and not using them solely as means to one's own ends, not doing any harm, telling the truth, keeping promises, treating people fairly and without discrimination, not depriving people of basic rights, such as the right to free speech and association'. Although these authors do not specifically refer to legal compliance, it is implicit both in their general specification of duties as well as in their expanded list that this includes being truthful in recruiting, equal pay for equal work, fair policies, and avoidance of the use of invalid and discriminatory selection and other HR systems.

The behaviour of some employers would suggest that not all agree with each and every one of the objectives stated by the Society for Human Resource Management. Certainly one would not have to ponder for long about whether many HR managers comply with the Fisher, Schoenfeldt, and Shaw (1999) ethical behavioural requirements. In the first case, American survey evidence tells us that a little more than half of the HR professionals who responded to a 2003 business ethics survey felt at least some pressure to compromise their organization's ethical standards (Schramm 2003). Second, there are not many HR practitioners that would be willing to tell applicants that there were unsuccessful because they were considered 'too old', or the 'wrong race' or whatever other bias the line manager (or they) may have brought to bear in the selection process!

Yet, it is HR managers that are often cast into the role of guardian of organizational ethics, so what is the HRM role and what does this mean in reality? In this chapter the focus will be on the ethical duty of legal compliance so the question that will be addressed is 'Can or should the HR managers be the agents of the state in ethical issues?' Although the discussion could address any number of HR areas, I have chosen to focus on one specific area that is clearly within the bailiwick of HRM and one that has a clear legal foundation, that of EEO/AA.

Background

In most countries the volume of both common law and statute law that imposes duties on employers has burgeoned over the last 20–30 years. This is particularly the case in respect to the functions often associated with personnel or HRM departments (e.g. recruitment, selection, occupational health and safety, promotion, separation). The responsibility is often delegated to people with titles such as HR managers, personnel managers, HR advisors, AA managers, EEO managers, diversity manager, EEO counsellor, people and performance managers, compliance officers, governance officers, and so on; the title varying depending on a variety of factors including the origin of the company and the nomenclature of its relevant legislation.

The law generally sets minimum standards. It might be criticized as falling far short of ethical goals by some and, by others, as possibly not even ethical. Viewed on a continuum, Baytos suggests that it operates along the lines of 'unfair...unethical...illegal' (cited in Grensing-Pophal 1998), but for the purpose of this chapter and, at least in the first instance, adherence to the law will be treated as the minimum requirement for ethical behaviour. It is acknowledged though that this assumption cannot uniformly apply, especially under unethical legislative regimes.

The possible consequences for the HR managers, encompassing all of the roles listed above and when acting as agents of the state (or the guardian of the ethical and legal duties imposed by the various laws), in the anti-discrimination or EEO area will be examined. The challenges of supporting and enforcing EEO principles in organizations will be made especially clear by case law from the USA which indicates that the courts do not see HR managers as advocates of EEO beyond quite strict boundaries within organizations and that in many cases HR managers have been excluded from the legislated whistle-blowing protections.

Equal employment opportunity

Equal employment opportunity is the focus of this chapter because it is a basic human right and is argued to be one of the most serious issues in HRM today (Cascio 1998; CCH 2003; Lutz 2001). It is so basic in fact that it has not only been covered by a plethora of laws in many countries but, albeit in a somewhat limited way, has also been included by umbrella organizations such as the United Nations as well as voluntary associations of businesses connected with the CSR and sustainability 'movements' (Florini 2003).

There are many areas of employment activity that can be affected by breaches of EEO and there is ample evidence that the number of cases in this area is increasing, especially in the United States (Mello 2000). One of the most important is that of employment recruitment and selection, as it is the least open to scrutiny of any HR processes (Petersen, Saporta, and Seidel 2000) and there is evidence that discrimination in these processes is commonplace, in both Western and non-Western countries (Bennington 2001; Collinson and Collinson 1996; Noon and Ogbonna 2001). Protecting EEO rights is both a legal and an ethical issue (Martin and Woldring 2001). Most countries have anti-discrimination laws in one form or another, but, along with educative approaches and the so-called 'business case for EEO', expectations of significant changes in outcomes have not been fulfilled (Dickens 1999).

There is even concern that there may be negative changes in the state or public sector that has (with some exceptions) also been subject to EEO laws.

This is of concern because in many cases it has been the public sector that has been the role model for EEO policies and adherence to EEO laws. Undoubtedly, this was the case when HRM was strong and centralized in the public sector, but with the reforms accompanying the paradigm of public sector management known as New Public Management—in which the public sector has been called on to become more like the private sector (Hughes 1998)—it is possible that EEO has either been forgotten or conveniently overlooked. This has occurred in a context of the devolution of HRM responsibilities, outsourcing, contract rather than tenured employment, and results-based rather than rule-based approaches to public sector management. Authors such as Kellough (1999) have argued that controls over consistency, fairness, and equity in personnel systems have broken down. Bertok (1999), in his work for the Organization for Economic Cooperation and Development on public sector ethics, believes that problems such as this arise from low-quality legislation and weak public institutions that do not enforce such laws.

In the specific area of EEO, the reasons for lack of adherence to EEO appear to be manifold. At one level, we know that employers do not necessarily subscribe to the benefits of EEO legislation (Bennington and Wein 2000a) and blatant flouting of anti-discrimination laws has been noted in Canada, the USA, and New Zealand (Harcourt and Harcourt 2002). Second, external recruitment consultants, who now conduct much of the recruitment work across sectors, do not universally adhere to EEO laws (Bennington 2001, 2002). Finally, individual job applicants and employees do not appear to be able to protect themselves, either because they have trouble detecting discrimination or, even if they can and do, they are reluctant to lodge complaints (Bennington and Wein 2000b).

What of the other institutions that might act as a positive influence in this area? For example, one might think of considering the church and trade unions. However, given the ongoing debate amongst the clergy in respect to the role of women any argument for the positive influence of the church might well be regarded as somewhat thin. Unions, on the other hand, have a somewhat more mixed record but do have a potential contribution to make given their formal role in employment relations in jurisdictions such as Australia. But British writers, Noon and Hoque (2001), in raising criticisms of trade unions, have questioned whether unions are appropriate to consider as guardians of equal opportunities, and the evidence shows that they too have been perpetrators or, at the very minimum, non-advocates for anti-discrimination (Yelnosky 1999). On the other hand, even though trade union membership has reduced in the UK and Australia over the last twenty or so years, data from the 1995 AWIRS shows that there is a significant difference between unionized workplaces and non-unionized workplaces in respect to having EEO/AA policies and training in these areas (Deery, Walsh, and Knox 2001). This same data set (AWIRS) also shows that unionized workplaces are more likely to have HR and/or ER managers, but it is possible that there may be some confounding of variables and thus one needs to be careful about attributing causation to unionization status. It is this role of HRM that is our focus here, even though, according to the AWIRS study, less than half of Australian organizations have such roles (Deery, Walsh, and Knox 2001).

The HRM role

The role of HRM deserves special attention for a variety of reasons, none the least of which is the ambivalence with which it is held and the changes that it has purportedly undergone in recent years. Therefore, this section will discuss the various roles of HR in respect to governance and legal compliance.

It is interesting to consider approaches to HRM developed in the UK as well as in the USA. For example, a little over ten years ago Storey (cited in Caldwell 2003), in discussing HRM within organizations, proposed two bipolar dimensions to differentiate HR managers: intervention versus non-intervention and strategy versus tactics resulting in a fourfold typology of personnel roles in the UK: advisors, handmaidens, regulators, and change-makers. Although adherence to EEO was not described as fitting within any of these categories specifically, it could be seen to fit in any or all of the roles, depending on how one perceives the value of EEO. For example, the business case for EEO might argue that it fits well with the change-maker role and that this will add significant value to the organization in the form of organizational justice perceptions, ease in recruiting, selection on merit, better decision-making, opening of new markets, etc., apart from avoiding law suits based on allegations of discrimination. Hunter argues that the costs of unethical behaviour should not be underestimated and suggests that these include 'deterioration of relationships; mistrust; negative impact on employee productivity; stifling of employee creativity; information flows throughout the company become ineffective; employee loyalty declines and absenteeism and labour turnover increases' (cited in Kantor and Weisberg 2002: 688). On the other hand, some might perceive attempts to regulate or monitor EEO as a regulatory role and one which might interfere with the achievement of business objectives.

A different approach was offered by Ulrich (1997) in the USA. He suggested that it was time for HR practitioners to throw off their marginalized positions and to become 'champions of competitiveness in delivering value'. Ulrich's dimensions were based on two axes: strategy versus operations and process versus people resulting in four roles: strategic partner, change agent, administrative expert, and employee champion. Again, it is debatable where adherence to EEO principles fits in this model, although it is likely that it would be perceived to fit within Storey's regulator role. Respondents in Caldwell's study (2003) of HR managers in the UK suggests that some managers thought that the regulator role might be rekindled by the new social and employment legislation but overall they thought that the role had declined.

Others still view HRM as having a role in compliance with employment law and EEO/AA legislation, for example Baron and Kreps (1999) and Woodd (1997). Grensing-Pophal asserts that 'one value shared by virtually every HR manager is to be an advocate for employees' (1998: 116). It certainly used to be assumed that HR had a strong role in EEO as it was believed that this function inherently upheld desirable social justice values (Trice, Belasco, and Alutto 1969). HR was always involved in recruitment, selection, and all other key staffing processes, but, increasingly, together with the devolution of many HR responsibilities (Torrington and Hall 1996), these important roles have assumed less importance or perhaps preference has been given to external providers who are less likely to oppose discriminatory practices in their quest to meet client expectations and obtain repeat business (Bennington 2001). On the positive side, research has found that the HR function is the main driver of change on equity issues (Cattaneo, Reavley, and Templer 1994), and even where there is support from senior managers, it has been found that diversity initiatives (the follow-on from EEO), have been driven by HRM (Miller and Rowney 1999). Moreover, it has been argued that one of the most significant effects associated with AA has been the elaboration of the HRM function (Konrad and Linnehan 1999).

It is very easy to become despondent about many of the published approaches to HRM as they appear to put superficial assessments of business requirements above ethical behaviour. However, recent work in the USA has been more heartening. After urging HR managers to be business partners for about a decade, the new call is for HR to become 'players' rather than simply 'partners' (Beatty, Ewing, and Tharp 2003; Ulrich and Beatty 2001). To become a 'player' it is argued that HR managers need to learn to coach, lead, architect, build, facilitate, and to become the conscience to employers (Ulrich and Beatty 2001). Of particular relevance to us are the roles of leader and business conscience. Under this approach, the HR manager should model the required behaviours for all managers (in respect to people and gover- nance issues), ensure that HR is governed as it should be, and ensure that 'organizations play by the rules' (Ulrich and Beatty 2001: 305). These authors suggest that HR is better placed than other functions such as finance and legal because they usually find out about legal and ethical issues too late for problem prevention. Ulrich and Beatty (2001) now argue that it should be HRM that ensures that organizations are successful but only when they are playing by the rules. The fact that the proper exercise of this role may result in job loss and ongoing retaliation is acknowledged but they argue that HR managers must be prepared for such risks!

Beatty, Ewing, and Tharp (2003) argue that if HR managers perceive customers and investors as more important than top management then taking such risks is less difficult. Moreover, they extend their argument by stating that it is HRM that needs to influence behaviour such that a culture of openness and willingness to confront wrong-doing is created. In respect to legal breaches, such as a breach of an anti-discrimination law, they point out that HR has a fiduciary responsibility to ensure compliance.

However, the role of the HR manager is still far from clear in most organizations (Gibb 2000). In fact, there has been a continuing concern about the role and perception of HR staff (Eisenstat 1996). Most appear to have a poor perception of HR (Gibb 2000). Seldom have HR decisions been viewed as a source of value creation (Becker and Gerhart 1996), although, controversially, Hart (1993) argued that HRM is concerned with adding value but often in the ways that are managerial and amoral! The movement in HR values towards the managerialist has led to strong criticism of the profession (Galang and Ferris 1997). Yet, prior to this, HR managers were described as inflexible and focused on rules, policies, and procedures (Church and Waclawski 2001), so it is not surprising that we often hear calls in the literature for more flexible HRM systems. But does this mean that HR should have flexible ethics and not worry about compliance with the law?

While employees might like to think that the HR manager will be employee focused, and an advocate for their rights, the changes over the last decade or so have clearly tipped the balance towards a corporatist focus and away from the so-called radical or employee focused approach. In the meantime, HR managers have struggled to attain credibility (Wright et al. 2001*b*) and have had to continually justify their existence to prevent their roles from being outsourced or downsized (Mitchell 2000). In these circumstances, it could hardly be expected that HRM would whole-heartedly embrace the EEO role, especially as no matter what the origin of the role, it does not seem to have been well received (Cassell 1997; Noble and Mears 2000). Even the newer role of diversity manager has been criticized as being 'captured by the systems they are trying to change, trivializing discrimination . . . and relinquishing critical human rights issues to the discretion of management' (Sinclair 2000: 239).

The pressures that this context creates do not bode well for those who believe that it is the role of the HR manager to promote, if not ensure, compliance with the relevant legislation, especially if there are senior managers who do not share the same views. Yet, as Mello points out, the literature is 'conspicuously silent concerning any examination or study of this potential conflict of interest' (2000: 12). In the UK, Collinson and Collinson (1996: 240) report that:

Attempts by personnel managers to ensure that recruitment practices were formal, consistent, and lawful were frequently undermined by divisions and conflicts based on function (between personnel and line): space (corporate/local); hierarchy (senior line manager/subordinate personnel); age; gender; and managerial ideology.

In fact, this study found that junior personnel managers reported that they would be labelled as troublemakers and their careers could be negatively affected if they strongly advocated for employee rights at the expense of managerial prerogative (Collinson and Collinson 1996). As we will see from the USA, this is exactly what has occurred in a number of reported cases.

The US context and cases

The USA has numerous federal and state laws that prohibit discrimination in employment (e.g. Title VII of the Civil Rights Act of 1964, the Americans with Disabilities Act, the Equal Pay Act, Age Discrimination in Employment Act, etc.). Employers are expected to maintain their own internal compliance mechanisms (Mello 2000), but where employees believe that they have been discriminated against it is expected that they will raise their concern with the appropriate person in their own organization and follow the grievance procedures stipulated in their employer's policies. There is also the option for employee grievances to be taken to an external body such as the US Equal Employment Opportunity Commission (EEOC).

Whistle-blowers are purportedly protected from reprisal, retaliation, or victimization by their employers. For example, Title VII prohibits two forms of retaliation. The first is known as 'opposition retaliation' which occurs as a result of an employee opposing an unlawful practice by conveying their concern or objection to the employer and explicitly stating that the behaviour or practice constitutes a form of employment discrimination that is unlawful. In theory, adverse reactions by the employers (such as a reassignment of duties, insufficient resources to perform the job properly, demotion, firing) that can be connected causally to opposition behaviour by the employee are prohibited.

The second type of retaliation may arise when an employee participates in a discrimination matter by 'making a charge, testifying, assisting, or participating in any manner in an investigation, proceeding or hearing' (Weatherspoon 2000) and is known as 'participation retaliation'. The penalty (compensatory and punitive damages) for retaliation, depending on the size of the employing organization, can be up to $300,000 (Ray 1997), although state law may allow for higher penalties. For example, in *Woodson* v. *Scott Paper Co.* the pay-out amounted to $1,557,845 (Ray 1997). Thus it might be expected that this type of behaviour would occur rarely but nearly one quarter of all EEOC cases are based on complaints of employer retaliation (Shapiro cited by Mello 2000).

In operationalizing EEO, it is common for employers to delegate much of the responsibility for compliance to an EEO/AA manager who may work within the HR division or who may be independent from HR, although the latter is perhaps more likely to occur in larger organizations that can afford the luxury of someone checking up on the gatekeepers to the organization who are also the advisors to managers. The Code of Federal Regulation outlines the EEO/AA employee's duties as including the development of policy statements, AA programmes, internal and external communication techniques; assisting in the identification of problem areas; designing and implementing auditing and reporting systems to ensure the effectiveness of programmes; serving as the liaison between the organization and enforcement agencies; and serving as the liaison between the organization and minority organizations and groups concerned with employment opportunities for marginalized groups such as women and minorities. Weatherspoon (2000) reports that it is typical for EEO job descriptions to require the EEO/AA employee also to investigate complaints of discrimination, to recommend disciplinary actions for employees who violate anti-discrimination laws and policies and to alert the public and federal agencies of discriminatory practices.

Clearly, this role is fraught with a variety of minefields in which the HR employee is between a rock and a hard place. Weatherspoon (2000) argues that it is not infrequent that the EEO employee has to advise their employer that the law has been breached and this in itself may well result in reprisal from the employer, even though the same employer probably hired the EEO officer to monitor this area.

Under common law, every employee, no matter whether in management or even at the EEO officer level, has a duty of loyalty and confidentiality to their employer and a clear duty to protect the employer's interests (Larmer 1992). This concept of loyalty is common across many countries; it is not unique to the USA. In fact, Aaron (1999), in his overview of the laws governing loyalty in countries including Australia, Canada, England, France, Germany, Italy, Japan, New Zealand, Sweden, and the USA suggests that it is commonly held that employees must behave in ways that enhance rather than detract from the interests of the employer. Pfeiffer agrees but adds that this should not be in a manner which is illegal or unethical (1992, citing Michalos). From the employer perspective, a 1997 House of Lords decision pointed out that employers, similarly, must not behave in a manner that serves to damage the trust and confidence between themselves and their employees (Hepple 1999; McCallum and Stewart 1999). An obvious conflict arises when issues of alerting public and federal agencies about non-compliance comes into play. However, even in these cases, it might also be thought that those who have been appointed to take care of this important area of EEO would also be covered by legislative protection and the Pfeiffer caveat should assist. However the American case law does not always provide support for this belief. An examination of some of the landmark cases is instructive.

The author acknowledges the work of Bales (1994) and Weatherspoon (2000) in identifying these cases and in the analyses provided by these authors, which are heavily drawn upon in this chapter.

The decision in *Holden* v. *Owens-Illinois, Inc.* is a frequently cited precedent. Holden, a female African American, had been hired to manage the firm's AA programmes but was apparently fired within 6 weeks of her commencement for, according to the district court, aggressively pursuing non-discriminatory employment practices. In this case the district court stated that the employer was merely practising window dressing by the token employment of minority individuals and was not serious about the issue. However, the decision was appealed and the complaint by Holden was dismissed with a statement from the court that Holden's activities did not constitute protected activity under the opposition clause of Title VII because this law does not require the implementation of AA, notwithstanding that the enforcement of an AA plan is consistent with the enforcement of Title VII (Weatherspoon 2000). The basis of this decision has been followed in other cases. For example, the same rationale was applied in the case of *Phillips* v. *Pepsi Cola General Bottlers, Inc.*, after which Weatherspoon (2000) concluded that the courts were taking a very narrow view of the law and that the EEO/AA employee basically had little or no protection in their roles. Once the term AA comes into the equation the American courts seem to be very wary and quite protective of employers.

In *Johnson* v. *University of Cincinnati*, a case related to a university vice president of human resources and human relations, the operation of the double standards are clear. In Johnson's case he was hired not just to ensure compliance with the regulations and the university's AA plan, but his job was to change the culture of the organization such that diversity would be accepted. After a couple of years Johnson became concerned that the AA processes were not effective so he wrote to the cabinet members of the university questioning the commitment to AA. Subsequently, his performance was criticized which culminated in Johnson filing a formal complaint with the EEOC complaining that he was being discriminated against on the basis of his race and due to his advocacy on behalf of women and minorities. Just over a month later his employment was terminated. In the first instance, Johnson was unsuccessful in that the court determined that the precedent in the Holden case mentioned above is the one that should apply. This decision was not concurred with by the court of appeals. His case was differentiated from Holden by the fact that he explicitly protested that discrimination had occurred in the hiring process.

It is possible that the devil is in the detail though and that the American courts expect an extremely high level of legal sophistication from plaintiffs (or complainants), which I would submit is totally unreasonable. It appears that the 'opposition' must include a clear statement that the employer is violating Title VII and that the simple description of how the violation is occurring is not adequate. The court drew our attention to this possibility in the case of *Coleman* v. *Wayne State University*. In this case Coleman, a personnel officer, claimed that he suffered from retaliation and constructive discharge due to his opposition to racism and the lack of AA in his university. Coleman was 'successful' because the court perceived that he had specifically expressed his opposition to racial discrimination in employment which is clearly protected under Title VII.

The next hurdle arose when the court had to determine whether the claim had been raised in a reasonable manner. Smith (2003) states that the legislative history is almost silent on the employee's latitude to oppose unlawful job practices. Assuming that the employee opposed what they reasonably believed was unlawful and that the employee acted in good faith, a number of tests seem to be applied at this point: did the employee's protest interfere with his or her ability to effectively perform the job for which he or she were hired? Did the employee breach any company policies, rules, or commands? Did the opposition result in disruption to the workplace and were the company's goals interfered with? In other words, if the opposition was disruptive then the conduct will not be protected!

It is probable that meaningful opposition to discrimination will be disruptive to someone in the organization and the treatment of this issue appears to drastically underestimate the emotional impact discrimination can have on employees. Smith (2003) reasons that it is necessary for the context to be understood and, in referring to the Holden case, suggests that the complainant (or plaintiff, using the American terminology) reaction to the discrimination by her employer was both a symptom of the injury she personally experienced as a black person as well as a self-defence against the employer's marginalization of other black people. Also it is known that minorities are more likely to perceive certain events as discriminatory than are white persons and this must influence how opposition is perceived.

Furthermore, Smith (2003) argues that not to engage in some form of opposition would result in greater injury because it would result in internalization of anger about the discrimination. The courts should therefore examine the total context of the emotional distress created by discriminatory behaviour. One of the best examples here is that of Becky Clark, who found out that her husband, who had been hired at the same time as her by the same firm which had a policy of pay confidentiality, was paid less than her husband to do the same work. She protested about the unequal salaries for women and threatened to contact the relevant external authority. This was done in the presence of other employees as was the supervisor's response which was to 'do just that'. Becky Clark then left the workplace and did not work the overtime agreed to earlier in the day. Even though backpay was awarded in this case the court agreed that the employer was justified in discharging her because she had failed to fulfil her agreed overtime and that there was an expectation that she should have expressed her grievance in private rather than in front of other employees. This decision shows very limited understanding of 'normal' human behaviour.

In a second case described by Bales (1994) an employee's complaints to her supervisor about racial discrimination received no adequate response so she then went one level higher. This resulted in the termination of her employment on the grounds that she bypassed her supervisor albeit that this was consistent with the company's policy. The court regarded this behaviour on the part of the employee as disruptive. The test in these cases arises from the case of *Hochstadt* v. *Worcester Foundation for Experimental Biology* in which the employee constantly complained about sex discrimination to her colleagues and it was alleged that this damaged relationships and interfered with their work. The court held that there must be a balancing of the employee's right to air her grievances with the employer's right to run his business. In this case the balance did not exist when conduct of this type was exhibited and the court found that such 'serious acts of disloyalty provided the employer with a legitimate, non-discriminatory basis for discharging' her (Bales 1994: 113). Bales also points out that all challenges to an employer's conduct will create some degree of disruption, and worries that the courts have not set clear standards to guide an employee in this position so that they can manage their conduct in such a way that they will be protected.

Hyman (1997) has summarized the activities of non-HR/EEO employees that do not appear to be protected. These include blocking traffic, refusing to perform duties, interfering with co-workers, disrupting the workplace, engaging in violence, and stealing or copying confidential documents. Presumably, much of the information that HR managers would wish to rely upon would be in the form of confidential information or 'confidential documents'.

Turning to the second form of retaliation which is, broadly speaking, related to participation in a discrimination matter. This may even be in the form of a letter of complaint rather than a formal charge or even a threat to take action, as well as action on one's own behalf or on behalf of another.

An employee is protected if the employee encourages co-workers to enforce their Title VII rights..., refuses to sign an inaccurate affidavit on behalf of an employer,... testifies on behalf of a co-worker,... participates in a conciliation meeting on behalf of a co-worker,... submits affidavits on behalf of a co-worker to the EEOC,... or submits non-confidential documentary evidence to an agency investigating a discrimination complaint.... (Bales 1994: 104–5).

As Weatherspoon (2000) points out, it would not be unreasonable to think that EEO/AA employees should be protected when trying to enforce anti-discrimination measures in their organizations to achieve legal compliance, and that they should also be protected if they make complaints on their own behalf. However, the courts have sometimes held that the EEO/AA officer is really there to protect the interests of the employer, and 'participating' in discrimination claims, is necessarily in direct conflict with the purpose of their job. This is where the issue of loyalty and the primacy of commerce over the law and human rights becomes an interesting one. For the naive and simple person, it would be very easy to assume that the law should take precedence. One might readily assume that the state would be very concerned that employers are not complying with the law and that it would ensure that those who engage in whistle-blowing activities, or simply provide information as part of their jobs that is required in discrimination cases, receive the utmost protection. But this does not appear to be so: Bales (1994) illustrates just how the courts give far less protection to personnel managers than to any other employee classification.

Loyalty to the employer appears to be seen as the primary duty. Yet, as Pfeiffer (1992) argued, loyalty is context specific and a relative concept. By reporting discriminatory behaviour after exhausting all best endeavours to change the situation may in fact be the most ethical and legal thing to do. According to Larmer, 'loyalty amounts to acting in a person's best interests and it can never be in a person's best interests to be allowed to act immorally' (1992: 128).

Baytos (cited in Grensing-Pophal 1998) suggests that HR managers have to be prepared to take risks if they feel strongly about an issue, but this is easy advice to give when not facing retaliation risk as well as, quite possibly, an unsuccessful court case and resultant lack of income: Bales (1994) summarizes the legal treatment of personnel managers in the USA by suggesting that the nature of the job description and the level of the job will come into play, so the higher up in management the less protection is likely and if the person was hired to represent the company 'against' employees who file claims then greater loyalty is expected. Absent is the suggestion of loyalty to 'right', lawful, or ethical behaviour! Thus it is not surprising that a survey by Weatherspoon (2000) of randomly selected members of the American Association for AA found that 67 per cent had faced reprisal in their position, but only 4 per cent had filed a complaint against their employer and only a further 8 per cent wanted to.

Discussion

In an era when CSR and alternatives to the overriding obligation to the economic model are being countenanced quite widely, it is perhaps disconcerting that HR managers are not obviously enforcing EEO obligations and when they do, at least in the USA, insufficient protections exist. This is particularly alarming when many codes of ethics specifically refer to an obligation to obey the law. Indeed, in an analysis of the codes of ethics of professional business organizations in the USA, Gaumnitz and Lere (2002) found that 60 per cent included a statement about obligation to obey the law.

The conflicts that arise in this area of ethical behaviour create significant issues for HR managers. Similar issues might be purported to exist for employee lawyers (Kandel and Kilens 1999) and accountants (Lovell 2002). However, HR managers have a unique role and unique associated issues. Marchington and Wilkinson (1996: 3) argue that HR managers are able to 'make a distinctive contribution by adopting a clear ethical and professional stance on issues which some other managers might wish to ignore'. Beatty, Ewing, and Tharp (2003), too, point out that HR has a fiduciary responsibility to ensure legal compliance, and that as research indicates that HR managers are more likely to act on legal and ethical issues than other employees, it follows that if HR managers do not adopt the role of agent of the state in EEO matters, then possibly no one will. Thus there is little doubt that the HR manager role is different to other professionals—they need to serve the employer, the interests of individual employees, and the society (Miller cited in Hart 1993).

But, it is probably impossible to uphold this trifold responsibility without conflict. Some managers will often choose to subordinate their knowledge of legal requirements in order to satisfy the expressed or implied requirements of the employer. Being a team player, a valued member of management (Losey 1997), aligning oneself with the objectives of the business and so on are argued as having the predominant influence on behaviour. Not diverting the attention of the business from profit objectives and not disrupting the business are seen to be important. Perhaps, too, there is an acknowledgement that HR is relatively powerless to bring about the kind of social change that would be required (Torrington 1993).

British authors, Winstanley and Woodall (2000a) have called for the ethical 'rearmament' of HR to provide some balance. They argue that business will be more successful anyway if it is ethical. However, when the courts do not support or protect HR managers in opposing unlawful discrimination and unethical conduct, it is understandable that many will choose to act with 'rational bias' or self-interest. In the USA the right of the employer to breach the law seems almost more acceptable than for an HR/EEO professional to act honestly, professionally (showing due care), and ethically, in cases of employer discrimination. HR managers are all too often forced to confront difficult ethical decisions: they can tow the company line and face their own internal psychological consequences of feeling powerless and not act ethically, or they can oppose discrimination and face the consequences which may be some form of retaliation by the employer. Sometimes this retaliation may be immediate or, as shown in a number of the American cases, the more sinister employer may bide their time and concoct other reasons for termination. This form of retaliation may have a more insidious effect on the career of the HR practitioner.

If HR managers are to return to their role as guardians of EEO, and accept the challenge of Ulrich and Beatty and their colleagues, they may well have to distance themselves from line management again, even though they have worked very hard to move closer to their group and to be perceived as 'aligned' with the interests of the business. The risk of course is that their HR role will be dispensed with altogether unless there is some legislative backing for the role as occurs in Germany. Assuming that their role exists in organizations, at the same time, senior management will need to be open to 'bad news' and challenge on ethical issues because unless HR managers can act without fear of retaliation, CEOs may well find that issues will escalate and create even further problems and costs (Trevino et al. 1999). Employee 'voice' is an important human rights issue for all employees, not just HR managers, and with the relatively low percentage of HR managers in businesses these days (at least in Australia), the outsourcing of HRM and the use of contract workers reductions in voice might be expected (Davis-Blake, Broschak, and George 2003), so the likelihood of HRM acting as the ethics agent is even further reduced.

External auditors might also be considered to provide independent assessments of compliance but much of the discrimination that occurs in organizations is not recorded and experiences reported by Florini (2003) on the external auditor who avoided the sensitive areas in a voluntary compliance audit would tend to suggest that this activity also may have limited benefit. The appointment of independent board directors to whom HRM can have direct access (as suggested by Beatty, Ewing, and Tharp 2003) may provide some additional value and some protection for the HRM, but these directors need to be from a different mould to line management. Elsewhere, I have argued for a more proactive approach to monitoring discrimination (by the relevant government authority) is necessary (Bennington and Wein 2000a) and I think that the same argument applies to ensure compliance with other areas of HRM that are covered by legislation. As Bertok (1999) has stated, problems will remain unless there are strong public institutions to enforce the law.

In conclusion, this chapter has only highlighted some of the issues for HR managers who adopt the role of ethics agents for the state in one particular area, that of EEO/AA. However, unless we are serious about the issue and protections are provided for HR managers then the state can expect little improvement in employer conduct and will need to look to other means of ensuring compliance with its legislation.

9 The ethical basis for HRM professionalism and codes of conduct

David Ardagh

Introduction

In this chapter the extent, feasibility, and desirability of the professionalization of HRM and HRM professionalism are discussed. It is argued that there are three broad marks of a profession. First, it meets a human need. Second, it applies knowledge to this need, and third, a profession has a social grant of authority. More specific criteria can be found in the literature, for example, one condition of full professionalization is a self-enforced code of ethics and conduct. The question of feasibility and desirability of professionalization is explored using the more specific criteria and the ethical framework of Neo-Aristotelian Virtue Ethics (NAVE). The chapter explores how HRM presently lacks some professional features but advocates pursuit of the professionalization of HRM via adoption of the 'concessional', constitutional model of corporations (Bottomley 1990, 1997; Dine 2000, 2005) and the addition of some features to reflect the monitoring role and contribution of HRM as corporate 'conscience'.

Neo-Aristotelian virtue ethics and needs

First, I want to address the idea that the mark of a profession is that it meets a human need. What are such needs? NAVE isolates one normative meaning of need: needs as ethically justified wants for those 'goods' which are needed for at least threshold operation of a human capacity. The ideal object and end of all human capacities is, from a NAVE perspective, 'well-being' or 'eudaimonia', abstractly conceived as 'living and acting well' (Ardagh 1979; Austin 1967). This Aristotelian idea of basing ethics on actualizing capacities and perfecting virtues is found today in the works of analytic Neo-Thomists like Geach (1978) and Haldane (1998) and Neo-Aristotelians such as Foot (1978), Nussbaum (1993), and Nussbaum and Sen (1993). For them, the perfecting end or goal of a natural capacity is a good, and our pursuit of this good (and the correlative need-satisfiers) is enhanced or perfected via what are called its virtues. The moral virtues are understood to enhance those capacities that will help us attain eudaimonia and more particularly are taken to govern our feelings and actions. Courage, for example, is a moral virtue that moderates how much and when to feel fear as well as how much and when to act on this fear. As such it is a virtue that helps us to pursue eudaimonia in the right way given the particular fearful circumstances we are facing. The capacity that we call 'intellect' has truth and knowledge as its end or goal, and the intellectual virtue that helps us to perfect or enhance the intellect we call wisdom.

Eudaimonia: a more determinate conception

Adding specificity and depth to the notion of eudaimonia, for Neo-Aristotelians there are more specific ingredient ends or goods that make up or concretize the notion of well-being. Any end can be identified as needed for well-being by meeting certain criteria or marks identified by wise people. For Aquinas in his *Summa Theologiae* (I–IIae, q. 2–8, 182), for example, the objects or ends which display the marks are:

(a) *The highest objects of the highest human powers:* They are the highest objects that can be assimilated by our 'highest' human powers, intellect, and will. Aquinas thought this included God, but we might say consciousness, or other humans and their works, as apprehended and enjoyed by means of these capacities.

(b) *Perfecting:* Ingredient goods help to exercise, perfect, and enhance the capacities of the human agent, especially the higher most distinctive capacities of thought and will.

(c) *Ultimate ends, not instrumental only:* Ingredient goods are capable of being desired for their own sake even if they also serve as means to other ends.

(d) *Relatively permanent:* The ingredient goods have a cumulative, relatively permanent, and continuous nature that can be left and returned to without difficulty.

(e) *Autonomy/self-sufficiency:* Ingredient goods express or enhance a person or group's human self-sufficiency and autonomy, and decrease unwanted dependency on luck or scarce external material resources.

(f) *Delight:* The ingredient goods meeting (a)–(e) are also enjoyable and result in deep satisfaction.

For a person to achieve eudaimonia, the attainment of goods of capacity which accord with these marks is needed. Where a person is not able to attain these ingredient goods of well-being, they can be said to have a need. This inability

Table 9.1. Examples of ingredient good ends and needs-satisfiers of well-being or eudaimonia

• Meditation/ contemplation of 'highest' objects of the highest powers • Knowledge of cause(s) of being, truth and goodness	• Love, friendship intimacy 'I thou' relationships • Making a free contribution to a person or project	• Creativity • Aesthetic or cultural activity (art, music, drama, dance, literature, etc. not driven by social, profit, commerce concerns) • Good work	• Information • Learning • Understanding • Philosophy • Science • Meaning in life • Freedom and identity; service	• Sports • Eating well • Clean habitat • Law and order • Health

may arise through privation or lack of sustenance, or some sort of involuntary disorder or because they occupy all their time pursuing goods that do not accord with the marks listed above. We call ingredient goods 'needs' in this normative sense because they are things that we all require if our common human capacities are to function normally. We want to remedy defects and disorders of capacity; attain goods without which we will suffer harm, including social and psychological deprivation; and enhance our understanding. We have consequent needs for such complex goods as security, shelter, food, public health (physical); basic information and education, fair treatment, social identity and recognition, culture (social); and autonomy (personal). Examples of needs in this sense are set out in Table 9.1.

NAVE and the socio-political remit

Each individual pursues the good within a complex matrix of social and political arrangements, which straddle the public, professional, and private sectors. In Neo-Aristotelian teleological representations of the relations between the individual and this broader social matrix, the human good ought to be articulated and pursued through the application of ethics by practical moral reason in a social and political context as shown in Figure 9.1. Public, professional, and private sectors are distinguished by the goods they focus upon; by reference to the breadth and nobility of their ends and purposes; the scope and target of their delivery; their funding base; and the specific mode and degree of moral necessity of their practice. Public sector decision-making in regimes of modern 'State-Welfare-Capitalist' (SWC) democracy (Shaw and Barry 2001: 149) ideally pursues opportunities for the achievement of the common good. This means facilitating threshold-level attainment of the co-operatively attainable common goods by all citizens. To do so requires SWC governments to largely set the legal and other boundaries for professions, businesses, and NGOs to operate within.

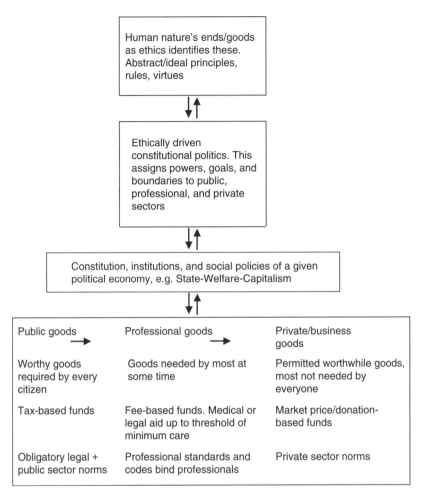

Figure 9.1 From human goods and needs to embodying social arrangements

Ideally the state partly determines professional authority, funds infrastructure and sites like courts and hospitals (Daniel 1990) and this is the reflection of the fact that the professional sector is purportedly oriented towards public goods and needs satisfaction and the private sector towards at least the ethically permissible. The arrows in Figure 9.1 are intended to indicate the direction of practical rational determination. Given the priority of ends over means in practical reasoning, the model calls for the normative priority of ethically warranted goods to be facilitated within 'welfare capitalist' social policy settings including corporate law. That is, ethically warranted human ends enjoy primacy over more specific sectoral means and their institutional embodiments. Nevertheless, the vertical arrows in Figure 9.1 linking the boxes in both directions indicate that practical organizational arrangements, brought into existence as means to the 'higher' more ultimate ends of ethics and politics, use resources which constrain realization of the ends themselves.

Public sector decision-making in a modern democracy therefore ideally seeks the achievement of the common good by all citizens, and should set legal and other boundaries within which professions, businesses, NGOs, and non-profit organizations operate. It has in some ways a broader legislative mandate allowing it to be directive of all of the domains, if only in some respects which we will examine presently. The view that business requires a social remit is supported in the business corporation case by the so-called 'dual concession' theory of the corporation (Bottomley 1990, 1997) and Dine (2000, 2005), and their 'constitutional' model of the corporation. Broadly, the state is seen as granting authority to constitute and then operate a corporation for any permissible purpose provided that it has fair procedures, does no harm, and does some social good.

Professions

Professions may be understood as constituting a hybrid sector between public and private, run autonomously in some ways, following a set of cognitive and moral norms via codes of ethics and conduct. From a teleological and virtue ethics perspective, the professions, like the public sector, pledge to provide certain specific public goods and human needs of individuals (Brock 1998; Koehn 1994; Oakley and Cocking 2001). In the paradigm cases of law and medicine, the profession of law is targeted on the provision of justice for individuals and medicine is targeted towards the provision of health for individuals. Professions can either be seen as being an autonomous sector serving the public good, or belonging within the public sector funded by taxes to threshold levels of service provision. Unlike private sector organizations, professions should meet morally warranted individual needs in a distinctive manner. The idea is ancient and has changed over time as have most social constructs, but the core values, goods, and needs (ethically warranted wants) remain relevant to society today (Alkire 2000; Bok 1995; Brown 1991; Finnis 1983; Walzer 1994).

NAVE and the applied knowledge requirement

There is also a broad expectation currently that a profession applies a body of systematic knowledge to need satisfaction. The candidates for the more specific kind of systematic knowledge include: theoretical, experimentally tested, inherited, empirical, practical, and normative knowledge, but none seems to be obviously paramount or essential. Rather than prejudging exactly what kind of knowledge is required I will simply list all the criteria of a profession, mentioning knowledge-related ones as they appear amongst the other criteria. There will be mention of theory, inherited tradition, practical judgement, expertise, and an ongoing empirical support basis, peer review, and other features. It does not however seem to be necessary to resolve this issue by privileging one or two over others 'once and for all' in order to recognize this cognitive and educational requirement as essential.

In compiling the list of criteria I discard uses of the term 'professional' where it means simply doing something to earn a living; or doing it very skilfully, and so 'professionally'. A professional is someone who meets a human need or normatively warranted want in a skilled and virtuous way, drawing on a body of systematic knowledge, and granted a social licence to practise as such. Based on an analysis of the literature I would claim that the criteria listed below are the marks of a profession and can be verified as such by paradigm cases of the professions such as law and medicine.

The criteria for a profession

A set of marks of a profession can be canvassed from the philosophy literature on what makes a field of practice into a profession (Battin et al. 1989; Bayles 1989; Callaghan 1988; Coady and Bloch 1996; Koehn 1994; Lawrence 1999; Solomon 1993, 1997). Most of these are mentioned in the sociology literature, which we will set aside in the interests of brevity (see Lawrence 1999 for most of the important sociological references). The paradigms are law and medicine closely followed by psychiatrists, academics, architects, accountants, dentists, natural scientists, teachers, and engineers. Although long self-styled as professions, clergy, armed forces, and police are, for some, questionable as professional groups, especially in the lower ranks. A third aspiring group includes nurses, journalists, computer specialists, pharmacists, radiographers, librarians, veterinarians, social workers, bankers, financial planners, and realtors. The marks listed below, I would claim, apply at least to the paradigm cases of professions and professionals—law and medicine. To be graduated as a profession a set of practices must meet some adequate subset of these marks. Some of these marks are internally complex and will be denoted by a letter after the number, for example, 9(c).

1(a). Professionals are *called to meet a specific, profession-defining need of the client*. Examples are justice and health for lawyers and doctors respectively. 1(b). In acquiring the skills and virtues used to meet the need, professionals take up a specific *calling, career, or vocation.* Clients may not want what the professional holds they need, but the goal is clients' empowerment. Code: *NeedVoc*

2. Professionals *apply an evergrowing body or store of systematic, specialized knowledge and associated norms* to cases involving contact with individuals or organizations. Code: *SpTK*

3(a). Professions require for entry *an extensive multi-year mandatory period of training.* Besides knowledge and understanding of theory, this involves a period of apprenticeship, or a transition from the status of novice to that of master, in order to apply skills and norms benignly to practical problems. 3(b). There is a taxonomy of types of case, principles, and precedents, and one studies and imitates the master's diagnosis, prognosis, and therapy, using the distinctive *mode of practical reasoning called casuistry* applied to judgements in particular cases, often involving a measure of autonomous discretion. 3(c). Commonly, diagnosis is *guided by client report of an issue.* (In emergency care this is set aside, but application of scientific truth in normal consultations cannot start till the patient/client tells the professional what the issue/problem is, and/or where it hurts.) Code: *TrCaCID*

4(a). Given criteria 1–3, an authoritative self-governing institutional body, drawn from practitioner ranks, *self-administers a grant of authority/licence/right* to practitioners. Professionals usually do their own peer assessment. 4(b). The inductees *thereafter become authoritative and autonomous experts,* with 4(c). *indirect social government cooperation and oversight of duty compliance* vested in society's representatives. Once inducted, professionals are credited *with* authority to speak on relevant social matters of importance (Battin et al. 1989). Since the technical nature of the work and expense precludes every citizen receiving training, some degree of 4(d). *social trust in a ruling expert subgroup,* the professional body, is necessary, to administer their grant of authority. They are not expected or required to make money for the body. Code: *Selfad/Auth*

5. The grant of authority or *licence* is conditional on a *public test (examination) of expertise* of some sort. Code: *Exam*

6. Professions are 'democratic brother/sister-hoods' *socially approved as quasi-monopolies* or quasi-guilds/solidarities. They have *the power to limit the number of trainees.* Unlicensed competition is discouraged, and government may intervene to assure this, through immigration policy (Flexner and Greenwood, cited in Lawrence 1999: 72–3). The charges against them of being closed shops, designed to drive up costs, can be answered to the extent that there is a case for limiting the

accessibility of costly professional training on a personal capacity/social cost basis. Permission to engage in the professional practice in the relevant system is seen as correlative to the right and duty of the public to receive the knowledge given in 1 above by a public grant of authority. Code: *App/Monop*

7. Practitioners retire and die, taking their knowledge to the grave. The education and training confers the *social gift* of the systematic body of (usually) *socially conserved knowledge* targeted towards attaining the relevant ultimate human good, one to be *passed down* (Latin, *traditio*). With a new science the tradition begins from scratch. One is expected to share the gift made possible by specialization, and *inter-generational succession planning*. Code: *Trad*

8. Since a profession is a vocation, involving social trust and care of needs with moral significance, not only a wealth creation device, *a code of ethics and conduct* for all individual practitioners is promulgated by the licensing body for members. Koehn (1994) agrees that such codes form the basis of an informal expectation and contract, but holds that contract is posterior to the *trustworthiness of the professional pledge of service reflected in the code*. Contracts often betoken a lack of trust. The intent of codes is to segregate professionals from commercial inducements to corrupt practice, and from conflicts of interest eroding trust, and by *delineating accountability* to minimize the risks to them and the professional group arising from malpractice. The rash of lawsuits against professionals may indicate some waning of this ideal's prominence and enforcement. Code: *EthCode*

9(a). *Codes of conduct, suspended from the code of ethics, specify certain role-relative privileges or duties*, for example of arms-bearing (military/police) confidentiality (lawyers/doctors), or truthful disclosure (accountants) within a context. *Informed consent* is often vital. Under their restricted role-prerogatives, expertise must be applied either under authority in rule-bound ways under strict conditions, or even-handedly to all members within the client base, *even to unsavoury clients* at least if accepted as clients. The need must be met in a specific, complex way, unlike the need for food or shelter. 9(b). Professionals must maintain *disclosure or silence to select inquirers*, often listed by an authoritative body mediating the conducting of the contract or grant of authority from the state to the client. 9(c). The rules and subjects of such privilege of disclosure are crafted by and within the system relative to a social need or *the patient's or client's welfare*, not that of the provider. 9(d). A grant of authority to practise is often given (see criteria 4–6) following an *oath of professional altruism*, to put public and professional good ahead of self-interest, and to avoid malpractice in an institutionalized system (e.g. courts/hospitals). 9(e). There is often an induction ceremony and sometimes a *uniform worn either on* (barrister/doctor) *or even both on and off the job,* for example, soldier/priest signifying *a right/duty to do what others may not.* Where there is a uniform, there is often also a line and staff command structure which often rules out substantive professional discretion for all but superior officers. Code: *Spec/Cond*

10. Codes in 8–9 provide group identity and culture through *gazetted enforcement of a range of sanctions* including de-registering or financial or other legal punishment for malpractice, and requiring indemnity insurance to cover civil claims. Professionals are deemed culpable for poor performance, which is the sanction side of accountability mentioned in 8 above. Code: *Expel*

11. Given the exacting cognitive requirements set down under mark 2, 3, 5, and 7 above, *Continuing education in the expertise is mandatory.* Code: *Contin/Ed*

12. Professionals provide service on the basis of *unequal knowledge to the client,* thus requiring trust and a *fiduciary relationship,* with some paternalistic features in tension with the idea of client autonomy. People who suddenly become severely sick will depend on their doctors and cannot always 'shop' as consumers of care as they would for clothes. Clients often consult professionals at the stage of *strong vulnerability.* The relation is one of inequality in this sense, although the client must be honest about their situation. Code: *Fiduciary*

13. *Professional detachment* from the individual client is needed, combined with proper attention to their lives as a whole. Professional satisfaction arises from mediating ultimate goods to persons, but does not require professionals to like clients or hold absolute attachment to them. Code: *Detachment*

14(a). A professional mediates the client's access to goods which is a matter of *distributive social or economic justice,* rather than personal 'desert' or ability to pay. Professionals operate in a 'field' identified as professional because activity specific to *this role delivers an important expert service needed by clients and the public,* one dealing with ultimate goods and ends such as life, security, health, justice, identity, reputation, income and means of sustenance, freedom from violence and arbitrary incarceration. 14(b). In paradigmatic cases of professional service, it is authorized for *delivery as a right to any applicant who is a citizen* without discrimination and ideally without excessive monetary charge. Code: *Distjus*

15. Closely connected to this a professional has a *right or duty to practise on behalf of all*. A defence force or police officer, assuming they are professionals, protects all citizens. The state ideally provides a 'floor' for minimal professional care of all including the indigent. For example, legal aid, or publicly available health services, are common in developed states. Accountants have to answer to the tax office on behalf of all clients, and professionals like engineers, science experts, medical researchers, and academics, are often consulted as witnesses in public policymaking contexts. Code: *PubCitclaim*

16. Being open to anyone passing the exam under mark 5 above, assists professionals in attaining moral autonomy and independence. This means there is always *a strong possibility that they will be in conflict with their managers in an employing organization* and with the institutions of SWC over poor funding of quality services, especially in for-profit organizations. They may be ordered to 'dumb-down' their expertise through overspecialization of skill merely for the sake of increased profitable task throughput. Whistle-blowers are often professionals working in large public corporations. Other problems surround intellectual property in science, often codeveloped by professionals, but controlled by bureaucrats or business managers. Code: *Whistle-blower*

17. A variable *fee for service structure is common, but not essential* and where present is not driven only by market price but provided on an autonomously crafted and variable schedule, often taking ability to pay into account rather than adopting a 'one size fits all' billable hours basis. Tax funds are commonly provided in SWC and *remuneration is usually substantial*. Code: *Variable fee/Floor*

18. Professionals are pledged to uphold and balance claims in *the public interest* in several senses there is an expectation of noblesse oblige, provision for *pro bono* service and *on call* requirements. Public interest is meant here in the following four senses. The first is the sum of the goods of individuals; the second, the structure for effective citizen action; third, the system for balancing of individual's competing goods against state and corporate power; and fourth, balancing actual and potential client claims (see: Koehn 1994: 155–81). Code: *Pro Bono*

19. Professionals initially apply their diagnostic knowledge to a client by appointment on a one-to-one basis in a *designated public facility or private chamber/clinic* usually with a shingle for identification and support staff suitable for the role. Code: *Shingle*

20. Under the implicit social contract, they enjoy *high social status* as professionals *qua* being engaged in non-manual work; enjoying *autonomy in the setting of their work conditions*, and are usually well remunerated

as noted above. Few are explicitly unionized, but their collective power is very similar. Like union members, their autonomy is being eroded as they become employees of larger, multinational organizations. Code: *Status*

My claim is that professionalizing a practice would require that most of the above features be established, at least the first eleven and arguably the first sixteen. What more has been added to the broad 3-point account with which I began? Mainly an emphasis on continuity in knowledge and skill updating, self-governance through peer review, social ethics and monopoly, and particular judgement. The more specific notion in the paradigm cases now is:

1. *Professionals employ high-level, peer-attested cognitive, and practical expertise.*
2. *They exercise self-governing virtue, giving impartial service to individuals in need and to society, applied in wise particular judgement.*
3. *This activity of the practitioner presupposes some social grant of positional authority and autonomy, as well as a role in an organized system. There is social monopolizing of function, and social funding, particularly for fair systemic service provision to the indigent.*

It must be conceded that professions are historically social constructs, which change over time. The graduates of early universities in Byzantium, and later Bologna, Paris, and Oxford were mainly clergy, state officials, scientists, doctors, and lawyers (Patterson 1989). But if the criteria above and a supportive neo-Aristotelian account are accepted, there are logically consistent and coherent connections between members of the set.

In summary, a mark of the professional is cognitive and moral virtue, applied to need; a pledge of adherence to the social good via a self-enforced code, embodying impartiality and altruism. Failure leads to sanctions imposed by a socially accepted professional authority. Professional prerogatives and restrictions outlined in codes of conduct devised by institutions are granted to make the system within which the professional operates, for the common good, viable and distributively just. Services are ideally made accessible to all including the financially needy through a socially funded safety net. Professionals will have to whistle-blow on their employing organization when this sort of systemic social justice condition is not met.

The HR profession?

Do HR practitioners meet the twenty criteria discussed above any better than say the business entrepreneur? Are there parts of the role that would be made clearer and easier if HRM could invoke professional status? Is it possible and indeed desirable to bring into being any absent features? I would argue in the affirmative. Such a move is desirable because the HRM and ethics literatures show that HR practitioners do face dilemmas of a professional type, many involving lack of clarity with respect to roles and responsibilities in contexts involving conflicts of organizational, civic, and individual need. These conflicts are in effect 'where the rubber of social policy hits the road of application' (Ardagh and Macklin 1999; Macklin 1999). These conflicts can only be resolved by an ethico-political analysis, by reference to the human goods of the practice, its institutions, sector, and domain norms, and by casuistry.

I take an HR practitioner to have at least the following features: HR practitioners deal with that aspect of the organizational task which requires someone authorized to find and appoint staff and ensure that people do execute tasks and successfully meet the organization's needs. Such a role requires: (a) Designing, identifying, and filling jobs and running systems; (b) Maintaining and developing staff learning and skill at all levels; (c) Performance management; and (d) Monitoring and mediating fair relations between all staff, outside stakeholders, and their use of resources and the environment (De Cieri and Kramar 2005).

Role (a) includes such things as job design, recruitment, induction, and redundancy; (b) is concerned with maintaining motivation, training, and succession planning; (c) implies setting reasonable and fair criteria for, and judging, performance; and (d) involves managing conflicts between the officers in the various levels of authority set down by the corporate structure, external perceptions of corporate repute, and evaluation of the organization's use of the environment. Roles b–d require the trust of others in the HR practitioner's moral integrity. They require precise definition of the professional expertise that must be demonstrated wherein failure means the practitioner will risk facing accusation of malpractice or negligence.

Organizations can be ascribed goals and needs analogically, and HR practitioners must meet these organizational needs (Ardagh 2001), as well as some of the personal needs of employees (e.g. fair treatment, safety, and the power to acquire their personal goods). It is clear that their role is replete with ethically demanding concerns. Needs are met at both personal and organizational levels. The HRM role can meet the most important criterion for a profession—the pledge of wise and ethical need satisfaction and service to clients. To perform b–d above well, an HR practitioner must be an intelligent, articulate, and ethical persuader. In addition, the practitioner must be respected and trusted as a negotiator and conflict resolver, capable of inspiring people by invoking a clear vision of the best the organization can achieve, building an ethical culture, and monitoring the fairness of its social and environmental behaviour.

Specific application of criteria to HRM

To evaluate the proposed professionalization of HRM in more depth one must ask whether it meets most of the important marks of a profession. The national context will vary even in the English speaking First World, but let us evaluate each in turn:

1. *The client has a need, which the provider's vocation meets.* Vocation might look too strong a word for the role, but many would agree on the crucial importance for well-being of work and dignity at work. There is arguably no one specific need for the practice of HRM in the way that justice stands to law and health stands to medicine. Nonetheless HR practitioners do have to manage a cluster of specific individual *needs-satisfiers for persons in organizations, and the needs of organizations themselves.* These include: equity and fairness (EEO and AA), fidelity (employment contracts), procedural justice (performance management and promotion policy), and opportunity for development and self-perfection (training), not to mention fun (culture of informal behaviour) and friendship; conflict, resolution processes; freedom from fear of danger, violent conflicts, and environmental hazards (occupational health and safety). These responsibilities suggest the role already has an implicit de facto grant of authority from society through a board of management or other government structure. There is a moral need for respect for staff members' personal dignity, relevant organizational information, job safety and security, equitable pay, and positive and negative freedoms. Additionally HR practitioners have to meet a cluster of organizational needs—for example recruitment and retention of qualified staff for task accomplishment, job analysis, performance management, and training. HRM passes this test. Code: *NeedVoc*

2. The existence of a growing *body of systematic, specialized, knowledge, practically applied.* This test seems to be essential and is listed in all discussions of the nature of professions. The HRM knowledge base and conflict resolution skill-sets, both draw on the standard applied social science-based curriculum. It has a theoretical and empirically tested aspect. It could be leavened by introduction of more normative ethics, politics, and social policy education; and the concessional and constitutional corporate model in corporate law and economics, taught with its individualistic assumptions and classical prescriptions laid bare. But HRM arguably can pass this test. Code: *SpTK*

3. *Mandatory training period.* There are professional associations but no professional licence issuing body exists. The nearest equivalents are tertiary level degrees, certificates, and specialization within broader

credentials. There are ample continuing education opportunities, but these are not usually mandatory. Required HRM education and training could be introduced by an emergent professional body, recognized in social policy and augmented to meet the mandatory training requirement. Casuistry in some form, and the need for mentoring of the young novice as an apprentice in case study, is certainly critical in HR and the overall role includes an obligation to respond to individual client-identified issues. Therefore, HRM only passes part of this test. Code: *TrCaCID*

4. *Grant of authority by a self-regulating body issuing licences with government oversight.* In the USA and UK, HRM has moved some of the way towards formalization of such an institution and approximates a mandatory continuing education requirement. Provision of HRM in other countries might be encouraged to advance along the same path. Code: *Selfad/Auth*

5. *National public exam.* This is not necessary in most regions where tertiary or university level education is sufficient. The present day institutions of HRM therefore do not meet this test, but social policy could be introduced for testing its capacity to implement all of the core HR practices. Code: *Exam*

6. *Publicly approved quasi-monopoly.* Here, there is a big gap for HRM to fill. The institutions of HRM are not granted monopoly status by society and do not yet meet this criterion. If HRM did, then entry would become restricted. Over time employers might demand a credential held by HR practitioners. Code: *App/Monop*

7. *Passed on by practice as a social gift.* There is *ex hypothesi* no long-standing tradition of HRM, but perhaps there are some traditional HRM-relative norms and skills in human relations. Succession planning for organizations involves building and handing on an ethically responsive corporate culture. The lack of an analogue here is a weakness for HRM as an aspirant profession. Code: *Trad*

8. *Code of Ethics.* There are both extant and draft codes of ethics and professional conduct, for example, in the USA, the Society for Human Resource Management, Code of Ethical and Professional Standards in Human Resource Management, 2002, *http://www.shrm.org/ethics/default.asp?page=code-of-ethics.htm* and in the UK, the Chartered Institute for Personnel and Development, Code of Professional Conduct *www.cipd.co.uk*. HR practitioners can seek to have their organization adopt *an organizational code of conduct*. Often, HR policy is formalized and in practice many norms are almost universally observed. For example, the norm of confidentiality to all but the authorized inquirers concerning employee contract conditions is a more or less universally respected norm. Research has shown HR practitioners view themselves

as responsible for the practical application of ethical principles, have a realization of their advocacy role on behalf of employees, play the role of organizational conscience (Macklin 2001), and have a duty of consistent enforcement of rules. Arguably there is a pass on this test. There remains though the problem that HR practitioners have not been held liable for bad job design in the way that, for instance, engineers are held accountable and face litigation for faulty material designs. Code: *EthCode*

9. *Code of conduct specifying specific prerogatives, role relative duties, and altruistic duty to clients.* There are no explicit rights corresponding to arms-bearing, oaths of profession or occupational norms requiring client welfare to be paramount. But a code such as this could be devised where not yet present. Selective confidentiality and disclosure are a clear need and duty in the role. Although organizational and sectoral codes are common, specific codes of conduct for HR practitioners are not uniformly found or enforceable. Code: *Spec/Cond*

10. There is no *de-registering mechanism*. HR practitioners are not usually sued for bad risk management or professional malpractice. Code: *Expel*

11. Little or no *continuing education* is mandatory, but ongoing up-to-date knowledge is essential. Code: *Contin/Ed*

12. *Unequal knowledge, fiduciary relationships, and vulnerability of the client* are quite strongly featured in the HRM role. HR practitioners monitor organizational policy on interview panels, promotion meetings, with respect to enforcement of EEO, etc. But the organizational context and contractual status mean there is a countervailing duty of loyalty to the organization, picked up again at mark 16 under whistle-blower. We will return to this matter in the conclusion. Code: *Fiduciary*

13. *Professional-like detachment* is required in many situations, although firms may not at present support independent judgement by HR practitioners. The special kinds of intrinsic satisfaction which attend professional life, due to the ultimate goods/needs which it mediates, can apply to an HRM job well done. Code: *Detachment*

14. The goods and rights at stake in HRM disputes such as EEO and freedom from danger and harassment have *strong public ethics/justice relevance.* Code: *Distjus*

15. *Right to appear/advocate/practise within an institutionalized system.* An industrial advocate is often permitted to appear before an industrial tribunal on the basis of HRM expertise or standing, and need not be a lawyer. But there is no equivalent to the right to appearance within the adversarial structure of criminal law or the right to practise in a clinic or hospital. Code: *Pub/Citclaim*

16. *Expectation/legitimation of potential clashes with organizational policy* or particular management demands (e.g. to downsize or fire on the spot). These clashes are alas common, and some management actions are and ought to be resisted on the basis of perceived violations of ethics or injustice. At present the practice of HR practitioners is variable. Code: *Whistle-blower*

17. *Differential professional fees for service* are rarely charged except as a budgeting mechanism, indeed neither are fixed fees, unless the HR practitioner is an employee of a consulting firm. Code: *Variable fee/Floor*

18. *Pro bono and on call work* is not presently required for HR practitioners. *Many worker rights (EEO, safety, privacy, and free association) are of a sort the employee ought to have protected as a citizen*, not just an employee. Code: *pro Bono*

19. The HR practitioner will usually have a private office and one-on-one meetings with staff as 'clients'. An HR practitioner is *using diagnostic and remedial skills* that are often of a high order. Code: *Shingle*

20. *The social status* varies with organizational size and rank and is not particularly high at the lower levels of authority. The autonomy of the HR practitioner in the work setting is not marked. Code: *Status*

HRM's scorecard

At present the case is strong in some areas but not overwhelming. HRM meets criteria 1–2: vocation and systematic body of knowledge. It could probably be self-organized, and then with some corporate law changes towards a more concessional corporate model, be socially authorized to meet, all the criteria 3–7: mandatory training process, self-licensing, exams/induction, monopolies, and tradition. It might then meet 10, gazetted expulsion. To generate the requisite 'social remit' dimension something like the 'corporate constitutionalism' of Bottomley (1990, 1997) and Dine (2000), which sees the company as a state concession, and having its own integrity apart from shareholders, would need to be adopted. Here, the company can more easily and explicitly avow an ethical and social purpose. Within the European Union, such social models, including two-tier and compound boards of governance which presuppose the arrangements depicted above in Figure 9.1, are more familiar (Charkham 1994). At present HRM does try to meet criteria 8–9. Codes of ethics, a crucial mark, are emerging and so are codes of conduct. But it struggles against the prevailing individualist and contractualist corporate law model. At present one can work without professional membership and there is no clear and specific risk assumed, corresponding to that assumed by the doctor, lawyer, or engineer for incompetent work. CEOs and other board members get punished for failure in ways that HR practitioners generally do not. Continuing education (mark 11) occurs but is not mandatory. On 12–15, HRM does better. Fiduciary relations are recognized by HR practitioners and so too are their social justice and advocacy roles. But on 16, whistle-blowing is rare. As managers, their first loyalty is to the organization in a way that is not professionally sequestered. Most probably a more uniformly coordinated education and training and an enforced code of ethics and conduct could greatly improve HRM's independence of top management, the HRM voice within it, and client service.

Conclusions

There are obstacles created by the presently dominant individualistic Anglo-American corporate models, the form of employment contract, and the consequent lack of autonomous status for HR practitioners. Of comparatively negligible importance are lack of variable fee for service, *pro bono* work, and a shingle. For HR autonomy to be increased, both some measure of monopoly and increased admission and training barriers, and obstacles to employers' substituting of alternate untrained staff, must be shown to be needed. An analogue of social remit and professional prerogative would have to be introduced and justified.

HR practitioners do face ethical dilemmas arising from the clashing roles which they are now asked to perform. They need some role clarification and prerogatives such as confidentiality protection. They are enforcers of company policy, instruments of downsizing, builders of positive culture, and change managers. They are also neutral conflict resolvers, communicators, and mediators between levels of the organization. And they are seen as advocates of employees' rights and counsellors. In the first bracket of roles they are often the bearers of bad tidings from management regarding decisions over which they have had little say. On the other hand, like professionals, they are systems and job designers and keepers of confidences on some matters. Many HR practitioners see themselves as 'the meat in the sandwich' (Ardagh and Macklin 1999), subject to conflicts of interest when dealing with top managers and unions, often possessing sensitive information of use to both parties.

Enhancing their professional status would depend on clearly establishing that they are managers and not union leaders, but developing stronger codes and practices around the 'corporate conscience' role: pledge of altruism, fiduciary relation, distributive justice, professional detachment, and whistle-blowing. In favour of the professionalization argument and associated proposal is the consideration that organizations are ideally the important delivery vehicles of normatively construed needs-satisfiers like dignified work, and of ethical goals. HR practitioners have a key moral obligation to respect, and see that the organization enforces, state law and its own ethical norms and codes, especially in the area of justice. This social justice requirement is at present largely enforced informally.

Professionalization would underline the fact that although senior HR practitioners are following CEOs on most issues, they can, should, and do refuse some requests from them and also from unions and outsiders, and this parallels the lawyer's and doctor's autonomy. A clearer position within the ethical organization would need to be spelled out, and a more 'social ethics-friendly' theory of the corporation specified along concessional model lines.

By professionalizing and specifying an interdisciplinary social policy, justice, and corporate governance curriculum grounded in the alternative corporate governance models, and a binding enforced code of ethics and code of conduct for all practitioners, HRM would gain in status and moral accountability. This might actually diminish one of the main ethical hazards of professionalization: that it would entail more responsibility, but no increased power. The danger that it would be subverted in the business sector (as individual accounting and law professionals have been in Enron-type fiascos) by incorporation into huge globalized transnational HR consulting firms, with no ethical allegiance to any particular state or region, is not increased by professionalization. If anything, it might be reduced by the proposed changes. More positively, it would guide HR practitioners in their role as the central clearing house between the top and bottom of the organizational structure.

There are other areas where the conflict of justice, organizational performance, and their personal morality is manifested. Professionalization might help to clarify their ethical focus in some of these areas (Macklin 2001). The USA and UK cases suggest that to some degree it is within the power of HR practitioners to put their own house in order, and then apply for recognition from outside.

Against the feasibility of professionalization de facto in Anglo-American contexts is the current economic and power dependency often presently written into their employment contracts, even at senior levels of HRM. Especially in the business sector which is arguably the least morally constrained sector because it permits pursuit of any ethically permissible good for profit, they have at present no area of presumptive ultimate authority. Even when they have a seat at the high table where decisions on strategic matters are made by leadership groups acting as the organizational 'intellect and will', mere professionalization without a change in their organizational power and authority might make things worse. HR practitioners would bear the heavy burden of being the conscience of the organization in that challenging private sector, but without any ultimate area of authority within the decision-making process.

It will be necessary to define the four HRM management roles—system and job design and recruitment, motivation and training, performance management, and cross-level conflict avoidance and resolution—in relation to a more ethically informed conception of the organizational or corporate purpose and of corporate governance. The conscience role of the HRM in the organization could then be more plainly tied in to that structure. The fact that HR practitioners are de facto the most important 'top-down' and 'bottom-up' communicators and mediators between the organizational stakeholders could be highlighted, within the emerging concessional and constitutional theory of corporate governance, as a vitally important condition of good governance. This being their role would even allow for a charge of professional negligence or malpractice to stick. Post-Enron, major changes in corporate practice, law, or structure are actively discussed across disciplines and might be accepted as part of the drive to develop more accountability.

This may create a new space in which it will be possible to give HR practitioners more autonomous discretion even within the business sector. Even if we agree to sequester them from responsibility for making some kinds of ultimate business decision currently reserved for boards and the CEO, we could hold them to account for providing professional advice grounded in the institutional ethics of their practice. The senior HR practitioners would contribute to conscience within the leadership 'intellect and will' group of the organization. This would place them at the top of the authority structure with a professional ethical 'voice' which would at least be heard even if it was outweighed.

10 Engineers of human souls, faceless technocrats, or merchants of morality?: changing professional forms and identities in the face of the neo-liberal challenge

Michael I. Reed

Introduction

Contemporary social science and social commentary are dominated by an incurably pessimistic metaphysical pathos over the 'professional society or state' (Perkin 1989). Although professions have been under attack, from one ideological direction or another, the virulence of contemporary critiques of the inherent immorality of unaccountable professional power reflects deeper structural movements and political shifts that seem to sound the death knell of professionalism. Not only are they now seen as a 'conspiracy against the laity', but they are also charged with the ultimate sin in the 'age of enterprise'. Professions are considered as constituting a fundamental institutional obstacle to market-led reforms, indeed transformations, in the way that expert knowledge and work are organized and controlled. Quasi-monopoly control over the institutionalized provision of specialized knowledge and skill is now understood to be inimical to the efficient and effective operation of expert labour markets dedicated to satisfying customer demand and need.

Abbott (1988) had reasonable grounds for concluding that professionalism and professions, as the dominant principle and mode of occupational control over highly abstract and specialized 'expert labour', could successfully withstand and adapt to market-driven knowledge commodification and managerially driven knowledge rationalization. Nonetheless, a decade and a half later, his confidence, as that of others (Ackroyd 1996; Macdonald 1995), in the underlying institutional resilience and innate organizational flexibility of professionalism and professions may look significantly less secure in a contemporary world that values, indeed vaunts, 'market populism' as a universal solution to all our economic, social, and ethical ills (Frank 2000).

When this state-sponsored and elite-supported, political drive to confront professional power and to control professional autonomy is combined with capitalist-led corporate restructuring and technologically driven work rationalization, it seems that 'the writing is on the wall' for professionalization and professionalism as the dominant means of organizing and institutionalizing expert services. It is at least conceivable that major restructuring of the international expert division of labour over the last two decades, as it responds to the combined effects of economic, technological, political, and cultural change, will have long-term implications for the system of professions and its constituent member groups (Reed 1996). In so far as the power struggle over abstract knowledge and the technical autonomy and cultural legitimacy or 'institutionalized trust' that it conveys has become more intensely contested as a result of these structural changes, then the work autonomy and control of professional workers is likely to be fundamentally effected (Hanlon 1998, 2004). Further, the competition and status divisions between and within professional associations and groups are likely to become more intense as the jurisdictional domains, labour market niches, and organizational locales in which they operate become more crowded, contested, deregulated, and fragmented.

Indeed, as Freidson (2001: 212), a lifelong, if realistic, supporter of professionalism as the 'third logic' of work organization and occupational association, has indicated in his most recent publication, it is highly likely that *many, if not most, professional workers* are fated to become 'merely technical experts in the service of the political and cultural economy'. In turn, Freidson (2001) continues, this will probably produce even greater inter- and intra-occupational conflict and polarization between and within professional associations and groups. They will become even more internally divided and stratified between an elite group, working more intimately with governmental and corporate elites, and a large group of technical specialists performing increasingly routinized and standardized tasks. Indeed, some researchers (Leicht and Fennel 2001) have gone as far as to suggest that elite managers are emerging as the 'new professionals' within a radically reconfigured international expert division of labour.

Global corporate restructuring and the long-term effects of market-driven government policies have forced professional associations and groups into a more accommodating political stances towards extensive and intrusive auditing and surveillance mechanisms.

Adapting to the political and economic realities of contemporary professional life within a political culture that is ideologically hostile to the normative authority and moral claims of the professional becomes the 'ontological priority' for the majority of professional workers (Dent and Whithead 2002). As a result, all pretence to the 'natural' moral and cultural authority that flows from indeterminate professional cognitive, symbolic, and technical power is washed away in the maelstrom of economic, technological, and political transformation now coruscating through late-modern societies. This does not necessarily entail the complete eradication of professionalism as, an always contested, principle and terrain of work organization and control. Rather, as Scarbrough (1996: 25) suggests, professionalism continues to evoke powerful meanings and identities such that the 'idea of professionalism' is likely to endure as an ideological resource for managers and expert groups.

Given the wider political and institutional context outlined above, the purpose of this chapter is to review and evaluate *three very broad, ideal-type, projections or models of possible 'professional futures' that draw on a wide range of cultural values and structural mechanisms conventionally associated with professionalism in modern industrial societies* (Reed 2004). The first of these ideal-typical prognostic models envisages something of a return to the halcyon days of unchallenged professional authority and autonomy when, to invoke Stalin yet again, the professions were truly *engineers of human souls*. Very few, if any, social scientists would wish to hold to this interpretation in its most optimistic form. However, there are a number (Ackroyd 1996; Freidson 1994; Kirkpatrick, Ackroyd, and Walker 2005; MacDonald 1995) who would suggest that professionalism and professions will reassert themselves as the dominant principle and form of organizing and controlling expert knowledge and skill in the twenty-first century. The second vision is one of *faceless technocrats* suggesting that, in so far as they have any sort of a future, the professions must come to terms with the managerialist ideologies and technocratic practices that now bestride contemporary work organizations in globalized capitalist political economies. Only by flexibly adapting to these new realities, and the power structures from which they have emerged and on which they continue to depend, will the contemporary professions be able to survive in the 'brave new world' of globalized markets for expert knowledge and skill and the multinational corporate structures through which they are serviced (Brock, Powell, and Hinings 1999; Cohen et al. 2003). Finally, a third prognosis will be considered; one that rejects the naïve political optimism of the engineers of human souls vision and the explicit technological determinism of the faceless technocrats interpretation. This final vision of professional futures anticipates a situation in which the professions have been forced to trade, even more skilfully and manipulatively than in the past, on their position and status as *merchants of morality*. Such a prognosis places the cultural, ethical, and symbolic power of experts at the very centre of the increasingly dispersed and complex, social, and organizational networks emerging in a postmodern society where uncertainty and ambiguity abound and trust, particularly institutionalized trust, is at a premium.

By putting their expert knowledge and skill at the disposal of an anxious and distrustful public on the one hand and an increasingly powerful but uncertain corporate elite on the other, contemporary professional groups and associations will be better placed to sustain their pivotal role as purveyors of ethical meaning and personal identity in a world continually on the edge of disorder and chaos. As it develops, the chapter will also consider the intra-organizational *surveillance and disciplinary regimes* to which professional workers are now routinely subjected (Fournier 1999) and their longer-term impact on the formation of professional identities. Overall, it seeks to demonstrate how a deeper appreciation is needed of the underlying material conditions and structural mechanisms that shape occupational and organizational change.

Professions in crisis?

The last two decades or so have not been the easiest of times for professionalism and professions. It is worth reminding ourselves though that there are very considerable national, sectoral, and jurisdictional variations in the scale and intensity of this putative crisis in professionalization (as an occupational control strategy), professionalism (as a principle of work organization and control), and professions (as occupational associations and groups). In broad terms, the Anglo-American and northern European political economies and welfare states seem to be experiencing a far deeper and fundamental questioning of institutionalized professional power, status, and control than their central and southern continental European counterparts (Clarke, Gerwitz, and McLaughlin 2000; Cohen et al. 2003; Dent and Whitehead 2002; Ferlie, Hartley, and Martin 2003; Freidson 2001; McLaughlin, Osborne, and Ferlie 2002; Pollitt and Bouchaert 2000).

Nevertheless, there are sufficient empirical and theoretical grounds for suggesting that very significant changes have already occurred, and will occur even more so in the future, in the dominant occupational strategies and organizational modes through which professionalization is pursued as a power game and mobility project (Larson 1977, 1990; Murphy 1990; Parkin 1979). It can also be argued that these changes are most appropriately explained as a configuration of collective responses to deeper, underlying structural movements that have confronted established professional groups with intensifying force and constraint since the early 1980s.

Five major structural movements can be identified. First, the global reach and impact of a revived neo-liberal ideology that generated a series of highly complex waves of *state-initiated* programmes of marketization and deregulation throughout the 1980s and 1990s (Frank 2000; Harvey 2003). Second, a continuing 'information and communication technology revolution' and the shift towards institutional and managerial governance through markets and networks, rather than through hierarchies, that this generated (Castells 1996, 2000; Thompson 2003*a*; van Dijk 1999; Webster 2002). Third, the move towards a highly individualized and consumption-dominated culture in which collectivist and production-based occupational cultures and organizational identities becomes much weaker and difficult to sustain (Alvesson and Willmott 2002; Giddens 1990, 2000). Fourth, the emergence of a globalized, 'post-industrial' political economy that is dominated by the provision of services, rather than the manufacture of products, and the much more complex 'knowledge-intensive' forms of work organization and openly contested and fragmented 'expert-based' occupational niche labour markets that this generates (Freidson 2001; Heckscher and Donnellon 1994; Lash and Urry 1994). Finally, the expanding influence of 'managerialism', in all its multifarious forms, as the dominant policy paradigm informing both private- and public-sector restructuring and the new surveillance and control technologies that it promotes (Enteman 1993; Exworthy and Halford 1999; Gabriel and Sturdy 2002; Reed 1999, 2002).

Of course, the precise nature, dynamics, interconnections, and consequences of these putative structural changes are hotly contested within the social science community and beyond (Jessop 2002; Thompson 2003*b*). Professionalization, professionalism, and professions face a series of threats, as well as opportunities, that question the underlying 'rules of the game' shaping the development of professionalized institutional forms and organizational structures for more than a century (Hanlon 2004). The collective capacity to achieve and sustain effective monopoly control over specialized knowledge and expert skill, as well as over the jurisdictional work domains in which they are exercised, has been substantially weakened. Thus, the incipient political, organizational, and ethical crisis that the established 'liberal-independent professions' are facing can, in very broad terms, be explained as a gradual 'draining away' of material, cultural, and moral capital consequent on the decline in elite and state support and the much more openly contested and fragmented 'system of professions' that this has produced.

Professionalization was the dominant strategy and process of occupational closure and control that most 'service class-based' occupational groups depended on to realize their 'mobility projects'—that is for improved economic reward, enhanced social status, and extended work-based decision-making discretion and autonomy—in the post-Second World War period (Butler and Savage 1995; Crompton 1990; Goldthorpe 1982, 1995; Hanlon 2004; Larson 1977; Scott 1997). The rapid expansion of white-collar bureaucracies, in both the private and public sectors, during this period and the expanded commercial opportunities that it provided to professional services firms generated very favourable material, structural, and cultural conditions in which professionalization flourished as a highly successful strategy of occupational closure and control. The expansion of large-scale corporate bureaucracies, resulting from the growing concentration of private capital and the centralization of public control from the 1930s onwards (Hanlon 2004), provided the material and structural conditions in which elite service class professional groups and managerial service class professional groups could launch successful *mobility projects* aimed at institutionalizing their economic, political, and social power.

The propertied elite and private sector-based professional (Savage et al. 1992) groups have always been in a relatively stronger position than their public sector-based counterparts. The former have accumulated, monopolized, and controlled liquid and transferable assets that are much more powerful in their spatial reach and material impact than the more restricted and immobile organizational assets available to public sector professional and semi-professional groups (Savage et al. 1992). This latter group has also experienced a steady decline in the power and influence of their 'organizational assets' as these have been further eroded through technological and managerial rationalization. The 'organizational professions'—predominantly located in public sector-based or dependent agencies and organizations—are in a much more exposed position when threatened with political, economic, and cultural change potentially undermining their power base and the public service ideology through which it has been legitimized (Clarke and Newman 1997).

Downsizing, delayering, decentralization, deregulation, and delegation have become widespread throughout the private and public sectors during the 1980s and 1990s. These changes have more often than not eroded *professionalization* as a strategy of occupational closure and control, *professionalism* as a mechanism of work organization and management, and *professions* as the dominant source of expert culture and identity formation in a meritocratic society (Dent and Whitehead 2002; Scarbrough 1996; Scarbrough and Burrell 1996). The longer-term consequences for professional groups of these exercises in institutional and organizational 'creative destruction' are the subject of much debate and controversy ranging from 'guarded optimism' (Ackroyd 1996; Brock, Powell, and Hinings 1999; Hanlon 2004; Kirkpatrick, Ackroyd, and Walker 2005; Kitchener 2000; Leicht and Fennel 2002; MacDonald 1995; Whittington, McNulty, and Whipp 1994) to 'unrestrained pessimism' (Aronowitz and DiFazio 1995; Burris 1993; Ehrenreich and Ehren-reich 1978; Haug 1973; Johnson 1972; Webb 1999). But whatever the longer-term prognosis, there is an underlying general agreement that successive waves of restructuring have produced a much more fragmented, polarized, and contested system of professions in which the dominant occupational strategy, organizational mechanism, and work identity is struggling to maintain its position.

As a result, what Freidson (2001) calls the third logic of professional work organization and control in advanced capitalist societies seems to be in some considerable trouble, if not terminal decay. He argues these essentially struc-tural changes in political and economic control will have a major impact on the cultural legitimacy and identity of 'professional work' and the people who perform it. Capital-led marketization on the one hand and state-led rationalization on the other have fundamentally weakened the credibility and sustainability of a once dominant, professional ideology and morality that is ultimately grounded in notions of judgemental indeterminacy and task autonomy protected both by the law and by quasi-judicial administrative con-ventions. Reviving this compromised ideology of professional independence and objectivity becomes doubly difficult when the system of professions is racked by material and status conflicts and increasingly divided into a rela-tively protected, elite core and an increasingly exposed periphery. The decline in institutionalized trust consequent on these developments is likely to have fateful consequences for the ways in which professional workers see themselves and are seen by the rest of society.

Recent work in the area of professional ideology, culture, and identity (Dent and Whitehead 2002; Fournier 1999; Freidson 1994; Sennett 1998) would suggest that the conventional public image of the professional (as someone who is naturally trusted, widely respected and well-rewarded in return for expert knowledge and skill wisely deployed to protect the collective good and enhance individual well-being) is in desperate need of a radical over-haul. Indeed, many have argued that this stereotype of the professional 'no longer exists... swept aside by the relentless, cold, instrumental logic of the global market, and with it the old order has been upturned' (Dent and Whitehead 2002: 1). In its place, we are offered an ideological and cultural simulacrum of 'professional performativity' that simulates many of the old values and norms but within a fundamentally transformed institutional envi-ronment and organizational context where the power of managerialism and management seems unassailable. Yet, this new 'identity formation' does little to soothe, much less appease, the deep-seated uncertainties and ambiguities that remain for the professional worker and for the client or customer alike. Once we accept that the stereotype of the 'true professional' has been funda-mentally compromised, how then is institutionalized trust, as the structural cornerstone and cultural lodestone of professionalism, to be generated and sustained in an economic, social, and political environment dominated by unregulated market competition, unrestrained consumerism, and rampant individualism?

Engineers of human souls

The idea that modern day professionals constitute a 'republic of experts' who *benignly* exercise their technical power and social authority on behalf of the collective good of society and the individual well-being of its citizens has exerted a powerful cultural and political hold over the historical development and structural formation of professionalism (Hodges 2000; Marquand 2004). Indeed, from Saint-Simon to Daniel Bell and on to Manuel Castells, modern social theory and analysis has played a major intellectual and ideological role in identifying and celebrating the rise of a professional elite cadre, and its supporting cast of scientific, technical, and managerial middle-level under-labourers, as one of the, if not the, 'axial' institutional features of industrial and post-industrial society (Bell 1973, 1999; Castells 1996, 2002; Wolin 1960, 2004). This broadly based 'service class' of professional, scientific, technical, and managerial expert labour, with all its internal structural contradictions and ideological tensions, has been the focus for both the party-political and wider socio-political power struggles and competition within the social democratic state that emerged out of the Second World War. Thus, the post-1945 'social democratic contract or settlement' between capital, labour, and the state gave a critical role to formally autonomous professional occupational associations and organizations in return for their, admittedly grudging, acceptance of a limited degree of social regulation and administrative control (Clarke and Newman 1997; Hodges 2000; Leicht and Fennel 2001).

The service class of professionals, managers, and technicians within industrial/post-industrial capitalist societies has always been stratified along economic, technical, and cultural lines. But the divisions and tensions that this inevitably generates have become more marked and potentially destabilizing as the underlying dynamic and trajectory of contemporary structural change further fragments and polarizes the collective interests and values of various expert groups differentially located within the emergent expert division of labour. Thus, the intimate historical and structural link between expert 'knowledge' and power, that has so powerfully shaped the social and organizational development of the modern professions becomes potentially disabling. Repairing and sustaining institutionalized trust in professionalism, within a social and historical context that is endemically suspicious of, indeed downright hostile to, the republic of experts as an irreplaceable repository of moral authority, social wisdom, and technical proficiency, would not be easy. Once the naturally given authority to exercise judgemental autonomy, and the 'moral mysteries' in which this technical or operational power was traditionally surrounded, become increasingly exposed to and invaded by 'the market' or by those acting as its delegated agents, then sustaining professional claims to elite status and rewards is much more problematic.

Recently, Hodges (2000: 175–8) has argued that the 'politics of expert power and reward' in advanced capitalist political economies will revolve around group struggles to access and control sources of relative labour market advantage in distinctive jurisdictional sectors or domains within an increasingly demystified and delegitimated professional state. This analysis of an increasingly structurally fragmented and politically fractured 'professional class' operating within a highly complex contemporary division of expert labour in which specialist knowledge is increasingly becoming deregulated, demystified, and delegitimated is also reflected in Stehr (1994) and Leicht and Fennel (2001). Stehr (1994) contends that the dynamic of technological, economic, and cultural change relentlessly restructuring 'knowledge bearing and disseminating occupations' is generating a proliferation of occupational groups and organizational practices geared to producing, packaging, and applying specialist knowledge and skill in ways that do not, and cannot, conform to established professional forms and norms. The 'new' or 'entrepreneurial professions' are emerging as the key producers, interpreters, and mediators of specialist knowledge and skill outside the purview and control of the institutionalized jurisdictional work domains in which the 'liberal professions' have fashioned their power base. In time, it is extremely likely that the entrepreneurial professions will make significant incursions into the jurisdictional work domains of the liberal professions as they move to extend their technical reach and political influence within a globalized market for expert services.

Stehr's analysis is echoed in Leicht and Fennell's identification (2001) of the 'neo-entrepreneurial workplace' as the emerging institutional setting and organizational locale within which the changing balance of expert power and control has been developing over the last two decades. They see this, flatter, more flexible, porous, post-unionized, and virtualized, organizational form as being based on the logic of coordination and control radically at odds with the core structural principles and cultural norms of the established liberal professions. Thus, they see the role of middle-level management as almost completely disappearing, while the 'professional' power, authority, and prestige of top and senior level corporate management, particularly, but not only, within the private, for-profit sector being considerably strengthened and extended. The latter are increasingly seen, and see themselves, as 'on par with physicians and lawyers in their ability to establish and maintain independent, fee-for-service practice delivery to corporate clients' (Leicht and Fennell 2001: 81). They further extend this analysis by suggesting that managerial and professional work, and the occupational interest groups clustering around these jurisdictional domains, may be 'changing places'.

The 'professional project' has been driven by the attempt to carve out and defend work-based decision-making domains against actual and potential competitors, while simultaneously seeking the support of the state and other key institutional actors and stakeholder agencies in order to legitimate and regulate ('at a distance') the material and cultural rewards that it delivers. On the other hand, 'the managerial project' has been focused on securing absolute social and organizational control over the material and HR that are required in order to maximize shareholder returns in the private sector and to meet public accountability norms as they are determined by the political party in power at a particular point in time.

In the post-Second World War period, roughly speaking mid-1940s to the late 1970s/early 1980s, a negotiated bargain or contract was struck between the professional and managerial projects that ensured, an often somewhat uneasy but relatively stable, collective deal that successfully contained the endemic contradictions and conflicts between them. But, Leicht and Fennell (2001) maintain, this contract or deal has been slowly but surely coming apart at the seams over the last two decades. A series of neo-liberal inclined governmental administrations, backed by their ideological and political supporters in private sector multinational corporations (particularly those in the cultural and media industries), have incrementally undertaken a series of strategic policy changes detrimental to the professional project. They have substantially increased the power, authority, and control of private and public sector-based managerial elites at the expense of the established liberal professions. Institutional reconfiguration and collective intent have been combined in an innovative, but potentially destructive, package of reforms for the republic of experts. Macdonald (1995), a highly sceptical evaluator of the 'deprofessionalization thesis', analyses this mounting threat to professional cognitive, and hence cultural-cum-political, exclusivity as testing the capacity of such groups to annexe and retain professional knowledge.

It is this, socially and politically pivotal, 'cultural work' that seems to be most under threat from the conjuncture of structural, cyclical, and policy changes that have been reviewed in previous discussion. Much of this literature has a strong 'Anglo-American' quality to it—that may be in need of considerable qualification when relocated within a continental European context. But, at the very least, it raises a series of fundamental questions over the 'social engineering' occupational ideology and identity that has underpinned the professionalization project's dominant strategy and form for institutionalizing the provision of expert services in the post-1945 era.

Faceless technocrats

The strong version of professional autonomy and control, based on institutionalized trust and cognitive-cum-technical exclusivity, may have been under extreme pressure in recent years. But it is possible that this once-dominant, professional occupational ideology and identity may mutate into something rather different within a social and historical context much less sympathetic to the professionalization project?

The 'technocratic imperative' inherent in modern, twentieth century professionalism as compared to the more traditional, nineteenth century form of professionalism, has been analysed most recently by Marquand (2004). For him, the latter was based, ideologically and organizationally, on the interconnected themes of service, equity, and trust contextualized, institutionally and culturally, by a strong 'public domain' of common citizenship and the reciprocal rights and duties that membership conveyed. In contrast, twentieth century, modern professionalism based its claims on the possession and application of specialized technical qualifications, knowledge and skill that were functionally indispensable to the governance and management of advanced capitalist political economies and welfare states.

Credentialism, meritocracy, and technocracy (Burris 1993; Collins 1979) came together to form a powerful ideological and organizational allegiance that legitimated the exclusion of 'non-professional laity' or even 'semi-professionalized' occupational groups from the key decision-making arenas. Over time, it accrued additional layers of ideological justification in an attempt to look somewhat more inclusive of the general public and its constituent stakeholder interest groups, such as consumer pressure groups. The ideology and practice of technocratic power and control, exercised by highly technically specialized and socially remote professional elites, seemed however increasingly at odds with the 'consumer populism' aggressively promoted by successive government regimes and its supporters in private and public sector corporations. A major aim was to breakdown the exclusionary jurisdictional domains constructed and protected by professional technocrats and to expose them to the full 'levelling effects' of 'consumer-based democracy'. Serving the wider public interest became radically redefined through a series of ideological and discursive shifts that placed technocracy—that is, rule by experts—and meritocracy—that is, entry to and movement within the technocracy through credentialized performance—in a much more unfavourable light. Thus, 'consumer populism' and 'market-based managerialism' have released the contemporary need for technocratic professionalism to redefine and realign itself with the prevailing ideological and political forces. One attuned to the role of twenty-first century professionals as 'servants of the people'—primarily in their role as consumers of expert services—rather than as 'servants of power'.

The collective identity of faceless technocrats in Bell's ideal (1999) typical post-industrial society, objectively and clinically serving the technical and planning requirements of the economic, scientific, and political elite, would seem to be increasingly anachronistic in a market-oriented and consumer-dominated society. Twenty-first century professionals are much more likely to define their strategic role in relation to meeting the heterogeneous cognitive, cultural, and personal needs of a newly empowered and enfranchised consumer democracy in which populist norms and values outweigh any residual commitment to internalized elitist ideology and control.

Yet, as Bell's 'Foreword' to the 1999 edition of *The Coming of Post-Industrial Society* makes clear, this 'New Service Class' of market-driven professionals are likely to be even more 'conservative', in ideological and political terms, than their more technocratically inclined forebears. They will be much more closely linked to business owners and executives through extensive elite social networks and intimately aligned with ideological prejudices and political preferences grounded in consumer populism and neo-liberal free-market economics. Of course, this is not the only possible outcome. Albeit from a 'British social democratic' perspective, Marquand (2004) holds out the distinct possibility of a revived and renewed professionalism inextricably linked, ideologically and institutionally, to a stronger public domain. In turn, he foresees a strengthening of the core civic values and virtues through which the public domain and its liberal-independent professional classes can be revitalized and sustained as central institutional components of twenty-first century socio-political life. This 'projected professional future' is far from impossible, and is echoed in the works of other, liberal progressive and social democratic writers such as Hutton (2002) and Sennett (1998). But the structural, political, and cultural preconditions required to make it a viable possibility as a projected professional future are very difficult to imagine, given the current ideological climate and policy context.

As new discursive formations of 'individualization', 'customization', and 'personalization' emerge, a redefinition of professional occupational identities and work cultures is occurring. The once dependent users or clients become redefined as 'commissioners' or 'coproducers' of the expert services that they receive and evaluate according to predetermined levels of customer service and care. As coproducers of professional services, the customers now directly participate in the decision-making process through which service design, delivery, and accountability are legitimated. The professionals no longer dominate and lead the process through which problems are defined, acted on, and outcomes assessed. They are transformed into 'honest brokers', advisors and intermediaries who assist 'coproducers' in finding the best way to deal with their problems for themselves (Leadbeater 2003). Professional power, authority, status, and reward are tamed, or certainly diluted, by the countervailing power of consumer choice and the 'personalization' of expert services made possible by globalized and deregulated markets in which the intensified competition between expert groups reduces the risk of monopolization and exclusion.

This scenario takes us a long way from the revival of the liberal progressive model of professional identity and role envisaged by Marquand and other commentators working in the social democratic tradition. It also undermines the technocratic vision of professional power and authority residing in unchallenged expert knowledge and skill that provides the cognitive and ideological basis for exclusive control over defined jurisdictional domains and the material and symbolic rewards that it conveys. Instead, the consumer choice-driven regime of expert service provision and organization envisages a future in which traditional professional authority and identity is gradually superseded by a much more 'flexible' and 'adaptable' model of professionalism, and, by logical extension, professionalization, in which issues of trust and control are left to market forces.

Merchants of morality

By the time we reach the third and final vision of professional futures surveyed in this chapter, we have reached a point where much of the historical, analytical, and ideological baggage that conventionally accompanied the study of professionalization, professionalism, and professions may need to be jettisoned. However, even in its darkest hour, mainstream studies of professionalism have assumed that professional structures and systems will adapt to whatever challenges are thrown at them (Ackroyd 1996; Freidson 1994; Kirkpatrick, Ackroyd, and Walker 2005; Macdonald 1995). As recently as 1990, Derber, Schwartz, and Magrass confidently predicted that professionals would not become proletarianized in the same way as assembly line operatives, craft workers, and even white-collar clerical, administrative, and middle-managerial staff. Indeed, they insisted that professionals have carved out a unique niche in the division of labour overseeing remarkable fiefdoms of capital and knowledge.

While highly critical of the 'mandarin class power and status' aspirations of modern professionals, Derber, Schwartz, and Magrass were convinced that they could more than hold their own in the much more competitive and fragmented socio-economic structures taking shape at the end of the twentieth century. However, that underlying confidence in the durability and continuity of established professional occupational strategies and forms may need to be revised, or at the very least revisited, at a time when the challenge and threat to their long-term viability seems to be at its zenith. 'Proletarianization', as the most radical and fundamental form of de-professionalization, is not the only game in town. The 'proletarianization thesis' as advocated most recently by

Aronowitz and DiFazio (1994), Burris (1993), and Murphy (1990), contends that professionals can be seen as 'technical intellectuals' who find themselves in a situation where they are increasingly exposed to the rationalizing and deskilling forces previously reserved for more routine white-collar occupations and workers. As a result, 'real control' (as opposed to 'formal control') of the new, knowledge-based productive and administrative apparatus required to manage advanced capitalist economies and welfare states passes from the technical intelligentsia into the hands of the corporate and governmental elite. The latter is supported by a transnational capitalist class of highly mobile and specialized technical experts who provide the specialized knowledge and control technologies required to keep the system going by satisfying the profit-driven culture ideology of consumerism (Sklair 2001).

While identifying the immense pressure that the professions are under to conform to the latest structural and organizational dictates of 'the global market' or 'international competitiveness', the proletarianization thesis may be guilty of oversimplifying both the process and outcomes of professional change in advanced capitalist societies. Many of the underlying structures and mechanisms that have generated and sustained professionalization and professionalism since the eighteenth century cannot be properly accounted for in this way.

Hanlon (1998) identifies a long-term process of 'creeping commercialization' in which the established professions are allowed to regain and retain some semblance of legitimacy and autonomy, but only if they submit themselves to the new surveillance technologies and disciplinary regimes taking root in the business and state apparatus. They are forced to renegotiate their occupancy of and control over various jurisdictional domains in terms that are more consistent with the ever-changing requirements of international competition and the demand for more entrepreneurial forms of expert service provision consistent with a 'minimal state'. Thus, the established professions are only able to maintain their economic and political power base, and the cultural and symbolic capital that flows from it, if they drop the pretence to generalized moral authority. They are forced to become much more politically realistic about the 'terms and conditions' on which their, now much more restricted, occupational exclusion and control will continue to be tolerated and the wider implications of these newly imposed structural limitations for their cultural authority and identity.

However, Hanlon's analysis also raises further questions about the cognitive and technical knowledge base on which conventional professional authority and identity has rested. This analysis would suggest that the more this cognitive and technical knowledge base is penetrated by 'alien' values, norms, and practices, the weaker it is likely to become as an effective institutional protector of established cultural authority and symbolic status.

Surveillance and disciplinary regimes

If the symbiotic link between 'knowledge/power' is broken, or at the very least eroded and diluted, by economic, political, and ideological forces that increasingly regard professionalism as a major obstacle to necessary social and cultural change, then the need for a thorough 'identity make-over' becomes very pressing indeed. This intimate 'knowledge/power' relation, and its crucial implications for professional identity formation, needs to be located in a longer-term historical context in order that the more recent 'crisis in professionalism' can be properly analysed and evaluated.

As Foucault (2003) argued, the emergence and subsequent development of what he calls 'disciplinary or non-sovereign power', as a primary mechanism or structure of social control and organizational surveillance, was closely aligned to the rise of the medical and human sciences and their associated expert or 'professional' groups from the eighteenth century onwards. This new mechanism of power and control was applied primarily to bodies and the temporal sequences and social spaces through which they moved and developed. It required constant, rather than discontinuous, surveillance. This, in turn, 'presupposed a closely meshed grid of material coercions rather than the physical presence of a sovereign, and it therefore declined a new economy of power based on the principle that there had to be an increase both in the subjugated forces and in the force and efficacy of that which subjugated them' (Foucault 2003: 36).

The expert groups and professional associations that crystallized around this new economy of disciplinary power were bound up with the expansion of professionalized scientific and technological knowledge. The latter provided the necessary theoretical and technical means that disciplinary power required to sustain itself and gradually to expand into all areas of biological and social life in modern societies. What we have here is an alternative historical and analytical narrative of the emergence, development, and domination of professional power and control. Now this story is told from the standpoint of the 'delicate mechanisms and instruments' through which professional power and control are achieved, rather than the overarching ideologies of rationality, truth, and service from which the 'professional story' is normally narrated.

The Foucauldian narrative of professional power and control seems increasingly apposite in a contemporary historical and social context that is radically subversive of the 'official' story of professionalization and professionalism (Gane and Johnson 1993; Johnson 1993). It is a story that is now 'told from below' rather than 'from above'. From the point of view of the detailed and delicate mechanisms of exclusion and surveillance that were put in place as 'micromechanisms of power' by professional groups acting as the agents of social order and control within an economically and politically unstable socio-historical context. It is a story that is told from the point of view of 'the subjugated'; that is, from the perspective of those subjected to these new surveillance and control mechanisms as they became economically profitable and politically useful to dominant elites and classes. It is a story that strips bare the moral rhetorics and intellectual discourses that have surrounded and mystified professionalization to show them for what they really are—that is, as discursive practices and technical instruments that operationalize and obscure 'the material agency of subjugation' (Foucault 2003: 28).

Professionalization is now redefined as a socio-historical process and organizational form that comes into play at the lowest levels of society and the key role that it fulfils in normalizing those who present an imminent or potential danger to 'normal society'. It is reworked as a practical discursive matrix and tool geared to the fabrication and implementation of new forms of power and control in newly 'professionalized' organizational settings such as asylums, schools, clinics, and prisons. Professionals now become the new merchants of morality at an historical juncture and within a social context in which moral and political realism is at a premium. Those to whom they minister ('the subjugated') are now seen as active agents in their own self-management and control. But they routinely resist, in some form or another, the new surveillance and disciplinary technologies to which they are subjected.

Over the last ten years or so a 'Foucualdian school' of 'professional studies' has emerged that has provided very different accounts and analyses of the rise, power, and position of expert groups within modern societies to those provided by mainstream sociologists and historians. These studies encompass both the 'old, established professions' of medicine, law, architecture, and accountancy, as well as the 'new, emergent professions' of criminology, psychology and psychiatry, social work, nursing, and management (Dean 1999; Dent and Whitehead 2002; Du Gay and Salaman 1992; Gane and Johnson 1993; Garland 1990; Grey 1999; Halford and Leonard 1999; Knights and McCabe 2003; Miller and Rose 1990; Power 1997; Rose 1990, 1991, 1996, 1999; Scarbrough and Burrell 1996; Thrift 1999, 2002; Townley 1994). They 'demystify' professional knowledge and the power that emerges from it, but not in any classical neo-Marxist critique of professional 'false consciousness'. Instead, they follow Foucault's original example of tracing and mapping the multifarious ways in which 'professional knowledge' becomes operationalized in detailed procedures, instruments, techniques, and practices within a wide range of organizational settings dealing with human beings and their problems as their raw material. They focus on the indispensable role that professionals play in providing the theories, programmes, and technologies that make modern forms of institutional governance and organizational management practically realizable mechanisms for dealing with 'control issues' at a local level.

If, in Marx's terms, capitalists eventually become their own grave-diggers, then, in Foucauldian terms, the creators of the 'disciplinary society' eventually become the agents of their own disempowerment. They design, implement, and refine the very surveillance and control technologies that will be turned back in on them by new expert groups working to very different political agendas. As Rose (1999) has argued, advanced neo-liberal forms of government, that depend on very different 'governmental rationalities' and control technologies than their social democratic predecessors, have transformed the governability of professional activity in ways that enclose them within far more restricted and visible local sites of service delivery. These have further exposed the inherent weaknesses of professional codes of conduct and modes of professional self-governance that have traditionally buttressed orthodox models of professional identity and status. Yet, many professional and semi-professional groups have been complicit in this continuing process of demystification and de-institutionalization to the extent that they have played critical roles in providing the innovative calculating and control technologies through which they themselves are to be submitted to new regimes of accountability and control. All they are left with is a now badly compromised, professional morality and an increasingly restricted technical autonomy as a basis on which to reconstruct and sustain some semblance of cultural authority and identity.

In a somewhat less apocalyptic register, Hanlon (2004: 205) concludes that, though much has changed, 'professional service markets and organizational forms are still based on trust, homology, and reputational capital'. But he also suggests that each of these key factors are having to readjust and to be substantially renegotiated within a dynamic temporal and structural context that challenges the institutional bedrock on which they have traditionally rested. This process of radical readjustment will, as Rose and other 'Foucauldian governmentalists' indicate, also require substantial changes to the institutional context and organizational control regimes within and through which professional service work is structured and legitimated. In turn, this is likely to mean that the orthodox occupational identity formation associated with the true professional will be increasingly subsumed, and consequently further diluted and weakened, under the dominant global culture of consumerism, individualism, and managerialism (Dent and Whitehead 2002: 1–18). The gradual displacement, if not marginalization, of the once privileged knowledges and practices of the old professional elites, also seems increasingly probable. But their capacity to resist further incursions into their power base and its legitimatory supports, even if this entails more internal restructuring that divides and polarizes the controlling elites from the rank and file routine workers, should not be underestimated. If something like this does happen, then the possibilities for creating and sustaining a strong or high 'trust culture' (Misztal 2002) within the professions and between them and the wider general public may become very limited indeed.

Conclusion

This chapter has provided a very broad overview and evaluation of the challenge that 'disjunctive change'—that is, deep-seated, system-wide structural transformations in the established institutional and ideological landscape—presents to the professions and the occupational structures and organizational strategies through which they generate and sustain socio-economic and political power. It has also considered the ways in which the professions have responded to this mounting challenge to their dominant position within the expert division of labour and the longer-term implications of these responses for established occupational identities and forms. Overall, the chapter has suggested that the more apocalyptic projections of 'professional meltdown', as conveyed in the proletarianization thesis, are unlikely to be realized. The triptych of professionalization, professionalism, and professions, it has been argued, retains structural power and cultural capital, as well as inherent organizational flexibility and adaptability, sufficient to resist the radical form of deprofessionalization projected in the proletarianization thesis.

Nevertheless, the chapter has indicated that a somewhat more contained, deprofessionalizing dynamic is at work within a number of Anglo-American political economies and welfare systems that is presenting a very substantial threat to established professional power and authority. There are clear signs of a partial convergence between macro-level structural and ideological transformation, meso-level occupational and organizational restructuring, and micro-level technical and discursive innovation sufficient to weaken the third logic of work organization and occupational association in advanced capitalist societies. This weakening or undermining of professionalism as the third logic also has deleterious consequences for established professional identity and the dominant cultural frameworks and discursive forms through which it is legitimated and communicated. From the established professions' collective viewpoint, they seem to be 'turning in on themselves'. As the pressure to become more open, transparent, competitive, entrepreneurial, and meritocratic intensifies, so intra-occupational fragmentation and inter-occupational polarization increases and begins to eat into the very ideological and intellectual muscle on which the social cohesion and organizational power of the system of professions depended.

Yet, prognoses of 'possible professional futures' anticipating an inevitable and irreversible decline in professional power and authority are counter-balanced by contrasting scenarios that point to the inherent flexibility, adapt-ability, and longevity of professionalized modes of expert power and control—even within a much more competitive and fragmented labour market for expert services and the organizational locales in which they are provided. What is clear, however, is that the 'politics of expertise' in advanced capitalist societies is becoming increasingly complex and uncertain as to its longer-term implications for the preservation of existing professional power structures and jurisdictional domains. Given this highly dynamic and uncertain institutional environment, professional forms, and identities are likely to become even more intensely contested, fragmented, and polarized in ways that we can only begin to appreciate at the present time.

11 Ethical Leadership in Employee Development

Ashly H. Pinnington and Serkan Bayraktaroglu

Economic capital and cultural capital

If HRM has an ethical purpose we argue it must involve more than 'following' the strategy of the business and likewise employee development means a lot more than developing human 'assets'. Ethical leadership in HRM would require at the very least that due attention be given to matters of both economic capital and cultural capital. In this chapter we examine the potential of Pierre Bourdieu's theory of practice for its capacity to consider these capitals within diverse political and societal contexts. We present two empirical case studies of typical corporate stances on HRM and then make some tentative recommendations for more ethical leadership in employee development.

Organizational leadership in the practice of HRM?

The arguments for and against HRM have been well rehearsed over the last twenty years. Its detractors have cogently argued that HRM's core concepts are contradictory (Keenoy 1990*b*; Legge 1989, 1995). For instance, highly individualized employee treatment can never be synonymous with a primary orientation towards team work and developing a unitarist company culture will never be entirely consistent with highly flexible employment practices. Some of HRM's proponents however have steadfastly countered these criticisms arguing that alternative forms of organization such as trade unionized employment relations are inherently conflictual and ultimately are less effective than HRM (Kearns 2003). Their defence of HRM often revolves around sets of organizational tenets and processes which are thought to inherently bring benefit to the individual, the workplace, and the national economy (Beer et al. 1984; Walton 1985). A demanding test of the successful implementation of HRM then is its capability for leading a variety of stakeholders especially owners, their agents, and employees (Guest 1987; Kochan and Osterman 1994; Schuler 1995; Watson 1986).

During the last fifteen or more years, there has been a strong interest in the relationship between employee development and organizations' success or competitive advantage. Learning organization theorists have expounded at length on the significance of employees' learning and organizational learning (Pedler, Burgoyne, and Boydell 1991; Senge 1990). Knowledge management practitioners and academics have proposed ways that knowledge should be created, transferred, absorbed, and appropriated by organizations. Often, they have accorded a central role to elite sections of the workforce (e.g. knowledge workers) in addition to making more general observations about the culture, structure, and systems of organizations (Flood et al. 2001; Kamoche 1996; Kamoche and Mueller 1998; Nonaka and Teece 2001). Others have drawn attention to the evolution of international HRM emerging partly as a result of the increased regional and transnational mobility of employees. This movement in people has created new opportunities and more demands on employees to work with and learn from economic and cultural diversity (Barney et al. 2001; Ferner 1994, 1997; Schuler 2001).

Typically, the policy and practice of HRM has been set within changing national contexts characterized by reduced trade protection and other practices aiming to promote globalization. The increased marketization of goods and services has taken place alongside developments in employment law and IR leading to a burgeoning complexity of individual rights and legislation operating within states and across continental blocs (Bamber and Lansbury 1998; Deery and Mitchell 2000; Dickens and Hall 2003). People working on HRM-related activities therefore are part of a complex and changing world of business involving ethical choices and dilemmas.

The purpose of this chapter is to identify ways that HRM can contribute to the fulfilment of organizational goals and employees' interests (Pinnington 2003). Our assumption is that HRM policies and practices often overplay the significance of the organization's part of the bargain and consequently fail to exercise leadership by so blatantly favouring one party in the employment relationship. In other words, the institutions and ethical practices of HRM are in question. HR practitioners and academics are employed within often ambiguous and biased organizational circumstances, which mean that HR practitioners do not have sufficient access to impartial institutional rules or normative guidelines (Foot 1977: 14–15; Rawls 1955, 1993) by which they can evaluate their actions and make ethical decisions. Our aim is to encourage employers and employees to identify stronger ethical bases for HRM policy and practice. Our hope is that this endeavour will make some contribution to the achievement of mutual benefits for organizations and employees (Tourish and Pinnington 2002).

HRM—bias towards organizational outcomes and lack of emphasis on employee outcomes?

The field of HRM has accountabilities for both organizational and employee outcomes. Many of the organizational considerations have been specified and elaborated since the beginnings of the debate on 'HRM versus personnel management'. The hard HRM thesis (Fombrun, Tichy, and Devanna 1984) was famed for its foregrounding of the bottom line benefit and competitive success of the organization and the soft HRM thesis (Beer et al. 1984) has been renowned for its emphasis on employee outcomes (most notably 'employee influence'). These original positions have since been elaborated in other academic frameworks and models. In general, theories have sought to understand possible lines of causation or influence between the organization's strategic position, vision, and mission, through to HRM. They endeavour to describe or predict the creation of HRM policies, and then move on to the implementation of HRM practices, and finally, the achievement of overall business and HRM outcomes (Boxall and Purcell 2003; Pinnington and Lafferty 2003).

George Strauss (2001) has argued persuasively that there are long-standing historical differences of belief between the USA and the UK/Australia/New Zealand on the nature and character of HRM. Strauss claims that the USA has never really evolved from the personnel management perspective whereby concern is with maximizing employee contribution and minimizing social obstacles (including satisfactory compliance with employment legislation) to the achievement of business objectives. The UK/Australia/New Zealand view, he proposes, is very different due to its stronger commitment to pluralist values of collective rights to trade union organization and employee influence in management. In support of his argument, he notes the consistency of subject matter and overall orientation in US business courses and textbooks throughout the last four decades of the previous century. He contrasts this continuity in the USA with the sudden disruption and heated debate occurring between IR specialists and the new HR specialists in the 1980s and 1990s in the UK, Australia, and New Zealand.

A body of interesting research work has evolved out of this fierce debate on collective IR versus individualized employee relations. It concentrates on the new partnership roles for trade unions and on ways of encouraging more 'employee voice' in both unionized and non-unionized organizations. One of the surprising findings of the empirical research in this field has been that HRM has been found to be *more frequently* present in unionized than in non-unionized organizations (Pinnington and Edwards 2000). This is somewhat counter-intuitive, especially for people maintaining a vigorously managerial viewpoint, because it demonstrates paradoxically that HRM policy and practice is more likely to be present in organizational settings said to be resistant to HRM. This is not to say that the work on employee voice commends unions as being essential to the practice of HRM rather it proposes there exist continua of choices (Marchington and Wilkinson 1996) ranging, for example, from 'trade unionized' to 'non-trade unionized' organization and from highly 'individualized' settings to highly 'collectivist' settings (which may not be union-oriented).

In our view, a strongly managerialist prescription for HRM runs the risk of short changing employees in both the economic and ethical senses. Paul Kearns' book (2003) on HR strategy is illustrative of the way HRM thinking consonant with managerialism underplays desirable outcomes for employees (Pinnington 2004). Kearns rails against 'blame cultures' and organizations where political infighting or rigid command structures exist contending that Toyota is the only place he has come across that has a long-term business strategy simultaneously combined with a long-term HR strategy. Kearns recommends HR strategy nonetheless as appropriate for maximizing organizational performance although he paints a somewhat dismal picture of the effectiveness of HR strategies in most organizations. He defines HR strategy, however, in normative terms as the 'conscious and explicit attempt to manage the organization's HR to gain a competitive advantage' (Kearns 2003: 10).

The principles Kearns considers to be fundamental to HR strategy are: honesty, added value, 'individually centred', measurement, and accountability. HR strategy he portrays as being about working within these principles to get the best out of people, which he asserts must mean ensuring that employees' values are aligned with the values espoused by the organization (2003: 76). In the closing pages, he says that business leaders are not guided primarily by ethical considerations, but that many of them feel that they have to work within two different and distinct parameters: (business) value and ethics (2003: 197). His overriding message is that to contribute to organizations and society, HR strategy must focus on (business) value rather than ethics.

Lepak and Snell (1999, 2002) take a very different line approach on HRM to the managerial instrumentalist line of argument articulated by Kearns, although their approach is similar in so far as they highlight HR–organizational outcomes and correspondingly reduce attention to HR–employee outcomes. Lepak and Snell predict that there will be observable relationships between employers' employment policies and configurations of HRM practices. Their position is broadly consistent with configurationist approaches adopted in the strategic management literature (Miller 1987) and more recently configurationist research within the academic discipline of HRM. The fundamental assumption here is that different types of HRM orientation and implementation will be characterized by different 'bundles' or configurations of organizational policy and practice (Delery and Doty 1996).

Lepak and Snell have applied this idea to the study of HRM and employment relations predicting alternative bundles of HRM practice according to whether the employment relationship is focused on: the core employees in the organization or a job-based approach to employees or an organizational alliance approach to employment or a short-term contract-based approach to employment. One of the central conclusions of their recent empirical work exploring the theory was that employers are somewhat inconsistent in their approach to HRM and employment relations. This problematic finding of Lepak and Snell (2002) is consistent with a large volume of studies within the literature on IR and HRM. Indeed, where consistency in HRM vis-à-vis organizational performance has most often been found, is in the broad-based tendency of organizations to limit their implementation of HRM during problems in organizational performance (Truss et al. 1997).

A group of HRM researchers then, first in the USA and more recently in the UK, have claimed over the last ten years that bundles or configurations of HRM practices can lead to superior organizational performance (Delery and Doty 1996; Huselid 1995; Ichniowski and Shaw 1999; Ichniowski, Shaw, and Prennushi 1995; Macduffie 1995). This research finding has been somewhat constrained by the noticeable tendency (Arthur 1994; Becker and Gerhart 1996) of 'universalist' (one size fits *all*) approaches to HRM being more frequently linked to high organizational performance than 'contingent' studies (e.g. 'cost leadership strategies *causally* imply a different bundle of HRM practices to quality differentiation strategies'). One major explanation for this discrepancy between theoretical prediction (use consistent bundles or configurations of HRM) and empirical reality (this somewhat arbitrary universal list of HR practices are reported to be statistically associated with high performance more so than theoretically predicted contingent clusters/bundles) are the overly simplistic typifications of universalist and contingent HRM (Boxall and Purcell 2003; Purcell 1999; Wood and Albanese 1995). The research studies in particular on contingent HRM have tended to rely on very bland, somewhat a-historical, non-processual academic stereotypes of strategy. For example, they have been based on rather stereotypical concepts of cost/quality/innovation derivative from Porter (1985) or alternatively draw from Miles and Snow's typifications (1984) of 'defender, prospector, and analyser' strategies.

Another problem with this whole line of configurationist research is that it seeks to reduce issues of organizational and employee outcomes to benchmarks driven primarily by an interest in economic capital. Its focus is on general financial indicators (e.g. profit per employee), financial indicators specific to the industry (e.g. scrap/waste measures, productivity per employee, quality management measures), and financial indicators specific to HRM (employee turnover rates, proportional cost of employees). Such measures are central to any business undertaking and we are not seeking to cast disdain on their significance, all the same, greater attention we feel should be given to employee considerations. Before turning to our two case studies, in the next section we outline the responsibilities of HRM in the light of economic and other alternative, significant forms of capital, which we refer to from here onwards as 'cultural capital'.

HRM—twin servant to economic capital and cultural capital

A more helpful way of understanding ethical issues in HRM we suggest is to see it as involved in the creation, accumulation, and distribution of different types of capital: *economic* wealth and *cultural* wealth. By cultural wealth we understand it as encompassing a broad range of ethical issues. We view it as inclusive of a variety of distinctive types of capital other than economic capital such as:

- educational achievement,
- cultural achievement,
- social status,
- social reputation,
- social respect, and
- symbolic power.

This definition of cultural capital is consistent with the work by the late sociologist and interpretive researcher, Pierre Bourdieu. Without going into detail, the following paragraphs provide an overview of his work to assist the reader with assessing his relevance for ethical analysis and reasoning. We will identify the relevance of his approach for inquiry on ethical issues and review some of the major critiques. Then we explain his concept of fields and their resources of economic and cultural capital (Pinnington 2002).

In management and organization studies, there has been comparatively substantial uptake of theories and concepts from Bourdieu's contemporaries, notably Foucault and to a lesser extent, Derrida. Much of this interest appears to be related to the 'linguistic turn' in progressive management studies as has been demonstrated in areas such as narrative and discourse research (Boje 2001; Hardy, Lawrence, and Grant 2005). Bourdieu's work has had significant impact within the discipline of sociology and been influential within anthropology and applied subjects, such as education (Bourdieu and Passeron 1977; Bourdieu and Wacquant 1992). By contrast, Bourdieu's work has been relatively ignored by researchers publishing in the major North American and

European academic management journals (Oakes, Townley, and Cooper 1998 is one of just a few notable exceptions).

His writings periodically criticize adopting language as a root metaphor for social studies, portraying theorizing and academic explanation that is fundamentally based on linguistic forms of analysis as being overly scholastic in approach to everyday social practice (Bourdieu 1977, 1998). His antipathy towards the linguistic turn, given its popular currency, goes some of the way towards explaining the comparatively lukewarm reception of his work in management and organization studies. Nonetheless, Bourdieu is not entirely alone in being circumspect on the fruitfulness of isolated forms of linguistic analysis, for instance, Mary Warnock (1966: 144) concludes:

One of the consequences of treating ethics as the analysis of ethical language is, as I have suggested earlier, that it leads to the increasing triviality of the subject. This is not a general criticism of linguistic analysis, but only of this method applied to ethics. In ethics, alone among the branches of philosophical study, the subject matter is not so much the categories which we use to describe or to learn about the world, *as our own impact upon the world, our relation to other people and our attitude to our situation and our life.* (emphasis added)

Moreover, Bourdieu was never a strong advocate of postmodernist academe, which contributed further to alienating him from an influential contemporary group of thinkers. Arguably, Bourdieu retained a somewhat traditional conceptualization of sociological methodology (Bourdieu 1984) at least up until publication of *Misère du Monde 1999 (Weight of the World)*. His work, through all of its phases, consistently portrays the role of the intellectual as a potential revolutionary force within society, albeit one that does not strike a chord with either Marxist ideologies or Sartrean existentialist notions of the free intellectual (Bourdieu 1993a; Sartre 1948). This has rendered Bourdieu open to criticism from many sides. On the one hand, he can be seen as a product of the 'old school' by failing to understand postmodernist enthusiasms for portrayal of ambiguities of social identity and fragmentation of theory. Then, on the other hand, he has been perceived by old school elements of leftist academe as uncommitted to revolutionary ideology (a notable exception to this stereotyping is the edited collection by Shusterman 1999).

Bourdieu's approach seeks to overcome traditional dualisms common to the social sciences such as the distinctions made between agency and structure or between individual and collective. He is not alone in this endeavour, however, his stance has attracted substantial criticism. Mouzelis (2000) censures Bourdieu for attempting to transcend the duality of structure and not retaining a dualistic ontology of social practice. Mouzelis proposes that distinct senses of *subject* and *object* should be maintained in social research and not conflated through attempts at theoretical transcendence. Jeffrey Alexander in his

1997 book *Fin de Siècle Social Theory* has argued from a similar perspective, criticizing Bourdieu still further for his 'failed synthesis'—reductionism and determinism.

Bourdieu frequently responded to these criticisms, nevertheless, there are shortcomings in his empirical research, possibly which concern less the problem of failed synthesis than his limited theoretical conceptualization of subjectivity. Bourdieu maintained the working assumption that if researchers seek to get too close to subjective experience it eludes subject and researcher at the very point when they think they have captured it! A demonstration of this dilemma common to phenomenological modes of analysis is offered by Wittgenstein (1978: 21) who challenges his readers to reflect on how hard it is to disentangle motives from causes because there is no unique, privileged means of unequivocal resolution:

… In a law-court you are asked the motive of your action and you are supposed to know it. Unless you lie you are supposed to be able to tell the motive of your action. You are not supposed to know the laws by which your body and mind are governed. Why do they suppose you know it? Because you've had such a lot of experience with yourself? People sometimes say: 'No-one can see inside you, but you can see inside yourself', as though being so near yourself, being yourself, you know your own mechanism. But is it like that? 'Surely he must know why he did it or why he said such and such.'

Bourdieu's theory of practice conceptualizes social activities such as management or employee practice as situated in multiple social fields, which he asserts possess a measure of autonomy of operation according to their own (field-based) principles. Fields have been conceptualized in many different ways in research, and Bourdieu's concept of field was developed independently and prior to the institutionalist theories that grew in the USA during the late 1970s and throughout the 1980s. Fields investigated empirically by Bourdieu during his lifetime included: the pre-modern and religious, the artistic and literary, the intellectual and academic, and the educational (Bourdieu 1988, 1990*a*, 1990*b*, 1996). His field concept is sociological rather than psychological, and applies to areas of specialist and popular discourse within society (Bourdieu 1987, 1991, 1993*b*). Fields, in Bourdieusian theory, are seen as hierarchically organized and depend for their continuing existence on the heteronomy of overarching economic and political fields. Fields are assumed to operate with a measure of autonomy accorded them in their relations to other fields. Their autonomous principles of operation constitute a game and stakes that have to be observed if one wishes to participate in the game and be recognized by others. According to *Bourdieu's theory of practice, fields will always have a structure and distribution of capital. He divides capital into two major symbolic forms: economic and cultural.* These can be converted from one to the other, but he believes tend to be in opposition to each other.

In short, Bourdieu offers a relational theory of individual action and societal structure that assumes all social relations have a tendency towards being dominated, stratified, competitive, and bound by individuals' dispositions; inculcated and shaped primarily by family and, in modern societies, schooling experiences (Pinnington, Morris, and Pinnington 2003). Bourdieu argues from a broadly relativist and instrumentalist perspective that individuals and groups strategize in an overall field of power, which subdivides into dominant and dominated groups. Within the dominant field of power, further fields and subfields exist operating partly on the basis of their own principles. Each field possesses varying allegiances to economic and cultural capital comprising an autonomous pole functioning according to cultural capital and a heteronomous pole based on economic capital. A Bourdieusian concept of strategizing can be counterposed to rational actor models of strategic decision-making, some of which tend to theorize economic activity as the consequence of individuals making calculative, self-interested, profit-maximizing decisions.

Bourdieu's approach portrays individuals' strategizing as relational rather than the consequence of aggregated individual decisions. Strategy, he claims, is shaped first by individuals' dispositions, and second, by aspirations guided by objective opportunities afforded in the structure of relations within and between fields. Strategic positions are said to be taken by individual actors or institutions seeking through practice to maximize the opportunities available within the field. It recommends that understanding their practice should be through understanding individuals or social groups as invariably being historically situated in social fields. Application of Bourdieu's theory of practice therefore requires that researchers and practitioners in HRM sustain a critical perspective on the changing distribution of economic and cultural capital within social fields over time (Pinnington 2005).

So, summarizing this section along with the previous one, the twin capital approach inspired by Bourdieu demands that researchers and practitioners become more rigorous in their ethical understanding of HRM outcomes. Kearns bemoans finding little evidence for the consistent practice of HRM because, we feel, he chooses to ignore the multiple bases of organizational action based on cultural capital rather than admit his frame of reference emphasizing economic capital is too limited. From a very different theoretical perspective on human capital, Lepak and Snell (2002) uncovered inconsistencies in HRM and employment practices not least because employers' policies and practices are motivated by other things in life than simple economic principles and (economically) consistent HR decisions.

The challenge for ethical practice in HRM then to our way of thinking is to attain willing acknowledgement from elite economists on the one hand and wealth-creating employers on the other hand of the multiple economic and cultural bases for HRM. The stakes are high because ethics is in danger of being compromised by HRM. As Barbara Townley (1994: 166) has claimed, ethics is central to the conduct of HRM:

The criteria I have used to critique personnel raise one central question: how might we conduct ourselves in our relations with others? This is an ethical question. To raise it is to place ethical considerations at the heart of political action.

Method

Our investigation was confined to one area of HRM—employee development. We interviewed managers who held responsibility for employee development in two corporate companies that were deliberately chosen because they had reputation for innovation in employee training and development. The first company was an automobile company at the time of the research soon to be split up with different units under American and German ownership, and the second was a privatized UK company operating primarily in the telecommunications industry. Influential stakeholders were selected as initial interviewees and then further subjects identified on the basis of recommendation, following the tracer study approach (Hornby and Symon 1994). The process of selection continued until the major reference network was exhausted. The managers were all interviewed using a semi-structured schedule of questions. The content covered: their background and work experience, the role and structure of technology-based learning (TBL), their knowledge of the use of multimedia programmes, decision-making processes in training, and external and internal factors influencing the design and implementation of training and TBL. The interviews were audiotape-recorded and transcribed. Their accounts and responses to questions were treated as potential individual agenda for employee development containing themes and actions. The data were content analysed for their individual themes and actions.

Sample

The job backgrounds of the managers in the automobile company were varied, but most were long-term employed by the company for twenty or more years, and individuals from all major UK plants were interviewed. The common initial career was in technical training and the majority had worked on several sites and had been employed for a period of time in areas such as engineering, production, or personnel. Interviews were held with seventeen individuals occupying roles titled: manufacturing manager, manager–young people development, project manager, training manager, IT advisor, learning media manager, skills development manager, open learning centre manager, learning and development manager, leadership development manager, dealer training manager, and change management leader.

In the telecommunications company, the network studied was twice the size of the one in the automobile company. Twenty-seven employees, training and development specialists, and influential line managers, were interviewed in the organization. They held positions within a broad range of the company's HR training and development function related to TBL. The sample of interviewees included: sponsors (individuals who are instrumental in identifying and meeting training opportunities and most often are responsible for budget allocation and authorization), internal customers (employees using training products via different media), and suppliers (training and design and delivery). All were either specialists or held key responsibilities for training and employee development. Six were based at a major technical training centre; two were based in the London headquarters; one in a major research installation, and the remainder were working in a training and development centre based in the Midlands.

Results

EMPLOYEE-CENTRED LEADERSHIP STYLE IN AN AUTOMOBILE COMPANY

Managers in the Group Training and Development Unit often spoke about three issues of employee development. First, encouraging employee development through an innovative leadership style incorporating a flexible training system approach. Second, taking a long-term view on employee development and using up-to-date training technologies, and third, dealing with the recurrent obstacles to employees being released from production tasks and other related problems of low attendance in the open learning centres.

The consensus to adopt a facilitative leadership style towards employees' development was supported by the general expressed aim of encouraging employees to have a greater desire for learning. The company's strategy identified employee development as necessary for achieving its vision and targets.

… But one of the things we have got to do is to create a desire to learn within the organization. Because you can have as much technology arrange as you want, if people do not want to learn they will not. So, you have to create the desire. That is very important. So, we put quite a lot of effort into creating that desire. (Manager, Young People Development)

Managers in the Group Training and Development Unit appeared to be most comfortable when discussing how the training and development function can assist the achievement of specified business objectives. The interviewees rarely related employee development from the perspective of the employee. Noticeably, when they did so, much of their accounts concerned employees' failure to achieve management's objectives. For example, difficulty in persuading employees to attend associate development centres (open learning centres located on each company site) was explained by some as a result of employees having had negative experiences of education during school years and being uncomfortable with individualized learning approaches. Further, some interviewees explained away the limited uptake of technology tools for employee development as caused by 'technophobia'. This condition, they suggested, was less prevalent in the company than it had been in previous years because employees had new role models especially in the home—seeing their children enthusiastically interacting with computer games and videos.

Mixed attitudes were expressed on the role and significance of technology tools for employee development. On the one hand, technology was presented as having a positive role for employees who were not intimidated by associate development centres. These employees were often seen as having a stronger intrinsic interest and desire for learning. On the other hand, technology was described as being of low worth, partly as a consequence of line managers' reluctance to support higher utilization of open learning and partly due to technology media's tendency, in their experience, to produce isolated and sporadic learning.

The development of employees was described by interviewees as beleaguered by obstacles. Three commonly identified problems were that: line managers often were uninterested in supporting employee development; only a small proportion of the total employees were intrinsically motivated to learn and use the associate development centres; and the technology tools suffered serious limitations creating isolated instances of learning. Partial resolution of these difficulties was presented as requiring an improvement in the status and authority of HR compared to other business functions, in this way employees may become more frequently released from their work tasks. Also, most of the interviewees appeared to be optimistic for the future believing that young people would be more amenable to technology training interventions through being better educated than the current generation of employees and by being more 'technology literate'.

BUSINESS-DOMINATED LEADERSHIP STYLE IN A TELECOMMUNICATIONS COMPANY

This company had a 25-year-long reputation for innovation in training technology. Interviewees' accounts of employee development and the role of TBL were replete with reference to the company's situation. They emphasized the need for social cohesion within the function, acknowledged senior management to have substantial capacity for initiating change in new directions, and most voiced a general concern over their employment security. Employment levels in the 'HR, Training and Development' function had experienced downsizing from 1,500 full-time people at its height down to 750 at the time of the interview study, and further reductions were expected. This is not to say that there was a pessimistic tone to their responses. Rather, the message was one of hope that, so long as in-house training provision was found to be competitive when assessed against external training providers and according to the evaluations of key internal customers in the business units, then, the training and development function would profit and grow.

... I do not believe, it is currently seen as important as it should be. First of all, our communication tech and blue chip company, and we should be using the technology that we look to see outside of [the company], inside [the company]. That has not got a high level profile. So, I do not believe it is seen by all people in [the company] as important. Some of the problems with that is the different pieces of hardware that people have. We also have to work with lowest common denominator, different hardware, different software packages, different e-mail packages. That has proved a problem to us in the past. But, I believe that it is critical for our success. Absolutely critical. And we need to be able to have a clear strategy in terms of how multimedia will be used for development strategy in [the company]. (Management Development Specialist, HR and Development Services)

Analysis of the themes and actions expressed in the interviewees' responses suggested that their priorities concerned, first, increasing employee development through technical development of 'training solutions' implemented by distance delivery. Second, their agendas attended to harnessing the design power of the company for training and development by focusing on the internal and external markets for TBL products. Third, they concerned the felt imperative to serve business goals.

Within employee development, there were only a few accounts indicative of a deliberate strategy by the middle and senior management to distribute employees' knowledge and skills. For example, there were not that many accounts of moving employees around the company from one location to another nor much talk of transforming the processes of 'learning-by-doing' such as in relocating employee development activities by transferring them from one medium of learning and communication to another. Similar to the automobile company, interviewees' expressed ambition was that the future generation would furnish the company with employees who were more receptive to TBL than the current workforce. They were optimistic that employees of the future would welcome computer-mediated forms of communication because it was offered by some interviewees as being self-evident that young people are more conversant than older people with computer technology.

Designers and developers were central in exhorting the role of youth as being critical to TBL design and use. Designers were conceived of as primarily being young people who would design and deliver technology-based training solutions by consumption primarily by young employees, but that this must be governed by the dictate and vicissitude of business need. Interviewees' accounts frequently made managerial assertions on the unity of good design with good business. This was epitomized in the oft-used jargon phrase, 'training integration'. It was commonplace for interviewees' accounts of employee development and training solutions to emphasize that solutions were easier to apply in some areas of the company than in others. Business and commercial areas of the company were reported to be more receptive to TBL than employees from engineering and technical services. We interpret this 'receptiveness' as partly a consequence of changing management priorities within the company. The internal environment (of the company) attached increasing importance to the commercial and business areas and was less willing than before to be led by product values dominated by professional and technical values and commitments.

TBL was however not popular with all of the employees in HR, Training and Development who were sometimes disparagingly referred to by interviewees as the 'delivery army'. Employees from HR, Training and Development were said to be resistant for two main reasons. First, TBL threatened to put them out of work, and second, it was believed to be ineffective for some training and development goals, particularly whenever face-to-face communication was considered central to achieving intended learning outcomes. There was an overriding sense in many of the interviewees' accounts that TBL was unpopular with people from engineering and technical backgrounds.

Old people were characterized by interviewees as employees most likely to be resistant to training solutions whereas young people were described as being more comfortable with computer technology and appreciative of its potential. Employee resistance to TBL was characterized by interviewees as caused by technophobia or 'unwillingness to change'. Designers and developers nevertheless were espoused to be passionate about the new technology and therefore were the reverse of the stereotype of an older employee. Designers and developers were described by their managers as motivated by the challenges of creative, professional, and technical work, and consequently, were said to be in need of constant reminding of the importance of serving customers and evaluating products according to business objectives.

Discussion—leadership and employee development in HRM

The above company case studies depict two very different stances on employee development. The approach taken in the automobile company was typical of a soft HRM approach with its emphasis on encouraging employees to feel they had real influence over their job, skill development, and ultimately, the success of the company strategy. The management with key responsibilities for training and development evidently paid attention to fostering a culture of EI, but were unable to secure the full cooperation of many other parts of the organization in their endeavours (Pinnington and Bayraktaroglu 1998, 1999). Consequently, employees' development was seriously confined to sporadic and individual exercise of initiative rather than a concerted programme of collective skill development. Unfortunately, one outcome of this for the company was that it gained a reputation in some quarters for failing to commit to the quality and development strategy that had been agreed in partnership with the trade unions.

One way of learning from the case studies is to reflect on the company's experience asking how, in the future, managers and employees in similar circumstances might act? Prima facie, managers with responsibilities for employee development must deal proactively with obstacles within the organization, and employees probably could have asserted themselves more forcefully to grasp the opportunities available to them. One shortcoming that was identified at the time within the automobile company in another research study on quality management (Hammersley and Pinnington 1999*a*, 1999*b*; Pinnington and Hammersley 1997) was that top-level management were steadfast in their commitment to economic capital and its productivity objectives, but ambivalent in their support for cultural capital and employee development goals. So, without digressing into a debate on the significance of senior management commitment, the main problem as we see it is: How should HRM *follow the strategy of the business* (primarily economic capital development) *and concurrently serve its employee development function* (cultural capital development)?

The evidence in the automobile company case study is that whether by design or by chance, people working with the HRM function chose to focus chiefly on their sphere of activity and to exert influence cognizant of the realpolitik of employee development. A stronger and more ethical stance we propose would have been appropriate. Ultimately, increased exertion of will and a more apparent management effort towards securing achievement of development goals has the potential to benefit the company and its employees. Managers and employees faced a myriad of decision points and interpersonal events when they could have legitimately and efficaciously asserted the cultural capital of employee development. In both companies, exercise of innovative leadership style could have further developed its system strengths in the rigour and daily detail of the implementation of flexible training methods. The implementation of up-to-date but unproven training technologies can be targeted to development goals where achievement is evident both for individual learners and their work groups. Failure to achieve training objectives can be addressed by dealing with obvious bottlenecks and constraints on development such as the line managers' and supervisors' refusal to release employees from production tasks and employees' unavailability or reluctance to attend open learning activities.

Ways that employees have developed habits of thinking and communities of practice which fail to effectively use available cultural benefits of technology tools need to be better understood. The tactics employed by HRM have to move beyond stereotyping 'technology literacy' into being the premium territory for young people, and instead treat the issue as a collective responsibility for continuous learning and adaptation. This means interpreting the cultural capital of employee development as requiring more democratic distribution rather than overconcentration in the hands of arbitrary elites, for example, managers, technical specialists, young or old groups of people (Pinnington 1992).

The stance adopted during the time of the case study research in the telecommunications company was more typical of a hard HRM focus on employees as resources and a means to the achievement of the strategy of the organization (Gratton et al. 1999). During the period of the case study research, they were one of the largest in-house groups of developers of TBL content in the UK and were under pressure to optimize the utilization and returns from the training materials development. The organization has a long history in training technologies (Bayraktaroglu 1999; Hawkridge, Newton, and Hall 1988) and the company's experience in using educational and training technology at the time of writing stretches for over three decades (Pinnington 1990). It was a pioneer user in the UK of programmed learning (TICCIT and PLATO) during the early 1970s.

The vigorous pressure from top management to focus on costs and the continuous cycle of organizational downsizing had had its effect on morale in the company (Stiles et al. 1997) so that employees working in the HR function were encouraged to think very much in market terms converting issues of employee development (cultural capital) into issues of internal and external markets for their products and services (economic capital).

The structure of the HRM group (known at the time of the case study research, 'Group Personnel') was subdivided into two areas: HR and development services. This structural division stimulated a business-dominated focus within the function because it was widely understood that productivity and profitability of the groups was key to determining budget allocations and cuts. The head of HR services and solutions worked closely with the business unit leaders respectively for commercial services and engineering. He was presumably convinced that integrated technology-based solutions made available on-the-job were the most cost effective for training all of the management grades and customer sales. His leadership style was highly dominated by business considerations so that people working for him in training services and solutions were encouraged to see themselves as members of project teams responsible for 'deliverables' measured according to the company's business need, strategy, budgets, and cost cutting.

The overall atmosphere seemed to be a complex mixture of job insecurity and technological innovation. Employees within HR services and solutions portrayed themselves as dealing with 'technology resistance' in the company. Much of this resistance was understood to emanate from old people many of whom had either left or were thought likely to be downsized in the future. The future prospects for TBL were seen as positive overall because the younger generation of employees had grown up with computers and were considered able to use and learn from technology training solutions driven by business need. Essentially, training was presented by HR managers as being a 'business within a business', serving its 'consumers' and senior management whose view counted most.

Despite the fact that HRM in the telecommunications company was much more highly resourced for expenditure on employee development than was the automobile company, its obsession with cost justification and cost control meant that development opportunities were being missed and the collective competence of the organization was at risk of being ignored (Pinnington 1990). The telecommunications company was more sophisticated in its business leadership of training and development activities, however, there was scant evidence that the obsession with converting cultural capital into issues of economic capital was assisting with skill development in large sections of the company, particularly its clerical support side and its technical and engineering base. In short, we interpret that the downsizing of the company was actually being supported by a 'hollowing out' of employee capabilities due to HR slavishly seeking to operate as a business within a business. Consequently, short-term top management goals of cutbacks were being reinforced but the consumers (i.e. employees) were being starved of development opportunity with perhaps the exception of immediate training needs related to short-term job tasks.

Our overall evaluation of the situation is that employee development was out-of-sync with even a purely instrumental company analysis of training and development needs. The marketization of the training function and its attendant conception of employees as consumers did not have either an intrinsic or a thorough instrumental rationale for employee development. The employees were not being treated as consumers for their own sake (Pinnington 1991).

Further, neither were they treated in accordance with a rational hard HRM logic which uses employees as resources that are instrumental to achievement of the business strategy. Where effective on-the-job training and employee development outcomes did occur, we would suggest that they therefore were due to fortuitousness combined with resilience on the part of managers and employees. This might be called 'leadership-by-default' whereby positive leadership arises out of lack of institutional leadership in HRM; and often can be traced back to managers and other employees who resist becoming enchanted by a pervasive mode of thinking such as one overdominated by matters of economic capital.

Concluding remark

The argument of this chapter has been that organizations and employees are influenced by diverse resources of *economic* and *cultural* capital, but the preference within the field of HRM is to defer to economic capital which often has been to the detriment of employees' development and cultural capital. The two case studies of employee development in an automobile company and telecommunications company reveal the need for a stronger ethical basis for the pursuit of HRM. Below are our tentative recommendations for improved ethical leadership in HRM.

Recommendations for leadership and employee development

ECONOMIC CAPITAL IN THE FIELD OF HRM

Philosophy

1. Seek to understand and communicate mutual gains (for employers and employees) to senior management
2. Encourage long-term commitment: challenge economic reductionism especially when it has an exclusively short-term focus

Everyday practice

3. Communicate wealth generation arising from HRM rather than be reliant on the cost-centred approach
4. Monitor and influence the distribution of economic capital available for HRM

CULTURAL CAPITAL IN THE FIELD OF HRM

Philosophy

1. Seek to understand and communicate the complex diversity of cultural capital in HRM decisions and action
2. Encourage a long-term commitment to the multi-level institutions of cultural capital—societal, organizational, group, and individual

Everyday practice

3. Communicate employee-centred development in cultural capital arising from HRM
4. Deliberately address and act on multiple issues of cultural capital.

12 Ethics and work in emergencies: the UK fire service strike 2002–3

Tom Sorell

Talk of employee relations has become more common than talk of IR in HRM, but collective action organized by trade unions has not disappeared from employment relationships. Collective action by trade unions operating in emergency services has traditionally been regarded as morally sensitive: it has taken on new significance throughout the West since September 11. In this chapter, I consider ethical issues raised by the strike in 2002–3 carried out by the UK fire services.

The strike was declared by the Fire Brigade Union (FBU) in November 2002. The union had asked employers for a significant pay increase for full-time and part-time firefighters, and the government refused to fund it. As it went on, the strike was directed against the recommendations of a government-commissioned review chaired by Sir George Bain (2002). Bain called for a radical restructuring of the fire service, including a reduction in numbers employed and changed shift patterns. The strike did not leave Britain entirely bereft of a fire and rescue service. The military was able to provide limited cover, but with antiquated emergency vehicles and relatively inexperienced, unsatisfactorily trained firefighters. When serious fires or car accidents were reported, pickets from a relevant fire station sometimes went back on duty to assist. Strike action was taken for relatively limited periods of a day or days at a time. Although the strike was protracted, lasting until February 2003, it passed with relatively little loss of life or serious injury.

Was the strike morally justified? This question is hard to answer properly without broaching some of the topics considered by the Bain Report. But there are also more general issues, to do with the demands of working in the emergency services generally. The FBU sometimes argued that the pay and working conditions of firefighters were reasonably viewed on the model of those in the police service. Journalistic, academic, and trade union discussions often speak of 'emergency service workers', including under that phrase not only firefighters and police, but paramedics and ambulance drivers among others. Later I argue that undifferentiated talk of emergency services clouds thinking about the work, responsibilities, and rights of paid firefighters, police, and paramedical personnel. There are important differences between the risks of firefighting and policing, and between both of these and the work of paramedics. There are corresponding differences between the moral risks of mismanaging these different personnel. To insist on these differences is not to deny that the psychological and social pressures associated with emergencies can be similar across professional boundaries. These similarities can co-exist with moral differences, for example because the official purposes of fire and police services are typically quite distinct.

My discussion reflects some of the peculiarities of a fire service and of the circumstances of the UK fire service strike in 2002–3. But there will be implications for our attitudes to emergency services in general. It is very important to the background of ordinary and official thinking about the emergency services that there is a difference between routine and manageable incidents on the one hand (Sorell 2002), and disasters on the other. The greater the frequency or risk of disasters, the more an emergency service will seem necessary, even if it is inadequate to the tasks it faces. When routine and manageable events are the rule, on the other hand, it becomes relevant to consider whether they are readily preventable. If they are, the non-emergency work of prevention can start to displace the emergency work of responding to incidents, with the result that the emergency work starts to seem less and less essential. The routine emergency work of the UK fire service has been downgraded in this way, and yet the service has also been given a new mandate for dealing with natural and terrorist disasters. The collision between a vision of a compact fire prevention service and that of a disaster-relief agency invites different kinds of injustice to firefighters. But since the ingredients of the UK case are present internationally, its lessons may be of general interest.

The UK fire service: perceptions and realities

If an emergency is understood as a situation in which there is a present danger of significant harm or loss to the public, then, in the UK, the fire service is the emergency service par excellence. It is the service called upon to deal not only with the threat to life and property from fires, but also from floods and other weather disturbances, earthquakes, explosions, releases of dangerous chemical substances, as well as major road traffic and rail accidents. The police service in the UK also attends some of these incidents, particularly road traffic accidents, and it is the front-line service for dealing with threats of harm or actual harm to individuals from assault. But its range is smaller than that of the fire service.

The ambulance service is likely to attend many of the incidents to which the fire service is called, but often the work of the fire service has to be done before theirs can begin. So even among front-line services, the fire service is often foremost.

Unlike many others in the world, the UK fire service is legally able to take industrial action. It does so infrequently. The strike of 2002–3 was the first in twenty-five years. The fact that it seldom takes strike action and only then with considerable reluctance; the fact that its members face danger, sometimes extreme danger, in the course of normal duties; the fact that the fire service performs well by many measures of response to incidents: all of these things contributed to the considerable sympathy the public displayed towards the strikers in opinion polls and in shows of support for pickets, at the beginning of the strike in November 2002. The firemen's demand for a 40 per cent wage increase was not greeted as excessive, because people agreed that their salaries were very low, unfairly low in comparison to those of the police. A poll conducted three weeks after the beginning of industrial action showed more that 53 per cent of the public in support of the strikers, up from 47 per cent at the very beginning of the strike (*The Guardian*, 19th November 2002).

These attitudes are unsurprising if people believe that the UK fire service is routinely called upon to face dangers that most people never face, and, in particular, that much better paid people never face. A certain amount of FBU campaigning material suggested precisely this. 'Would you do all this for £6 an hour?' an FBU poster asked, over pictures of firemen attending major train accidents and fires. An FBU website which reproduced the poster, directed visitors to comparisons of firefighters' pay with the pay of politicians (FBU 2002). Unchallenged data in the Bain Report, however, shows very clearly that, in recent history, the UK fire service has *not* routinely been called upon to face extreme danger. In 2000–1, under half of the incidents attended by the fire service were fires of any description, and attending to these consistently occupies no more than 10 per cent of fire service time (Bain 2002: §3.6). The proportion of call-outs for real fires (42 per cent) is virtually equal to the number of false alarms (41 per cent) (see Bain 2002: Figure 3.1), and real fires can include fires that are not a major threat to life or property. Rescues bring the proportion of genuine incidents to 47 per cent. There is a concentration of call-outs for real fires at night, so that fire service personnel on day shifts may have long periods of relative inactivity or routine and *safe* duties. This is not to say that the firefighter's job is not demanding. A high degree of physical fitness has to be maintained and training regimes see to this. Again, regular training includes practices and exercises that can themselves be dangerous. But these facts do not bear out the implication of the FBU poster—that only £6 per hour is paid for what is routinely highly dangerous work. As a rule £6 per hour or more is paid for work that need not be and more often than not actually *isn't* dangerous. Indeed, a high proportion of some shifts can be stand-down time, when no particular duties are carried out at all, but where fire service staff have to be ready to respond quickly to an emergency (see Bain 2002: Figure 3.14).

Facts about the shift pattern in the fire service also put the question of salary in an unexpected light. The pattern of about 95 per cent of full-time firefighters in the UK is two day shifts followed by two night shifts followed by four days off. This pattern permits staff to take second jobs, and many (Bain does not say exactly how many) do. So it becomes a question what is meant by a full-time job in the fire service, and also how many hours of stand-down time, which at night can be hours of sleep, are paid for at the same rate as hours of duties. There are further questions about the timings of shifts, and especially about the effectiveness of having shift changes at times of heavy demand for the fire service (Bain 2002: §§3.30–3.38). The shift pattern in the fire service does not seem to have even a rough counterpart in the police service, and independent studies commissioned by Bain found police service duties at different ranks more onerous than those in the fire service (Bain 2002: §§8.12–8.13). Attempts since the end of the strike to introduce some paperwork duties during stand-down time have been strenuously resisted, to such an extent that there was a recurrence of industrial action as late as May 2004 in some places in England, including Salford in Greater Manchester.

It might be thought that what makes the job of firefighter unusually demanding is not *actually being called upon* to risk one's life, but having to be prepared to do so whenever one is on duty. If this is right, then the FBU poster may not be so misleading after all. But compare firefighting to military service in peacetime. In that case, too, there is a preparedness to go into action that is potentially lethal, but the chances of doing so are far less than during military service in war. Active service in war comes much closer to the threshold of routine life-risking than either military service in peacetime or normal fire-service work. An intermediate case might be ordinary fire fighting duty during a drought in a highly forested area, or ordinary firefighting duty in an area where even false alarms usually expose fire crews to attacks from hostile inner city youths. Outside these cases the moral weight attaching to being prepared to risk one's life is probably slight, because the chances of actually being called upon to risk one's life are slight.

Even when firefighting is indisputably life threatening, there is something wrong with the FBU's implication that not many members of the public would attempt it for £6 per hour, and something wrong also with the popular idea that one needs to have heroic impulses to go into firefighting. First, as Bain makes clear, there are forty applicants for every fire service vacancy in the UK (Bain 2002: §3.39). Second, there is a difference between, on the one hand, someone properly trained and equipped to take life-threatening risks, and, on the other, someone who makes, as we might say, a superhuman effort against great odds. It might take heroism for an ordinary agent to attempt what a trained firefighter is used to doing when fighting fires. It would only take heroism in a trained and properly equipped firefighter to attempt *more* than his training and equipment prepared him for. Presumably, even the risky work of fighting an average fire is open, through training, to an ordinary human without exercising superhuman efforts. Otherwise it would make no sense to recruit firefighters from the general public. And so even though this work is dangerous, it is wrong to associate it with heroism. Heroism comes into its own with an emergency on a large scale. Thus, many of the firemen who attempted to rescue people in the Twin Towers on September 11 were heroes, because of the mammoth demands made on the fire service by that event, and by the willingness of fire crews to rise to the occasion; but not every call-out, even for a moderately big fire, is necessarily an occasion for an effort that stretches people enough to make heroes out of them. Even a major fire may be manageable work for every member of several crews working at once. Disasters, on the other hand, by definition overwhelm the available personnel.

It is probable that there are aspects of the firefighter's job that are traumatic and therefore highly demanding even when they do *not* put any firefighter's life at risk. For example, 4 per cent of the UK fire service's time is spent on road traffic accidents, and this work, as well as rescue from collapsed buildings and major weather incidents, can be very harrowing. Viewing and handling badly mutilated bodies, and especially the bodies of children, is particularly stressful. It is singled out as the single most stressful part of the job by Australian firefighters (Moran and Colless 1995: 410). Again, in a study of DPS, 'a public-sector provider of pre-hospital emergency care' in Australia, Boyle and Healey found considerable psychological disturbance arising from exposure to death, and also in balancing emotional reactions to the extreme circumstances of road accidents and normal life away from work, or periods of inactivity at work (Boyle and Healy 2003: 357). Like the UK fire service, DPS has an overwhelmingly male workforce, organized along strict hierarchical, quasi-military lines, and this sometimes seemed to pose an obstacle to emotional balancing. Further, even more routine, aspects of the job can also make it stressful. There is the shift system, with its impact on sleep patterns and the continuity of family life. There is the strict, military-style hierarchy, with its inflexibilities and lack of channels for ordinary criticism and accountability. Then, because of severe gender and racial imbalances in some emergency services, notably the fire service in the UK, there are problems of sexual harassment and racism (Bain 2002: §3.41. The ILO discussion document, op. cit. pp. 30ff samples imbalances internationally). When these are combined with the life-risking aspects of the job, even if they are not everyday aspects, they make a difficult job harder, especially for women and members of racial and ethnic minorities.

It does not follow from the fact that the job is difficult that the FBU's strike action was justified. Even if the pay for the job was inadequate—a claim the Bain Report implies is debatable—the general disruption and potential threat to life of a non-functioning emergency service makes industrial action highly questionable morally. This is so even though fire crews did often respond ad hoc to serious incidents when officially on strike.

The challenge of terrorism

Emergency services can be victims of their own success, as the case of the UK fire service shows. Not only has it reduced the number of fires by campaigning for improved building techniques and by carrying out good inspections; it has raised consciousness of fire risks and persuaded the public to purchase devices that give early warning of fire. Bain found that the number of fires in the UK had fallen markedly after a peak in 1995, albeit with a slow increase at the end of the 1990s. Internationally, the incidence of dwelling fires in developed countries from 1996–2000 fell by between about 1 per cent in Britain and about 11 per cent in the USA and New Zealand, with the incidence of deaths from such fires falling much faster (Bain 2002: Figure 3.4). This background of success prompted Bain to conclude not only that the fire service might be reduced in size, but that it could be reorganized to respond better to places and times that posed the highest fire risk.

This approach makes sense if the main task of the fire service continues to be fighting fires, and if the trends described in Bain continue. Matters are complicated, however, by the fact that the fire service is the emergency service par excellence, and by the fact that the potential demands on its services may not be confined in the future to fires. There is an acknowledgement of this fact in the UK government's 2003 White Paper on the Fire and Rescue Service. It explicitly looks to a role for the fire service in which firefighting intervention is increasingly the exception due to a concentration on fire prevention. But at the same time, it envisages a much bigger role for the fire service in the management of natural disasters and terrorism (HM Govt. White Paper 2003).

This shift of policy is philosophically interesting, because it suggests a recognition of a difference between, so to speak, a normal emergency and an abnormal emergency. A fire in a dwelling or industrial property is a normal emergency, a commonly encountered and normally manageable one, for which there are established and effective remedies. It may even be that fires are coming to be seen by the UK government as largely preventable emergencies, in contradistinction to extreme weather conditions and terrorism. Terrorism, especially in the form of chemical or biological attack, is both abnormal and virtually unpreventable, two things fires are not. Again by contrast with fires, terrorism is an object of considerable general public fear, and a major preoccupation for governments in the West.

Now the reclassification of the hazard traditionally assigned to the fire service as readily preventable, and the new emphasis on fire prevention, indicates a move away from conceiving the fire service primarily as an emergency response organization. On the other hand, there is evidence in the White Paper of a wish for a fire service that will become a *new* sort of emergency response organization. These contradictory tendencies seem to point to a downgrading and an upgrading of the fire service at the same time. Both tendencies carry moral risks. First, the policy of reducing the size of the fire service can intensify the sense of being undervalued that was widely expressed during the FBU strike. This can compound the demoralization that is bound to be felt already by the fire service in the face of the high and increasing numbers of malicious false alarms. Second, the downgrading is not likely to be counterbalanced by the 'upgrading' just mentioned. On the contrary, assigning particularly daunting new hazards to the fire service can be a threat rather than a morale-boosting opportunity, since the chances of mishandling the abnormal and hard-to-control are bound to be high.

Terrorism in particular needs to be considered. The September 11 attacks in New York City led to the deaths of 343 firefighters, including very senior and experienced officers. These people were not readily replaced, and their loss affected the capacity of the Fire Dept of New York to attend even to normal emergencies immediately after September 11. The FDNY's strategic plan for 2004–5 highlights the challenge posed by terrorism, and also indicates the huge scale of the task of becoming prepared for a repeat of September 11 in a city like New York. About 150 locations have been identified as high-priority risk sites, and plans for protecting only 65 are being developed to begin with (NYC strategic plan 2004).

Although New York and other major American cities are particularly vulnerable to the sort of high-profile attack that Al Qaeda seem to prefer, the threat from that group has already been shown to be international. The bombing of a commuter train in Madrid; the firebombing of nightclubs used by Western tourists in Bali; these are a sample of what could easily be reproduced virtually anywhere. Britain has already been singled out as a priority target, and the July attack on the London underground may well be followed by even worse things. This probably poses more of a problem for the London Fire Brigade than for the UK fire service in general, but one of the lessons of September 11 is that a successful attack can leave casualties in sufficient numbers to require some sort of pool of trained personnel as possible replacements. This pool would presumably be made up of firefighters from brigades outside London. In this way the problem of terrorism for a major city can become a problem for a fire service nationally.

Terrorism is not a preoccupation of the Bain report, and the relative neglect of the problem may call into question Bain's vision of a fire service with a smaller workforce engaged in a decreasing number of fires, and with a bigger role in fire prevention. The government White Paper makes more room for the terrorist threat, but without altering very much the Bain vision of a fire service better adapted to the normal emergency. Yet a fire service adapted to the demands of terrorism is not likely to be as compact or as cheap as a Bain fire service.

The tensions in the UK government position extend to moral tensions. It is undoubtedly a leading responsibility of government to protect its citizens from violent attack and to minimize the after-effects when an attack cannot be prevented. But the organizations it calls upon to discharge these responsibilities are, by the same token, important for a government not to disable or demoralize. In the UK the demands of keeping public spending under control, and the prevailing vision of the fire service as an organization for dealing with increasingly preventable normal emergencies, may have led to a demoralization of the fire service during the period of the FBU strike; if so, the fire service is not well situated to take on new and demanding responsibilities so soon after that strike. It is not insignificant that, in the very recent industrial action in Greater Manchester, it was new equipment for dealing with terrorist incidents that firefighters were refusing to train on.

The UK government's role in relation to the fire service and terrorism is more complicated than may first appear. First, the size of the threat from terrorism is affected by ongoing government policymaking, especially foreign policy decisions, to which terrorism is sometimes a reaction. Like the army, the fire service is sometimes in the front line when government policy is badly thought out or dangerous. It has to be there to pick up the pieces when things go wrong in the form of terrorism, and sometimes, as in New York, it suffers the first casualties. These are new risks, and they are not likely to be taken on enthusiastically in a cost-cutting climate or in the face of government commissioned reports that suggest that there are too many firefighters chasing, so to speak, too few fires. The moral is not that the government should have agreed to the firefighters' demands before November 1992. Nor is it that the FBU strike was justified after all. The FBU strike was unjustified, and the government's refusal to pay 40 per cent was justified—so long as the job of firefighters was normal firefighting. When the role of the fire service was reconceived, as in the White Paper, there was a new need to enlist the goodwill of the firefighters by acknowledging, inviting a discussion of, and perhaps proposing improved pay for, a new role, especially in major cities. What appears to have happened is that new responsibilities have been quietly grafted on to the post-Bain fire service, as if terrorism and natural disasters might naturally fill the free time created by successful fire prevention. This seems to be a kind of injustice, as well as being politically inept.

Other emergency services

I have been arguing that the new terrorism duties of the UK fire service significantly strengthen the fire service's claims to be given exceptional treatment in pay negotiations. Not only are the new duties likely to be onerous when discharged; exercising for them and devising plans for protecting the public will be substantially new and possibly dangerous tasks as well.

Why, if at all, is it any different for the other services involved in emergency work? Won't the police and ambulance service and, for that matter, the army, have to rethink their roles and rise to a new challenge posed by terrorism? When their jobs become dangerous in the new terrorist climate, won't they be dangerous for the same reasons as firefighters' work will be dangerous? Yes and no. Here it is important not to lump together different services involved in emergency work, or their different current circumstances. Police services seem to me to be emergency services incidentally, and other kinds of service first of all. In the UK, for example, only 5 per cent of officers at any one time are available for front-line work, including emergencies, the rest being involved in such activities as training, administrative work, and court appearances (http://www.polfed.org/). This is not to say that non-front-line work is a distraction from the real business of the police. Administrative work may be, but courtroom appearances definitely are not. A main function of the police service in the UK and elsewhere is to collect and present evidence for the prosecution of criminal offences. Although this work takes police off the streets, it does not take police away from legitimate police work. The fact that the public in the UK wishes that the police were more visible on the streets and deterring crime and disorder does not mean that invisible police work is any less police work. Undercover detection work is not, for example. But, to return to our main topic, very little of what counts as front-line work in the police need be emergency work. Front-line work typically amounts to routine patrolling. This, and the proportion of front-line work to police work as a whole, is what makes the classification of the police as an emergency service questionable.

Even if the proportion of UK police time spent on proper emergency work were much higher than it actually is, the circumstances of the police service are not comparable to those of the fire service. Numbers in police services have been rising in many countries and are due to go on increasing. Between 1998 and 2000 there was a growth of 70,000 or about 9 per cent in the police and detective force of the USA, with a predicted further growth of 21 per cent for the period 2000 to 2010 (*Occupational Outlook Quarterly* 2002). This compares to a predicted growth in firefighter numbers of only 9 per cent, this increase in turn being largely accounted for by volunteer firefighters going into full-time employment (*Occupational Outlook*

Quarterly 2002). In the UK, police numbers in England and Wales rose to over 136,000 in 2003, up from about 124,000 in 2000 (BBC News 2nd October 2003 http://news.bbc.co.uk/1/hi/uk/3157138.stm). Against this background, a new mandate for police to be involved in terrorist work would not be being addressed to a declining workforce, or to one that felt it was particularly badly paid.

Ambulance services are more centrally emergency services than police services and are to that extent comparable to the fire service. Indeed, in Ireland, firefighters even alternate as ambulance personnel (ILO discussion document 2003 op. cit. 22). In the UK, the ambulance service was for a long time seen as the transport arm of the UK health service rather than as a first responder to medical need; historically the occupation of 'emergency medical technician' in the USA grew out of voluntary transportation work (Nelsen and Barley 1997). The first responder role is now gaining in prominence according to the UK Commission for Health Improvement study of ambulance services published in 2003.

Morale in the UK ambulance service has lately been low, mainly on account of the struggle to meet response time targets. Other problems have been due to administrative reorganization. Ambulance services have become National Health Service (NHS) trusts, and, like other trusts, their managements have been distracted by having to make decisions about merging with other trusts for financial reasons. Like the fire service, the ambulance service in its current demoralized state is being asked to take on new responsibilities for emergency preparedness in connection with terrorist action. New emergency powers legislation in the UK makes the ambulance service a category 1 responder, on a par with the police and fire service. It does not appear that this role is registered in increased pay, and day-to-day operations are dominated by normal emergency rather than abnormal emergency preoccupations.

Like the fire service, then, the ambulance service seems to me to have been drafted into preparations for disaster work without much fanfare or evident consultation. It is not clear that there will be more money to assist with its new tasks. Elsewhere, ambulance services are earmarked for financial cuts. Even in New York, the Fire Department introduced an 8 per cent reduction in ambulance shifts in 2002 (ILO discussion paper op. cit. 23). Though ambulance workers may not face all the hazards that go with firefighting, they face many of the same sources of psychological stress. In the UK there is a considerable risk of their being bounced into even more difficult work. Or, in other words, there is a risk of reproducing the injustice facing UK firefighters.

To conclude, the UK fire service strike demonstrates the need to disaggregate the general category of emergency service work and occupations. It also shows the need to analyse more carefully the fairness of allocation of responsibilities and tasks within an occupation such as the fire brigade or the police. I have argued that politicians, public service officials, employers, and employees have opportunities to make their policies morally defensible, namely by attending more rigorously to the distributive and procedural justice of the organization and reorganization of work for firefighters, police, and ambulance services.

Part III

Progressing Human Resource Management

13 HRM, ethical irrationality, and the limits of ethical action

Tony J. Watson

Introduction

'I remember when I was a young personnel officer, a view that HR—the personnel function as it was then called—should be the conscience of the organization. I think I wrote an essay on this when I was studying for IPM [Institute of Personnel Management] grad[uate] membership. I wish I could find it for you. But then perhaps not! It might be embarrassing. I probably wrote to support the proposition. I was naïve in those early days, thinking that personnel was the "people" part of management and therefore had to take on the caring part of, you know, the management of the business. And "doing the right thing by people" was obviously part of that caring thing. If I remember rightly, the IPM's mission statement was about balancing "efficiency and welfare" in managing people. And, of course, that's been dropped now. We all know that any talk of welfare, caring or ethical practice is only acceptable in managerial circles if it is a means to a business end. The idea that I might go to the Board here to say to them "We must do this because I, Bob Davern, believe it is ethically right" would be to risk my job. And there is just one thing that would be more dangerous to my future. If I were to say that my professional body—the chartered institute as it's soon going to be—would be unhappy with the company going down a certain line on employment matters on ethical grounds ... well, they'd send for the men in white coats.'

The above statement was made by an HR director who was being interviewed as part of a project on how HR managers were talking about the likelihood of their professional association gaining a royal charter. The context in which these (previously unpublished) words were uttered was a discussion about HR work and what I conceptualized in the research as discourses of professionalism (Watson 2002). We return to what this individual had to say about HR as a profession later on but, for now, his words can usefully be read to illustrate the broad argument being put forward in the present chapter. This is the argument that the scope for HR managers to make ethical interventions in the conduct of their employing organizations is extremely limited and is, in fact, practically non-existent unless it is connected to a claim that the ethical act in question (whether it be to treat employees in a 'more ethical way' or to avoid treating them in a potentially 'unethical way') will, in one way or another, be 'better for the business'.

This argument is supported in two ways: theoretically and empirically. Sociological theorizing will be deployed at two levels; the level of ethics in human societies generally and the level of the institution of HR management in industrial capitalist societies specifically. Empirical material will be drawn upon throughout in outlining these theoretical ideas, this being taken from personal research on HR practices and practitioners carried out over several decades, some of it deriving from interview-based investigations but much of it coming from ethnographic participant research in corporate HR departments. The theoretical framing of this research evidence is especially important here. Merely reporting relatively 'raw' empirical evidence to support a negative does not in itself determine the argument that organizational research therefore shows certain things are unlikely to happen. Nevertheless, there is one fairly straightforward statement that is possible at this stage. I can say that after years of personal research on HR practitioners and practices, I have never witnessed a case of a significant employment management decision being influenced by ethical arguments expressed by an HR practitioner *in straightforward ethical terms*—without reference, that is, to the business/corporate advantages or disadvantages of acting in particular ways. This does not mean, as we shortly see, that HR managers are simply corporate lackeys, unable to exert any ethical influence whatsoever.

Ethical irrationality, unintended consequences, and HR decision-making

The first stage in considering the possibility of HR practitioners making ethical interventions in the conduct of business in their organizations must be to reflect on just what it is to 'be ethical'. The complexities of this are examined in various chapters of the present volume. For present purposes, and to cut through much of the standard discussion of the varying types of ethical scheme and the variety of criteria of ethicality available to managers and others, it is helpful to look to the analysis of Max Weber and his concern to understand the place of value-oriented actions in the 'modern' world. In some ways his thinking anticipates more recent postmodernist or post-structuralist ideas in his recognition that, as Willmott puts it (1998: 105), 'no set of values is intrinsically any better than any other', and that 'instead, there is an endless clashing of many competing and irreconcilable value orientations'.

At the core of Weber's notion (1949) of ethical irrationality is the belief that no ethical system can be established that will make every value consistent with every other or ensure that right actions always lead to right outcomes— or, indeed, wrong actions necessarily lead to wrong outcomes. This creates enormous problems for anyone trying to generalize about how HRM, or any other activity for that matter, can be made 'more ethical' in any incontestable manner. Weber wrote that 'it is not true that good can follow only from good and evil only from evil, but that often the opposite is true' (2005: 267). He reinforces this point powerfully: 'Anyone who fails to see this is, indeed, a political infant' (Weber 2005). Here we see the *axiological* dimension of the irrationality principle that the social world is full of different human goals, interests, purposes, and values and that these are often irreconcilable.

The relevance of this axiological principle to HR work can be illustrated with a set of events I observed and participated in when working in the HR department of an aerospace company. During some rather difficult business circumstances, a decision was required about how to handle the employment of a long-serving and very senior engineer who had, in the past, made innovations which had benefited the business considerably. With changes in technology, this individual's services were deemed to be no longer required. One senior director argued that it would be 'wrong' to make the man redundant given his deep loyalty and long-standing commitment to the company, together with the economically significant contributions he had made in the past. Another director, however, said it would be wrong to continue to give him what he called a 'dummy' job—an internal consultancy role which, in effect, added practically nothing to the effectiveness of the design function. This, it was argued, was morally dubious because it meant patronizing the individual and denying him the sort of satisfaction he would gain from doing 'a real job'. The decision was referred to the divisional HR manager with whom I was working.

Either solution to the problem of the ageing designer, we saw, could be defended as morally correct and each, equally, could be condemned as morally wrong. After considerable discussion, it was suggested, and eventually accepted, that the man be made a personal and highly confidential offer of a financial settlement that 'would reflect his outstanding contribution to the company' if he chose to resign from the business. And how was this justified? It was justified primarily on the grounds that the trend in the business was towards much tighter cost controls on the personnel front and that to keep the man in employment (distracting others from their main tasks, we were informed by a local personnel officer) would only delay the 'correct business decision' to bring about the departure of this employee. But does this mean that we, as HR managers, were ignoring moral issues which go beyond concerns of business expedience? Indeed not, we were taking into account the variety of competing value positions. And—rather importantly as far as I and my colleague were concerned—we felt *personally* that this was the right thing to do in broad ethical terms, given that the man was still young enough to get a job with another company. This was a possibility that would probably disappear if his departure were delayed and he became too old to get re-employed. Personal ethical criteria were being used by us as private individuals. But they were being used in conjunction with the business-oriented criteria which were formally presented in support of the formal HR decision.

The second dimension of Weber's ethical irrationality principle is the *paradox of consequences* (Albrow 1970). This recognizes that the means that are socially devised to achieve certain ends (e.g. bureaucratic structures) can readily come to undermine the very ends which they were devised to achieve. A clear example of how this can come about in HR work arose in the course of an ethnographic study of managerial life in a telecommunications development and manufacturing company (Watson 2001). This episode, not reported previously, involved the increased HR support provided to one of the largest employing departments on the site. It had been observed that a series of problems in this part of the factory, varying from poor quality work performance and disciplinary problems to high levels of labour turnover and minor shop-floor disputes, were coming to the attention of senior management. The explanation generally agreed among HR people and the senior line managers was that the managers within the department were lacking in 'people management' skills. Consequently, a personnel officer was directly attached to the department to support and develop the skills of this group of junior line managers. The person undertaking this task was well aware that she needed to avoid undermining the authority of the supervisory line and she also appreciated that a key part of her role was to develop the skills of these men. However, the outcomes were far from those intended. In Kay Rhodes' own words, in conversation with the researcher:

'I was determined to help these managers learn how to be better managers. But I think I have learned a lot more than they have. And what I think I have learned is the sheer impossibility of this job.'

'*Do you really mean that?*'

'Not really I suppose. But it has seemed that every time I achieve a step forward I get kicked two steps back. I think that I have excellent relationships with the managers here—at a personal level. Do you agree?'

'*They certainly don't seem to resent you personally, anyway. They love to talk about hating Personnel though.*'

'Oh yes, I pick that up all right. I thought this was just a wind up at first. But I reckon that much of the time they treat everything that I help them achieve as an excuse for them to do the next thing badly. I've tried so hard to avoid them getting dependent on me. But, the minute there's anything tricky to handle, they say "get Kay to sort it". When I tell them that I am there to help them do it themselves they sort of laugh and say "But we couldn't do it as well as you, Kay". Half the time they tell me—apparently sincerely—that I am brilliant. The other half of the time they say things like "Ooh we're not personnel, we couldn't handle that"'.

'*What's going to happen, then?*'

'I am going to talk to Martin about it. He might as well pull me out. OK, as an experienced HR person, I can solve a lot of the HR problems that come up in manufacturing. But a lot of the time, I fear, my presence is creating as many problems as it is solving. I've tried to develop these managers. But they would probably develop better if I weren't there—they'd bloody well have to learn for themselves, wouldn't they. A lot of what they have got to learn is how to treat the people who work for them as people. The bottom line is that they've just got to act as nicer people. They've got to treat people properly. As an HR person I can't do that for them.'

'*And you won't have a sense of failure if Martin does pull you out?*'

'I don't think so. Actually, I think it's the right thing to do. I feel, personally, that it would be the wrong thing to do to continue.'

'*How do you mean "the wrong thing"?*'

By holding the hands of those manufacturing supervisors and managers I am stopping them ever doing a good job for the business. Also—how can I put it?—I am taking responsibility away from them. I believe in respecting people's right to get it wrong as well as to get it right. Let them do what they are paid to do or look elsewhere for a job.'

There is a sting in the tail of Kay's last statement. There was a lot of emotion involved in the situation in which she found herself. But she is introducing various ethical criteria into the discussion. She talks of some of her personal ethical thinking—about giving people responsibility for their actions and, it would seem, about people fully deserving the pay they receive. Her personal values, however, are secondary to the business ones: it is the importance of these men's 'doing a good job for the business' that is given priority. That, however, is not the only point that emerges from this episode from the ethnographic study. This situation only arose because of the coming into play of the Weberian paradox of consequences: A formal HR presence in this part of the factory was intended to improve the quality of day-to-day management. The unintended consequence of its introduction was, however, to make things worse. As Kay put it in a later conversation: 'Everything about my going there was right. It was right for the business and it was right for the people. But it turned out to be wrong for the business, wrong for the staff, wrong for the manufacturing supervisors and, yes, wrong for me.' With the words 'right' and 'wrong', Kay is mixing together ethical principles and expedient considerations in a way that was observed more widely in the study of the company. Generally, the 'principles which appeared to underpin managers thinking' were ones which combined 'moral categories with pragmatic conceptions of what "will work"—what will work in the sense of helping managers carry out the tasks for which they are responsible' (Watson 1996). Ethical thinking, it would appear, is not something that researchers can readily separate from everyday practical managerial thinking. This is perhaps not surprising, given the irrationality of the world and the mass of competing values, interests, and understandings pointed to by Weber.

HR managers as the agents of industrial capitalist corporations

The analysis so far has established how ambiguous, muddled, and contradictory the role of ethical considerations is in HR work. There is no such simple matter as either the individual HR manager or the HR function becoming more ethical. Yet we have seen quite clearly that ethical considerations of various kinds come into play in the making of HR-related decisions. And individual managers are not without scope to throw into the mix of decision-making criteria some personal ethical considerations of their own. But the two cases we have seen so far would suggest that the potential here is limited. It is to the degree to which this potential is generally limited that we now turn. And to do this we need a theory of HR management which recognizes its role both as an institution at the level of an industrial capitalist political economy and as a function within work organizations. Let us consider the broader picture first.

The main argument of my study of the personnel occupation (Watson 1977) was that it can be understood sociologically as an institution of industrial capitalist societies which, alongside other institutions like trade unions and the state, helps deal with the conflicts, tensions, contradictions, and unintended consequences of a type of political economy at the centre of which is the institution of *employment and rational organization of free labour*. This is a way of organizing economic and social life which 'works'. But it has to be made to work: tensions, conflict, and contradictions which run through it have to be 'managed'. In later developments of this thinking (Watson 1986, 2006) it is argued that the central contradiction which HR helps to manage is that between the principles of *controlling* the activities of organizational employees (a principle which is inherent in the institutions of employment and the rational or bureaucratic organization of work) and the principles of *freedom*, *choice*, and *autonomy* that are implicit in the basic capitalist principle of free labour and the political institutions of democracy. Given this role in the world, we cannot expect HR managers to introduce ethical criteria *in their own terms* into decision-making. To manage all the conflicts and tensions with which they are concerned they will nevertheless have to deal with ethical and moral matters every day of their lives—but their task is one of dealing with ethical problems and demands that arise with respect of employment matters in the organization, not as ethical issues in their own right but in terms of their relevance to the longer-term continuation of the organization.

The main logic of managerial work in modern corporations is one of maintaining the long-term viability of the corporation which pays the managers—with issues like profitability, market share, service to the public, and so on, being means towards this rather than ends in themselves (Watson 2001, 2006; note the continuity between this type of analysis and that of Boxall and Purcell, as it was introduced by Pinnington, Macklin, and Campbell: pp. 1–20). The main task of HR people, their rationale, the logic of their existence is to 'keep the organizational show on the road'. It is not to bring ethical considerations that seem important or attractive to members of the HR occupation as private citizens or members of a professional body into the interplay of values and the conflicts of interest among the various constituencies with which the organization that employs them has a resource-dependent relationship. Managers are agents of the organizations which employ them and are bound, given the political-economic system within which they are working, to deal with labour 'in terms of the return that can be obtained from it', this meaning that an HR manager who 'deviated markedly from these criteria, putting employee welfare before (longer-term) organizational advantage, would be *failing to do their job*' (Watson 1977: 196). And the same conclusion can be drawn from reference to the classic identification of the key principles of bureaucratic organization (Weber 1978) which observes that the bureaucrat (and all managers are bureaucrats, in these terms) cannot treat their post as their own property or private territory. They are required to make all decisions and judgements impersonally and neutrally, without personal preference or prejudice. Bureaucracy, as du Gay (2000) emphasizes, has its own ethic—one which separates administrative work from the exercise of 'private moral absolutisms'.

It is important to stress that the above analysis is very much a sociological one. It identifies the basic logics or principles underlying the social institutions of modern societies and the bureaucratic work organizations within which HR managers operate. In practice, there will be considerable divergence from the ideal typical patterns which sociologists (and economists and political scientists for that matter) identify when characterizing different societal forms. We have already noted that the ambiguities of life in organizations are such that scope can be found for individual managers to bring personal ethical concerns into decision-making situations, at least at the margins. Also, it is becoming increasingly clear that strategic decisions in organizations are not simply reactions to structural circumstances and contingencies but are chosen by managers as part of a strategic *choice* process (Child 1972, 1997) in which personal values and preferences play a part. And strategists' own identities and life priorities influence strategy making generally (Schoenberger 1994) and with reference to HRM specifically (Watson 2004). The question of whether all of this gives HR people scope for anything more than marginal independent ethical action is something to which we will return. What it is vital to recognize, however, is that the basic systems and institutions within which HRM operates are ones which, in principle, formally rule out the right to introduce into HR decision-making and actions ethical criteria which are not consistent with corporate priorities.

Just what 'corporate priorities' are, in practice, is inevitably open to managerial interpretation. In principle, I have argued, these are ultimately a matter of working towards continuation of the organization into the longer term. This, however, still leaves scope for interpretation. But what were referred to as 'forces beyond our control' were pointed to as illustrating the limits which 'the system' puts upon moral choices made by managers in a recent interview with Kevin Musson, an HR manager from a large distribution business (an 'opportunistic' interview carried out with the present chapter in mind):

'I have to say that I have considerable moral qualms about some of the things we have been doing recently. I have spent a lot of my time on what amounts, if I can put it this way, to *culling* our middle managers. Now, let me say that I have been aware from the start that making people redundant, as well as sometimes sacking people for various offences, goes with the territory in HR management. Nobody these days thinks we are there primarily to look after people. We are business people first and foremost, with the people side of the business being our focus. OK? I can't say I have ever been happy taking people's jobs away from them. But I think I have been lucky for most of my career. I'm lucky because I have always seen the *need* for losing those people. A lot of us in this business... uhm.'

'*Your own business or the logistics business generally, Kevin?*'

"No, I mean the HR business. Sorry about that. Anyway, I am sure that a lot of us in HR justify the redundancies that we carry out by saying that if we don't lose a proportion of the current headcount now we will lose a lot more of them in the future. OK?'

'*Yes, you are saying that you have to lose the jobs of a minority to protect the jobs of the majority?*'

'You've obviously been there. Yeah, that's it. And that's been OK with me.'

'*And when you say "justify"—justify to whom?*'

'Obviously to the people that are going to lose out. But, yes, I think we justify what we are doing to ourselves in ways like this, don't we?'

'*I suppose we do. But I was interrupting. Do go on.*'

'Well, I think that we have a problem with such a justification in the present situation in our business—in our company, I mean. I know that my job is not one of providing people with jobs. But I feel strongly that if I can do this [provide jobs], and in doing it, help along the business that gives *me* a job then I am acting in accord with both my Christian values and my job demands. Now where was I?'

'*You were going to tell me about the new situation you are in.*'

'Thanks. I actually felt in a recent board meeting that I had to get up and say that the currently proposed redundancy exercise is quite immoral. It's not often that one is able to do this, is it?'

'*Why not?*'

'Come on, you've been there. We are not meant to talk like that are we? We are meant to be hard-headed businessmen in that room'.

'*But can't you be hard headed and ethical?*'

'Precisely. That's exactly it. I always try to be hard-headed and moral. What I am struggling to say here is that making these managers redundant is only hard-headed in City investor terms. Our board know damn well that our share price will suffer—and everything that follows from that (customer confidence and so on and so on)—if we don't cut costs somewhere. And people, especially middle managers these days, are an easy option, at first sight anyway. I ... er ... '

'*Go on.*'

'I can't say I was completely surprised but the CEO himself said he agreed with me that the cost-cutting was, as he put it, a "bit of blood letting" for the city. It was not really necessary for the business, given the orders that we feel fairly confident we are going to get in the next year. And, he went on, he could not see how we could make the sort of savings required in any other way than by cutting the managerial head count. "Right or wrong in our own eyes, we have got to do it", he said. That's it.'

'*That was the end of the argument?*'

'It was. "It's the system that we live in, like it or not", he went on. At least I'm gratified that he admitted that he didn't like it. I just had to go along with the idea of forces beyond our control.'

'*But you are left uncomfortable?*'

'Very.'

'*So what will you do?*'

'I think you know very well what I'll do. We do it a lot in HR, don't we, when we have to implement decisions we don't like.

'*OK, I think I can guess. But please put it in your words.*'

'Yes, I deal with my conscience by doing my damndest to make the redundancy as painless as I am able to do. I'll argue for the best possible terms and do as much as I can to help people find other jobs—before they actually leave here if I possibly can.'

As with the other HR managers we have heard from in this chapter, we see clear indications of ethical concerns on the part of the HR manager. We also see indication of Kevin Musson's desire to act ethically, within his own terms, as far as he is able to do. (We must note though that Kevin, although keen to imply that he is no different from other HR managers, is conscious that he is being interviewed about ethical matters. This may have coloured his account. Also, his Christianity is an important part of his personal identity, which may make him especially keen to accentuate his personal ethicality.) The main point that is illustrated by this interview, for the present argument, is the extent of the social structural or political-economic limitations upon managerial ethical choices.

HR, professionalism, and the battle for occupational legitimacy

In the interview segment with which this chapter opened, Bob Davern told us that if he were to tell his senior managers that his professional body [now the CIPD] 'would be unhappy with the company going down a certain line on employment matters on ethical grounds ... well, they'd send for the men in white coats'. This makes clear sense in the light of the emphasis given earlier to the fact that managers are employees of corporations who are paid to work to the bidding of their corporate employers. It is hard to imagine non-HR managers being very concerned with the ethical views of the HR colleagues' 'professional body'. Sociologically, the situation of the manager is utterly different from that of the archetypal professional, who was an independent fee-paid expert belonging to a professional body with an ethical code of conduct with which the practitioner either had to comply or lose their licence to practise (Millerson 1964). Over the past century, many occupations whose members lack this traditional self-employed status have sought to increase their social standing and their relative autonomy vis-à-vis employers by taking on certain characteristics of the old 'learned' professions (Abbott 1988; Freidson 2001; Larson 1991). And Personnel or HR management has been one of these occupations.

Professionalization has always been a double-edged sword for members of the HR occupation. It has all the status-giving attraction that is traditionally associated with membership of a qualifying association. But as Goldner and Ritti (1967) argued as far back as the 1960s, 'to be identified as part of a "profession" would preclude concurrent identification as general management' (1967: 493) and this statement had to be read in the light of the recognition that 'The history of personnel specialists as a group is the history of a struggle for status to become full members of the management team' (Anthony and Crichton 1969: 165). There is nothing to say that this situation has changed over the subsequent near half-century. The tensions between line and HR managers identified by Legge (1978) and Watson (1977) continue to exist

(Caldwell 2003). This can be explained sociologically, in structural terms. Much of the time HR specialists work *with* other managers to maintain control over employee activities and to maximize the corporate benefits to be derived from those activities. At other times, however, they find themselves working *against* line managers. Line or departmental managers are constantly faced with short-term and localized pressures. And this means that HR managers come to clash with them. This happens as a result of what we might call the essentially *strategic* function of an HR department which requires HR managers to consider the longer-term implications (as opposed to immediate problem-solving pressures) and more corporate implications (as opposed to local or sectional preferences) of human resourcing decisions and actions (Watson 1986, 2006).

Although we can identify structural reasons for the continuing tensions between line and HR managers, we need to give full recognition to the historical fight of personnel specialists to overcome their marginality—a marginality very much associated with the welfare associations of the occupation's history. The very hint that an HR manager might be some kind of 'do gooder' is, as much or more than ever it was, the kiss of death in terms of managerial credibility. And to talk of being a 'professional' who wanted to bring ethics to the boardroom table would be to risk an invitation to find the boardroom door—unless that introduction of ethical concern was one pertinent to the success or otherwise of the business. To talk of 'good behaviour' per se is to invite in the men in white coats that Davern talks of. As Reed (chapter 10) shows, the discourses and practices of 'professionalism' are not ones towards which we can in general realistically look for an injection of ethicality into the conduct of business and administration in the contemporary world. As I have shown elsewhere (Watson 2002) the UK HR manager's professional body has more or less reinvented itself in the process of gaining state recognition as a chartered body. Its Director General, in setting out the stall for what he aims to be 'a pathfinder for professional institutes in the twenty-first century', makes no reference to the ethical dimension of the older type of profession; for him the CIPD is 'a professional institute that adds value to its members in the performance of their jobs...' (Crabb 1999: 44). All its activities, it would seem, are aimed at helping its members to be better servants of those who employ them.

Conclusions

Altogether, it would appear that there is very limited, if any, scope for HR managers as individuals or as members of an organizational HR department or as members of an occupational association to intervene in organizational decisions and events to make decisions or actions more ethical per se. The reasons for this lie in part in the nature of ethical systems or schemes themselves, as social constructions devised by members of various cultures throughout the evolution of the human species to handle problems of order and existential challenge—schemes which, as a result of the very nature of the social world, both clash with each other and contain internal contradictions. There can be no absolute or incontestable notion of what is more or less ethical. But the difficulties with the idea of a more ethical HRM also relate to the nature of the industrial capitalist political economy and culture of which HR institutions are an element. HR managers are part of the control apparatus of employing organizations and they are paid to service those corporations. To bring in extraneous considerations into the daily managerial toil, whether these be ethical or any other kind of consideration, is to risk being marginalized, with all the career implications it has for the HR manager or the HR department. But note the use here of the word 'extraneous'. It is talk of ethics in the abstract ('abstract' in business terms) that gets the HR manager shown the door. Our sociological and structural analysis does not have to take us completely down the pathway of pessimism and determinism. There are two ways in which we can qualify the argument that HR managers cannot be looked to as a lever for making managerial and organizational work more ethical.

The first qualification to the basic case being made is to point out that ethical considerations are relevant, from beginning to end, to doing HR work. Every action affecting employees of the organization has an ethical dimension. Every pay rise that is envisaged has to be considered, in part, in terms of whether it is fair or unfair. Every appointment that is contemplated has to be considered, in part, in terms of equal opportunity criteria. Every job redesign or organizational restructuring that is planned has to be considered, in part, in terms of the ways in which it will enhance or worsen the quality of work life of the people who will fill those jobs and animate those structures. All of these considerations are alongside, or secondary to, the main 'business' considerations that enter this decision-making process. Or perhaps it is more realistic to say that, if they are to be considered at all, ethical issues are part and parcel of the business-oriented calculation. The HR manager must be sensitive to the fairness of the proposed pay deal because, if mistakes are made in this respect, employees may leave the organization or enter a grievance mode of action which undermines productive cooperation between managers and workers. Fairness for the HR manager is thus a business matter. The HR manager must think about how a new appointment is to be perceived by organizational members, again in terms of the costly grievances that might ensue if dissatisfactions are created, with a possible turning to the law which would risk bringing negative publicity to the employing organization. Equal opportunities are thus also a business matter for the HR manager. And the HR manager must look at the various gains and losses that employees are going to experience when jobs and structures are changed—yet again because of the risks of bringing about negative perceptions and consequent poorer performances. Qualities of work experience, issues of consultation versus unilateral action, possibilities of enhancing or harming trust relations are all business matters for the HR manager involved in organizational changes.

Organizations are resource dependent on many constituencies and the HR function has a particular responsibility for managing the organization's dependence on employee constituencies. Part of the managing of that dependency is dealing with the question of how ethical or otherwise the treatment of employees is perceived to be by various parties whose cooperation might be withdrawn if negative conclusions are drawn (e.g. employees themselves, the state, ethically concerned customers). But note the full logic of this: if an employing organization were to find no objections raised to its treating of its employees as semi-starved slaves, with the effect the workers continued to do the required work, state agencies raised no objections, and customers were untroubled by the experiences of the workers making their clothes or growing their food, then any HR manager raising ethical objections to such a regime would be a prime candidate for being escorted off the premises.

Again we see pessimism alongside the optimism. And if we remember that HR management occurs in organizations across the globe, with all the inequalities prevailing in an allegedly globalizing world scene, we come to recognize just what we are up against if the best that we can do is unsubtly to invite those managers to 'be more ethical, please'. But let us try to end on a relatively optimistic note. Throughout a predominantly structural analysis in this chapter we have encountered the possibilities of individual HR managers finding 'spaces' within the business-dominated decision-making in which they were engaged to bring to bear ethical considerations that were personally important to them. In a close study of one especially ethically self-aware manager (not, in this case, an HR specialist, however) I have shown the possibilities of the manager doing more than 'going with the flow' of the pressures coming from resource-dependent constituencies (Watson 2003). This relatively 'ethically assertive' manager looked for opportunities to pursue her personal environmentalist, humanist, and feminist ethical agenda through her work. But in every case where she has achieved anything in this respect, she insists that she did it by tying that ethically positive action to an action which she was able to persuade her senior managers would either be of benefit to the organization or would avoid dangers that the organization might get into. To this extent, then, we can possibly argue that HR managers might be more ethical and, where they can find an elective affinity between business interests and 'positive' ethical moves, they might be able, at the margins, to make the world a better place.

Ethically assertive managerial action can only be effective, it has to be reiterated, at the margins. Efforts to make serious changes in the ethicality of employment practices, this notwithstanding all the problems of the irrationality of the social world, must come from argument and debate within the democratic processes of the societies in which HR management operates, not from within HR itself. Matters of morality, ethics, and the pursuit of the good life are far too important to leave to HR managers.

14 Expanding ethical standards of HRM: necessary evils and the multiple dimensions of impact

Joshua D. Margolis, Adam M. Grant, and Andrew L. Molinsky

Ethical challenges abound in HRM. Each day, in the course of executing and communicating HR decisions, managers have the potential to change, shape, redirect, and fundamentally alter the course of other people's lives. Managers make hiring decisions that reward selected applicants with salaries, benefits, knowledge, and skills, but leave the remaining applicants bereft of these opportunities and advantages. Managers make promotion decisions that reward selected employees with raises, status, and responsibility, leaving other employees wondering about their future and their potential. Managers make firing and lay-off decisions in order to improve corporate performance, all the while harming the targeted individuals and even undermining the commitment and energy of the survivors. Even when managers complete performance appraisals and deliver performance feedback, they may inspire one employee and devastate another. For each HR practice, there are winners and there are losers: those who get the job, or receive a portfolio of benefits, and those who do not.

It is therefore a reality of organizational life that managers engage in acts that harm people. These tasks have important consequences for individuals, organizations, and society. Although individuals might prefer to avoid performing them altogether (Bazerman, Tenbrunsel, and Wade-Benzoni 1999; Folger and Skarlicki 1998; Tesser and Rosen 1975), failure to accomplish these tasks threatens the greater good for which they are intended. Failure to perform them also threatens to harm the welfare and dignity of the harmed parties (Bies 2001; Molinsky and Margolis 2005), as well as the HR professional's own sense of morality and professional competence. When the task constitutes a fundamental part of one's role or professional socialization, failure to get these tasks done, and done well, has an even larger effect on the person asked to perform them.

How can organizational scholarship be a useful guide for HR professionals who are called on to perform these ethically challenging tasks? One set of guidelines is provided by research on procedural justice, a term that refers to people's perceptions of how fair decision-making processes and interactions are (Brockner 2002). A central premise of procedural justice is that people must be treated in a consistent and equitable manner. That manner has been operationalized in at least three ways: (*a*) granting voice: giving those affected by a practice or outcome the opportunity to offer input (Folger 1977; Lind and Tyler 1988); (*b*) providing justifiable explanations to those affected by a practice or outcome, as well as information that the decisions and actions which brought about the practice or outcome were fair and unbiased (Bies and Shapiro 1988; Brockner, et al. 1990); and (*c*) interpersonal treatment that shows concern or compassion for those affected by a practice (Frost et al. 2000), which is sometimes deemed interactional justice (Bies and Moag 1986). Research has shown that when accorded procedural justice, people are more willing to accept negative outcomes and less likely to respond in a destructive manner (e.g. Greenberg 1990, 1993; Sheppard, Lewicki, and Minton 1992; Tyler 1999).

Procedural justice would appear to be an important ethical standard for guiding the practice of ethically challenging tasks, such as firing someone, delivering negative feedback, and denying bonuses—tasks in which a manager must cause pain or discomfort to another person in the name of a greater good (Molinsky and Margolis 2005). However, treating the recipient well is only one of the ethical challenges elicited by these tasks.

Managers face a crucial internal ethical challenge when called on to cause harm to another human being. Do they acknowledge the trade-off between harming one party and advancing the interests of others? Do they sustain uneasiness, even repugnance, about causing one person harm, about distributing benefits and opportunities to some and denying them to others—albeit in the name of an organizational objective—or do they suppress all questions and queasiness, rationalizing the harm in a way that erases doubt?

Where is the organization in this drama? That question introduces another ethical concern elicited by the distributive judgements HR practices entail. Organizational objectives carry moral weight, but it is easy for them to be eclipsed in discussions of managerial ethics. Organizational objectives may sometimes come at a cost to some human beings, but the capacity of an organization to function effectively may require HR practices that benefit some people and harm others. In wrestling with this trade-off, and in treating targeted individuals with procedural justice, managers doing the work of HRM may misplace the organizational objective itself—superior performance, better teamwork, or recognition of outstanding effort.

In this chapter, we propose an ethical compass to guide the work of HRM—in particular, those tasks in which harm is being done to another human being for the purpose of achieving a greater good. This ethical compass builds on previous research on procedural justice, extending it to the full range of ethical challenges elicited by these difficult tasks. We elaborate three ethical standards to guide HR practices, and we illuminate the conceptual and practical challenges entailed in meeting these standards. We then suggest some levers that can help managers move towards fulfilment of these standards.

We draw on two streams of research and theory to lay out the three ethical standards, the challenges they pose, and the levers for equipping managers to address the challenges and live up to the standards. One stream of research focuses on ethically challenging professional tasks deemed 'necessary evils' (Molinsky and Margolis 2005): tasks that entail causing harm to another human being in the name of a perceived greater good or purpose. These tasks call upon a professional to knowingly and intentionally cause psychological or physical harm to another human being in the service of achieving some perceived beneficial outcome. Necessary evils have important consequences for individuals, organizations, and society, but individuals often attempt to avoid performing them altogether (Bazerman, Tenbrunsel, and Wade-Benzoni 1999; Folger and Skarlicki 1998; Tesser and Rosen 1975). Research into how necessary evils are performed lends insight into ethical standards for guiding HRM and for realizing those standards in practice.

The second stream of research focuses on the other side of the ledger, positive impact (Grant, forthcoming). When performing a task, people who perceive the positive impact of their actions on other people end up experiencing a range of benefits (Grant, forthcoming; Grant et al., forthcoming). The challenge lies in raising HR managers' levels of awareness of the potential for their actions to positively affect others. That is no small challenge, we suggest, since HRM so often entails necessary evils that raise vexing questions about ethics.

Three ethical standards for HRM

We propose three ethical standards for governing HR practices. Each of these standards embodies a core principle and protects a prominent constituency whose interests and well-being hinge on the work of HRM. We first specify the standards, and then for each one, we explain its intended function, the constituency whose interests it protects, and the problems, both practical and conceptual, confronting the standard. We begin simply by proposing the three standards:

Standard # 1: *Advance the organization's objective.* Execute the task in question so that progress is made towards the objective that calls for it to be done in the first place.

Standard # 2: *Enhance the dignity of those harmed by the action.* When managers distribute opportunities and benefits, there are those who do not receive those opportunities and benefits—or who receive fewer than others. When companies go through cycles of destruction—restructuring, downsizing—individuals get harmed. In both instances, those who lose out are due treatment that respects their standing, fosters their resilience, and enables them to continue to function effectively.

Standard # 3: *Sustain the moral sensibility of those executing morally ambiguous tasks.* Someone must deliver the poor performance appraisal, announce the lay-off, or shutter the manufacturing facility. The ambivalence induced in performing these tasks reflects an underlying uneasiness about fair treatment and fair outcomes, and managers ought to remain attuned to that uneasiness.

To explain why we specify these three standards and what normative weight they carry, we now outline the function each is designed to serve, the constituencies to which it responds, and the problems posed in attempting to fulfill it.

STANDARD # 1: ADVANCE THE ORGANIZATION'S OBJECTIVE

It would seem to go without saying that hiring and firing decisions, performance appraisals, and even downsizings should serve a central organizational objective. However, it does tend to go unsaid, and even worse, in the doing of these tasks, the underlying organizational objective is often utterly misplaced. By making the organization's objective explicit, the aim of this ethical standard is to align the specific HR practice with a clear grasp of the objective it is designed to advance.

This ethical standard therefore serves two functions. First, it requires managers to identify the objective that their actions are intended to serve. It prompts careful consideration of the objective these practices serve, initiating a process of thoughtful due diligence to ensure that the purpose does warrant the practice. Imagine managers working in a company with a forced-ranking performance evaluation system. They must explain to those receiving below-average appraisals why they are ranked as they are. The need to deliver these negative appraisals does not itself make the practice wrong. It does make the practice difficult, and it does inflict emotional and material harm on some people. Clarity about the objective can help managers weigh the difficulty and harm, and it can push them to question whether the objective really necessitates the practice and whether the practice really advances the objective. Might there be alternative ways of advancing the objective? Perhaps not, or perhaps ways that are not as effective, but the process of clarifying the objective and questioning its connection to the practice solidifies the importance of the practice and aligns it with the objective it serves.

This ethical standard also serves a second function: it makes the underlying objective psychologically salient. Too often, legal requirements and administrative rituals shape HR practices, eclipsing the purpose those practices are meant to serve. The law certainly needs to be followed, and administrative routines certainly preserve consistency, but they are insufficient guides for action. When performing tasks that leave some people less well off or that fracture an organization as it goes through change, managers need a meaningful sense of direction.

In general, a clear and engaging direction tends to enhance motivation and performance in work tasks (Hackman 2002; Locke and Latham 1990, 2002), but it is even more essential in the painful side of HRM. Research on delivering bad news (Tesser, Rosen, and Tesser 1971) indicates that people simply avoid delivering it, perhaps anticipating the distress others will feel (Folger and Skarlicki 2001) or responding empathically to the experience of those being harmed (Molinsky and Margolis 2005). In general, it is reassuring to know that human beings cringe at the prospect of hurting others, but there are some purposes that require people to harm others, at least to some limited degree (Blass 1991; Milgram 1974). Making those purposes clear enables people to make sense of the harm they are doing, understanding what they are doing at a level of meaning that accentuates the larger purpose served (Vallacher and Wegner 1987).

Some might fear that this amounts to mere rationalization. The risk does exist that people will grasp for any purpose that can excuse otherwise questionable conduct. However, our aim in suggesting this ethical standard— advance the organization's objective—is to reduce the likelihood of rationalization and increase the likelihood of careful deliberation, of considered judgement in performing HR practices, so that even those that raise ethical questions have been checked against underlying goals. Necessary practices that have been weighed seriously against their intended organizational objective may nonetheless entail harm. Clarity about the underlying objective enables those performing these practices to connect psychologically to the objective and perform what otherwise would be experienced solely as a harmful task.

Advancing the organization's objective reflects the interests and needs of three central constituencies. It captures concern for those who benefit from the organization's ongoing and effective operation, typically owners, shareholders, clients, and employees. Terminating a contract employee, denying a promotion, or shutting a plant should all be designed to ensure the ongoing effective functioning of the organization. Presumably, the effective operation of the organization benefits those who continue to use its products and services, those who remain employed making those products and services, and those who gain economically from the company's production of those goods and services. In addition, advancing the organization's objective also provides a degree of protection for the harmed targets of HR practices. It ensures that serious thought and consideration have gone into why this practice and its outcomes are warranted. It also places boundaries around the harm that can be done, invoking managers to limit the harm to only that necessary to advance the now-salient objective.

Conceptual and practical challenges confront this standard. Conceptually, no matter how aligned hiring, firing, compensation, or appraisal practices are with an organizational objective, that objective might not justify the practice. Promoting or rewarding one person rather than others, or demoting an under-performing team member, may clearly serve the purpose of enhancing performance quality or productivity, but does that objective necessarily warrant the practice? In addition, the injunction to advance the organizational objective may focus effort and increase the likelihood that the practice will serve that objective, but seldom can we know with certainty ahead of time whether a practice will produce its intended consequence. Even in those instances when the objective unequivocally justifies the practice, what if the practice turns out not to advance the objective? Will a downsizing truly save a company, preserving shareholders' investment and other employees' jobs? What if it fails to do so? We simply cannot augur whether the desired outcome will emerge from the harmful action, or whether the distribution that leaves some better off and others worse off will indeed benefit the organization. And even if the benefit materializes, is it sufficient to justify the harm done?

The practical challenge follows from these conceptual dilemmas. Is it even possible for individuals in organizations to align their practices with under-lying organizational purposes? Much as managers might engage in what they experience as a conscientious process of aligning HR practices with organiza-tional purposes, managers might fall far short of actual alignment. Human faculties of deliberation are limited (March and Simon 1958), biases creep in (e.g. Tversky and Kahneman 1992), and time and other organizational demands constrain the extent of deliberation. It is impossible to generate all available options, construct the full set of options that may serve the desired objective while unleashing less harm, or even weigh whether a single practice advances its intended objective and whether that objective grants sufficient permission to perform the practice. The overwhelming power of institutional pressures (DiMaggio and Powell 1983; Dobbin and Sutton 1998) even suggests that the HR practices chosen are far less subject to deliberate choice. Rather, they are selected off-the-shelf of accepted or mandated routines and customs, and a convenient rationale follows, making them seem far more rationally chosen than they are (Dobbin and Sutton 1998; Haidt 2001).

Managers face another practical challenge when engaging in HR practices. The organizational objective can be misplaced altogether amid the storm of emotion and anxiety unleashed when bad news and bad outcomes must be delivered. The risk is great that the task itself will not get done (Bazerman, Tenbrunsel, and Wade-Benzoni 1999). The sway of raw visceral forces (Loewenstein 1996) in the moment of task execution may keep the manager from delivering candid feedback, announcing the true extent of the lay-off, or reporting the blunt fact of bonus distributions. The task may not get done and the organization's objective may fail to be advanced.

We do not deny these challenges. In fact, they motivate the introduction of this first ethical standard. The conceptual and practical challenges exist even without the first ethical standard in place. But insisting that HR practices should advance organizational objectives opens the possibility of a more intentional, mindful (Langer 1978; Weick, Sutcliffe, and Obstfeld 1999) approach to weighing and adopting specific practices. The first ethical standard cannot eliminate these challenges—organizational life makes these challenges endemic to HR practices. However, the second and third ethical standards address the inevitable presence of these challenges.

STANDARD # 2: ENHANCE THE DIGNITY OF THOSE HARMED BY THE ACTION

This second standard differs from and augments procedural justice in an important way. Procedural justice seeks to embody fundamental respect for human beings by treating people with just procedures. In so doing, theorists and researchers find that people abide by decisions and feel those decision outcomes were arrived at fairly. A premise of procedural justice is that people must be treated in a consistent and equitable manner. Research has shown that when accorded procedural justice, people are more willing to accept negative outcomes and less likely to respond in a destructive manner (e.g. Greenberg 1990, 1993; Lind et al. 2000; Sheppard, Lewicki, and Minton 1992; Tyler 1999).

Whereas procedural justice is foremost a defensive standard, designed to prevent the violation of rights and the impairment of human beings, dignity lays out an affirmative standard, designed to promote the effective functioning of human beings. Although dignity is often mentioned in discussions of procedural justice (Tyler and Lind 1992), here we use dignity to signify something distinct and specific. Dignity refers to individuals' capacities to exercise those faculties that identify a person as distinctively human, faculties that endow each human being with the capacity to develop and pursue purposes (Margolis 2001).

Dignity expands the lens of procedural justice. Procedural justice revolves around concern for harmed individuals' perceptions and experiences of the harmful act itself. The second ethical standard we propose revolves around harmed individuals' capacities to operate constructively *after* the harmful act. This second ethical standard serves a different function from procedural justice. Procedural justice functions to impart a sense of fairness and ensure acceptance of the outcome, thereby limiting potential repercussions and negative emotions for victims and witnesses. Dignity functions to preserve and restore the capacity of harmed individuals to act effectively. As suggested by research indicating that procedural justice has a more significant effect on negative emotions than it does on positive emotions (Weiss, Suckow, and Cropanzano 1999), procedural justice prevents the downside; conversely, dignity fosters the upside. Dignity focuses on preserving and enhancing the faculties and sense of identity people need in order to get on with life.

Why does this matter to HRM? When practices entail distributions, some will lose out on what is being distributed—jobs, promotions, opportunities, rewards. Focusing on dignity expands the distributive pie for those who end up worse off. They may be denied opportunities or have their jobs and lives disrupted, but attending to their dignity ensures that another good is distributed to them. Enhancing their dignity means equipping them with the ability to move on and restoring their sense of self-efficacy (Bandura 1997), so that they can cope with the blow, rebound, and move forward.

The challenges inherent in the first ethical standard also make this second standard especially important. In an imperfect world, managers do not have time to perfectly determine if a practice is indeed justified, and even if justified, whether it will indeed advance the organization's objective as intended. Certainly, managers can take actions to ensure that a worthy purpose is being advanced and that the organizational purpose warrants the harmful practice. However, the reality is that some people do end up with less in distributive decisions and that some people do carry the burden of displacement and restructuring—at times, even unjustifiably absorbing these negative outcomes. Dignity introduces a commitment to them, a responsibility to distribute to them the capacity to be creative agents in the aftermath of the harm. This is a compensatory standard, ensuring that those harmed by HR practices, however justifiably they may be harmed, emerge with their human faculties intact.

The conceptual difficulty of this second standard lies in its asymmetric function. Enhancing the dignity of victims does not redress the underlying wrong. A HR practice that harms one party to advance an organizational purpose might nonetheless still be unjustifiable or, worse yet, might in fact fail to advance the objective. How does preserving the dignity of targets speak to this problem? We acknowledge that it does not speak directly to the problem, but no practical solution can; the underlying ethical problem cannot be redressed. There will be instances when downsizing might not be ethically justified, even if it preserves a company, saves jobs, and permits a profit. The only option resides in asymmetric response, a response that (*a*) recognizes the realistic possibility of distributive injustice and the possibility that some people will be unjustifiably harmed and (*b*) responds to those possibilities through the distribution of alternative creative resources.

The practical problem with enhancing the dignity of those harmed by HR practices is that it is not easy to do. From the perspective of the target of harm, preserving their sense of self-efficacy and equipping them with skills and capabilities to move forward is akin to teaching people to swim *after* throwing them into the middle of a pool. The overwhelming sinking feeling of the experience makes it difficult to develop the skills and orientation that would prevent sinking (Zajonc 1965). From the perspective of those called upon to perform the harmful practice, it is challenging enough to deliver the harmful blow (Molinsky and Margolis 2005)—to deny opportunities or end relationships, for example. Amidst the welter of emotion, those doing the work of HRM must master the experience of the situation to respond appropriately to the harmed individuals. This is one of the most difficult tasks that a manager can face, and later we illuminate two mechanisms for helping managers meet this challenge.

STANDARD # 3: SUSTAIN THE MORAL SENSIBILITY OF THOSE EXECUTING MORALLY AMBIGUOUS TASKS

As the two prior standards indicate, HR practices focus foremost on the human beings they are intended to affect and on the organizations those practices serve. Human Resource practices rarely take into account the practitioners of HRM, whether a HR manager or a general manager. Although hiring, firing, promoting, appraising, rewarding, and restructuring are actively carried out by people, the people who perform these tasks have largely been neglected.

Neglecting the practitioners of HRM seems especially problematic because the enactment of HRM is both practically and ethically challenging. As we argued in proposing the first ethical standard, often HR practices raise irresolvable ethical conflicts, and as we suggested in proposing the second standard, performing HRM effectively may entail simultaneously delivering a blow and restoring the humanity of the person absorbing the blow. Tasks that remain morally ambiguous and that require opposing actions require at least some consideration of how those charged with these tasks can carry them out.

Our third ethical standard brings into consideration the people doing the work of HRM. The function of this third standard is to set out a criterion that recognizes the realistic psychological challenges confronting those who must implement HR practices. We propose that HR practices should be designed to help those who perform them to sustain their capacity to ask moral questions and to deliberate seriously, rather than reach for rationalizations and convenient escapes from responsibility.

Practices that distribute opportunities and advantages to some but not others, or that demolish aspects of a company in order to preserve or open opportunities, leave those performing these practices with a choice. They can live with the noxious feeling of dissonance, wondering, 'Do the gains really justify the harm I am doing?' Or they can release the dissonance by accepting the justifiability of the cost absorbed by those who lose out. Research indicates which way managers will lean: most human beings naturally seek to resolve cognitive dissonance (Cooper and Fazio 1984; Festinger 1957; Heider 1958; Schachter and Singer 1962). They will find it difficult to live with the possibility that a bonus was given to the wrong person, that a lay-off was not needed to save the company, or that a negative performance appraisal of one individual, even if it improved the team's performance, might have harmed the individual too significantly.

So, too, when dealing face-to-face with the human beings who lose out. The overwhelming cocktail of emotion experienced by those who deny the opportunity or impose the cost can drive the most conscientious HR practitioner either to dodge the task altogether or to do it in a manner that reduces his or her own anxiety (Molinsky and Margolis 2005). In these cases, the dignity of the target does not register, even as an afterthought. The pressures and psychological weight of the situation make one's own experience as the executioner the sole preoccupation.

To espouse ethical standards for guiding HRM requires attending to the experience of those who must perform the work of HRM. Our third ethical standard does not magically enable managers to live with ambivalence and satisfy heightened demands. It does, though, call attention to the experience of managers. It creates an imperative for designing HR practices so they foster the capability of HR practitioners. Specifically, this third ethical standard calls upon organizations to (*a*) foster HR practitioners' capacities to retain, rather than resolve, qualms and moral conflicts, and (*b*) provide means for HR practitioners to learn how to achieve multiple objectives when performing acts that affect others.

Human resource practices are difficult enough to devise, especially practices consistent with standards of morality. Introducing concern for the agent enacting those practices makes them more difficult to devise. Conceptually, it also raises the question of which party takes precedence: the organization, the target, or the practitioner? Whose concerns should anchor HR practices? Which of these ethical standards takes precedence? Our aim in introducing this third standard is not simply to complicate matters. Rather, the capabilities of the person performing the HR practice must be taken into account if the HR practice is to be performed proficiently and in accordance with ethical standards. Simply leaving the performer out of the picture does not remove the problem; it overlooks, and potentially exacerbates, the problem.

The practical challenge lies in equipping managers to perform unnatural acts. Human beings seek to evade or reduce noxious experiences, whether it is the dissonance of questionable practices or the anxiety of witnessing the target's experience. How can managers be equipped to live with negative emotions, with qualms, and with multiple demands to meet organizational needs and enhance the dignity of victims, yet remain capable of offering a job to one person and not others, deliver a performance review, and transfer jobs from one location to another?

One reason for introducing this ethical standard, much as with the other two, is to pose these questions. Where should the crafting of HR practices start—with concern for whom?—and how should HR professionals be equipped? We do not pretend to have answers. These ethical standards indicate the need for organizations to develop responses that protect the welfare of the organization, victims, and managers in order to address the ethical questions that HRM raises.

A family of ethical standards

The three standards function as an integrated set. The first insists that the purpose of the HR practice be considered and that the practice be carefully aligned to fulfil that purpose. This neither guarantees that the purpose indeed warrants the practice, nor that the practice will indeed fulfil the purpose. It does increase the likelihood that hiring one person rather than another, delivering negative feedback, or laying off part of the workforce will occur after deep consideration of both the purpose these practices are intended to serve and the cost of advancing that purpose through those practices.

Practices will no doubt be performed that fail to realize the purpose and, even in realizing the purpose, exact a toll on harmed parties. Thus, the second standard insists that the methods used to perform these HR practices provide some asymmetric compensation. The justifiability of HR practices that dole out gains and losses to some and benefits and wins to others cannot be guaranteed in the imperfect world of organizations. Since some people absorb the costs while others enjoy the benefits, then those who suffer the harmful, perhaps unjustified, consequences are due something in return. Our second ethical standard proposes that they be granted treatment that reinforces their creative potential.

Human resource management means meting out benefits to some and harms to others. The ethics of this work is destined to remain unresolved.

Every instance in the workplace is likely to be ambiguous; we cannot know if denying an applicant a job offer or firing an underperformer serves the organization well until the consequences tell us so, and even at that, we cannot determine if the organization's benefit warrants the harm done to those who lose out. How, then, can people live with the unresolved ethics of HR practices while performing those practices and extending special efforts for those negatively affected? Our third standard indicates that it begins with an ethical injunction to attend to the moral development of those called upon to perform these tasks.

The ethics of HRM is about more than treating people sensitively or being fair and measured. Human resource management entails consideration of the organization, the target of harms, and the HR managers themselves. There will certainly be trade-offs between these three standards, and those trade-offs merit attention in future conceptual and empirical work. For now, we close by drawing on two streams of research that indicate two levers that managers might use to begin making the three proposed standards more of a reality in organizations.

Levers of intervention

If the three proposed standards bring awareness to the broader ethical challenges embedded in HRM, how might those challenges be met? Drawing on two streams of research, we suggest two unconventional means of intervention. The first underscores the positive impact managers can have on others, even as they perform necessary evils that leave some people worse off. The second applies subtle shifts to the implicit identities people have when they are called upon to perform practices that have negative outcomes for others.

POSITIVE IMPACT

Grant (forthcoming) proposes that the relational design of work—structuring jobs and tasks with attention to their potential to foster interpersonal interactions and connections—can enable performers to become more aware of the impact of their actions on beneficiaries. Grant et al. (forthcoming) conducted three experiments to examine the effects of heightened contact with beneficiaries.

The first experiment took place in the field with callers responsible for soliciting alumni donations to a university. These donations provided student scholarships, but the callers had no contact with the students who were receiving these scholarships. Callers in the experimental condition read a letter by a student scholarship winner explaining how the scholarship had made a difference in his life, and then had the chance to ask him questions for five minutes. Callers in the control condition were not exposed to this brief intervention. One month after the intervention, over the course of one week, callers who met the beneficiary displayed significantly higher persistence (47% more minutes on the phone) and job performance (45% more pledges and 120% more donation money) than callers in the control condition. Compared with their baseline levels two weeks before the intervention, callers who met the beneficiary displayed significant increases in persistence (142% more minutes on the phone) and job performance (84% more pledges and 171% more donation money). Callers in the control condition did not change in persistence or job performance over this time period.

In another experiment, Grant and colleagues found that performers who merely saw a beneficiary, without interaction, spent more time on impactful tasks than performers who did not see the beneficiary. Performers also reported higher satisfaction with these tasks. Merely seeing a beneficiary was sufficient to motivate performers to care about the welfare of the beneficiary, which increased performers' task persistence and satisfaction. These findings suggest that contact with beneficiaries is highly motivating.

How might this be applied to circumstances when decisions distribute gains to some and losses to others—the classic situation of HRM? It is tempting to suggest that those doing the work of HRM be exposed as much as possible to the winners—those who get the job, receive the bonus or dividend, or keep their employment during a lay-off.

We suggest the contrary. Organizations can help HR managers perceive the benefits they can produce for the victims—the individuals harmed. That can then enable those doing the HRM, when in contact with those victims, to experience more palpably the benefit they are having. To put this in terms of our three ethical standards, if managers can be oriented to see their roles in terms of enhancing the dignity of those losing out (standard two), then they may be motivated to aid and assist those being harmed when in contact with them, thereby coming closer to fulfilling standard three, sustaining their own moral sensibility rather than withdrawing or resolving dissonance.

IDENTITY

How people implicitly see themselves has tremendous influence on their behaviour (e.g. Bargh and Chartrand 1999; Grube and Piliavin 2000; Nelson and Norton 2005). For example, a series of experiments we conducted indicates that in imperfect situations, implicitly seeing oneself as a helper rather than just as a messenger makes a significant difference in a person's conduct (Grant et al. 2006).

In two experiments, we primed half of the performers with prosocial identity using a scrambled sentence task that included words such as helping, compassionate, altruistic, and kind. The other half completed a control task. We then asked performers to deliver bad news: to write a letter informing honours thesis students that their thesis grants were being taken away. The organizational purpose was that the department was short on money and other students needed the funds. We varied procedural justice by informing one group that the process for deciding who would lose the scholarships was fair, and the other group that the process was biased (a faculty member chose to give the money to his own students). In the control condition, for which we did not manipulate the identity of participants, performers in the unfair condition felt worse and expressed more compassion in their letters than those in the fair condition. These results conformed to our predictions.

In the other condition, in which we primed participants' prosocial identity, prosocial identity actually reversed reactions to procedural justice. Performers whose prosocial identities were activated actually felt *worse* and expressed *more* compassion when the process was *fair* than when it was *unfair*. This result surprised us.

To understand this counter-intuitive result, we conducted a second experiment using the same design to examine whether the effect would recur with a different behavioural outcome: the degree to which performers would recommend that the department financially compensate the victims. We did indeed replicate the result of the first experiment. Performers in the control identity condition offered more compensation to the victims when the process was unfair, but the effect was reversed for performers whose prosocial identities were activated. When in a prosocial mindset, participants actually offered more compensation when the process was fair.

Further inquiry into the results—and into the mechanisms that account for those results—revealed the importance of identity and inferred roles. When prosocial identity is not activated, participants intuitively see themselves as messengers, focusing on *communicating* the bad news to victims. When the process is fair, these performers have a relatively easy time delivering the news of fair procedures. When the process is unfair, these performers' beliefs in a just world are threatened (Lerner and Miller 1978). They feel worse and attempt to compensate the victims in order to restore justice.

Alternatively, when prosocial identity is activated, participants intuitively see themselves as helpers, focusing on *assisting* the victims in coping with the news. When the process is unfair, performers have the opportunity to blame the unfair process as a reason for the victims being harmed. They grant assistance by explaining away the outcome. When the process is fair, performers lack an explanation to provide to the victims, and thus they cannot fulfil their inferred role of assisting the victims. Accordingly, they feel worse and attempt to compensate the victims in order to restore justice.

The results of these experiments suggest two important implications for managing the ethics of HR practices. First, examining the control identity condition, procedural justice can have divergent and counterproductive effects. Fair procedures result in a more comfortable experience for the performer, but those same fair procedures also reduce the performer's expression of interpersonal sensitivity to the victim; the unfair procedures, although psychologically taxing, increase interpersonal sensitivity. Second, a performer's identity drives his or her experience and execution of practices that entail harming another person. When procedures are unfair, a prosocial mindset helps those performing the harmful tasks express more interpersonal sensitivity.

Does this mean that organizations should jettison procedural justice? Not at all. Instead, our findings suggest that in a world in which even fair procedures do not guarantee ethical outcomes, it would be constructive to help those doing the work of HRM to see themselves as more than mere messengers. Sustaining managers' moral sensibility and orienting them to enhance the dignity of those affected negatively by HR practices may very well improve their capacity to deliver treatment experienced as affirmative and constructive. Some people are burdened with harmful and unfair outcomes that cannot be fully justified, and those doing the work of HRM, oriented correctly, can ease that blow.

Conclusion

We have proposed three ethical standards to guide the practice of HRM. Advancing the organization's purpose, enhancing the dignity of harmed parties, and sustaining the moral sensibility of those performing the task provide a small, simple, but illuminating set of standards. These standards highlight underlying ethical challenges that arise in performing the work of HRM, and they orient managers towards not only the targeted party, but also to themselves and to the organization as a whole. As important as procedural justice is, it becomes more powerful when standing alongside ethical standards that promote due consideration of organizational objectives, active efforts to promote the dignity of harmed parties, and care and development of the very people asked to perform the tasks of HRM.

15 Strategy, knowledge, appropriation, and ethics in HRM

Ken Kamoche

Managing people and knowledge 'strategically'

Are people valuable to the organization? Do they add value? Do they constitute a strategic asset? These are some of the questions that have shaped the HRM debate particularly in the last decade or so. They are important questions, and the associated debate has spawned an extensive literature which continues to bring us closer to understanding what it really means to manage people (Kamoche 2001; Legge 1995; Mabey, Salaman, and Storey 1998; Storey 1992). The interpretations of what is really happening in HRM range from the sceptical and cynical to the optimistic and laudatory. The debate now needs to go further, and in our view there are two interrelated questions that must be addressed more critically: first, how are organizations going about the task of appropriating the value inherent in HR; and, second, what are the ethical implications of these appropriative actions? Some authors are now recognizing that employees do not always willingly allow the organization to appropriate their knowledge (e.g. Currie and Kerrin 2003). We build on this argument and develop a more critical perspective of the problematic nature of appropriation including the ethical questions arising therefrom. The problematic nature of the appropriation of HR value has been highlighted in particular by Kamoche and Mueller (1998) who argue that the purpose and mechanics of appropriating value needed to be recognized more explicitly than has been the case so far if we are to grasp the full meaning of strategic HRM. In this chapter, attention shifts to the appropriation of knowledge and in particular tacit knowledge which is recognized as more difficult to manage and diffuse than the more visible forms of explicit/codified knowledge.

We begin by recognizing the pivotal role played by developments in the SHRM debate especially the role of the RBV. This is because an understanding of the dynamics of the creation, diffusion, and appropriation of knowledge attributable to HR requires that we appreciate how the rationale for appropriation has come about, whether it is recognized as such or not. Once it became clear, and generally accepted that HR constitute a source of strategic value which is appropriable by the organization, the knowledge HR generate inevitably came to be seen as potentially appropriable by the organization. This raises some difficulties because the organization's proprietorial claims over HR become equally controversial when applied to the knowledge they generate. These difficulties in turn assume an ethical dimension not only because the organization's claims to ownership over its workforce are suspect, but also because it is often not explicitly recognized that the workforce itself retains any proprietoral claims over the knowledge it generates. The extreme situation is one in which the organization seemingly rationalizes the appropriative exploitation of the vitality of people in a manner akin to vampirism, which Garrick and Clegg (2000) refer to as 'organizational gothic'. For our purposes the important question is how does the organization assume these appropriative powers, and on what basis are they legitimized to the exclusion of other relevant stakeholders, in particular the employees who are directly involved in generating knowledge? These are the issues that this chapter intends to grapple with.

The origins of the RBV can in fact be traced back to the work of Edith Penrose (1959) and even earlier. The debate remained dormant and only began to be revived in the early 1990s (e.g. Barney 1991), and went on to make a substantial impact, which predictably, began and stubbornly remained largely within the strategic management paradigm. This perspective has directly or indirectly shaped our views on the utilization of HR, especially with the gaining popularity of SHRM onwards from the late 1980s and early 1990s. As a result of these developments, HR increasingly came to be viewed as one of many different types of assets whose purpose is to facilitate the achievement of strategic objectives. Strategic objectives thus assumed preeminence, and have, over time, become the vehicle through which profitability and productivity are nurtured, measured, and realized. The inclusion of a strategic dimension within the HR discourse achieved a number of significant objectives. In addition to the more controversial views about enhancing the perceived status of HR practitioners and the HR function, it also reaffirmed the status of the HR as a valuable asset. This gave rise to the axiom 'human resources are our most important asset'. Some would argue, however, that given the flippant manner in which hire and fire decisions are made particularly in difficult economic times, this axiom is but an empty platitude. The ambiguity surrounding the question of what exactly is a resource has also spawned a number of interpretations which ultimately attach a notional monetary value to people. One example is the idea that people are valued only to the extent that they generate financially quantifiable outcomes. When they cease to justify themselves financially, they are considered as expendable as any other asset that has ran its course. If this makes economic sense on one level, it ignores the possibility that financial measures themselves may be faulty or inappropriate, particularly when it comes to the provision of services through tacit knowledge. How do we compute the financial value of an administrative clerk, a police officer on the beat, or an accountant for that matter? We explore the problematic nature of these interpretations in the sections that follow.

The human resource, human capital, and knowledge management

There is no denying that the strategic perspective played a remarkable role in highlighting the importance of people for the organization. In fact the very idea of strategy, a notion that is more readily applied to military manoeuvres as in the dictionary meaning—the art of planning operations in war—implies the skilful utilization of resources in the most efficient and effective way. This importance attaches primarily to the skills, competences, and knowledge people bring to the organization. The challenge for managers is thus cast in terms of how best to utilize these skills and competencies in order to achieve organizational ends. While this perspective might be seen as offering a new interpretation of the nature of human skills, it also reaffirms the view of labour as a factor of production. What is new about this 'people are an important asset' argument is that it does not restrict itself to shop-floor workers and those in the lower echelons of the organizational hierarchy. Instead, it encompasses a different section of the workforce, primarily the white collar and professional cadres. In fact until recently, many observers have been restricting their discussion on knowledge management to so-called knowledge-workers, that is technocrats and IT people, and in the process limiting themselves to the purely technical aspects of knowledge management which in fact merely boils down to information management.

The recognition that people constitute 'human capital' has fostered a resurgence of interest in how to 'manage' this resource in order to maximize benefits to the organization, while at the same time responding to the often complex needs of these individuals. The concept of human capital acknowledges that the skills and knowledge people bring to the organization have value in and of themselves (see also Nahapiet and Ghoshal 1998). The task for managers is to tap into this value and utilize it in the quest for attaining organizational objectives, and to help build a competitive advantage. This is achieved through the process of appropriation, which we consider in more detail below. The justification for tapping into this unique value is provided by the treatment of the resource as strategic, which also implies it is at the disposal of the organization.

This scenario is exemplified in the emerging debate on knowledge management, in particular the challenge of managing tacit knowledge (Nonaka and Takeuchi 1995; Schultz and Jobe 2001). The knowledge debate has developed along a number of directions, ranging from the earlier concerns with what it entailed (e.g. Nonaka 1994) and the importance of so-called knowledge-intensive firms and knowledge workers (Starbuck 1992), to questions about the unique problem posed by the tacit component (e.g. Kogut and Zander 1993; Schultz and Jobe 2001; Schultze and Stabell 2004), and the dimension of power and conflict (e.g. Alvesson and Karreman 2001; Hayes and Walsham 2000). While recognizing the difficulties involved in managing and diffusing knowledge flows that involve tacit knowledge, some commentators offer codification as a possible solution. For instance, Schultz and Jobe (2001) suggest that codification can be achieved through encoding knowledge in formulas, codes, expert systems, budget information, and so forth. Recognizing a human component to 'knowledge flows', they suggest that codification can also be achieved by depositing it in employees who visit or rotate between different subunits. These authors treat codification as a prerequisite for transmission, especially in the case of multinational firms. It is assumed that people will absorb and internalize these explicit artefacts of knowledge as they come into contact with different sections of the organization, interact with others, and as they engage with different processes.

Codification of course raises the prospect of 'involuntary transfer'. An important strand in the knowledge management debate therefore relates to how to protect organizational knowledge from dissipation or spillage. Scholars as well as managers recognize the need to protect this valuable resource and retain it within the organization using protective mechanisms such as patents, copyrights, and in the case of HR, the use of isolationism and physical controls (e.g. Liebeskind 1997). These developments in knowledge management have reignited debate on the critical question of how best to utilize existing resources for organizational ends. In the section below, we examine this question through the conceptual lens of appropriation.

The challenge of appropriation

Developments in the SHRM debate in recent years have brought to the fore the important question of appropriation. This question first took root in the early 1990s with the re-emergence of the RBV of the firm as noted above. It had of course always been recognized that it was in the firm's interest to seek to retain the added value from utilizing the resources available to it (Nelson and Winter 1982). In fact, this has been a central question throughout the history of economic thought and organized capitalism. In contemporary scholarship, much of the debate has taken place in strategic management and the management of innovation (Cohen and Levinthal 1990). The latter is particularly helpful for our purposes here because it deals with the embodiment and manifestation of knowledge through innovation.

As interest began to focus on the value of human capital and SHRM, it became apparent that the value inherent in HR was subject to dissipation and spillage if the firm did not take effective measures to appropriate such value. Kamoche and Mueller (1998) argue that the debate on the appropriation of HR must be preceded by a more fundamental question in organizational sociology, that is, why people participate in organizations in the first place. They call upon managers and scholars to recognize explicitly that the exercise of managing people 'strategically', is ultimately about appropriating the value derived from utilizing HR. If through their pronouncements and actions managers demonstrate that people are valued only to the extent that they contribute to measurable bottom-line outcomes, HRM as a function thus boils down to the appropriation of value from the human 'resource', or organizational gothic and the extraction of human vitality in Garrick and Clegg's terms (2000). Thus the strategic management of people as a process should not be couched in ambiguous terms that obscure the real purpose of managing people. It is important to call a spade a spade.

The appropriation process involves a plurality of stakeholders, and the extent to which each party can appropriate value depends, *inter alia*, on their relative bargaining power (Coff 1999). An even more accurate picture of the nature of appropriation has been emerging in recent years as attention shifts to knowledge management. It is becoming more evident that managing people is about extracting the skills and knowledge people possess and building these into the organizational productive processes. In the sections below we examine an important aspect of this process: the question of participating in the organization and consenting to transfer and share knowledge. Hence, to what extent is the individual a willing participant in the organization's efforts to extract his or her 'HR vitality' for the corporate good?

Knowledge diffusion and sharing

Nonaka and Takeuchi's study (1995) of knowledge creation in Japanese firms holds that the 'knowledge conversion' process is a social process between individuals, and is not confined solely within an individual. For these authors, the importance of social interaction and sharing cannot be overemphasized. It is taken as a given, while attention quickly shifts to the interaction between the various forms of knowledge, for example tacit and explicit. This perspective has fostered the impression that knowledge is created internally through intense social interaction and diffused throughout the organization by employees *willingly* sharing with workmates. It is assumed that the knowledge is so intricately intertwined with the knowledge-creators that it is meaningless to contemplate the need for a separate process of appropriating such knowledge. The appropriation process takes place both at the office and at informal 'brainstorming camps' such as those at Honda where participants (presumably all male) 'discuss difficult problems while drinking sake, sharing meals, and taking a bath together in a hot spring' (Nonaka and Takeuchi 1995). These scenarios also illustrate the notion of 'oversocialized' people responding to norms, values, beliefs, and attitudes developed consensually and internalized through socialization (Granovetter 1985).

These camps provide opportunities for sharing tacit knowledge and building trust. Versions of such gatherings and social activities can be found in other cultures and are not uniquely Japanese. The point to note is that the Japanese experience has led others to believe that bringing people together in these sorts of social contexts will automatically lead to knowledge-sharing. The idea of sharing knowledge *willingly* has subsequently come to be taken for granted by scholars who tend to ignore the very unique features of the Japanese industrial practices which render it feasible there and possibly untenable elsewhere. As Glisby and Holden (2003) point out, knowledge sharing and transfer in Japanese firms must be understood with reference to their embeddedness in Japanese social and organizational culture and related value systems.

The circumstances that facilitate widespread diffusion include the distinct possibility or explicit promise of lifetime employment, a high degree of commitment, extensive socialization, and relatively limited opportunities for cross-organizational knowledge diffusion through employee mobility. This latter is facilitated in part by a high degree of firm-specificity in the knowledge itself and the processes through which it is created. Where these circumstances do not hold, and where career advancement is typically individual or profession rather than organization-oriented, the appropriation of knowledge becomes a much more problematic issue than in the case of Japanese firms. Organizations in such environments are therefore likely to put in place more explicit mechanisms for protecting their knowledge from what they consider to be dysfunctional spillage or dissipation. Even so, the challenge of appropriation has not been fully understood within the HRM domain. While the work on employee surveillance and control (e.g. Ogbonna 1992) implicitly acknowledges the organization's need to guard against dysfunctional knowledge spillage, this is never explicitly recognized as a problem of appropriation. In a recent contribution, Currie and Kerrin (2003) observe that employees may be reluctant to share knowledge particularly if they fear this will hurt their careers, and also that organizations may be unable to appropriate knowledge that is situated in informal social groups. Theirs is a rare attempt to analyse the connection between employees sharing knowledge with each other and the contribution of HRM to knowledge management.

In the majority of cases, the problem is more likely to be framed in terms of protecting knowledge from appropriation by rivals. Both scholars and managers appear to be so preoccupied with the external competitive context that they have ignored the more complex equation defining the competitive and inherently contested organization–individual interface. In her analysis of protective institutional mechanisms, Liebeskind (1997) details the effectiveness and costs associated with rules, compensation schemes, and structural isolation vis-à-vis appropriation by rivals. While correctly recognizing that knowledge is embodied in employees and in the 'knowledge products' produced by employees, for example, plans, products, processes, and machinery, Liebeskind (1997: 625) argues that:

Much of this knowledge can be transmitted from one firm to another by moving either the knowledge products or the employees themselves. Thus, firms have both the motive for, and the means of appropriating knowledge from rivals.

This perspective deals with inter-firm appropriation and does not recognize the individual–organization appropriation interface, except to the extent that individuals are perceived as disinterested agents in the transmission of knowledge, not for their own use, but for the use of a rival organization. Therefore, this perspective endorses the dominant strategic management view underpinning the creation and utilization of knowledge: organizations retain the rights to knowledge and the individual's stake is immaterial. Tackling the appropriation issue exclusively at the inter-firm level ignores the very critical role individuals play or are likely to play in the knowledge creation, diffusion and utilization process, as well as facilitating and/or preventing inter-firm diffusion. This role can constitute an obstacle in the organization's appropriative efforts and it is erroneous to assume it can be addressed fully through the governance structures and protective mechanisms that Liebeskind (1997) considers appropriate for HR and products.

In large Japanese firms, it is presumed that people willingly share their knowledge with colleagues and do so with a view to making a contribution to the organization. It is suggested here that in non-Japanese organizations, this idea of willing contribution needs to be treated with more caution. In more individualistic contexts, and also where commitment to the organization is not considered so much of a 'fait accompli' as it is in large Japanese firms, individual choice cannot be wished away when it comes to sharing/participation. Even where you have coercive management, or where highly directive leadership styles and lack of empowerment appear to negate individual choice (in any sort of organization, including Japanese), individuals often retain some degree of discretion on the nature of their contribution to the organizational purpose, that is to the corporate good. This is simply because the organization cannot exercise absolute control over individuals' choices and actions. This leads to the question how willing are individuals to share their knowledge with other organizational members for the good of the organization? The nature of tacit knowledge lends itself to a certain degree of ambiguity in this respect. Tacit knowledge is said to have a 'personal nature' (Polanyi 1967), is manifest in action, and has a distributed character (Blackler 1995; Tsoukas 1996). Tacit knowledge is difficult to formalize and communicate, thus rendering it sticky (von Hippel 1994). We can apply this notion more generally to work itself. In developing their notion of work as disputed terrain, Kruger, Kruse, and Caprile (2002: 203) argue that:

the capacity to work (and therefore the work actually performed by individuals) is not divisible, because work is an important constituent of personal identity and the individual's participation in life in its widest sense.

This characterization of work has important implications for the management of knowledge vis-à-vis industrial and labour relations. For example, when management undertake work re-organization and other forms of organizational change, the impact is not only felt in operational workplace outcomes but also in the changes to the forms and degrees of control workers have over the work process and hence over the knowledge creation process, or work process knowledge. Individuals therefore emerge as agents with a capacity to shape the work flow process and *ipso facto*, a capacity to impact on knowledge diffusion. The polarities, real or potential, between the individual and the organization as regards the execution of work and knowledge diffusion are made more complex by the fact that work is attached to personal identity, and the choices are not as clear-cut as merely spelling out the individuals' respective duties and obligations. The appropriation regime thus goes beyond structure and hierarchy, and embraces questions like motivation and commitment (Kirkpatrick and Ackroyd 2003).

Individual motivation has an important role in determining the extent to which an individual is prepared to contribute effort and knowledge towards organizational objectives. Therefore, managers need to appreciate what individuals want and how the perceptions about the way they are treated affect their choices, in particular how they position themselves in the appropriation regime. Efforts to explain motivation range from transaction cost economics with its emphasis on opportunism and self-interest and the need for institutional mechanisms (Williamson 1985) to the concern with more intrinsic and behavioural perspectives which introduce notions like psychological contracts and identification with the firm (Rousseau 1995). Furthermore, withholding tacit knowledge is likely to involve the more complex issue of shirking and free riding (Kandel and Lazear 1992). In this case, Osterloh and Frey (2000: 545) argue that employees cannot be identified and sanctioned if they hold back their tacit knowledge, and therefore, 'an intrinsic motivation to generate and transfer tacit knowledge cannot be compelled but can only be enabled under suitable conditions. By its nature, intrinsic motivation is always voluntary'.

A question of ethics

In recent years, more attention has been given to ethics in the HRM domain. The initial developments appear to have taken place in the broader domain of business ethics (e.g. Donaldson 1989; Snell 1993). The debate has received further impetus following a spate of widely publicized business and financial scandals in the financial capitals of the West. These are merely the tip of the iceberg; corruption, misuse, and outright theft of corporate assets, abuse of high office, and greed are common features of business around the world. In this chapter, our specific concern is how the emergent developments in ethics in HRM resonate, if at all, with the appropriation of knowledge. We can begin by noting that the business ethics debate has revolved around the obligations business has towards specific stakeholders and the society at large.

The issue of how ethics or an ethical dimension can be fostered amongst managers has been one of the more prominent themes (e.g. Snell 1993) especially where there are serious concerns about widespread corruption and other questionable business practices. In understanding the connection between ethics and HRM, there still remains much work to be done. Researchers have been grappling with the philosophical roots of the ethical dimension, and ways in which an ethical dimension can be built into the HRM debate (e.g. Legge 1995; Miller 1996; Winstanley and Woodall 2000b). Others have focused their attention on the ethical dilemmas faced by HR specialists and how they resolve these dilemmas that result from business demands (e.g. Foote and Robinson 1999; Snell 1996). Similarly, Foote (2001) found that organizational values have an impact on ethical behaviour yet there are issues of ethical inconsistency and even hypocrisy in the link between values and the management of people in charities. According to Winstanley and Woodall (2000a: 5), the debates on ethical perspectives pertain largely to business ethics and 'only touch on employee interests as one of several stakeholders or only to the extent that employees might suffer adversely in terms of health and personal integrity as a consequence of their role in producing the organization's goods and services'.

These authors seek to show that given the neglect of the ethical perspective by HRM, both HR academics and professionals should concern themselves with raising ethical awareness and sensitivity. However, creating greater awareness and sensitivity is easier said than done. This is particularly difficult to achieve across the organization in its entirety, and has led some observers to the conclusion that the HR function is the right place to locate the conscience of the organization and therefore the most appropriate locale for assembling and disseminating this elusive ethical dimension. For example, Woodd (1997) sees HR professionals as playing a crucial role by virtue of their input into policy design and implementation. She urges HR professionals to take on the responsibility of raising awareness, facilitating learning, and ensuring that high standards of ethical conduct are maintained and implemented through HR policies and practices. This argument echoes the assumption that the HR function is the conscience of the organization. It however, raises an important question: where does that leave small and medium-sized firms with no distinct HR or personnel function? Employees in such firms tend to be prone to abuse particularly in sweatshops and family owned firms which are also typically non-unionized. An additional problem with this 'conscience-of-the-organization' scenario is that locating the responsibility for ethical behaviour in one function potentially absolves other managers from any such responsibility, and yet it is the line and senior managers themselves whose actions/decisions actively drive the organization.

In fact when we consider the extent to which the HR leadership is routinely ignored or relegated to an advisory role (in spite of claims that HR is a strategic partner), it is doubtful whether senior (line) managers will listen to HR managers pontificate on ethical issues. In an organization where the HR officers are not accustomed to being heard on matters of critical, long-term strategic interest, why should we expect things to be any different when it comes to business ethics? Such efforts are more likely to succeed when they are spearheaded by the top management because it is the top management that sets the ethical climate for an organization's business activities, much as it does corporate culture. Connock and Johns (1995) make a similar point when they comment on the ethical responsibilities of all managers in general.

Ford and Harding (2003: 1145) argue the case for bringing the study of emotions into the management theory debate. They do so by exploring the ethical circumstances surrounding the apparently inhumane treatment of managers by organizations going through mergers. They propose the need for axiological models of ethics to be applied to HRM, that is 'models containing an ethic of value which validates feeling rather than purpose or duty and represents forms of care that a person might take in life' (Ford and Harding 2003: 1145). Their analysis also serves as a critique of researchers and managers who are implicated—in the view of these authors—in organizations' lack of ethics by focusing only on the economic consequences of managerial action. Their critique may well be legitimate; however, it echoes concerns that have been raised before. For example, Legge (1998) has questioned whether the management of people can be truly ethical. In other words, can HR seriously address issues like rights, justice, fairness, and trust? The evidence seems to suggest that the emphasis is on organizational commitment, unitarist ideology, and the pursuit of power through utilitarian instrumentalism (see also Townley 2004). In an earlier contribution, Legge saw this as the triumph of the technical-scientific (bureaucratic control) over the notion of management as moral order (Gowler and Legge 1983).

In the 'real world' is a 'care ethic' (Ford and Harding 2003) therefore tenable? The evidence would suggest that the ethical dimension is pursued because it makes good business sense. The argument goes that it is not sufficient for managers to be cognizant of the ramifications of their actions and those of their organizations for the society at large; instead they must pursue an ethical dimension because it serves the strategic and financial interests of their organizations in addition to enhancing the managers' own careers. In this regard, Watson (2003: 172) argues that:

> For an organization to survive into the long-term, its managers cannot afford to lose the support of the state, public opinion, communication media, and, especially, clients and customers. If it offends what journalists take to be important moral values, it is likely to suffer damaging publicity. If it offends social moralities embedded in state legislation, it is likely to be punished and possibly put out of business by the law. If it ethically offends employees and potential employees, it may find itself without the labour resources and commitment it requires to stay in operation. And if customers see the organization in a morally offensive way, they may take their trade elsewhere.

The argument above seeks to highlight the commercial sense of being ethical, which would challenge the significance of the notion of 'caring' as proposed by Ford and Harding (2003). In his paper, Watson (2003) analyses the views of a manager who is steadfast in offering 'business grounds' as a rationale for making the morally correct decisions and arguing against those he or she perceives to be morally untenable. This perspective effectively combines utilitarian (actions compatible with commercial interests), deontological (relating to fairness), and emotivist principles of ethics. In the literature, the utilitarian perspective features prominently, thus underpinning the centrality of business interests in the pursuit of the ethical dimension. Hence, an ethical perspective is pursued because it is commercially expedient, not because of other reasons which are likely to be morally ambiguous and which might run against or even contravene personal, cultural, and possibly religious preferences. The message seems to be: 'Let's keep it simple, if it's good for business, let's do it'.

Relating this to our theme of appropriation, it becomes evident that the pragmatism inherent in the 'business interests' argument is consistent with the rational approach to the justification of interest in HR as 'strategic assets' and the subsequent preoccupation with codification of knowledge. As we argue above, people are valued in the organization because they are perceived as strategic assets, and this rationale in turn serves to justify investments in training and development, empowerment, and all those other initiatives currently associated with enlightened or progressive management. It is often argued that the functionality and desirability of these initiatives can be verified through empirical observation and quantitative analysis. Typically, this means that to the extent that it can be demonstrated that HR add value, they earn the right to be treated as valuable. This argument was pivotal in the earlier phases of SHRM in the 1980s when personnel practitioners struggled to attain recognition for their function. It is not surprising that this argument has continued to underpin the emergent knowledge management debate, and as we have shown above, the ethical perspective as well.

As far as the knowledge debate is concerned, the weight given to codified and codifiable knowledge vis-à-vis tacit knowledge once more highlights the significance of the tangible and empirically verifiable, which echoes Gowler and Legge's 'techno-scientific' perspective (1983). This is in keeping with positivistic thinking and is pragmatic from a business perspective. It reminds us that even where reference is made to other supposedly important stakeholders, ultimately, business interests are defined very narrowly, and pertain largely if not primarily to shareholder interests. This leads us to an important question: how is the process of unilateral and unidimensional appropriation legitimized? We have observed that the pursuit of business objectives offers a rationale for the strategic management of people, which in turn demonstrates the extent to which people are considered a valued resource. Similarly, organizations appear to be guided largely by pragmatic, objective, and measurable reasons in the pursuit of business ethics.

Taken together, these two scenarios point to the suggestion that the appropriation of value (or human vitality) is legitimized on unitarist and clearly pragmatic grounds in which ethical considerations are distilled to the purely utilitarian. This appears to offer little scope for the consideration of other stakeholders except to the extent that business interests are maintained. Furthermore, it demonstrates how objectivity in performance parameters legitimizes asymmetrical power relations. Power formally embedded and institutionalized in the higher echelons of the organizational structure enables top management to determine both what constitutes knowledge and how the outcomes of the utilization of that knowledge are measured and distributed. Organizational members engaging in the creation and utilization of knowledge are, ultimately, relegated to serving the interests of enterprise and for them, the ethical question about unilateral appropriation remains unresolved.

This has important implications for the development of the ethical perspective in management and academic research. It suggests that the utilitarian perspective will remain predominant: to managers, the argument that an ethical perspective is good for business is more compelling than any pressures to display social responsibility for its own sake or indeed to ensure fairness in HR practices. In fact, these latter two acquire more weight if they themselves can be shown to be good for business. This view echoes the scepticism often expressed about similar management initiatives. Regarding initiatives like gain-sharing, empowerment, teamwork, and so forth, and what they have achieved for the intended beneficiaries, I have argued elsewhere (Kamoche 2001: 13) that:

The evidence is patchy and inconclusive....Part of the difficulty lies in the non-measurability of these initiatives, which may perhaps lead some to disregard the initiatives altogether as wishy-washy. On the other hand, there is a danger in taking on practices in order to be seen to be caring, or simply because the practice is 'flavour of the month'.

Similar questions need to be asked about ethics with regard to knowledge management and the implications for managing HR, and managers' motives for engaging with this ethical perspective. Knowledge management has now become a buzzword that helps refocus attention on performativity and competitive advantage, especially where objectively identifiable artefacts of knowledge are concerned, hence explicit or codified knowledge. We argue here that tacit knowledge will attract increasing attention because of its inherent qualities of causal ambiguity and 'personal nature' (Polanyi 1967), which pose a challenge of appropriation to the organization since the individual does not manifest his or her knowledge to the extent that the organization might require. Thus, tacit knowledge emerges as a potential source of competitive advantage, and since questions have been raised in the literature about the ability of management theory to deal exhaustively with issues of fairness, rights, and justice, as cited above, it is conceivable and worrying, that the appropriation regimes that will emerge will likely be built on shaky ethical foundations.

Conclusion

The scepticism in the argument above does not mean a genuine ethical perspective is untenable in the knowledge creation and diffusion exercise. It is achievable, but will require hard work and a willingness to question the organization's monolithic dominance in the knowledge creation and appropriation process. It will require managers and academics to rethink the assumptions currently underpinning appropriation. Managers in particular will need to reconsider the multifaceted nature of knowledge and the fact that the tacit component in particular is closely tied to the identity of the person.

It is unrealistic to expect, and hence ethically questionable, that knowledge can be extracted from an individual, as though it were a commodity, or that the willingness to engage in knowledge creation and diffusion on the part of the individual can be taken for granted. We have noted above that the Japanese experience offers interesting lessons but is culturally bounded and has little relevance in organizations that instrumentally place their own appropriative needs above those of their employees. In order to ensure fairness in the appropriation regime, it may be helpful for managers to offer specific incentives for people to share knowledge as well as to tackle the obstacles that so often prevent people from developing the sense of belonging that would facilitate this proactive contribution.

These obstacles are deeply rooted in the workplace, both in the private and public sectors, partly through tight competitive and financial pressures which have subsequently institutionalized a culture of cost management. They include the lack of job security, the failure to invest in training and development, the failure to provide real opportunities for creative input beyond the rhetoric of empowerment, and the deeply held beliefs by managers that employees cannot be trusted to work without close supervision and with strict management controls. As Currie and Kerrin (2003) point out, sharing knowledge cannot be engendered by merely creating 'informal' communities; such communities come about through voluntary participation. It is not surprising that in the absence of effective mechanisms to foster, protect, and reward the willing contribution of knowledge by employees, managers easily retreat behind the protective shield of utilitarian thinking.

16 The morally decent HR manager

Rob Macklin

Introduction

In this chapter, my aim is to help HR managers who wish to be decent and who wish to defend ethical decision-making. In order to do this, I describe the theory developed by the moral philosopher, Agnes Heller (especially 1987*a*, 1988, 1990, and 1996) and argue that her approach could be of use to HR managers who wish to be decent people when fulfilling their roles.

The rationale behind this chapter can be traced back to my experiences as a young HR officer and four events in particular. The first, a comment by an IR manager: 'the important thing is to have a good memory so that you don't contradict the lies you have told'. The second involved an interview for a vacant position in a plant that the personnel manager, to whom I reported, and I knew would probably soon close. At the end of his interview, the best applicant asked about job security (he had been retrenched over a short period of time from several positions). My manager answered that he could never give guarantees but implied the job was secure. The applicant took the job and was retrenched within a year. The third involved the 'on the spot sacking' of a supervisor by a senior manager after I complained that the supervisor had nearly created an industrial dispute. The manager subsequently told me the supervisor had an alcohol problem, thus, the sacking was necessary. The fourth event involved a senior manager demanding that I only employ men in production positions. I said this was illegal, he replied, 'yes, but you will nevertheless find a way to only employ men'.

Academic life has allowed me to reflect on my experiences and on whether the 'right' thing was done in each case. My intuition told me that it is better to tell the truth, that I should care for someone who has personal problems, and that I should uphold the principle of equal opportunity. But, I was also aware of claims that sometimes one has to make tough decisions, that the interests of the company must be paramount, and efficiency and profitability must be the dominant values. Since becoming an academic, I have asked HR managers who were also my students whether they have had similar experiences. Many had, and all acknowledged that HR management is an area where ethical dilemmas are ubiquitous and where people often face difficult moral decisions. Most said some guidance on how to do the right thing would be of great help.

I therefore turned to moral philosophy for guidance that I could give students and HR managers. However, moral philosophy is not a unified field with a single set of 'ready to hand' answers on how to do the right thing. It is rife with debate and polarized points of view. Debates about the foundations of morality, the extent to which there are universal moral norms and principles, and how any moral theory should portray the 'self' are ongoing. Given these difficulties, I set myself the task of finding a moral theory that adequately addresses the debates in moral philosophy and that has the capacity to be of use to HR managers seeking advice on how to be decent. After some investigation, I discovered Agnes Heller's work and suggest that it provides a way through the debates as well as a set of usable guidelines. I discussed her ideas in depth with a selection of HR managers and concluded that her moral philosophy would be of use to them, which I endeavour to demonstrate in this chapter. I interviewed twenty-three HR managers employed by Australian companies across a range of industries. The interviews explored the roles HR managers play, the goals they pursue, the moral norms and principles they follow, and the difficulties they face in trying to ensure justice and morality in HR management.

Moral problems faced by HR managers

Based on in-depth interviews (Macklin 1999), I suggest that HR managers find it hard to ensure just and moral processes in their organizations and that moral conflicts are frequent. In broad terms the reasons identified by the HR managers I spoke to for the difficulties in ensuring justice and morality included ambiguous criteria; partiality and discrimination; non-compliance with process; cynicism and poor training; the place of HRM in the organization; organizational history, culture, structure, and location; and the growth of the economic or performance imperative. Of special importance here, is the place of HRM. In organizations with a strong HR presence and especially a strategic input, it was suggested by many of my interviewees that they can wield more influence and thus have the power to ensure some level of justice and morality. Where this was not the case there is little that HR managers can do. In this regard, one HR manager spoke of HR professionals who are frequently members of interview panels and yet are unable to ensure justice because their hierarchical position means that it is easy for other managers to overrule or ignore them.

Senior HR managers argued that justice and morality is hard to guarantee, regardless of how entrenched they are in senior management circles and positions. The reason for this it was claimed has much to do with the fact that HR managers are but one decision-maker among many in an organization and are not the sole purveyors of justice. Responsibility for all decision-making is not in their hands but is diffused amongst many people. Moreover, their decisions are sometimes overruled and their advice sometimes ignored by CEOs and managing directors. In addition, part of the problem has to do with there being so many things 'lumped' under HR. This was particularly the case, it was argued, for HR managers who are generalists managing all facets of the HR function. Finally, it was also suggested that the 'will' and 'skill' of HR managers is very important to their capacity to achieve moral outcomes and processes.

Nevertheless, the HR managers I interviewed also stated that they are not powerless. In most cases while they may not possess much *formal* authority, their capacity to influence is significant. My interviewees suggested that the basis of HR managers' capacity to shape decisions varies, but four interrelated factors are common: their identification as 'experts' in people management, their ability to package agendas and messages in acceptable language, high interpersonal skills, and high levels of credibility.

Turning to moral conflicts, the HR managers tended to identify three broad dilemmas: clashes between justice and care, morality (including justice) and organizational performance, and confidentiality and honesty or openness. The interviewees claimed that clashes between the demands of justice (as fairness) and the need to care for particular individuals are major tensions. Ensuring absolute fairness between individuals *and* providing real care for a particular individual is difficult to achieve. Being just means being blind to the individual's particular needs, and caring adequately for one person can mean being unfair to many others.

Most of the HR managers also acknowledged that organizational performance as an ultimate goal is increasing in importance in HRM. For some, this undermines moral norms: they clash with performance and performance takes precedence. All saw the performance imperative as inexorable and while a few were supportive of its increasing priority, many were ambivalent about it and it was clearly an area of moral tension.

HR managers identified two types of clashes between confidentiality and honesty/openness. First, they spoke of the tension they feel when employees raise personal issues they wish to be kept confidential. This leads to moral conflict if the information could have an effect on company operations. The HR manager is torn between keeping a confidence and passing the information on to other managers. The second situation involves HR managers being privy to confidential information about impending company decisions. This creates dilemmas for HR managers when they talk to employees who may be affected or who ask about rumours they have heard.

It was clear from my interviews that all these areas, because they can lead to a compromising of moral norms, are causes of stress for HR managers.

Moreover, in discussing the pressure to compromise morality, many of the HR managers indicated that they would only go so far: that at some point they must 'draw a line in the sand'. The point at which this line is drawn varied across the HR managers interviewed and most said it was hard to draw a sharp line. They all strongly affirmed a desire to act decently but it was clear that knowing whether morality is at risk and, if it is, what a decent course of action is, is difficult to discern. This is an area where guidance can be helpful.

Agnes Heller's work as a path through debates in moral philosophy

Without undertaking an exhaustive review (see Macklin 2001 for a fuller description), any account of ethics should, in my view, address at least three contemporary debates in moral philosophy: debates about the foundations of morality, the universality of ethics, and the constitution of the self. The debate about foundations focuses on whether it is possible to ground morality outside human construction and whether an individual can assert moral claims as more than statements of personal preference. The debate about universality is concerned with the question of whether it is possible to identify or construct moral principles that are capable of applying universally to any human communities. Finally, the debate about the constitution of the self focuses on the relationship between the 'self' and community and at its extremes whether the self is prior to community or if it is the community that defines the self.

In broad terms, Agnes Heller has written her philosophy with a commitment to taking into account the situation and context that people face in contemporary societies. She seeks to provide a framework that allows for diversity and pluralism, recognizes the socially embedded nature of morality and still affords a basis for critique.

More specifically, and with respect to the foundations of morality, Heller does not rely on thick descriptions of the natural ends or goods of human life. She identifies in a number of places (see especially Heller 1987*a*, 1985) the development of endowments into talents and emotional depth in personal attachments as essential elements of the good life. In a later work (1996) she discusses the beautiful or sublime character and love which also points towards the importance of talents and emotional depth. However, they are not for Heller the direct foundations of morality. For her, decency is fundamental to a good life, but she does not contend that people should be decent because it will help them achieve a good life. In this sense, Heller's approach is not teleological or consequentialist. An act does not become moral simply because it will maximize the development of a person's endowments into talents or lead to greater depth in their personal relationships. Some acts with these good consequences may actually be immoral because they breach important moral norms.

Nor does Heller adopt a utilitarian orientation towards the grounding of morals. Indeed, in *A Philosophy of Morals* (1990: 144–5) she explicitly rejects a utilitarian moral philosophy:

> …a utilitarian moral philosophy is singularly unfit to provide general guidelines for decent persons who pose the question 'What is the right thing for me to do?'. And it is on the basis of my conviction that I state that the safest way to resist temptation is to figure out whether or not participation in an action or institution will allow you to live, think and behave in accordance with the principles, norms and maxims to which you otherwise subscribe.

However, in avoiding teleological approaches to grounding ethics, Heller does not ignore some of the insights that can be derived from classical approaches such as Aristotelian virtues ethics. Thus for example, Heller (1990: 64–5) speaks of the importance of virtues, which she roughly defines as 'character traits that predispose persons to promote and support as well as maintain certain values (common goods)', and as the 'backbone of a decent course of conduct' (1990: 70). With respect to morality or decency, virtues predispose us to do the right things. That is, they help us to be decent people. However, Heller departs from Aristotle (1941, 1984) in that she does not equate virtues with 'pre-established behavioural patterns, … "forms" into which the raw material of a person may be moulded' (1990: 70). That is, virtues and vices are not to be linked with one particular depiction of what amounts to a good life. Different people can have very different views about what constitutes a good life while simultaneously holding very similar views about what constitutes virtuous behaviour.

Heller also does not seek to develop a view that tries to quarantine community values or build an objective moral theory standing outside history. In this respect, she does not follow Kant by trying to transcendentally deduce moral maxims or Rawls (1971) by hypothetical deliberations behind a veil of ignorance. She does though discuss and advocate, akin to Habermas (1984), a principle of universalization for generating norms of social and political justice (see Heller 1987*b*). However, she does not use this principle as a base for grounding morality, nor as a mechanism for generating moral maxims. For Heller, moral maxims and norms are generated historically and dialectically. Thus, Heller's approach tends towards communitarianism: morality is embedded in historical and communally shared meanings.

However, Heller does not ignore the insights that can be provided by the classic works of writers such as Kant. In this respect, for example, she gives particular prominence to Kant's means–ends formula:

If he had formulated nothing else, Kant would remain the greatest genius of modern philosophy. He found the fundamental maxim (or imperative) from which all others spring. One can fully subscribe to this formula without knowing anything at all about Kant's philosophy. One need not understand its philosophical foundations in order to endorse the simplest, the most radical, the clearest and most sublime universal one can dream of, which prescribes that one should never use another person as a mere means but also an end. (1990: 105)

In applauding this maxim, however, Heller is not supporting or adopting Kant's broader philosophical approach. Her argument is that the means–ends formula was not invented by Kant so much as found by him. It is a historically devised, communally shared norm to which Kant provided his philosophical support.

In adopting a more communitarian perspective, Heller does not argue that morality can be understood only within the borders of particular communities. She claims that some moral norms do transcend communities and that there are universals to which all modern and decent people attend. Here Heller is somewhat in accord with writers such as Bok (1995), Walzer (1994), and Young (1990). However, she does not go so far as to ground her moral theory in the existence of universal moral norms and values that cover the community of humankind. Rather, for Heller it is the existence of decent people, who in modern societies must live with contingency, that grounds morality. Decency survives here and now not because it meets teleological ends, nor because it accords with reason, nor because we all blindly accept certain norms and values. It survives due to the existence of decent people who prefer to follow moral norms rather than break them and, indeed, would prefer to suffer wrong than breach norms. It is in the existence of such decent people that Heller grounds morality: morality survives because decent people exist.

For Heller it is better to suffer wrong rather than commit wrong. For Heller this is a confession of faith for which the decent person does not require any proof. Here, she comes close to articulating the more postmodern theme articulated by writers such as John Caputo (1993). However, she goes further by discussing the notion of an 'existential choice' that authentic moderns must make.

For Heller (see particularly 1993 and 1990) people in modern societies face a historico-social contingency. While everybody is born with a bundle of genetic capacities contingent upon who their parents are, people born into modern societies do not face a preset social role or *telos* already marked out for them by their parents' location in society. The situation into which a person is thrown conditions their chances of successfully choosing a particular pattern of life but nonetheless in modern societies no child is born into a socially predetermined role.

The consequence of historico-social contingency is that the modern person must choose a *telos* if he or she does not wish to lead a purely contingent life. The modern person thus must make an existential choice. This choice is not about instrumental rationality, it is a means and an end in itself. And one of the fundamental choices a person can make is the existential choice of decency. According to Heller, a person can make an existential choice under two broad categories: the category of difference and/or the category of universality. More particularly, a choice under the category of *difference* is the choice of a particular calling or cause that defines that person's life and destiny. Choosing under the category of the *universal* is to choose oneself as a decent person. A choice under the category of difference is a choice that separates individuals from each other. Everyone, she argues can choose to become or destine themselves to be a decent person.

This involves a person committing to being decent and in so doing choosing to accept themselves as they are. That is, in choosing decency we also choose to accept all our 'determinations, circumstances, talents, assets, infirmities: we choose our ill fate and good fate—in short everything that we are' (Heller 1990: 14). It also involves a person striving to have no compulsions built into their character and thus to take responsibility for all of their actions. This does not mean the existential choice should be understood in absolute terms: you either chose yourself entirely or you have not chosen at all (see Heller 1996). For Heller, decent people may choose themselves, but not completely: they may be blind to some of their frailties and on occasions they may lapse into inauthenticity. Moreover, the choice need not be a momentous episode but can involve a gradual dawning of awareness. It is not necessary for a person to recall significant validating episodes or well-thought steps to prove to themselves or others that they have chosen. The choice is proven in a person's behaviour as he or she struggles to be himself or herself.

Thus, morality exists because decent people exist and decent people exist because they have made an existential choice to suffer wrong if faced with the alternative of committing wrong.

Turning to the debate on universality, Heller recognizes that norms and values vary significantly across communities but, nevertheless, states that there are moral universals that all decent people in modern societies use to question or reject other normative criteria. The universal norms and values are largely orientative and abstract and thus are interpreted and followed in somewhat different ways. This means decent people do not submissively abide by norms and values. They discuss and deliberate on them in order to decide which to follow in particular situations and thus how to act.

The inclusion of discussion in decision-making here is important because it suggests that the decent person need not rely on his or her own resources when working out what to do. This is important because for Heller the existence of a plurality of communities, a diversity of norms, and the ultimate contingency of all decisions in modern societies complicates the task of the person who wishes to be decent. Decent people do not automatically know the right thing to do. They need support to help them to be decent. They turn to others for advice and in discussing what is right and wrong they find moral universals that can span modern and diverse communities.

It is from being part of such discussions herself that enables Heller to propose the universal norms and principles described in her books. These norms and principles are guidelines that she, as a moral philosopher, and as a person who also faces contingency, has identified and articulated through discussion with people who strive to be decent. They are not commandments but guidelines that people who have chosen themselves to be decent are party to developing and which they and all decent people can consult.

Thus, Heller's moral theory recognizes and transcends modern communities and does so without pretending to stand outside human construction. In making this point, however, Heller argues that it is important not to depict universal moral norms and values as governing the totality and minutiae of every moral decision that a person makes. Here Heller, in accord with postmodernists, claims that ultimately it is the individual alone who decides and is responsible. Every decision is a leap, not based solely on knowledge or rational choice; no moral principle can take us all the way. But as Heller states it is nevertheless imperative for most of us to have 'crutches' and this is where moral norms and values can be of use. They will not eliminate contingency or risk but they can help us to be the decent persons that we want to be. And importantly they allow us to evaluate a set of guidelines that HR managers in modern societies might be able to use.

Heller, provides quite robust guidelines, and meets a concern I have for providing HR managers with guidelines that are not so thin as to be of little practical use. Heller's books (particularly 1990 and 1987a), describe and articulate a large number of universals. The guidelines include an orientative principle of care, a constitutive moral principle (the means–ends formula), a maxim of justice, norms of giving and receiving, moral maxims, ultimate values, and a selection of virtues and vices, and values. In Table 16.1, I set out examples of some of the norms and maxims she suggests, which I have adapted to the HR manager's context.

Importantly, her catalogue is not a closed set to which nothing can be added or taken away. As Heller states of her orientative principle of care: 'I do not pretend to offer a catalogue of all principles' (1990: 44). Rather she suggests that '(e)very decent person can correct me as well as add his or her own principle to the list' (1990: 44). She also invites other people to add to her list of maxims. It is in accord with these invitations that I have evaluated Heller's moral philosophy and with this spirit that I have adopted her norms and principles. The example set out in Table 16.1 and my fuller catalogue reproduced elsewhere is a summary of what Heller has written, cast

Table 16.1. Sample of Heller's norms and maxims adapted for the HR manager's context

The Universal Orientative Principle of Care in Organizations

1. Have a proper regard for employees' vulnerability.
   (a) Do not offend employees in their person and in anything they hold dear.
   (b) Be civil and urbane, and learn to appropriately express your feelings towards employees.
   (c) Help employees to save face.

2. Have a proper regard for employees' autonomy.
   (a) Do not violate an employee's body.
   (b) Do not violate an employee's soul.
   (c) Do not manipulate employees.
   (d) Do not keep employees in tutelage.
   (e) Help employees achieve greater autonomy.

3. Have a proper regard for employees' morality.
   (a) If your opinion holds weight in the deliberations of employees you must warn them every time they embark on a wrong, bad, criminal, or evil course of action. Moreover every time the application of norms is flawed, you should stand up to protect the cause of justice.
   (b) Pay attention to the moral merit of employees.
   (c) Learn how and when to pass moral judgements on employees.
   (d) Learn when to forget and when to remember.

4. Have a proper regard for employees' suffering.
   (a) A decent manager notices the suffering of others.
   (b) A decent manager does his or her best to alleviate another person's sufferings.

5. Have a proper regard for the value of each employee*
   (a) Give credit to each employee for his or her contributions and opinions.
   (b) Foster each employee's sense of self-worth and esteem.

The 'Maxim of Justice'

Consistently and continuously apply the same norms and values to each and every employee member of the (organizational, divisional, departmental, occupational, professional, trade, or other) cluster to which the rules and norms apply.

Moral Maxims

The categorical and orientative universal maxim—never treat an employee as a mere means but also as an end in himself or herself.

1. *Categorical* (prohibitive): never commit acts, follow norms and values, join/remain in organizations that by definition or in principle use employees as mere means.
2. *Orientative*: never treat an employee as a mere means but also as an end in himself or herself.

First-order Maxims

Prohibitive Maxims

1. Do not choose maxims (or norms) which cannot be made public.
2. Do not choose values (or norms) the observance of which involves in principle the use of employees as mere means.
3. Do not choose moral norms (binding norms) the observance of which is not an end-in-itself.

Imperative Maxims

1. Give equal recognition to all employees as free and rational beings.
2. Recognize all human needs except those the satisfaction of which in principle involves the use of employees as mere means.
3. Respect (give esteem to, admire) employees only according to their (moral) merits and virtues.

*This principle is an addition to Heller's work.

in words relevant to HR managers and with a few added norms derived from my interviews with HR managers (Macklin 1999). The norms, principles, and maxims are primarily adapted from Heller (1990) Chapter 2 (for those in Table 16.1 see pages 44–9, 55, 107–8 and 111) and the full catalogue of my adaptation of her norms, principles, and maxims can be obtained from me.

I offer the catalogue as a set of potential guidelines but also as a starting point for further discussion by HR managers who wish to be decent. I suggest that decent HR managers as a group need to fashion their own moral supports and this catalogue could be a starting point for this task.

I fear the way I have set out the principles would overstretch Heller's patience. The discussion of principles in *A Philosophy of Morals* (1990) is more narrative in orientation and sometimes avoids the specification of lists, perhaps because of the importance Heller places on 'good judgement'. Heller argues that no ethical decision can be governed fully by detailed principles. Nevertheless, I have reproduced lists here because I wish to provide principles for HR managers that I think they might be able to refer to when they feel the need. It is in this spirit that I offer the catalogue, as an adaptation of her work.

Turning finally to the debates about the constitution of the self, Heller goes beyond the dichotomy of a completely encumbered or unencumbered self by suggesting that no individual is a simple subsystem of society or completely independent from it. She provides a differentiated view of the self that stresses, *inter alia*, every normal individual's *relative* moral autonomy. In Heller's view, we are not unfettered by the moral norms of our community but neither are we so encumbered that we cannot critically reflect on and resist or change them. We are neither absolutely autonomous nor absolutely heteronomous: we live with relative moral autonomy. And, by relative moral autonomy she means a person does not automatically obey every concrete norm but confirms them as valid or not with their conscience and guided by abstract norms and values. Individuals are able to compare their actions with those of others and to assess critically actions from the perspective of abstract norms, maxims, and values. This can involve an internal dialogue within the self, or a discussion or debate with others. Thus, the decent person is a person whose actions are not determined by concrete norms and values or by self-interests or blind passions. Rather the choice they have made to act in accord with norms and values they accept as good, determines their actions. Moreover, relative moral autonomy presupposes relative moral heteronomy. The decent person by virtue of being a decent person is subject to situational constraints that mean they must carry out some acts of moral relevance that they would not be willing to carry out if nothing constrained them. That is, decent people have to face situations where to follow moral norms means they must choose to suffer wrong rather than do wrong.

The efficacy of Agnes Heller's moral theory to HR managers

While I believe Heller provides an effective response to contemporary philosophical debates I also think that in the realm of applied ethics one must go beyond the philosophically robust to questions about the 'defendability' of an approach in everyday life. So is Heller's approach likely to be of use to HR managers who want to be decent and who wish to defend or advocate a moral approach? This is an important question for anyone seeking to help HR managers because, as indicated earlier, the HR managers I interviewed suggest that many HR managers rely on influence rather than formal authority when trying to ensure moral decision-making by others. They must persuade, defend, and justify rather than insist, order, and demand.

My interviews also suggest that many HR managers seek to justify good ethics by linking it to increased economic performance. While such appeals seem very politic, I worry about their sincerity and vulnerability. The impression I get from some HR managers is that they believe a positive link between being decent and high performance is not provable but nevertheless use it as an argument because they are committed to the pursuit of decency. The idea of promoting ethics using a possibly dishonest argument is problematic. Also of concern is the vulnerability of the argument. I can envisage a situation where HR managers are called to account on this claim—'You say good ethics is good for business. Prove it!' It may be the case that in some circumstances the claim can be substantiated, but I would be hesitant to universalize it. I suggest therefore that HR managers need to offer other justifications. My question is, can Heller provide some; is her approach to grounding ethics likely to be of use to HR managers? The answer I think is 'yes' for several reasons.

First, the basis on which Heller's moral philosophy rests is not a deduction from a posited fact of human nature, transcendental reasoning or a hypothetical discussion behind a veil of ignorance, nor is it an ideal speech act. Rather, it rests on reflections on the lives and discussions of people who live in modern societies. That is, her moral guidelines are not derived from or justified by abstractions distant from HR managers' everyday lives, rather they rest in the actions of people in their own societies. They are guidelines HR managers can justify by simply saying, 'This is what the decent person does in our society today.' They do not have to take themselves or their listener to positions unencumbered by community in order to prove that the guidelines are built on a solid base. The grounding is useful to HR managers because it is one they can easily understand and to which they can readily point to.

This is a real advantage. As I describe in Macklin (1999), according to the HR managers interviewed a real difficulty they face is getting other managers to do the right thing. Justifying to other managers that they should follow certain moral principles because they accord with unencumbered reason seems to me to be inherently more complicated than asserting that they should follow the principles because that is what decent people in the manager's own organization and wider community do. To say to resistant managers that they should follow a principle because 'it accords with what a group of people in an original position deliberating behind a veil of ignorance would agree to,' I suggest, is unlikely to succeed. The distance such a justification would have from the everyday life of the manager is likely to be far too great. The image of the decent person embedded in that manager's own community does not have to cross such a divide and is likely to be more persuasive.

Second, and related to the above, HR managers are likely to find Heller's approach useful because it appeals to principles that have emerged over time in discussions between decent people and thus it enables HR managers to point to the widespread acceptance of such principles within their community. Helpfully, the appeal will also be based in claims that the principles are universally embedded across modern societies and can be used because they are a part of the culture and history of such societies. This I suggest will be more convincing than arguments that they should be followed because they stand outside every community's history and culture.

Further support for the efficacy of Heller's argument here is that, given her guidelines are derived from discussion with decent people in modern societies, it is likely they will resonate in the lives of HR managers and that of managers they interact with. HR managers will be advocating principles that are not foreign to them nor to other managers. Research that I have undertaken (see Macklin 2001, 2003a) shows that many of Heller's norms and principles are similar to those advocated by HR managers and that they identify with many of the other norms and principles put to them from Heller's list.

Third, Heller's moral theory is useful to HR managers because it takes seriously the existence of moral diversity, but provides guidelines for accommodating differences. By articulating moral norms and maxims that span the cultural and moral diversity of modern societies, Heller provides a framework that enables HR managers to accept diversity but nevertheless make decisions or advocate conduct that transcend it. It was clear from my interviews that it is important for HR managers to accept diversity and not deride or judge individuals for their different beliefs, values, and needs. Heller's framework allows them to do this. However, it was also clear that HR managers have to draw a line at some point and Heller's universal norms, maxims, and values help them to do this as well. For example, when faced with tension between a diversity of behaviours and the call for some common code of behaviour, HR managers can use Heller's universals to make judgements about what behaviour they should support.

This aspect of Heller's approach would strengthen further the arguments of HR managers trying to influence others to do the 'right thing'. It does not require them to ignore diversity and demand people follow a closed set of concrete norms and values. Such a demand in modern organizations where often people have diverse backgrounds would likely create significant levels of resistance. Rather, the appeal will acknowledge and recognize the different values people hold and the various ways people wish to behave while, nevertheless, advocating the importance of not breaching certain overarching norms. These norms because they are universal in modern communities are likely to resonate with the many people HR managers must deal with and, thus, are less likely to generate strong resistance.

Fourth, Heller's reliance on the idea of an existential choice will be useful to HR managers because it does not require them to engage in lengthy and heated debate about *why* someone should do the right thing. For example, as Heller asserts we live in an age where many question the authority of religion. Expecting *all* HR managers to adopt and successfully advocate a set of moral norms and values because they represent the word of God is, I suspect, somewhat unrealistic. Many people demand more earth-bound reasons. As stated earlier, many HR managers appear to rely on the assumption that good ethics pay and this is an earth-bound reason. However, as I have argued, such a claim is at least suspect, for some HR managers too optimistic, and at the very least, requires stronger moral inquiry and justification.

The idea of decency taken as a matter of existential choice does not require appeals to religion or to empirical verification that decency will 'pay-off'. Moreover, it is an appeal to what I suspect is a commonly held view that one should do the right thing because to not do so means being untrue to oneself, lacking integrity, or undermining one's own dignity. In the interviews I held, HR managers made links between the idea of existential choice and upholding their own values. They argued that they would find it difficult to live with themselves if they did not do the right thing. In addition, integrity was identified as an important moral norm and defined, *inter alia*, as about holding onto and following one's own ethical values.

Adding to the usefulness of Heller's approach to HR managers here is that while the existential choice does not require an appeal to the divine it does not exclude such arguments. Heller suggests in *An Ethics of Personality* (1996) that many moral philosophies, be they religious or secular, can serve as a crutch. The central concept is that being decent is a fundamental choice. If such a choice is aided by a person's theology, so much the better. This I suggest opens the door for religious HR managers to accept Heller's approach to grounding morality. They might argue that ultimately choosing to be decent is about choosing to live with God's will, but clearly this does not undermine the importance of the moral choice. Likewise, I suggest that it increases the likelihood that the HR manager's advice will be taken seriously by other managers whose morality is theologically grounded. Finally, Heller's approach does not exclude a partial and measured appeal to possible benefits in performance terms of doing the right thing in certain circumstances. Again, the central concept is that being decent is a fundamental choice. If such a choice also can be legitimately shown to improve company performance then so much the better.

Despite all that has been said it is unrealistic to argue that Heller's approach to grounding ethics will be of use to all HR managers. Fundamentally, the natural addressee of her moral philosophy is the person who has chosen decency. It would be naive therefore to expect all HR managers to be interested in decency and it would be naive to expect all other managers to value it. In some cases, despite the power of decent HR managers' arguments, their pleas will be ignored. Heller's moral philosophy is designed for people who want to be decent. It is not designed to persuade people who see no value in decency to do the right thing.

This incapacity need not be seen as a serious weakness of the theory. Heller (1990) argues that decent people are not rare. I agree and contend that they will be found at all levels in any company. Nevertheless, the limitations must not be underplayed. Heller's moral philosophy will only be of use to HR managers who have chosen to be decent and who ask the question 'What is the right thing to do?' Further, most decent HR managers undoubtedly at some point in their careers must work within organizations that give them little room to move and will, as I did, face individuals who will not respond to their pleas. Decent HR managers will then be left with questions about what they should do next. Heller recognizes this as a possibility confronting all decent people and discusses how they can deal with such situations. She also discusses how decent people can deal with the difficult choices that must be made when two or more moral norms clash. Elsewhere (Macklin 2003*b*), I have reshaped some of this discussion into a set of guidelines for HR managers to consider, discuss, and possibly use. As with the catalogue of moral norms, these guides should be seen as crutches. They do not take away the responsibility for decision-making or the need to leap at some point and they should not be used in a mechanical way.

Conclusion

In this chapter, I have argued that the moral theory developed by the moral philosopher Agnes Heller provides an approach that addresses important debates in moral philosophy and is of potential use to HR managers who want to be decent and who wish to defend or advocate ethical decision-making. Heller provides an approach that is committed to taking into account the situation and context that people face in contemporary societies. It is a framework that allows for diversity and critique, while also recognizing the embedded nature of morality. Consequently, I think it is well suited for use by HR managers working in modern western societies.

It is acknowledged that Heller's moral theory will not meet the needs of all decent HR managers. It is all very well for me to use Heller's approach to say to HR managers that here is an argument that will always help you effectively prioritize moral considerations in all deliberations. However, I am no longer an HR manager having to face resistant managers and sometimes more senior ones, while worrying about my career prospects, my mortgage, or my family responsibilities. Heller suggests that being decent means preferring to suffer wrong rather than to cause wrong to others. She also argues that decent people will remain decent despite the social sanctions they face in doing so. These are easy things to write but carrying them out in practice can be difficult. Obviously, it would be absurd to claim that HR managers face extreme pressures when compared to the moral predicaments many individuals have faced throughout history, especially during times of war and genocide. Nevertheless, the pressure to pay mortgages and support families are not slight and neither are the pressures HR managers face in living in a society where 'success', efficiency, and profit are powerful imperatives regardless of someone's commitment to being decent.

I think that Heller addresses these issues and I think her principles and guidelines are a helpful step. However, it would be naive to suggest that this is all that decent HR managers will ever need to rely on. The pressure to push for performance in organizations is strong and when morality clashes with economic performance, the pressure for economic performance to come out trumps is significant. This may well be the case regardless of the broader economic system an HR manager finds himself or herself working in, but it is likely to be especially true in liberal market economies where the market mechanism is substantially left to coordinate activity in firms including the relationships between employers and employees (Hall and Soskice 2001). In such situations and in others where decent HR managers are seeking to do the right thing they may find that arguments presented within the bounds of morality will fail. Here decent HR managers may have little left to do but fall back on their courage and face the consequences of being decent or advocating decency. This may mean marginalization, reduced promotional opportunities, or termination of employment. Thus from Heller's perspective the decent HR manager may have to simply face, with courage, suffering as a consequence of being decent.

This may be a hard step for many HR managers to make here and now in our societies. But I also think it important not to exaggerate the frequency of such situations. Moreover, as many of the HR managers I interviewed stated, it is sometimes a question of timing and striving for gradual change. That is, without breaking moral norms and maxims themselves, when influencing others to abide by moral maxims decent HR managers can exercise prudence in determining exactly how far they should push in a particular set of circumstances. Nevertheless, there will still be occasions, and for some perhaps many, when following Heller's approach also means facing suffering with courage.

And it is on this last point that I would like to finish. For Heller courage is a crucial virtue and while she would undoubtedly agree that 'getting up the nerve' to be courageous can be hard she nevertheless encourages the decent to be courageous in the following way:

Ultimately, it is simple to be brave. Once one sees what the right thing to do is, one does it. Seeing what is the right thing to do is, in Kierkegaard's phrase, to be in an instant: there is no 'before' and no 'after'. One ceases to consider losses and gains; one stops imagining what is going to happen to oneself. In the 'instant' there is only the person and eternity. You close your eyes, take your hand off the rail you have been grabbing, and—there you go. Once in the water, you will swim. Have courage, be brave. (1990: 85)

Conclusion

Tom Campbell, Ashly Pinnington, Rob Macklin, and Sheena Smith

Ethics in employment and HRM

The contributors to this book present a wealth of alternatives for encouraging more ethical policy and practice in the discipline of HRM. The kaleidoscope of perspectives adopted reveals a consensus on the significance for HRM of specific ethics within business and of broader societal values. Notwithstanding, this common ground there are substantive differences between the contributors, and we hope that future HRM practice and research will be stimulated by their debates and by our closing reflections as to the nature, feasibility, and desirability of proactive and reforming modes of ethical HRM.

First, all agree that *there is tremendous scope for bringing about moral improvement in the treatment of employees.* Indeed, Walsh (see Chapter 6) cautions us to remember that moral choice is an integral part of market and of labour commodities, and therefore ethics is systemic to decision-making in business and employment relationships, whether the intentions and outcomes are good, bad, or indifferent. It is evident that regardless of the contributors' political perspective and approach to ethical reasoning, they are all somewhat restrained in their evaluation of the ethical impact of individual HRM practitioners. Furthermore and with only one exception, they do not say much about the potential and contribution of professional HRM associations and it is very clear that powerful social forces limit the freedom of action of individuals who are seeking to be ethical in business.

Implicit to the different arguments of all of the contributors is the idea that HRM systems are increasingly under the control of the higher management of private corporations whose principal interests relate directly to short-term stock market success. For a variety of reasons they can then be subdivided into roughly two groups, those who recommend a more comprehensive or focused system of balances and checks within the existing political and social system and those who are more pessimistic about the potential of organizational and societal cultures based on individualist employment relationships. The critical goals of organizational flexibility, labour productivity, and social legitimacy are often in tension with each other as they are also with ultimate business goals such as the continuing viability of the organization, obtaining adequate shareholder returns, and achieving competitive success (see Boxall and Purcell

Chapter 4). Guest (see Chapter 3) acknowledges such inherent conflicts and so far the limited adoption of proactive HRM policies such as in partnership arrangements between stakeholders, but like Boxall and Purcell, he remains positive overall about the potential of HRM within business and society. In contrast, Legge (see Chapter 2) is altogether more critical arguing that the reduction in collectivist arrangements is creating a divide between people such as elite groups of knowledge workers who can anticipate reasonable conditions of employment and fairer and more ethical treatment at work than is the deal for the bulk of employees. In contrast to the variety of political institutions and normative value systems within society, HRM therefore sometimes appears like flotsam on the surface of the seas (see Palmer, Chapter 1).

The second implication therefore, of the contributions taken together, is that such solutions as there are to the *critical ethical issues in HRM have to be addressed at both the macro- and the micro-level*, including issues of social and political philosophy, government regulation, board room policy, and CEO initiative, as well as line management and HR management. More specifically, HRM practitioners are in a weak position whenever they seek to implement ethical HRM without a framework of sensible legal regulation, the support of senior management and an agreed area of authority for decision-making (see Creighton Chapter 5). If HRM systems become too closely related to serving politically dominant ideologies and sectional interests, then the best ethical role available to even courageous HRM specialists may be to promote good and mitigate bad moral decisions taken elsewhere (see Pinnington and Bayraktaroglu Chapter 11).

Most contributors stress the substantial complexity of the ethical choices that arise with respect to HRM, the difficulty of determining the morally best HRM strategies, and what to do when faced by unethical and even illegal HRM practices. Moral judgement on such matters has to relate to the nature of the political, economic, and legal system in place, the cultural realities of the organization and sector in question, and the personal capacities and circumstances of the individual practitioner. Ethical HRM is a complex and multifaceted matter in which there are no easy solutions and few evidently correct answers. More attention should be paid to the distributive and procedural justice of work and employment relations and particularly to HRM's role in productivity improvement, work reorganization, organizational flexibility and change (see Sorell Chapter 12). This book demonstrates insights can be gleaned from a wide range of disciplines and debates in, for example, legal ethics, neo-Weberian sociology, stakeholder theory, utilitarian economic philosophies, Kantian ethics of respecting persons, Aristotelian concepts of virtue and capabilities, human rights and reflections as to how decent people behave in morally difficult situations, but there is no ready-made ethical theory from which uncontroversial HRM policies can be readily derived (see Macklin Chapter 16). Hence, we have not sought in this book to reduce the subject matter of HRM, ethics and employment purely to theoretical abstraction.

A third area of agreement and implication for ethical debates in HRM is that they can be *illuminated by reasoning based on specific theories and systems of ethics*. Creighton demonstrates the long-term influence of legal systems observing the latitude that remains within them for making moral choices and adopting different courses of action. Watson's (see Chapter 13) use of neo-Weberian sociology makes a similar point about agency and determinism noting the constraining but not exclusive role of business objectives when making ethical choices in work and employment; interestingly, Weber was himself trained in law and wrote extensively on its influence. Greenwood and De Cieri (see Chapter 7) applies stakeholder theory in a challenging way by adopting an implicitly utilitarian economic philosophy that eventuates in increased moral onus placed on managers through the concept of 'stakeholder engagement' that sees employees as moral claimants rather than simply strategic stakeholders. Kamoche takes a different approach to HRM more consonant with aspects of Kantian ethics of respecting persons as well as being similar in emphasis to discourse theory's preference for addressing issues of asymmetric power (see Chapter 15). He proposes that we reconsider the ethics of organization's appropriation of employees' knowledge and work efforts, thus presenting a strong moral challenge to business and management for greater ethical reflection and action more sensitive to employee considerations.

None of the contributors question that HRM has the capacity to treat employees instrumentally as a resource, but they differ in their evaluation of its core contention that people are a resource that must be strategically managed. Some strongly question the adequacy of HRM systems and strategies for managing the workforce (see Reed Chapter 10) whereas others see more scope for defining relevant outcomes but remain somewhat ambivalent on the sufficiency of HRM strategies for consistently attaining ethical employment (see Boxall and Purcell Chapter 4). There again, some doubt the capacity of companies to look seriously beyond their own bottom line (see Watson Chapter 13), whereas others argue that this is in effect tantamount to the rejection of the moral point of view (see Walsh Chapter 6).

A fourth area of general agreement between the contributors is that *any intellectually and morally acceptable approach to HRM must take account of a pluralism of partially conflicting interests*. A major part of the debate about ethical HRM concerns determining the right balance between the morally relevant competing interests affected by HRM practice. Unitarist theories that legitimate only stockholder interests are morally untenable and practically unrealistic. So, there is reason for caution in outlining a radical vision for ethical HRM in which the balance of economic efficiency and the more directly humanitarian elements of basic human decency is tilted in the direction of the rights and well-being of employees under the leadership of ethically enlightened senior management and HRM specialists. Quite apart from the idealism of attempting to implement such a vision, the consensus of the majority of the contributors is that its consequences would not be desirable for many, if not all, employees.

Within the knowledge of the shortcomings of idealism and abstract modes of ethical reasoning divorced from their social and moral contexts, a number of individual and collective alternatives are available for progressing HRM. Macklin (see Chapter 16) outlines the groundwork for a normative conception of individuals acting decently within any specific community. Likewise, Margolis, Grant, and Molinsky (see Chapter 14) offer genuine grounds for hope by challenging stereotypes of business decision-making as bereft of ethical content. These contributors present a framework for encouraging moral reflection and acting with integrity. They wrestle with understanding how managers, including HR managers, should deal with ethical dilemmas which frequently occur when people in authority have to perform 'necessary evils' for the greater benefit of all. Moreoever, at the collective level of HRM institutions, adopting a neo-Aristotelian virtue ethics perspective, Ardagh (see Chapter 9) advances a detailed programme of action for reinvigorating and strengthening HRM by setting demanding targets for professional organization.

Ethical standards in business and society

Having identified some of the common themes and agreement between the contributors, it is worth reflecting further on their overall significance for ethics within business, employment, and HRM. Assuming as all genuine ethical debate must assume, that all social institutions, including business, have to be morally justified, it is clear that at least part of that justification must derive from the evaluation of the purpose(s) of that institution. In the case of business, the main (but not necessarily the sole) legitimating objective is the generation of wealth, efficiently and effectively. Here 'wealth' is taken to be the sum of material goods and services generally considered desirable. Wealth is not to be equated with profit, although profitability is generally considered a prerequisite of wealth production in a capitalist system. Wealth creation in this sense is generally taken to be the prime moral grounding and legitimating goal of business in general. However other purposes, such as the provision of meaningful and fulfilling occupations, may be added to wealth creation as other or even as superior, legitimating objectives.

If the general justifying aim of business is the creation of wealth, conceived of as desirable material goods and services, this gives prima facie legitimation and hence conditional moral endorsement to the efficiently organized wealth creation of any business organization. The norms that state how this objective is best achieved may be said to constitute the 'internal' morality of business. In a liberal capitalist system the internal ethics of business include the prerequisites of an effective market, including the norms of open competition, commutative justice and transactional honesty. In this system profit is an integral part of the game but it is not the purpose of the game. Profit maximizing is justified only within the suppositions of a system designed to maximize global output, and that means real, honest, fair, and voluntary competition. That is an internal and distinctive core of business ethics in a market economy.

Recognition of an ethics internal to business is vital for the proper assessment of different forms of generic HRM. However, any account of business ethics must also involve recognition of 'external' ethical considerations and the moral requirement to behave humanely and decently towards people in the course of business, as in other spheres. Many of these external ethical considerations arise from the fact that business involves people and that people have certain rights, such as the moral right to be treated with respect as human beings, that is beings with the capacity to suffer, the ability to choose for themselves, and to have the chance to live a meaningful life. These moral imperatives may in general be equated with the human rights that all organizations ought to respect. As such, they may be viewed as considerations external to business which both limit and extend the moral legitimacy of business activity. Thus, human rights limitations on business identify those things that businesses may not do in the otherwise legitimate pursuit of profit in the process of wealth creation. On the other hand, human rights extensions to internal business ethics concern those goals that business ought to adopt in addition to the generation of wealth. A great deal of business ethics can be conceptualized as working out the specific obligations of businesses with respect to the human rights of those involved in and affected by business activity, and working out how compliance with these obligations is best achieved.

This broad conception of business ethics, distinguishing its internal and external aspects and incorporating moral debate about the proper scope and mode of business regulation, may seem rather grandiose to those who consider that the main issue in business ethics is simply how to get business people to 'walk the talk' and 'do the right thing'. It will certainly appear somewhat rarefied to the ordinary HR managers grappling with the mix of conflicting pressures and humdrum routine that characterize their daily work. It is, however, only by looking at everyday moral dilemmas in the context of business ethics that real progress can be made in articulating and responding to the normative questions that arise in HRM. For this reason, much of this book concerns the social and political legitimation of economic systems and the role that business institutions and organizations play within them.

Nevertheless, the limited contribution of contemporary HRM to the more external aspects of ethical work and employment cannot be ignored. Even if corporations have good business reasons to look after skilled and information service workers, the disposability of casual and lesser skilled workers and the increasingly weak bargaining power of such employees and contractors renders them vulnerable to the unjust and arbitrary exercise of power (see Legge Chapter 2). This is an ethically important aspect of the context in which both the moral risks and the moral potential of HRM must come under further scrutiny.

The key elements for establishing institutionalized ethical HRM must be directed to ensuring not simply that HR considerations are central to the development of business strategies and core business decisions, but that these considerations are framed in a way that identify and promote the ethical potential of HRM. At the very least, this is unlikely to be achieved without the authoritative presence at senior levels of management of HR managers with a strong professional ethos backed by an influential professional organization and appropriate legal requirements for the monitoring, reporting, and auditing of HRM within business organizations. The subordinated role of HRM, as illustrated by the continuous demand to prove its contribution to competitive advantage, combined with wide variation in the expertise of HRM specialists are unlikely drivers of change. HRM lacks promise with respect to either improving the internal business ethics that promote the legitimate goals of business as a whole, such as a fair and open employment market, or accommodating the more external demands that employment should contribute to the fulfilment of human potential for its own sake.

The contributors to this book are divided as to whether it is possible to turn the situation around within the context of systems of HRM. Clearly, to do so would involve a combination of factors, including a more profound commitment to CSR that goes far beyond the relatively superficial public relations exercise that are not untypical manifestations of CSR and a legal framework that gives more explicit recognition to the particular moral claims of employees. It would include monitoring and auditing going beyond areas of occupational health and safety and equal opportunity, and incorporate more oversight of such matters as training, dismissals, and redundancy conditions. Admittedly, this form of meta-regulation will not achieve very much without the appropriate ethical commitment and effective compliance programmes within organizations to back it up. However, it does provide a basis for according HRM greater status. It offers HRM specialists enhanced roles as instigators and implementers of strategies that blend the legitimate economic and human goals that we suggest should feature centrally in CSR norms. The upshot of this would be more powerful HR departments with more clearly defined roles, and strong representation at board level, operationalized with some consistency across the corporate world through various techniques of meta-regulation. In such circumstances, ethical conduct in the management of HR and treatment of employees in all categories would be less a matter of senior managerial discretion and more a formal matter of institutionalized and monitored rights and obligations.

Within this framework, HR specialists could have a leadership role in the business ethics of corporations that is relatively narrow in scope but of the highest priority in meeting corporate CSR obligations. As there are many different kinds of ethical issues in business and these relate more or less closely to the various management roles not everything that applies to HRM may be transferable. Even so, identifying how to ensure that corporations seriously consider the ethical concerns of their HR managers points to ways in which other management functions and specialists may be able to adopt similar techniques. In this way, HRM is one of the most promising ways of encouraging more ethical conduct in business in general. Without proposing that HR managers should carry the major ethical burden of a corporation, it offers them an opportunity to enact a specialized role for providing ethical input to business practice through motivating and monitoring ethical HRM.

Ethical HRM and the question of its professionalization

Beyond this, we suggest that progression towards a more ethical HRM through professionalization and reforms in corporate governance backed by changes to management practices may offer some palliative to the recent trends in employment relations, including increased uncertainty and insecurity of employment, the decline of trade unionism, and the impact of economic globalization (see Creighton Chapter 5). Ardagh's comprehensive consideration (see Chapter 9) of the criteria for recognition as a profession offers support to the idea that HRM can be the basis for a profession that has sufficient moral authority and organizational autonomy to justify being called a profession. As the medical profession is committed to the social value of health and the legal profession to that of justice, so the HRM profession could be seen as promoting the basic social need of 'well-being and dignity at work', as well as contributing to the productive efficiency of business. While doubts may be raised with respect to any quasi-monopoly claims that might be made about the exclusivity of such roles for HRM practitioners and the precise nature of the expertise claimed in discharging their responsibilities, it is plausible that there is the basis here for creation of a relatively autonomous profession that would have the clout, in such areas as equal opportunity procedures, which

Bennington (see Chapter 8) sees to be currently lacking, and be accountable for corporate failures in this regard in a way that Ardagh envisages. In such a context Rob Macklin's aspirational model (see Chapter 16) of the decent and courageous HR manager begins to seem more attainable.

Expanding on this idea somewhat and while mindful of the difficulties involved we suggest that the capacity of HR managers to support decent decision-making could be increased by HR managers becoming profession-alized in the same way accountants and social workers have been. Such a move we believe could provide HR managers with further steps to resort to prior to resigning, defying orders, waiving norms and rules, or whistle-blowing. Professional bodies such as those covering social workers and doctors are collective organizations that tightly restrict entry to the occupation (Kultgen 1988): in this respect, they can be seen as establishing something akin to a closed shop. While such bodies could be seen as requiring individuals to give up a certain amount of autonomy, they also provide individuals with a mea-sure of protection. When joining a professional body individuals must agree to abide by codes of practice and failure to do so can result in expulsion (Kultgen 1988). Given the closed-shop nature of the profession this means individuals can appeal to the codes if put under pressure by their employers to breach moral norms—so long as, of course, the norms are embraced by the codes. Our recommendation is that despite the disanalogies between HRM's work and that of paradigmatic professions like doctors and lawyers who are 'on-call' after hours in assigned blocks, and charge fees for service, HR managers as a group should work towards a similar status.

In making this suggestion we recognize that professionalization can have its own moral 'downsides' and note the doubts that have been raised in the book with respect to the likely prospect of professionalizing HRM specialists in a way that would provide them with any significant degree of autonomy and independence. Given the recent trend towards decentralizing HR tasks and skills, it is acknowledged that it will be more difficult for the HR profession to 'carve out' a privileged area of knowledge and professional jurisdiction.

Moreover, it must be recognized that professionalization as a path to a moderate model of ethical HRM seems to swim against the tide of change in professions and professional work as outlined by Reed (see Chapter 10) who gives a lucid account of the decline of the distinctively professional characteristics of professions. He explains how exclusive control of a body of knowledge has become both more contested and accountable as well as subject to increased moral criticism. What it may be asked is therefore the point of seeking professionalization of HRM in a world in which professionalism in general is under threat? Reed's own answer, to the effect that professions are most flexible and resilient as 'merchants of morality' can be interpreted as implying that an HRM profession will best be developed through reviving the idea that HR practitioners are the 'conscience of the corporation'. Reed's argument is informed by realist and Foucauldian analysis that explains but does not in itself morally justify having 'professions' that successfully claim such moral powers, indeed it is presented as a process of elite subordination. While his sociological analysis is persuasive, it may be argued otherwise that there are indeed instrumental reasons for supporting such developments in the rather amoral conception of HRM that is the current norm. If HR practitioners can succeed in passing themselves off as the moral merchants of employee interests, then this might help to provide an effective counter-influence to the exploitative tendencies of business in a neo-liberal economy to which attention is drawn in the Introduction. This may seem a somewhat cynical reason for promoting HRM professionalization but, as with the business case for CSR, anyone seeking to promote morally acceptable outcomes has to depend on utilizing social mechanisms that draw on demonstrating the benefits of self-interested conduct for the general good.

One of the conclusions that has to be drawn from Part I is that what is and what is not morally acceptable in HRM is a complex matter that is determined in part by prior views as to what constitutes ethically acceptable business practice within a particular type of economic system. If we accept, for instance, Palmer's and Sorell's analyses (Chapter 1 and Chapter 12) that the moral dilemmas that arise in everyday HRM practice manifest the conflicting values that exist in a pluralist world in which there are not only conflicting interests, but no agreement as to how these conflicts should be resolved, then it is not clear that there is sufficient practical agreement as to what constitutes 'well-being and dignity at work' let alone how achieving this is to be reconciled with the generation of wealth.

Given such complexity, it might be tempting to confine HRM to achieving professional status in the overall pursuit of employee well-being, leaving other spheres of management to deal with wealth generation. But that would be to go back on the essential core of specific HRM, namely the contribution of employee development to competitive advantage. Furthermore, it asserts an agenda for professionalization which lacks much justification and support from past, present, or anticipated generic HRM contexts, something that no contributor to this book recommends we should do. On the other hand, if we try to balance the twin ethical demands of effective wealth generation and wealth and decent employment conditions in the one profession, we not only render the boundary between HR managers and line management highly porous, but, by keeping generic HRM firmly within the management camp, we make it impossible to consider HRM practitioners as anything approaching an autonomous profession with overriding fiduciary duties to their 'clients' (Freidson 2001).

Some of these problems could be overcome, but it takes us back to the inevitable connection between HRM and an ethical/moral conception that goes beyond the narrow business case for valuing HR in business. In conclusion, ethical HRM means taking into account not only the internal morality of a liberal market system with its insistence on arrangements that promote the free market and not just the interests of particular businesses. It means ensuring wider commitment to making all employment experiences of individuals commensurate with their status as moral beings whose lives, interests, and development are ultimately the sole basis for 'designing' and supporting any economic system.

☐ BIBLIOGRAPHY

Aaron, B. (1999). 'Employees' Duty of Loyalty: Introduction and Overview', *Comparative Labor Law and Policy Journal*, 20(2): 143–53.

Abbott, A. (1988). *The System of the Professions: An Essay on the Division of Expert Labor*. Chicago, IL: University of Chicago Press.

Ackers, P. and Payne, J. (1998). 'British Trade Unions and Social Partnership: Rhetoric, Reality and Strategy', *International Journal of Human Resource Management*, 9(3): 529–50.

Ackroyd, S. (1996). 'Organization Contra Organizations: Professions and Organizational Change in the UK', *Organization Studies*, 17(4): 599–622.

Adler, P. S., Goldoftas, B., and Levine, D. I. (1999). 'Flexibility versus Efficiency? A Case Study of Model Changeovers with Toyota Production System', *Organization Science*, 10(1): 43–68.

Akyeampong, E. (1997). 'A Statistical Portrait of the Trade Union Movement', *Perspectives on Labour and Income*, 9: 45–54.

―――― (1999). 'Unionization: An Update', *Perspectives on Labour and Income*, 11: 45–65.

Albrow, M. (1970). *Bureaucracy*. London: Macmillan.

Alexander, J. C. (1997). *Fin de Siècle Social Theory: Relativism, Reduction, and the Problem of Reason*. London: Verso Books.

Alkire, S. (2000). 'The Basic Dimensions of Human Flourishing', in N. Biggar and R. Black (eds.), *The Revival of Natural Law*. Aldershot, UK: Ashgate, pp. 73–110.

―――― (2002). *Valuing Freedoms. Sen's Capability Approach and Poverty Reduction*. Oxford: Oxford University Press.

Alvesson, M. and Karreman, D. (2001). 'Odd Couples: Making Sense of the Curious Concept of Knowledge Management', *Journal of Management Studies*, 38(7): 995–1018.

―――― and Willmott, H. (2002). 'Identity Regulation as Organizational Control: Producing the Appropriate Individual', *Journal of Management Studies*, 39(5): 620–44.

Anthony, P. and Crichton, A. (1969). *Industrial Relations and the Personnel Specialists*. London: Batsford.

Appelbaum, E., Bailey, T., Berg, P., and Kalleberg, A. (2000). *Manufacturing Advantage: Why High Performance Systems Pay Off*. Ithaca, NJ: ILR Press.

Aquinas, T. (1963). *Summa Theologica*. London: Blackfriars with Eyre and Spottiswoode, New York: McGraw-Hill.

Ardagh, D. (1979). 'Aquinas on Happiness: A Defence', *New Scholasticism*, Vol. LIII, Autumn: 428–59.

―――― (2001). 'The Virtuous Organization: A Neo-Aristotelian Foundation', in D. Kantarelis (ed.), *Global Business and Economics Review*. Worcester, MA: Business and Economics International, pp. 1–15.

―――― and Macklin, R. (1998). 'Ethics and the Human Resource Manager', *Business and Professional Ethics Journal*, 17(4): 61–78.

―――― ―――― (1999). 'The Difficulties and Moral Compromises Faced by Australian Human Resource Managers Seeking to Create Decent Organisations', *Business and Professional Ethics Journal*, 18(3 and 4): 93–112.

Aristotle (1941). *The Basic Works of Aristotle*, R. McKeon (ed.). New York: Random House.

———(1984). 'Nicomachean Ethics', in J. Barnes (ed.), *The Complete Works of Aristotle. The Revised Oxford Translation*. Princeton, NJ: Princeton University Press, pp. 1729–867.

Aronowitz, S. and DiFazio, W. (1994). *The Jobless Future*. Minnesota, MN: University of Minnesota Press.

Arthur, J. B. (1994). 'Effects of Human Resource Systems on Manufacturing Performance and Turnover', *Academy of Management Journal*, 37(3): 670–87.

ASX (2001). *Guidance Note 10. Review of Operations and Activities: Listing Rule 4.10.17*. Australian Stock Exchange, pp. 1–12.

Austin, J. L. (1967). 'Ägathon and Eudaimonia in the Ethics of Aristotle', in J. Moravscik (ed.), *Aristotle: A Collection of Critical Essays*. New York: Doubleday, pp. 261–96.

Australian Government (2002). 'The National OHS Strategy 2002–2012'. Canberra: Australian Government, Department of Employment and Workplace Relations, Office of the Australian Safety and Compensation Council. http://www.nohsc.gov.au/nationalstrategy/

Baier, K. (1958). *The Moral Point of View*. New York: Cornell University Press.

Bain, G. (2002). *The Future of the Fire Service*. London: HMSO. Available at: http://www.irfs.org.uk/docs/future/

Bain, P. and Taylor, P. (2000). 'Entrapped by the "Electronic Panopticon"? Worker Resistance in a Call Centre', *New Technology, Work and Employment*, 15(1): 2–18.

Baldamus, W. (1961). *Efficiency and Effort*. London: Tavistock.

Baldwin, J. (1959). The Medieval Theories of Just Price: Romanists, Canonists, and Theologians in the Twelfth and Thirteenth Centuries. *Transactions of the American Philosophical Society*, 49(4): 1–92.

Bales, R. (1994). 'A New Standard for Title VII Opposition Cases: Fitting the Personnel Manager Double Standard into a Cognizable Framework', *South Texas Law Review*, 35: 95–136.

Bamber, G. J. and Lansbury, R. (eds.) (1998). *International and Comparative Industrial Relations: A Study of Industrialised Market Economies*. St Leonards, NSW: Allen & Unwin.

Bandura, A. (1997). *Self-Efficacy: The Exercise of Control*. New York: W. H. Freeman and Company.

Bargh, J. A. and Chartrand, T. L. (1999). 'The Unbearable Automaticity of Being', *American Psychologist*, 54: 462–79.

Barney, J. (1991). 'Firm Resources and Sustained Competitive Advantage', *Journal of Management*, 17(1): 99–120.

——— and Wright, P. (1998). 'On Becoming a Strategic Partner: The Role of Human Resources in Gaining Competitive Advantage', *Human Resource Management*, 37: 31–46.

——— Wright, M., and Ketchen, D. J. (2001). 'The Resource-Based View of the Firm: Ten Years after 1991', *Journal of Management*, 27(6): 625–41.

Baron, J. N. and Kreps, D. M. (1999). *Strategic Human Resources*. New York: John Wiley.

Bassett, P. and Cave, A. (1993). *All for One*. London: Fabian Society.

Batt, R. (2000). 'Strategic Segmentation in Front Line Services: Matching Customers, Employees and Human Resource Systems', *International Journal of Human Resource Management*, 11(3): 540–61.

Battin, M. P., Windt, P. Y., Appleby, P. C., and Francis, L. (eds.) (1989). *Ethical Issues in the Professions*. Englewood Cliff, NJ: Prentice Hall.

Bauman, Z. (1989). *Modernity and the Holocaust*. Oxford: Polity Press.

_____ (1993). *Postmodern Ethics*. Oxford: Blackwell.

_____ (1994). 'Narrating Modernity', in J. Burnheim (ed.), *The Social Philosophy of Agnes Heller (Poznan Studies in the Philosophy of the Sciences and the Humanities 37)*. Amsterdam-Atlanta, GA: Rodopi B.V. Editions, pp. 97–120.

_____ (1995). *Life in Fragments: Essays in Postmodern Morality*. Oxford: Blackwell.

Bayles, M. (1989). *Professional Ethics*, 2nd edn. Wadsworth, CA: Belmont.

Bayraktaroglu, S. (1999). 'Management Agendas for Technology-Based Learning Media', Coventry University. Ph.D. thesis, UK.

Bazerman, M., Tenbrunsel, A., and Wade-Benzoni, K. (1999). 'Negotiating with Yourself and Losing: Making Decisions with Competing Internal Preferences', *Academy of Management Review*, 23: 225–41.

BCA (2003). 'Speech by Katie Lahey CEO Business Council of Australia', paper presented at the Australasian Corporate Governance Congress, 19th–20th February.

Beatty, R. W., Ewing, J. R., and Tharp, C. G. (2003). 'HR's Role in Corporate Governance: Present and Prospective', *Human Resource Management*, 42(3): 257–69.

Beauchamp, T. L. and Bowie, N. E. (2004). *Ethical Theory and Business Practice*, 7th edn. Englewood Cliffs, NJ: Prentice Hall.

Becker, B. and Gerhart, B. (1996). 'The Impact of Human Resource Management on Organizational Performance: Progress and Prospects', *Academy of Management Journal*, 39(4): 779–801.

_____ and Huselid, M. (1998). 'High Performance Work Systems and Firm Performance: A Synthesis of Research and Managerial Implications', *Research in Personnel and Human Resource Management*, 16(1): 53–101.

_____ _____ Pickus, P., and Spratt, M. (1997). 'HR as a Source of Shareholder Value: Research and Recommendations', *Human Resource Management Journal*, 31(1), Spring: 39–47.

Beckett, R. and Jonker, J. (2002). 'AccountAbility 1000: A New Social Standard for Building Sustainability', *Managerial Auditing Journal*, 17(1/2): 36–42.

Beer, M., Spector, B., Lawrence, P. R., Quinn Mills, D., and Walton, R. E. (1984). *Managing Human Assets*. New York: Simon & Schuster Inc., The Free Press.

_____ _____ _____ _____ _____ (1985). *Human Resource Management: A General Manager's Perspective*. New York: The Free Press.

Beetham, D. (1987). *Bureaucracy*. Milton Keynes, UK: Open University Press.

Bell, D. (1973). *The Coming of Post-Industrial Society: A Venture in Social Forecasting*. New York: Basic Books.

Bell, D. (1999). 'The Axial Age of Technology' Forward to *The Coming of Post-Industrial Society*. New York: Basic Books, pp. ix–lxxxvii.

Bendix, R. (1956). *Work and Authority in Industry*. Berkeley, CA: UCLA Press.

Benhabib, S. (1992). *Situating the Self: Gender, Community, and Postmodernism in Contemporary Ethics*. Cambridge: Polity Press.

Bennett, L. (1994). *Making Labour Law in Australia: Industrial Relations, Politics and Law*. Sydney, NSW: Lawbook.

Bennington, L. (2001). 'Age and Carer Discrimination in the Recruitment Process: Has the Australian Legislation Failed?', in M. Noon and E. Ogbonna (eds.), *Equality, Diversity and Disadvantage in Employment*. Basingstoke, UK: Palgrave, pp. 65–79.

___ (2002). 'Who Should be the Guardians of EEO?', *Proceedings of the VIth IFSAM World Congress*, Gold Coast, 10th–13th July.

___ (2003). 'NPM, Ethics and the Need for Greater Whistle-Blowing Avenues in Victoria, Proceedings of the Toward Public Value?', *Management and Employment Outcomes Conference*. Melbourne: Monash University.

___ and Wein, R. (2000*a*). 'Anti-Discrimination Legislation in Australia: Fair, Effective, Efficient or Irrelevant?', *International Journal of Manpower*, 21(1): 21–33.

___ ___ (2000*b*). 'Job Applicants—Sometimes they Name, Infrequently they Blame and Rarely they Claim', in R. Dunford (ed.), *ANZAM 2000 Conference Proceedings*. Macquarie Graduate School of Management, Sydney, NSW, 3rd–6th December.

Berlin, I. (1958 [2002]). *Liberty (*incorporating *Four Essays on Liberty)*, in H. Hardy (ed.). Oxford: Oxford University Press.

Bertok, J. (1999). 'OECD Supports the Creation of Sound Ethics Infrastructure: OECD Targets both the "Supply Side" and the "Demand Side" of Corruption', *Public Personnel Management*, 28(4): 673–87.

Bies, R. J. (2001). 'Interactional (In)justice: The Sacred and the Profane', in J. Greenberg and R. Cropanzano (eds.), *Advances in Organizational Justice*. Stanford, CA: Stanford University Press, pp. 89–118.

___ and Moag, J. S. (1986). 'Interactional Justice: Communication Criteria of Fairness', in R. J. Lewicki, B. H. Sheppard, and M. H. Bazerman (eds.), *Research on Negotiation in Organizations*. Greenwich, CT: JAI Press, pp. 43–55.

___ and Shapiro, D. L. (1988). 'Voice and Justification: Their Influence on Procedural Fairness Judgments', *Academy of Management Journal*, 31(3): 676–85.

Blackler, F. (1995). 'Knowledge, Knowledge Work and Organizations: An Overview and Interpretation', *Organization Studies*, 16(6): 1021–46.

Blass, T. M. (1991). 'Understanding Behavior in the Milgram Obedience Experiment: The Role of Personality, Situations, and Their Interactions', *Journal of Personality and Social Psychology*, 60: 398–413.

Bloch, S. and Coady, M. (1996). *Codes of Ethics and the Professions*. Melbourne: Melbourne University Press.

Blyton, P. and Turnbull, P. J. (1998). *The Dynamics of Employee Relations*, 2nd edn. Basingstoke, UK: Macmillan.

Boje, D. M. (2001). *Narrative Methods for Organizational and Communication Research*. London: Sage.

Bok, S. (1995). *Common Values*. Columbia, MO: University of Missouri Press.

Boselie, P., Paauwe, J., and Jansen, P. (2001). 'Human Resource Management and Performance: Lessons from the Netherlands', *International Journal of Human Resource Management*, 12(7): 1107–25.

Bottomley, S. (1990) 'Taking Corporations Seriously: Some Considerations for Corporate Responsibility', *Federal Law Review*, 19: 203–11.

___ (1997). 'From Contractualism to Constitutionalism: A Framework for Corporate Governance', *Sydney Law Review*, 19(3): 281.

Bourdieu, P. (1977). *Outline of a Theory of Practice*. Cambridge: Cambridge University Press.

___ (1984). *Distinction: A Social Critique of the Judgement of Taste*. Cambridge, MA: Harvard Press.

_____ (1987). 'The Force of Law: Toward a Sociology of the Juridical Field', _Hastings Journal of Law_, 38: 805–53.

_____ (1988). _Homo Academicus_. Stanford, CA: Stanford University Press.

_____ (1990a). _Photography: A Middle-Brow Art_. Stanford, CA: Stanford University Press.

_____ (1990b). _The Logic of Practice_. Cambridge: Polity Press.

_____ (1991). _Language and Symbolic Power_. Cambridge, MA: Harvard Press.

_____ (1993a). _The Field of Cultural Production_. Cambridge: Polity Press.

_____ (1993b). _Sociology in Question_. London: Sage.

_____ (1996). _The Rules of Art_. Cambridge: Polity Press.

_____ (1998). _Practical Reason_. Cambridge: Polity Press.

_____ Accardo, A., Balazs, G., Beaud, S., Bonvin, F., Bourdieu, E., Bourgois, P., Broccolichi, S., Champagne, P., Christin, R., Faguer, J.-P., Garcia, S., Lenoir, R., Oeuvrard, F., Pialoux, M., Pinto, L., Podalydès, D., Sayad, A., Soulié, C., and Wacquant, L. J. D. (1999). _The Weight of the World: Social Suffering in Contemporary Society_. Stanford, CA: Stanford University Press.

_____ and Passeron, J.-C. (1977). _Reproduction: In Education, Society and Culture_. London: Sage.

_____ and Wacquant, L. J. D. (1992). _An Invitation to Reflexive Sociology_. Chicago, IL: The University of Chicago Press.

Bourke, J. and Ronalds, C. (2002). 'Discrimination Laws: Striving Towards Equality', in J. J. Macken, P. O'Grady, C. Sappideen, and G. Warburton (eds.), _The Law of Employment_, 5th edn. Sydney, NSW: Lawbook, pp. 593–647.

Bowie, N. E. (1998). 'A Kantian Theory of Meaningful Work', _Journal of Business Ethics_, 17(9/10): 1083–92.

_____ (2002). _The Blackwell Guide to Business Ethics_. Oxford: Blackwell.

_____ and Werhane, P. H. (2005). _Management Ethics_. Oxford: Blackwell.

Boxall, P. (1995). 'Building the Theory of Comparative HRM', _Human Resource Management Journal_, 5(5): 5–17.

_____ (1996). 'The Strategic HRM Debate and the Resource-Based View of the Firm', _Human Resource Management Journal_, 6(3): 59–75.

_____ (1998). 'Achieving Competitive Advantage Through Human Resource Strategy: Towards a Theory of Industry Dynamics', _Human Resource Management Review_, 8(3): 265–88.

_____ (1999). 'Human Resource Strategy and Industry-Based Competition: A Conceptual Framework and Agenda for Theoretical Development', in P. M. Wright, L. D. Dyer, J. W. Boudreau, and G. T. Milkovich (eds.), _Research in Personnel and Human Resource Management (Supplement 4: Strategic Human Resources Management in the Twenty-First Century)_. Greenwich, CT: JAI Press, pp. 259–81.

_____ (2003). 'HR Strategy and Competitive Advantage in the Service Sector', _Human Resource Management Journal_, 13(3): 5–20.

_____ and Haynes, P. (1997). 'Strategy and Trade Union Effectiveness in a Neo-Liberal Environment', _British Journal of Industrial Relations_, 35(4): 567–91.

_____ and Purcell, J. (2003). _Strategy and Human Resource Management_. New York and Basingstoke, UK: Palgrave Macmillan.

_____ and Steeneveld, M. (1999). 'Human Resource Strategy and Competitive Advantage: A Longitudinal Study of Engineering Consultancies', _Journal of Management Studies_, 36(4): 443–63.

Boyle, M. and Healy, J. (2003). 'Balancing Mysterium and Onus: Doing Spiritual Work within an Emotion-Laden Organizational Context', *Organization*, 10(2): 351–73.

Brock, G. (ed.) (1998). *Necessary Goods: Our Duty to Meet Other's Needs*. Lanham: MA: Rowman and Littlefield.

Brock, D., Powell, M., and Hinings, C. R. (1999). *Restructuring the Professional Organization: Accounting, Health Care and Law*. London: Routledge.

Brockner, J. (2002). 'Making Sense of Procedural Fairness: How High Procedural Fairness can Reduce or Heighten the Influence of Outcome Favorability', *Academy of Management Review*, 27: 58–76.

———DeWitt, R., Grover, S., and Reed, T. (1990). 'When it is Especially Important to Explain Why: Factors Affecting the Relationship Between Managers' Explanations of a Layoff and Survivors' Reaction to the Layoff', *Journal of Experimental and Social Psychology*, 26: 389–407.

Brodie, D. (1996). 'The Heart of the Matter: Mutual Trust and Confidence', *Industrial Law Journal*, 25: 121.

———(2001). 'Mutual Trust and the Values of the Employment Contract', *Industrial Law Journal*, 30: 84.

Brooks, A. (1988). 'Myth and Muddle—An Examination of Contracts for the Performance of Work', *University of New South Wales Law Journal*, 11: 48.

Brown, C. and Reich, M. (1997). 'Micro-Macro Linkages in High-Performance Work Systems', *Organization Studies*, 18(5): 765–81.

Brown, D. (1991). *Human Universals*. Philadelphia, PA: Temple University.

Brown, W., Deakin, S., Nash, D., and Oxenbridge, S. (2000). 'The Employment Contract: From Collective Procedures to Individual Rights', *British Journal of Industrial Relations*, 38(4): 611–29.

Budd, J. W. (2004). *Employment with a Human Face: Balancing Efficiency, Equity, and Voice*. Ithaca, NY: ILR Press, an imprint of Cornell University Press.

Burawoy, M. (1979). *Manufacturing Consent*. Chicago, IL: University of Chicago Press.

Burns, T. and Stalker, G. (1961). *The Management of Innovation*. London: Tavistock.

Burris, B. (1993). *Technocracy at Work*. New York, NY: State University of New York Press.

Butler, T. and Savage, M. (eds.) (1995). *Social Change and the Middle Classes*. London: UCL Press.

Caldwell, R. (2003). 'The Changing Roles of Personnel Managers: Old Ambiguities, New Uncertainties', *Journal of Management Studies*, 40(4): 983–1004.

Callaghan, J. (1988). *Ethical Issues in Professional Life*. Oxford: Oxford University Press.

Cameron, K. (1986). 'Effectiveness as Paradox: Consensus and Conflict in Conceptions of Organizational Effectiveness', *Management Science*, 32(5): 539–53.

Cappelli, P. and Neumark, D. (2001). 'Do "High Performance" Work Practices Improve Establishment Level Outcomes?', *Industrial and Labor Relations Review*, 54: 737–75.

Caputo, J. D. (1993). *Against Ethics*. Bloomington, IN: Indiana University Press.

Carroll, G. R. and Hannan, M. T. (eds.) (1995). *Organizations in Industry: Strategy, Structure and Selection*. New York and Oxford: Oxford University Press.

Carson, W. G. (1970*a*). 'White Collar Crime and the Enforcement of Factory Legislation', *British Journal Criminology*, 10: 383.

———(1970*b*). 'Some Sociological Aspects of Strict Liability and the Enforcement of Factory Legislation', *Modern Law Rev*, 33: 396.

——— (1974). 'Symbolic and Instrumental Dimensions of Early Factory Legislation: A Case Study in the Social Origins of Criminal Law', in R. G. Hood (ed.), *Crime, Criminology and Public Policy: Essays in Honour of Sir Leon Radzinowicz*. London: Heinemann, pp. 107–38.

——— (1979). 'The Conventionalisation of Early Factory Crime', *International Journal of the Sociology of Law*, 7: 37–60.

——— (1980). 'The Institutionalization of Ambiguity: Early British Factory Acts', in G. Geis and E. Stotland (eds.), *White Collar Crime: Theory and Research*. Beverly Hills, CA: Sage, pp. 41–72.

Cartier, K. (1994). 'The Transaction Costs and Benefits of the Incomplete Contract of Employment', *Cambridge Journal of Economics*, 18: 181–96.

Cascio, W. F. (1998). *Applied Psychology in Human Resource Management*. Upper Saddle River, NJ: Prentice Hall.

Cassell, C. (1997). 'The Business Case for Equal Opportunities: Implications for Women in Management', *Women in Management Review*, 12(1): 11–17.

Castells, M. (2000). *The Rise of The Network Society*, 2nd edn. Oxford: Blackwell, 1st edn. 1996.

Cattaneo, R. J., Reavley, M., and Templer, A. (1994). 'Women in Management as a Strategic HR Initiative', *Women in Management Review*, 9(2): 23–8.

CCH (2003). *Australian and New Zealand Equal Opportunity Commentary*. North Ryde, NSW: CCH.

Charkham, J. (1994). *Keeping Good Company: Corporate Governance in Five Countries*. Oxford: Clarendon Press.

Child, J. (1964). 'Quaker Employers and Industrial Relations', *Sociological Review*, 12(2): 293–315.

——— (1972). 'Organizational Structure, Environment and Performance: The Role of Strategic Choice', *Sociology*, 6(3): 1–22.

——— (1997). 'Strategic Choice in the Analysis of Action, Structure, Organizations and Environment: Retrospect and Prospect', *Organization Studies*, 18(1): 43–76.

——— Loveridge, R., and Warner, M. (1973). 'Towards an Organizational Study of Trade Unions', *Sociology*, 7(1): 71–91.

Church, A. H. and Waclawski, J. (2001). 'Hold the Line: An Examination of Line vs. Staff Differences', *Human Resource Management*, 40(1): 21–34.

Clark, C. M. H. (1978). *A History of Australia, Vol 4*. Melbourne: Melbourne University Press.

Clarke, J. and Newman, J. (1997). *The Managerial State*. London: Sage.

——— Gewirtz, S., and McLaughlin, E. (eds.) (2000). *New Managerialism, New Welfare?* London: Sage.

Claydon, T. and Doyle, M. (1996). 'Trusting Me, Trusting You? The Ethics of Employee Empowerment', *Personnel Review*, 25(6): 13–25.

Clegg, H. (1975). 'Pluralism in Industrial Relations', *British Journal of Industrial Relations*, 13(3): 309–16.

Coady, M. and Bloch, S. (1996). *Codes of Ethics and the Professions*. Melbourne: Melbourne University Press.

Coff, R. (1997). 'Human Assets and Management Dilemmas: Coping with Hazards on the Road to Resource-Based Theory', *Academy of Management Review*, 22(2): 374–402.

——— (1999). 'When Competitive Advantage Doesn't Lead to Performance: The Resource-Based View and Stakeholder Bargaining Power', *Organizaton Science*, 10(2): 119–33.

Cohen, G. A. (1993). 'Equality of What? On Welfare, Goods, and Capabilities', in M. Nussbaum and A. Sen (eds.), *The Quality of Life*. Oxford: Clarendon Press, pp. 9–29.

Cohen, L., Finn, R., Wilkinson, A., and Arnold, J. (2003). 'Professional Work and Management', *International Studies of Management and Organization*, 32(2): 3–24.

Cohen, W. M. and Levinthal, D. A. (1990). 'Absorptive Capacity: A New Perspective on Learning and Innovation', *Administrative Science Quarterly*, 35(1): 128–52.

Collins, H. (1990). 'Independent Contracts and the Challenge of Vertical Disintegration to Employment Protection Laws', *Oxford Journal Legal Studies*, 10: 353.

Collins, R. (1979). *The Credential Society*. Orlando, FL: Academic Press.

Collinson, D. and Collinson, M. (1996). 'Barriers to Employee Rights: Gender, Selection, and the Labor Process', *Employee Responsibilities and Rights Journal*, 9(3): 229–49.

Connock, S. and Johns, T. (1995). *Ethical Leadership*. London: IPD (Institute of Personnel and Development).

Cook, N. (2003). 'The Health and Safety Trainer', *Occupational Safety and Health*, 33(3): 32–5.

Cooper, J. and Fazio, R. H. (1984). 'A New Look at Dissonance Theory', in L. Berkowitz (ed.), *Advances in Experimental Social Psychology*, vol. 17. New York: Academic Press, pp. 229–66.

Cornelius, N. and Gagnon, S. (1999). 'From Ethics "by Proxy" to Ethics in Action: New Approaches to Understanding HRM and Ethics', *Business Ethics: A European Review*, 8(4): 225–35.

Coulthard, A. (1997). 'The Individualisation of Australian Labour Law', *International Journal Comparative Labour Law & Industrial Relations*, 13: 95.

——— (1999). 'The Decollectivisation of Australian Industrial Relations: Trade Union Exclusion Under the *Workplace Relations Act* 1996 (Cth.)', in S. Deery and R. Mitchell (eds.), *Employment Relations: Individualisation and Union Exclusion*. Annandale, NSW: The Federation Press, pp. 48–68.

Coupar, W. and Stevens, B. (1998). 'Towards a New Model of Industrial Partnership: Beyond the "HRM Versus Industrial Relations" Argument', in P. Sparrow and M. Marchington (eds.), *Human Resource Management: The New Agenda*. London: *Financial Times*/Pitman Publishing, pp. 145–60.

Coyle-Shapiro, J. and Kessler, I. (2000). 'Consequences of the Psychological Contract for the Employment Relationship', *Journal of Management Studies*, 35(4): 439–56.

Crabb, S. (1999). 'Seal of Approval', *People Management*, (19 August): 42–4.

Cragg, W. (2002). 'Business Ethics and Stakeholder Theory', *Business Ethics Quarterly*, 12(2): 113–42.

Crane, F. G. (2004). 'The Teaching of Business Ethics: An Imperative at Business Schools', *Journal of Education for Business*, 79(3): 149–51.

Creighton, W. B. (1979). *Working Women and the Law*. London: Mansell.

——— (1997). 'The Workplace Relations Act in International Perspective', *Australian Journal of Labour Law*, 10: 31.

——— (1998). 'The ILO and the Protection of Fundamental Human Rights in Australia', *Melbourne University Law Review*, 22: 239.

——— (2000). 'One Hundred Years of the Conciliation and Arbitration Power: A Province Lost?', *Melbourne University Law Review*, 24: 839.

_____ (2003). 'Modernising Australian Labour Law: Individualisation and the Shift from Compulsory Conciliation and Arbitration to Enterprise Bargaining', in R. Blanpain and M. Weiss (eds.), _Changing Industrial Relations and Modernisation of Labour Law_. The Hague: Kluwer Law International.

_____ and Mitchell, R. (1995). 'The Contract of Employment in Australian Labour Law', in L. Betten (ed.), _The Employment Contract in Transforming Labour Relations_. The Hague: Kluwer Law International, pp. 129–66.

_____ and Stewart A. J. (2005). _Labour Law: An Introduction_, 4th edn. Annandale, NSW: The Federation Press.

_____ Ford, W. J., and Mitchell, R. J. (1993). _Labour Law: Text and Materials_, 2nd edn. Sydney, NSW: Lawbook.

Crompton, R. (1990). 'Professions in the Current Context', _Work, Employment and Society_, 32(2): 147–66.

Cully, M., Woodland, S., O'Reilly, A., and Dix, G. (1999). _Britain at Work_. London: Routledge.

Cummings, S. (2000). 'Aesthetics of Existence as an Alternative to Business Ethics', in S. Linstead and H. Hopfl (eds.), _The Aesthetics of Organization_. London: Sage, pp. 212–27.

Currie, G. and Kerrin, M. (2003). 'Human Resource Management and Knowledge Management: Enhancing Knowledge Sharing in a Pharmaceutical Company', _International Journal of Human Resource Management_, 14(6): 1027–45.

Daniel, A. (1990). _Medicine and the State_. Sydney, NSW: Allen and Unwin.

Datta, D., Guthrie, J., and Wright, P. (2005). 'Human Resource Management and Labor Productivity: Does Industry Matter?', _Academy of Management Journal_, 48(1): 135–45.

Davidson, A. P. (1975). 'A Skeleton in the Cupboard: Master and Servant Legislation and the Industrial Torts in Tasmania', _University of Tasmania Law Review_, 5: 123.

Davis-Blake, A., Broschak, J. P., and George, E. (2003). 'Happy Together? How Using Non-Standard Workers Affects Exit, Voice, and Loyalty among Standard Employees', _The Academy of Management Journal_, 46(4): 475–85.

Deakin, S. F. (1998). 'Labour Law and the Evolution of the Contract of Employment, 1900–1950: The Influence of the Welfare State', in R. Salais and N. Whiteside (eds.), _Governance, Industry and Labour Markets in Britain and France—The Modernizing State in the Mid-Twentieth Century_. London: Routledge, pp. 212–30.

_____ (2000). 'Legal Origins of Wage Labour: The Evolution of the Contract of Employment from Industrialisation to Welfare state', in L. Clarke, P. de Gijsel, and J. Janssen (eds.), _The Dynamics of Wage Relations in the New Europe_. Dordrecht, The Netherlands: Kluwer Law International, pp. 32–44.

_____ (2005). 'The Origins of the Contract of Employment', in S. Deakin and F. Wilkinson, _The Law of the Labour Market: Industrialization, Employment, and Legal Evolution_. Oxford: Oxford University Press, Ch. 2.

Dean, M. (1999). _Governmentality: Power and Rule in Modern Society_. London: Sage.

De Cieri, H. and Kramar, R. (2005). _Human Resource Management in Australia_, 2nd edn. Irwin, Sydney, NSW: McGraw-Hill.

Deephouse, D. (1999). 'To be Different, or to be the Same? It's a Question (and Theory) of Strategic Balance', _Strategic Management Journal_, 20(2): 147–66.

Deery, S. and Mitchell, R. (eds.) (2000). _Employment Relations, Individualism and Union Exclusion_. Annandale, NSW: The Federation Press.

———— Walsh, J., and Knox, A. (2001). 'The Non-Union Workplace in Australia: Bleak House or Human Resource Innovator?', *International Journal of Human Resource Management*, 12(4): 669–83.

Delery, J. E. (1998) 'Issues of Fit in Strategic Human Resource Management: Implications for Research', *Human Resource Management Review*, 8(3): 289–309.

———— and Doty, D. H. (1996). 'Modes of Theorizing in Strategic Human Resource Management: Tests of Universalistic, Contingency and Configurational Performance Predictions', *Academy of Management Journal*, 39(4): 802–35.

Dent, M. and Whitehead, S. (2002). *Managing Professional Identities: Knowledge, 'Performativity' and the 'New' Professional*. London: Routledge.

DesJardins, S. and McCall, B. (eds.) (2005). *Contemporary Issues in Business Ethics*. Belmont, CA: Wadsworth.

DTI (Department of Trade and Industry) (2002). *Full and Fulfilling Employment*. London: DTI.

———— (2004). *Society and Business*. London: DTI. Available at: http://www.societyandbusiness.gov.uk/policy.shtml

Derber, C., Schwartz, W. A., and Magrass, Y. (1990). *Power in the Highest Degree*. Oxford: Oxford University Press.

Dickens, L. (1999). 'Beyond the Business Case: A Three-Pronged Approach to Equality Action', *Human Resource Management Journal*, 9(1): 9–19.

———— and Hall, M. (2003). 'Labour Law and Industrial Relations: A New Settlement?', in P. Edwards (ed.), *Industrial Relations: Theory and Practice in Britain*, 2nd edn. Oxford: Blackwell, pp. 124–56.

Dietz, G. (2004). 'Partnership and the Development of Trust in British Workplaces', *Human Resource Management Journal*, 14(1): 5–24.

DiMaggio, P. and Powell, W. (1983). 'The Iron Cage Revisited: Institutional Isomorphism and Collective Rationality in Organizational Fields', *American Sociological Review*, 48(2): 147–60.

Dine, J. (2000). *The Governance of Corporate Groups*. Cambridge: Cambridge University Press.

———— (2005). *Companies, International Trade and Human Rights*. New York: Cambridge University Press.

Dobbin, F. and Sutton, R. C. (1998). 'The Strength of a Weak State: The Rights Movement and the Rise of the Human Resources Management Divisions', *American Journal of Sociology*, 104(2): 441–76.

Donaldson, T. (1989). *Key Issues in Business Ethics*. London: Academic Press.

———— and Preston, L. E. (1995). 'The Stakeholder Theory of the Corporation: Concepts, Evidence and Implications', *Academy of Management Review*, 20(1): 65–91.

Du Gay, P. (2000). *In Praise of Bureaucracy: Weber, Organization, Ethics*. London: Sage.

———— and Salaman, G. (1992). 'The [Cult]ure of the Customer', *Journal of Management Studies*, 29(4): 616–33.

Duska, R. (2004). 'Whistleblowing and Employee Loyalty', in T. L. Beauchamp and N. E. Bowie (eds.), *Ethical Theory and Business*, 7th edn. Upper Saddle River, NJ: Prentice-Hall, Pearson Education, pp. 335–9.

Dyer, L. and Shafer, R. (1999). 'From Human Resource Strategy to Organizational Effectiveness: Lessons from Research on Organizational Agility', in P. M. Wright, L. D. Dyer, J. W. Boudreau, and G. T. Milkovich (eds.), *Research in Personnel and Human Resource Management*

(*Supplement 4: Strategic Human Resources Management in the Twenty-First Century*). Greenwich, CT: JAI Press, pp. 145–74 (also available as CAHRS Working Paper 98–12).

Effron, M., Gandossy, R., and Goldsmith, M. (2003). *Human Resources in the 21st Century*. New York: John Wiley & Sons.

Ehrenreich, B. and Ehrenreich, J. (1978). 'The Professional-Managerial Class', in P. Walker (ed.), *Between Capital and Labour: The Professional–Managerial Class*. London: Southend Press, pp. 5–45.

Eisenstat, R. A. (1996). 'What Corporate Human Resources Brings to the Picnic: Four Models for Functional Management', *Organizational Dynamics*, 25(2): 6–14.

Elliott, J. (2004). 'Business Schools and Social Responsibility: A Dean's Perspective, May 12 2004', *Business & Society Review*, 109(4): 567–76.

Enteman, W. (1993). *The Emergence of a New Ideology*. Madison, WI: University of Wisconsin Press.

Evan, W. M. and Freeman, R. E. (2004). 'A Stakeholder Theory of the Modern Corporation: Kantian Capitalism', in T. L. Beauchamp and N. E. Bowie (eds.), *Ethical Theory and Business*, 7th edn. Englewood Cliffs, NJ: Prentice Hall, pp. 101–5.

Evans, F. J. and Marcal, L. (2005). 'Educating for Ethics: Business Deans' Perspectives', *Business & Society Review*, September, 110(3): 233–48.

Evans, P. and Genadry, N. (1999). 'A Duality-Based Perspective for Strategic Human Resource Management', in P. M. Wright, L. D. Dyer, J. W. Boudreau, and G. T. Milkovich (eds.), *Research in Personnel and Human Resources Management (Supplement 4: Strategic Human Resources Management in the Twenty-First Century)*. Greenwich, CT: JAI Press, pp. 367–95.

Everett, J. and Jamal, T. B. (2004). 'Multi-Stakeholder Collaboration as Symbolic Marketplace and Pedagogic Practice', *Journal of Management Inquiry*, 13(1): 57–78.

Exworthy, M. and Halford, S. (eds.) (1999). *Professionals and New Managerialism in the Public Sector*. Berkshire, UK: Open University Press.

Fenwick, C. and Landau, I. (2006). 'Work Choices in International Perspective', *Australian Journal of Labour Law*, 19: 127.

Ferlie, E., Hartley, J., and Martin, S. (eds.) (2003). 'Changing Public Service Organisations: Current Perspectives and Future Prospects', *British Journal of Management*, Special Issue, Vol. 14, December.

Ferner, A. (1994). 'Multinational Companies and Human Resource Management: An Overview of Research Issues', *Human Resource Management Journal*, 4(3): 79–102.

—— (1997). 'Country of Origin Effects and HRM in Multinational Companies', *Human Resource Management Journal*, 7(1): 19–37.

Festinger, L. (1957). *A Theory of Cognitive Dissonance*. Palo Alto, CA: Stanford University Press.

FBU (Fire Brigade Union) (2002). Available at: http://www.fbu.org.uk/pay2002/pay2002main.html

Finnis, J. (1979). *Natural Law and Natural Rights*. Oxford: Oxford University Press.

—— (1983). *Fundamentals of Ethics*. Oxford: Clarendon Press.

Fisher, C., Schoenfeldt, L. F., and Shaw, J. B. (1999). *Human Resource Management*, 4th edn. Boston, MA: Houghton Mifflin Company.

Flew, A. (1976). 'The Profit Motive', *Ethics*, 86: 312–27.

Flood, P. C., Turner, T., Ramamoorthy, N., and Pearson, J. (2001). 'Causes and Consequences of Psychological Contracts Among Knowledge Workers in the High Technology and Financial Services Industries', *International Journal of Human Resource Management*, 12(7): 1152–65.

Florini, A. (2003). 'Business and Global Governance', *The Brookings Review*, 21(2): 4–8.

Folger, R. (1977). 'Distributive and Procedural Justice: Combined Impact of "Voice" and Improvement on Experienced Inequity', *Journal of Personality and Social Psychology*, 35: 108–19.

——— and Cropanzano, R. (1998). *Organizational Justice and Human Behaviour*. Thousand Oaks, CA: Sage.

——— and Skarlicki, D. P. (1998). 'When Tough Times Make Tough Bosses: Managerial Distancing as a Function of Layoff Blame', *Academy of Management Journal*, 41: 79–87.

——— and Skarlicki, D. P. (2001). 'Fairness as a Dependent Variable: Why Tough Times can Lead to Bad Management', in R. S. Cropanzano (ed.), *Justice in the Workplace: Volume 2—From Theory to Practice*. Mahwah, NJ: Erlbaum, pp. 97–118.

Fombrun, C. J., Tichy, N. M., and Devanna, M. A. (1984). *Strategic Human Resource Management*. New York: John Wiley & Sons.

Foot, P. (ed.) (1977). *Theories of Ethics*. Oxford: Oxford University Press (first published in 1967).

——— (1978). *Virtues and Vices and Other Essays*. Berkeley, CA: University of California Press.

Foote, D. (2001). 'The Question of Ethical Hypocrisy in Human Resource Management in the UK and Irish Charity Sectors', *Journal of Business Ethics*, 34(1): 25–38.

——— and Robinson, I. (1999). 'The Role of the Human Resources Manager: Strategist or Conscience of the Organization?', *Business Ethics: A European View*, 8(2): 88–98.

Ford, J. and Harding, N. (2003). 'Invoking Satan or the Ethics of the Employment Contract', *Journal of Management Studies*, 40: 1129–50.

Foucault, M. (2003). *Society Must be Defended*. London: Allen Lane.

Fourier, C. (1971). *Harmonium Man: Selected Writings of Charles Fourier* (edited with an introduction by M. Poster). New York: Anchor Books.

Fournier, V. (1999). 'The Appeal to "Professionalism" as a Disciplinary Mechanism', *Sociological Review*, 47(2): 280–307.

Fox, A. (1974). *Beyond Contract: Work, Power and Trust Relations*. London: Faber and Faber.

——— (1985). *History and Heritage: The Social Origins of the British Industrial Relations System*. London: Allen and Unwin.

Frank, T. (2000). *One Market Under God: Extreme Capitalism, Market Populism and the End of Economic Democracy*. New York: Secker and Warburg.

Freedland, M. R. (1995). 'The Role of the Contract of Employment in Modern Labour Law', in L. Betten (ed.), *The Employment Contract in Transforming Labour Relations*. The Hague: Kluwer Law International, pp. 17–27.

——— (2003). *The Personal Employment Contract*. Oxford: Oxford University Press.

Freeman, J. (1995). 'Business Strategy from the Population Level', in C. Montgomery (ed.), *Resource-Based and Evolutionary Theories of the Firm: Towards a Synthesis*. Boston, MA: Kluwer, pp. 219–50.

Freeman, R. and Medoff, J. (1984). *What Do Unions Do?* New York: Basic Books.

Freeman, R. E. (1984). *Strategic Management: A Stakeholder Approach*. Boston, MA: Pitman.

——— (1999). 'Divergent Stakeholder Theory', *Academy of Management Review*, 24(2): 233–6.

_____ and Phillips, R. A. (2002). 'Stakeholder Theory: A Libertarian Defense', *Business Ethics Quarterly*, 12(3), July: 331–49.

Freidson, E. (1994). *Professionalism Reborn*. Cambridge: Polity Press.

_____ (2001). *Professionalism: The Third Logic*. Cambridge: Polity Press.

Friedman, M. (1970). 'The Social Responsibility of Business is to Increase Profit', *The New York Times Magazine*.

Frost, P., Dutton, J., Worline, M., and Wilson, A. (2000). 'Narratives of Compassion in Organizations', in S. Fineman (ed.), *Emotion in Organizations*. Thousand Oaks, CA: Sage, pp. 24–45.

Gabriel, Y. and Sturdy, A. (2002). 'Exporting Management: Neo-Imperialism and Global Consumerism', in K. Robins and F. Webster (eds.), *The Virtual University?* Oxford: Oxford University Press, pp. 148–68.

Galang, M. C. and Ferris, G. R. (1997). 'Human Resource Department Power and Influence Through Symbolic Action', *Human Relations*, 50(11): 1403–26.

Gandz, J. and Bird, F. G. (1996). 'The Ethics of Empowerment', *Journal of Business Ethics*, 15: 383–92.

Gane, M. and Johnson, T. (eds.) (1993). *Foucault's New Domains*. London: Routledge.

Garland, D. (1990). *Punishment and Modern Society*. Oxford: Clarendon.

Garrick, J. and Clegg, S. (2000). 'Organizational Gothic: Transfusing Vitality and Transforming the Corporate Body Through Work-Based Learning', in C. Symes and J. McIntyre (eds.), *Working Knowledge: The New Vocationalism and Higher Education*. Buckingham, UK: The Society for Research into Higher Education and Open University Press, pp. 153–71.

Gaumnitz, B. R. and Lere, J. C. (2002). 'Contents of Codes of Ethics of Professional Business Organizations in the United States', *Journal of Business Ethics*, 35(1): 35–49.

Geach, P. (1978). *The Virtues*. Cambridge: Cambridge University Press.

Geare, A. J. (1977). 'The Field of Study of Industrial Relations', *Journal of Industrial Relations*, 19(3): 274–85.

Ghemawat, P. and Costa, J. E. (1993). 'The Organizational Tension Between Static and Dynamic Efficiency', *Strategic Management Journal*, 14: 59–73.

Gibb, S. (2000). 'Evaluating HRM Effectiveness: The Stereotype Connection', *Employee Relations*, 22(1): 58–75.

Giddens, A. (1990). *The Consequences of Modernity*. Cambridge: Polity Press.

_____ (2000). *The Third Way and its Critics*. Cambridge: Polity Press.

Glisby, M. and Holden, N. (2003). 'Contextual Constraints in Knowledge Management Theory: The Cultural Embeddedness of Nonaka's Knowledge-Creating Company', *Knowledge and Process Management*, 10(1): 29–36.

Godard, J. (2001). 'Beyond the High-Performance Paradigm? An Analysis of Variation in Canadian Managerial Perceptions of Reform Programme Effectiveness', *British Journal of Industrial Relations*, 39(1): 25–52.

_____ and Delaney, J. (2000). 'Reflections on the "High Performance" Paradigm's Implications for Industrial Relations as a Field', *Industrial and Labor Relations Review*, 53(3): 482–502.

Goldner, F. H. and Ritti, R. R. (1967). 'Professionalization as Career Immobility', *American Journal of Sociology*, 72(5): 489–502.

Goldthorpe, J. (1982). 'On the Service Class: Its Formation and Future', in A. Giddens and G. MacKenzie (eds.), *Social Class and the Division of Labour*. Cambridge: Cambridge University Press, pp. 162–85.

—— (1995). 'The Service Class Revisited', in T. Butler and M. Savage (eds.), *Social Change and the Middle Classes*. London: UCL Press, pp. 313–29.

Gospel, H. (1992). *Markets, Firms, and the Management of Labour in Modern Britain*. Cambridge: Cambridge University Press.

Gowler, D. and Legge, K. (1983). 'The Meaning of Management and the Management of Meaning', in M. Earl (ed.), *Perspectives on Management: A Multidisciplinary Analysis*. Oxford: Oxford University Press, pp. 197–233.

Graham, G. (2004). *Eight Theories of Ethics*. London: Routledge.

Granovetter, M. (1985). 'Economic Action and Social Structure: The Problem of Embeddedness', *American Journal of Sociology*, 91(3): 481–510.

Grant, A. M. (forthcoming). 'Relational Job Design and the Motivation to Make a Prosocial Difference', forthcoming in *Academy of Management Review*.

—— Campbell, E. M., Chen, G., Cottone, L., Lapedis, D., and Lee, K. (forthcoming). 'Impact and the Art of Motivation Maintenance: The Effects of Contact with Beneficiaries on Persistence Behavior'. *Organizational Behavior and Human Decision Processes*.

—— Molinsky, A., Margolis, J., Kamin, M., and Schiano, B. (forthcoming). 'The Performer's Reactions to Procedural Injustice: When Prosocial Identity Reduces Prosocial Behavior', Manuscript in preparation for publication.

—— —— —— Schiano, B., and Kamin, M. (2006). 'When Prosocial is Antisocial: Identity Moderates Reactions to Procedural Justice in the Performance of Necessary Evils', Manuscript in preparation for publication.

Grant, R. M. (1991). 'The Resource-Based Theory of Competitive Advantage: Implications for Strategy Formulation', *California Management Review*, 33(2): 114–35.

Gratton, L., Hope-Hailey, V., Stiles, P., and Truss, C. (1999). *Strategic Human Resource Management*. Oxford: Oxford University Press.

Gray, J. (1995). *Berlin*. London: Fontana.

Greenberg, J. (1990). 'Employee Theft as a Reaction to Underpayment Inequity: The Hidden Cost of Pay Cuts', *Journal of Applied Psychology*, 75: 561–8.

—— (1993). 'The Social Side of Fairness: Interpersonal and Informational Classes of Organizational Justice', in R. Cropanzano (ed.), *Justice in the Workplace: Approaching Fairness in Human Resource Management*. Hillsdale, NJ: Lawrence Erlbaum, pp. 79–103.

Greenwood, M. R. (2001). 'Community as a Stakeholder: Focusing on Corporate Social and Environmental Reporting', *Journal of Corporate Citizenship*, 1(4): 31–45.

—— (2002). 'Ethics and HRM: A Review and Conceptual Analysis', *Journal of Business Ethics*, 36(3): 261–79.

Grensing-Pophal, L. (1998). 'Walking the Tightrope, Balancing Risks and Gains', *HR Magazine*, 43(11): 118–19.

Grey, C. (1999). 'We Are All Managers Now, We Always Were: On the Development and Demise of Management', *Journal of Management Studies*, 36(5): 561–86.

Grube, J. A. and Piliavin, J. A. (2000). 'Role Identity, Organizational Experiences, and Volunteer Performance', *Personality and Social Psychology Bulletin*, 26: 1108–19.

Guest, D. E. (1987). 'Human Resource Management and Industrial Relations', *Journal of Management Studies*, 24(5): 503–21.

———(1997). 'Human Resource Management and Performance: A Review and Research Agenda', *International Journal of Human Resource Management*, 8(3): 263–76.

———(1998). 'Is the Psychological Contract Worth Taking Seriously?', *Journal of Organizational Behaviour*, 19: 649–64.

———(1999). 'Human Resource Management—The Workers' Verdict', *Human Resource Management Journal*, 9(3): 5–25.

———(2001). 'Industrial Relations and Human Resource Management', in J. Storey (ed.), *Human Resource Management: A Critical Text*, 2nd edn. London: Thomson Learning, pp. 96–113.

———(2002). 'Human Resource Management, Corporate Performance and Employee Wellbeing: Building the Worker into HRM', *Journal of Industrial Relations*, 44(3): 335–58.

——— and Conway, N. (1998). *Fairness at Work and the Psychological Contract.* London: IPD.

——— ———(1999). 'Peering into the Black Hole: The Downside of the New Employment Relations in the UK', *British Journal of Industrial Relations*, 37(3): 367–89.

——— ———(2000). *Change at Work and the Psychological Contract.* London: IPD.

——— and Hoque, K. (1994). 'The Good, the Bad and the Ugly: Employment Relations in New Non-Union Workplaces', *Human Resource Management Journal*, 5(1): 1–14.

——— and King, Z. (2004). 'Power, Innovation and Problem-Solving: The Personnel Managers' Three Steps to Heaven?', *Journal of Management Studies*, 41(3): 401–23.

——— and Peccei, R. (2001). 'Partnership at Work: Mutuality and the Balance of Advantage', *British Journal of Industrial Relations*, 39(3): 207–36.

——— Conway, N., and Dewe, P. (2004). 'Using Sequential Tree Analysis to Search for Bundles of HR Practices', *Human Resource Management Journal*, 14(1): 80–96.

——— ——— Briner, R., and Dickmann, M. (1997). *The State of the Psychological Contract in Employment.* London: IPD.

——— Mackenzie Davey, K., and Patch, A. (2000). 'The Employment Relationship, the Psychological Contract and Knowledge Management: Securing Employees' Trust and Contribution', *Proceedings of the Knowledge Management Concepts and Controversies Conference*, Warwick University, 9th–10th February.

——— Michie, J., Conway, N., and Sheehan, M. (2003). 'Human Resource Management and Corporate Performance in the UK', *British Journal of Industrial Relations*, 41(2): 291–314.

——— ——— Sheehan, M., and Conway, N. (2000). *Employment Relations, HRM and Business Performance: An Analysis of the 1998 Workplace Employee Relations Survey.* London: CIPD.

Gunningham, N. (1984). *Safeguarding the Worker.* Sydney, NSW: Lawbook.

Habermas, J. (1984 [1976]). *Communication and the Evolution of Society.* Cambridge: Polity Press.

Hackman, J. R. (2002). *Leading Teams: Setting the Stage for Great Performances.* Boston, MA: Harvard Business School Press.

——— and Oldham, G. R. (1976). 'Motivation Through the Design of Work: Test of a Theory', *Organizational Behavior and Human Performance*, 16: 250–79.

Hagan, J. (1964). 'Employers, Trade Unions and the First Victorian Factory Acts', *Labour History*, 7: 3.

Haidt, J. (2001). 'The Emotional Dog and its Rational Tail: A Social Intuitionist Approach to Moral Judgment', *Psychological Review*, 108: 814–34.

Haldane, J. (ed.) (2002). *Mind, Metaphysics, and Value in the Thomistic and Analytic Traditions.* Notre Dame, IN: University of Notre Dame Press.

Halford, S. and Leonard, P. (1999). 'New Identities?: Professionalism, Managerialism and the Construction of Self', in M. Exworthy and S. Halford (eds.), *Professionals and New Managerialism in the Public Sector.* Berkshire, UK: Open University Press, pp. 102–20.

Hall, P. A. and Soskice, D. A. (2001). 'An Introduction to Varieties of Capitalism', in P. A. Hall and D. A. Soskice (eds.), *Varieties of Capitalism: The Institutional Foundations of Comparative Advantage.* Oxford: Oxford University Press, pp. 1–70.

Hall, R. (1993). 'A Framework Linking Intangible Resources and Capabilities to Sustainable Competitive Advantage', *Strategic Management Journal*, 14(8): 607–18.

Hamel, G. and Prahalad, C. (1994). *Competing for the Future.* Boston, MA. Harvard Business School Press.

Hammersley, G. C. and Pinnington, A. H. (1999*a*). 'Quality Circles Reach End of the Line at Land Rover', *Human Resource Management International Digest*, 7(3), May–June: 4–6.

―――― (1999*b*). 'Land Rover Employees' Attitudes to Continuous Improvement Groups', *The TQM Magazine*, 11(1), January: 8–18.

Hanlon, G. (1998). 'Professionalism as Enterprise: Service Class Politics and the Redefinition of Professionalism', *Sociology*, 32(1): 43–63.

―――― (2004). 'Institutional Forms and Organizational Structures: Homology, Trust and Reputational Capital in Professional Service Firms', *Organization*, 11(2): 187–210.

Harcourt, S. and Harcourt, M. (2002). 'Do Employers Comply with Civil/Human Rights Legislation? New Evidence from New Zealand Application Forms', *Journal of Business Ethics*, 35(3): 207–21.

Hardy, C., Lawrence, T., and Grant, D. (2005). 'Discourse and Collaboration: The Role of Conversations and Collective Identity', *Academy of Management Review*, 30(1): 1–20.

Harley, B. and Hardy, C. (2004). 'Firing Blanks? An Analysis of Discursive Struggle in HRM', *Journal of Management Studies*, 41(3): 377–400.

Hart, T. J. (1993). 'Human Resource Management: Time to Exorcize the Militant Tendency', *Employee Relations*, 15(3): 29–36.

Haug, M. (1973). 'Deprofessionalization: An Alternative Hypothesis for the Future', *Sociological Review Monographs*, 20: 195–211.

Harvey, D. (2003). *The New Imperialism.* Oxford: Oxford University Press.

Hawkridge, D., Newton, W., and Hall, C. (1988). *Computers in Company Training.* London: Croom Helm.

Hayes, N. and Walsham, G. (2000). 'Safe Enclaves, Political Enclaves and Knowledge Working', in C. Pritchard, R. Hull, M. Chumer, and H. Willmott (eds.), *Managing Knowledge: Critical Investigations of Work and Learning.* London: Macmillan, pp. 69–87.

Heckscher, C. and Donnellon, A. (eds.) (1994). *The Post-Bureaucratic Organization.* Thousand Oaks, CA: Sage.

Heider, F. (1958). *The Psychology of Interpersonal Relations.* New York: Wiley.

Heller, A. (1985). *The Power of Shame: A Rational Perspective.* London: Routledge & Kegan Paul.

―――― (1987*a*). *Beyond Justice.* Oxford: Blackwell.

—— (1987b). *Radical Philosophy*. Oxford: Blackwell.

—— (1988). *General Ethics*. Oxford: Blackwell.

—— (1990). *A Philosophy of Morals*. Oxford: Blackwell.

—— (1996). *An Ethics of Personality*. Oxford: Blackwell.

Hendry, C., Arthur, M., and Jones, A. (1995). *Strategy Through People*. London and New York: Routledge.

Heneman, H. G. (1969). 'Toward a General System of Industrial Relations: How Do We Get There?', in G. G. Somers (ed.), *Essays in Industrial Relations Theory*. Ames, IW: Iowa State University Press, pp. 3–24.

Henriques, H. W. (1979). *Before the Welfare State: Social Administration in Early Industrial Britain*. London: Longmans.

Hepple, B. (1999). 'Employee Loyalty in English Law', *Comparative Labor Law and Policy Journal*, 20(2): 205–24.

Higgins, H. B. (1915). 'A New Province for Law and Order', *Harvard Law Review*, 29: 13.

HM Govt. White Paper (2003). 'Our Fire and Rescue Service', §§3.24–3.25. Available at: http://www.odpm.gov.uk/stellent/groups/odpm_fire/documents/page/odpm_fire_022968-06.hcsp#TopOfPage

Hochschild, A. (1983). *The Managed Heart*. Berkeley, CA: University of California Press.

Hodges, D. (2000). *Class Politics in the Information Age*. Urbana, IL: University of Illinois.

Hodson, R. (2001). *Dignity at Work*. Cambridge: Cambridge University Press.

Holman, D. (2003). 'Call Centres', in D. Holman, C. W. Clegg, T. D. Wall, P. Sparrow, and A. Howard (eds.), *The New Workplace*. Chichester, UK: John Wiley & Sons, pp. 115–34.

Hornby, P. and Symon, G. (1994). 'Tracer Studies', in C. Cassell and G. Symon (eds.), *Qualitative Methods in Organizational Research: A Practical Guide*. London: Sage, pp. 167–86.

Howe, J. and Mitchell, R. (1999). 'The Evolution of the Contract of Employment in Australia: A Discussion', *Australian Journal of Labour Law*, 12: 113.

Howell, C. (2004). 'Is There a Third Way for Industrial Relations?', *British Journal of Industrial Relations*, 42(1): 1–22.

Howells, R. W. L. (1972). 'The Robens Report', *Industrial Law Journal*, 1: 185.

HR Nicholls Society (1986). *Arbitration in Contempt*. Melbourne: HR Nicholls Society.

Hughes, O. E. (1998). *Public Management and Administration*, 2nd edn. London: Macmillan.

Huselid, M. A. (1995). 'Impact of Human Resource Management Practices on Turnover, Productivity, and Corporate Financial Performance', *Academy of Management Journal*, 38(3): 635–72.

Hutchins, B. L. and Harrison, A. (1926). *A History of Factory Legislation*. London: Frank Cass.

Hutson, J. H. (1983). *Penal Colony to Penal Powers* (rev. edn.). Sydney, NSW: Amalgamated Metal Workers and Shipwrights Union.

Hutton, W. (2002). *The World We're In*. London: Little Brown.

Hyman, R. (1987). 'Strategy or Structure? Capital, Labour and Control', *Work, Employment & Society* 1(1): 25–55.

—— (1997). 'The Future of Employee Representation', *British Journal of Industrial Relations*, 35(3): 309–36.

Ichniowski, C. and Shaw, K. (1999). 'The Effects of Human Resource Management Systems on Economic Performance: An International Comparison of US and Japanese Plants', *Management Science*, 45(5), May: 704–21.

——— ——— and Prennushi, G. (1997). 'The Effects of Human Resource Management Practices on Productivity: A Study of Steel Finishing Lines', *The American Economic Review*, 87(3): 291–313.

ILO (International Labour Organization) (1999). *Decent Work*. Report of the Director General to the 87th Session of the International Labour Conference, Geneva: ILO.

——— (2001). *Reducing the Decent Work Deficit*. Report of the Director General to the 89th Session of the International Labour Conference, Geneva: ILO.

——— discussion document (2003). Available at: http://www.ilo.org/public/english/dialogue/sector/techmeet/jmpes03/jmpes-r.pdf

——— (2004). International Labour Organization Mandate. Geneva: ILO. Available at: http://www.ilo.org/public/english/about/mandate.htm

——— (2005). *Report of the Committee of Experts on the Application of Conventions and Recommendations*. Report III (Part 1A), ILO: Geneva.

IPA (Involvement and Participation Association) (1997). *Towards Industrial Partnership: New Ways of Working in British Companies*. London: IPA.

Ivancevich, J. M. (1992). *Human Resource Management: Foundations of Personnel*. Boston, MA: Irwin.

Jacoby, S. (1998). 'Downsizing in the Past', *Challenge*, 41(3): 100–13.

Jennings, M. M. (2006). *Business Ethics: Case Studies and Selected Readings*, 5th edn. Ohio: Thomson.

Jessop, B. (2002). *The Future of the Capitalist State*. Cambridge: Polity Press.

Jessop, R. (1994). 'Post-Fordism and the State', in A. Amin (ed.), *Post-Fordism: A Reader*. Oxford: Blackwell, pp. 251–79.

Johnson, G. (1987). *Strategic Change and the Management Process*. Oxford: Blackwell.

Johnson, T. (1972). *Professions and Power*. London: Macmillan.

——— (1993). 'Expertise and the State', in M. Gane and T. Johnson (eds.), *Foucault's New Domains*. London: Routledge, pp. 139–52.

Johnstone, R. (2000). 'Occupational Health and Safety Prosecutions in Victoria: An Historical Study', *Australian Journal Labour Law*, 13: 113.

——— (2003*a*). *Occupational Health and Safety, Courts and Crime: The Legal Construction of Occupational Health and Safety Offences in Victoria*. Annandale, NSW: The Federation Press.

——— (2003*b*). 'Safety, Courts and Crime: Occupational Health and Safety Prosecutions in the Magistrates' Courts', *Policy and Practice in Health and Safety*, 1: 105.

——— (2004*a*). *Occupational Health and Safety Law and Policy*, 2nd edn. Sydney, NSW: Lawbook.

——— (2004*b*). 'From Fiction to Fact: Rethinking OHS Enforcement', in E. Bluff, N. Gunningham, and R. Johnstone (eds.), *OHS Regulation for a Changing World of Work*. Annandale, NSW: The Federation Press, pp. 146–78.

Jones, C., Parker, M., and Bos, R. T. (2005). *For Business Ethics*. London: Routledge.

Kahn, W. A. (1990). 'Psychological Conditions of Personal Engagement and Disengagement at Work', *Academy of Management Journal*, 33: 692–724.

Kahn-Freund, O. (1949). 'The Tangle of the Truck Acts', *The Industrial Law Review*, 4: 2.

——— (1954). 'Legal Framework', in A. Flanders and H. A. Clegg (eds.), *The System of Industrial Relations in Great Britain*. Oxford: Blackwell, pp. 42–127.

_____ (1967). 'A Note on Status and Contract in British Labour Law', _Modern Law Review_, 30: 635.

_____ (1977). 'Blackstone's Neglected Child: The Contract of Employment', _Law Quarterly Review_, 93: 508.

Kaler, J. (1996). 'Does Empowerment Empower?', paper presented at the Centre for Organizational and Professional Ethics, Institute of Education, University of London, Workshop on Ethics and Empowerment.

_____ (2002). 'Morality and Strategy in Stakeholder Identification', _Journal of Business Ethics_, 39(1/2): 91–9.

_____ (2003). 'Differentiating Stakeholder Theories', _Journal of Business Ethics_, 46(1/2): 71–83.

Kamoche, K. (1996). 'Strategic Human Resource Management Within a Resource-Capability View of the Firm', _Journal of Management Studies_, 33(2) March: 213–33.

_____ (2001). _Understanding Human Resource Management_. Buckingham, UK: Open University Press.

_____ and Mueller, F. (1998). 'Human Resource Management and the Appropriation-Learning Perspective', _Human Relations_, 51(8): 1033–60.

Kandel, W. L. and Kilens, K. W. (1999). 'In-house Counsel as Whistle-Blower: At-Will Employment on Trial', _Employee Relations Law Journal_, 19(1): 91–102.

Kandel, E. and Lazear, E. (1992). 'Peer Pressure and Partnerships', _Journal of Political Economy_, 100: 801–17.

Kant, I. (1956). _The Moral Law or The Groundwork of the Metaphysics of Morals_ (trans. H. J. Paton). London: Hutchinson.

_____ (1963). _Lectures on Ethics_. New York: Harper and Row.

_____ [1724–1804] (1996). _Groundwork of the Metaphysics of Morals_, in Mary Gregor (ed.), (and introduction by Christine Korsgaard). Cambridge: Cambridge University Press.

Kantor, J. and Weisberg, J. (2002). 'Ethical Attitudes and Ethical Behavior: Are Managers Role Models?', _International Journal of Manpower_, 23(8): 687–703.

Kaplan, R. and Norton, D. (1996). _The Balanced Scorecard: Translating Strategy into Action_. Boston, MA: Harvard Business School Press.

Kay, J. (1993). _Foundations of Corporate Success_. Oxford: Oxford University Press.

Kearns, P. (2003). _HR Strategy: Business Focused, Individually Centred_. Oxford: Butterworth Heinemann.

Keat, R. and Abercrombie, N. (eds.) (1991). _Enterprise Culture_. London: Routledge.

Keenoy, T. (1990a). 'HRM: Rhetoric, Reality and Contradiction', _International Journal of Human Resource Management_, 1(3): 363–84.

_____ (1990b). 'HRM: A Case of the Wolf in Sheep's Clothing?', _Personnel Review_, 19: 3–9.

_____ (1992). 'Constructing Control', in J. F. Hartley and G. M. Stephenson (eds.), _Employment Relations: The Psychology of Influence and Control at Work_. Oxford: Blackwell, pp. 91–110.

_____ (1997). 'HRMism and the Languages of Re-Presentation', _Journal of Management Studies_, 34(5): 825–41.

_____ (1999). 'HRM as Hologram: A Polemic', _Journal of Management Studies_, 36(1): 1–23.

_____ and Anthony, P. (1992). 'HRM: Metaphor, Meaning and Morality', in P. Blyton and P. Turnbull (eds.), _Reassessing Human Resource Management_. London: Sage, pp. 223–55.

Kellough, J. E. (1999). 'Reinventing Public Personnel Management: Ethical Implications for Managers and Public Personnel Systems', *Public Personnel Management*, 28(4): 655–71.

Kirby, M. D. and Creighton, W. B. (2004). 'The Law of Conciliation and Arbitration', in J. E. Isaac and S. Macintyre (eds.), *The New Province for Law and Order: 100 Years of Australian Industrial Conciliation and Arbitration*. Melbourne: Cambridge University Press, pp. 98–138.

Kirkpatrick, I. and Ackroyd, S. (2003). 'Archetype Theory and the Changing Professional Organization: A Critique and Alternative', *Organization*, 10(4): 731–50.

—— —— and Walker, R. (2005). *The New Managerialism and Public Service Professionals*. London: Palgrave.

Kitchener, M. (2000). 'The Bureaucratization of Professional Roles: The Case of Clinical Directors in UK Hospitals', *Organization*, 7(1): 129–54.

Knights, D. and McCabe, D. (1998). 'What Happens When the Phones Go Wild? Staff, Stress and Spaces for Escape in a BPR Telephone Banking Call Regime', *Journal of Management Studies*, 35(2): 163–94.

—— —— (2003). *Organisation and Innovation*. Berkshire, UK: Open University Press.

Kochan, T. A. and Osterman, P. (1994). *The Mutual Gains Enterprise: Forging a Winning Partnership Among Labor, Management and Government*. Boston, MA: Harvard Business School Press.

—— Katz, H., and McKersie, R. (1986). *The Transformation of American Industrial Relations*. New York: Basic Books.

Koehn, D. (1994). *The Ground of Professional Ethics*. London: Routledge.

—— (2005). 'Transforming our Students: Teaching Business Ethics Post-Enron', *Business Ethics Quarterly*, 15(1): 137–51.

Kogut, B. and Zander, U. (1993). 'Knowledge of the Firm and the Evolutionary Theory of the Multinational Corporation', *Journal of International Business Studies*, 24(4): 624–45.

Konrad, A. M. and Linnehan, F. (1999). 'Affirmative Action: History, Effects and Attitudes', in G. N. Powell (ed.), *Handbook of Gender and Work*. Thousand Oaks, CA: Sage, pp. 429–52.

Korczynski, M. (2002). *Human Resource Management in Service Work*. Basingstoke, UK: Palgrave.

Kretzmann, N. and Stump, E. (1988). 'Being and Goodness', in T. Morris (ed.), *Divine and Human Action: Essays in the Metaphysics and Theism*. Ithaca, NY: Cornell University Press, pp. 281–312.

Kruger, K., Kruse, W., and Caprile, M. (2002). 'Work Process Knowledge and Industrial and Labour Relations', in N. Boreham, R. Samurcay, and M. Fischer (eds.), *Work Process Knowledge*. London: Routledge, pp. 201–14.

Kultgen, J. (1988). *Ethics and Professionalism*. Philadelphia, PA: University of Pennsylvania Press.

Kuruvilla, S., Das, S., Kwon, H., and Kwon, S. (2002). 'Trade Union Growth and Decline in Asia', *British Journal of Industrial Relations*, 40(3): 431–61.

La Trobe/Melbourne Occupational Health and Safety Project (1989). *Victorian Occupational Health and Safety—An Assessment of Law in Transition*. Melbourne: Dept. of Legal Studies, La Trobe University.

Langer, E. J. (1978). 'Rethinking the Role of Thought in Social Interaction', in J. H. Harvey, W. I. Ickes, and R. Kidd (eds.), *New Directions in Attribution Research*, vol. 2. Hillsdale, NJ: Erlbaum, pp. 35–58.

Larmer, R. A. (1992). 'Whistleblowing and Employee Loyalty', *Journal of Business Ethics*, 11(2) February: 125–8.

Larson, M. S. (1977). *The Rise of Professionalism: A Sociological Analysis.* Berkeley, CA: University of Califonia Press.

——(1990). 'In the Matter of Experts and Professionals', in M. Burrage and R. Torstendahl (eds.), *The Formation of Professions.* London: Sage, pp. 24–50.

——(1991). 'On the Matter of Experts and Professionals, or How Impossible it is to Leave Nothing Unsaid', in M. Burrage and R. Torstendahl (eds.), *The Formation of Professions.* London: Sage, pp. 24–50.

Lash, S. and Urry, J. (1994). *Economies of Signs and Space.* London: Sage.

Lawler, E. (1987). *High Involvement Management.* San Francisco, CA: Jossey-Bass.

Lawrence, J. (1999). *Argument for Action: Ethics and Professional Conduct.* Aldershot, UK: Ashgate.

Leadbeater, C. (2003). *Personalisation Through Participation.* London: Demos.

Lees, S. (1997). 'HRM and the Legitimacy Market', *International Journal of Human Resource Management*, 8(3): 226–43.

Legge, K. (1978). *Power, Innovation, and Problem-solving in Personnel Management.* London: McGraw-Hill.

——(1989). 'Human Resource Management: A Critical Analysis', in J. Storey (ed.), *New Perspectives on Human Resource Management.* London: Routledge, pp. 19–40.

——(1995). *Human Resource Management: Rhetorics and Realities.* Basingstoke, UK: Macmillan.

——(1996). 'Morality Bound', *People Management*, 25(2): 34–6.

——(1998*a*). 'The Morality of HRM', in C. Mabey, D. Skinner, and T. Clark (eds.), *Experiencing Human Resource Management.* London: Sage, pp. 14–30.

——(1998*b*). 'Is HRM Ethical? Can HRM be Ethical?', in M. Parker (ed.), *Ethics and Organizations.* London: Sage, pp. 150–72.

Leicht, K. T. and Fennel, M. L. (2001). *Professional Work: A Sociological Approach.* London: Blackwell.

Lepak, D. P. and Snell, S. A. (1999). 'The Human Resource Architecture: Toward a Theory of Human Capital Allocation and Development', *Organization Studies*, 18(1): 43–76.

—— ——(2002). 'Examining the Human Resource Architecture: The Relationships Among Human Capital, Employment and Human Resource Configurations', *Journal of Management*, 28(4): 517–43.

Lerner, M. J. and Miller, D. T. (1978). 'Just World Research and the Attribution Process: Looking Back and Ahead', *Psychological Bulletin*, 85: 1030–51.

Letiche, H. (1998). 'Business Ethics: (In-)Justice and (Anti-)Law—Reflections on Derrida, Bauman and Lipovetsky', in M. Parker (ed.), *Ethics & Organizations.* London: Sage, pp. 122–49.

Liebeskind, J. P. (1997). 'Keeping Organizational Secrets: Protective Institutional Mechanisms and Their Costs', *Industrial and Corporate Change*, 6(3): 623–63.

Lind, E. A. and Tyler, T. R. (1988). *The Social Psychology of Procedural Justice.* New York: Plenum Press.

—— Greenberg, J., Scott, K. S., and Welchans, T. D. (2000). 'The Winding Road from Employee to Complainant: Situational and Psychological Determinants of Wrongful-Termination Claims', *Administrative Science Quarterly*, 45: 557–90.

Lindsay, J. (2001). 'The Implied Terms of Trust and Confidence', *Industrial Law Journal*, 30: 1.

Locke, E. A. and Latham, G. P. (1990). *A Theory of Goal-Setting and Task Performance*. Englewood Cliffs, NJ: Prentice Hall.

———— (2002). 'Building a Practically Useful Theory of Goal Setting and Task Motivation: A 35-year Odyssey', *American Psychologist*, 57: 705–17.

Loewenstein, G. (1996). 'Out of Control: Visceral Influences on Behavior', *Organizational Behavior and Human Decision Processes*, 65(3): 272–92.

Losey, M. R. (1997). 'The Future HR Professional: Competency Buttressed by Advocacy and Ethics', *Human Resource Management*, 36(1): 147–50.

Lovell, A. (2002). 'Ethics as a Dependent Variable and Organizational Decision Making', *Journal of Business Ethics*, 37(2): 145–63.

Lukes, S. (1974). *Power: A Radical View*. London: Macmillan.

Luthans, F. and Peterson, S. J. (2002). 'Employee Engagement and Manager Self-Efficacy: Implications for Managerial Effectiveness and Development', *The Journal of Management Development*, 21: 376–87.

Lutz, M. A. (2001). 'On the Norm of Equality', *International Journal of Social Economics*, 10/11/12: 782–99.

Lyotard, J.-F. (1984). *The Postmodern Condition: A Report on Knowledge*. Manchester, UK: Manchester University Press.

Mabey, C., Salaman, G., and Storey, J. (1998). *Human Resource Management: A Strategic Introduction*. Oxford: Blackwell.

Macdonald, K. M. (1995). *The Sociology of the Professions*. London: Sage.

MacDuffie, J. P. (1995). 'Human Resource Bundles and Manufacturing Performance: Organizational Logic and Flexible Production Systems in the World Auto Industry', *Industrial and Labor Relations Review*, 48(2): 197–221.

Machin, S. (2000). 'Union Decline in Britain', *British Journal of Industrial Relations*, 32(4): 631–45.

MacIntyre, A. (1981). *After Virtue: A Study in Moral Theory*, London: Duckworth.

———— (1988). *Whose Justice Which Rationality*, London: Duckworth.

Macintyre, S. (1989). 'Neither Capital nor Labour: The Politics of the Establishment of Arbitration', in S. Macintyre and R. Mitchell (eds.) *Foundations of Arbitration*. Melbourne: Oxford University Press.

———— and Mitchell, R. J. (1989). 'Introduction', in S. Macintyre and R. Mitchell (eds.), *Foundations of Arbitration. The Origins and Effects of State Compulsory Arbitration, 1890–1914*. Melbourne: Oxford University Press, pp. 1–21.

Macken, J. J., O'Grady, P., Sappideen, C., and Warburton, G. (2002). *The Law of Employment*. Sydney, NSW: Lawbook.

Maclagan, P. (1998). *Management and Morality: A Developmental Perspective*. London: Sage.

Macklin, R. (1999). 'The Difficulties and Moral Compromises Faced by Australian Human Resource Managers Seeking to Create Decent Organizations', *Business & Professional Ethics Journal*, 18(3/4): 93–112.

———— (2001). 'Justice, Morality and the Role of Human Resource Managers in Australian Organisations: An Evaluation of the Applicability of the Moral Theory and Philosophy of Agnes Heller', Ph.D. thesis, Charles Sturt University.

———— (2003a). 'The Moral Norms and Principles of HR Managers in Australian Organizations', Refereed *Proceedings of the 2003 Hawaii International Conference on Business*. Hawaii.

_____ (2003*b*). 'Guidelines for Dealing with Moral Conflicts in Human Resource Management', in P. Rushbrook (ed.), Innovations in Professional Practice: Influences & Perspectives— Refereed *Proceedings of the 2003 Continuing Professional Education (CPE) Conference.* Australian National University, 7th–8th March 2003.

March, J. and Simon, H. A. (1958). *Organizations.* New York: John Wiley & Sons.

Marchington, M. (2001). 'Employee Involvement at Work', in J. Storey (ed.), *Human Resource Management: A Critical Text*, 2nd edn. London: Thomson Learning, pp. 232–52.

_____ and Wilkinson, A. (1996). *Core Personnel and Development*, 1st edn. London: Institute of Personnel and Development (IPD).

Margolis, J. D. (2001). 'Responsibility in Organizational Context', *Business Ethics Quarterly*, 11(3): 431–54.

Markey, R. (1989). 'Trade Unions, the Labor Party and the Introduction of Arbitration in New South Wales and the Commonwealth', in S. Macintyre and R. Mitchell (eds.), *Foundations of Arbitration. The Origins and Effects of State Compulsory Arbitration, 1890–1914.* Melbourne: Oxford University Press, pp. 156–77.

Marquand, D. (2004). *Decline of the Public.* Cambridge: Polity Press.

Martin, G. and Woldring, K. (2001). 'Ready for the Mantle? Australian Human Resource Managers as Stewards of Ethics', *International Journal of Human Resource Management*, 12(2): 243–55.

Marx, K. (1954). *Capital*, vol. 1. Moscow: Progress Publishers.

Matten, D. and Crane, A. (2003). *Business Ethics: A European Perspective.* Oxford: Oxford University Press.

McCallum, R. and Stewart, A. (1999). Employee Loyalty in Australia. *Comparative Labor Law and Policy Journal*, 20(2): 155–83.

McCarry, G. J. (1984). 'The Employee's Duty to Obey Unreasonable Orders', *Australian Law Journal*, 58: 327.

_____ (1998). 'Damages for Breach of the Employer's Implied Duty of Trust and Confidence', *Australian Business Law Review*, 26: 141.

McKenna, R. and Tsahuridu, E. (2001). 'Must Managers Leave Ethics at Home? Economics and Moral Anomie in Business Organisations', *Reason in Practice*, 1(3): 67–76.

McLaughlin, K., Osborne, S. P., and Ferlie, E. (eds.) (2002). *New Public Management: Current Trends and Future Prospects.* London: Routledge.

Meisinger, S. (2002). Trust in the Top, *HR Magazine*, 47(10): 8.

Mello, J. A. (2000). 'The Dual Loyalty Dilemma for HR Managers Under Title VII Compliance', *SAM Advanced Management Journal*, 65(1): 10–15, 51.

Metcalfe, C. (1998). 'The Stakeholder Corporation', *Business Ethics: A European Review*, 7(1): 30–6.

Meyer, A. D., Tsui, A. S., and Hinings, C. R. (1993). 'Configurational Approaches to Organizational Analysis', *Academy of Management Journal*, 36(6): 1175–95.

Miles, R. E. and Snow, C. C. (1984). 'Designing Strategic Human Resource Systems', *Organizational Dynamics*, 13(1): 36–52.

Miles, S. and Friedman, A. (2003). 'Exploring the Social Construction of Stakeholder Management in the UK', paper presented at the Academy of Management Annual Meeting, Seattle, Washington.

Milgram, S. (1974). *Obedience to Authority*. New York: Harper & Row.

Miller, D. (1981). 'Toward a New Contingency Approach: The Search for Organizational Gestalts', *Journal of Management Studies*, 18(1): 1–26.

—— (1987). 'The Genesis of Configuration', *Academy of Management Review*, 12(4): 686–701.

Miller, G. E. and Rowney, J. I. A. (1999). 'Workplace Diversity Management in a Multicultural Society', *Women in Management Review*, 14(7/8): 307–16.

Miller, P. (1996). 'Strategy and the Ethical Management of Human Resources', *Human Resource Management Journal*, 6(1): 5–18.

—— and Rose, N. (1990). 'Governing Economic Life', *Economy and Society*, 19(1): 1–31.

Millerson, G. (1964). *The Qualifying Associations: A Study in Professionalization*. London: Routledge and Kegan Paul.

Mintzberg, H. (1978). 'Patterns in Strategy Formation', *Management Science*, 24(9): 934–48.

Misztal, B. (2002). 'Trusting the Professional: A Managerial Discourse for Uncertain Times', in M. Dent and S. Whithead (eds.), *Managing Professional Identities: Knowledge, 'Performativity' and the 'New' Professional*. London: Routledge, pp. 19–37.

Mitchell, M. E. (2000). Entrepreneurial Activities in Human Resource Management, *AIC Journal of Business*, 12: 12–27.

Mitchell, R. K., Agle, B. R., and Wood, D. J. (1997). 'Towards a Theory of Stakeholder Identification and Salience: Defining the Principle of Who and What Really Counts', *Academy of Management Review*, 22(4): 853–86.

Molinsky, A. and Margolis, J. (2005). 'Necessary Evils and Interpersonal Sensitivity in Organizations', *Academy of Management Review*, 30(2): 245–68.

Moran, C. and Colless, E. (1995). 'Perceptions of Work Stress in Australian Fire Fighters', *Work and Stress*, 9(2), p. 410. Cited in the International Labour Organization discussion document, 'Public Emergency Services: Social Dialogue in a Changing Environment' (2003), 72. Available at: http://www.ilo.org/public/english/dialogue/sector/techmeet/jmpes03/jmpes-r.pdf

Morehead, A., Steele, M., Stephen, K., and Duffin, L. (1997). *Changes at Work: The 1995 Australian Workplace Industrial Relations Survey*. Melbourne: Longman.

Mouzelis, N. P. (2000). 'The Subjectivist-Objectivist Divide: Against Transcendence', *Sociology*, 34(4) November: 741–762.

Mueller, F. (1996). 'Human Resources as Strategic Assets: An Evolutionary Resource-Based Theory', *Journal of Management Studies*, 33(6): 757–85.

Munro, R. (1998). 'Ethics and Accounting: The Dual Technologies of Self', in M. Parker (ed.), *Ethics & Organizations*. London: Sage, pp. 197–220.

Murphy, R. (1990). 'Proletarianisation of Bureaucratisation?: The Fall of the Professional?', in M. Burrage and R. Torstendahl (eds.), *The Formation of Professions*. London: Sage, pp. 70–96.

Nahapiet, J. and Ghoshal, S. (1998). 'Social Capital, Intellectual Capital and Organizational Advantage', *Academy of Management Review*, 23(2): 242–66.

Nash, J. (2000). 'Safety Education: The Method is the Message', *Occupational Hazards*, 62(7): 33–6.

Naughton, R. B. (1997). 'Implied Obligation of Mutual Trust and Confidence', *Australian Journal of Labour Law*, 10: 287.

Nelsen, B. J. and Barley, S. R. (1997). 'For Love or Money? Commodification and the Construction of an Occupational Mandate', *Administrative Science Quarterly*, 42(4): 619–53.

Nelson, L. D. and Norton, M. I. (2005). 'From Student to Superhero: Situational Primes Shape Future Helping', *Journal of Experimental Social Psychology*, 41: 423–30.

Nelson, R. (1991). 'Why Do Firms Differ, and How Does it Matter?', *Strategic Management Journal*, 12(8): 61–74.

Nelson, R. R. and Winter, S. G. (1982). *An Evolutionary Theory of Economic Change*. Cambridge, MA: Belknap Press.

Noble, C. and Mears, J. (2000). 'The Impact of Affirmative Action Legislation on Women in Higher Education in Australia: Progress or Procrastination?', *Women in Management Review*, 15(8): 404–14.

Nonaka, I. (1994). 'A Dynamic Theory of Organizational Knowledge Creation', *Organization Science*, 5(1): 14–37.

_____ and Takeuchi, H. (1995). *The Knowledge Creating Company*. New York: Oxford University Press.

_____ and Teece, D. J. (2001). *Managing Industrial Knowledge: Creation, Transfer and Utilization*. Thousand Oaks, CA: Sage.

Noon, M. and Hoque, K. (2001). 'Ethnic Minorities and Equal Treatment: The Impact of Gender, Equal Opportunities Policies and Trade Unions', *National Institute Economic Review*, 176: 105–16.

_____ and Ogbonna, E. (2001). 'Introduction: The Key Analytical Themes', in M. Noon and E. Ogbonna (eds.), *Equality, Diversity and Disadvantage in Employment*. Basingstoke, UK: Palgrave, pp. 1–14.

Nussbaum, M. (1988). 'Nature, Function and Capability: Aristotle on Political Distribution', in *Oxford Studies in Ancient Philosophy* (suppl.), 145–84.

_____ (1990). 'Aristotelian Social Democracy', in R. B. Douglass, G. M. Mara, and H. S. Richardson (eds.), *Liberalism and the Good*. New York: Routledge, pp. 203–52.

_____ (1993). 'Non Relative Virtues: An Aristotelian Approach', in M. Nussbaum and A. Sen (eds.), *The Quality of Life*. Oxford: Clarendon Press, pp. 242–69.

_____ (1995). 'Aristotle on Human Nature and the Foundation of Ethics', in J. E. J. Altham and R. Harrison (eds.), *Essays on the Ethical Philosophy of Bernard Williams*. Cambridge: Cambridge University Press, pp. 86–131.

_____ and Sen, A. (eds.) (1993). *The Quality of Life*. New York: Clarendon Press.

NYC Strategic Plan (2004). Available at: http://www.nyc.gov/html/fdny/pdf/pr/2004/strategic_plan/executive_summary.pdf

Oakes, G. (1990). *The Soul of the Salesman: The Moral Ethos of Personal Sales*. London: Humanities Press International.

Oakes, L. S., Townley, B., and Cooper, D. J. (1998). 'Business Planning as Pedagogy: Language and Control in a Changing Institutional Field', *Administrative Science Quarterly*, 43(2) June: 257–93.

Oakley, J. and Cocking, D. (2001). *Virtue Ethics and Professional Roles*. Cambridge: Cambridge University Press.

Occupational Outlook Quarterly (2002). Spring, 46(1), cited in ILO (International Labor Organization) discussion paper, op. cit. Table 2.6, p. 18. Available at: http://www.polfed.org/

Ogbonna, E. (1992). 'Organizational Culture and Human Resource Management: Dilemmas and Contradictions', in P. Blyton and P. Turnbull (eds.), *Reassessing Human Resource Management*. London: Sage, pp. 74–96.

Ohmae, K. (1989). 'Managing in a Borderless World', *Harvard Business Review*, 67(3): 52–61.

Oliver, C. (1997). 'Sustainable Competitive Advantage: Combining Institutional and Resource-Based Views', *Strategic Management Journal*, 18(9): 697–713.

Organ, D. and Moorman, R. (1993). 'Fairness and Organizational Citizenship Behaviour: What are the Connections?', *Social Justice Research*, 6: 5–18.

Osterloh, M. and Frey, B. S. (2000). 'Motivation, Knowledge Transfer, and Organizational Forms', *Organization Science*, 11(5): 538–50.

Osterman, P. (1987). 'Choice of Employment Systems in Internal Labor Markets', *Industrial Relations*, 26(1): 46–67.

Oxenbridge, S. and Brown, W. (2002). 'The Two Faces of Partnership? An Assessment of Partnership and Cooperative Employer/Trade Union Relationships', *Employee Relations*, 24(3): 262–76.

Palmer, G. (1986). 'Donovan, The Commission on Industrial Relations and Post-Liberal Rationalisation', *British Journal of Industrial Relations*, 14(2): 267–96.

—— (1989). 'Corporatism and Australian Conciliation and Arbitration', in S. Macintyre and R. Mitchell (eds.), *Foundations of Arbitration: The Establishment of the Compulsory Arbitration System 1890–1914*. Melbourne: Oxford University Press, pp. 313–33.

Parker, M. (ed.) (1998*a*). *Ethics & Organizations*. London: Sage.

—— (1998*b*). 'Against Ethics', in M. Parker (ed.), *Ethics & Organizations*. London: Sage, pp. 282–96.

Parkin, F. (1979). *Marxism and Class Theory: A Bourgeois Critique*. London: Tavistock.

Patterson, G. (1989). 'The Evolution of the University', Occasional Paper # 2 Palmerton North: Department of Management Systems, Massey University, New Zealand.

Patterson, M., West, M., Lawthorn, R., and Nickell, S. (1998). *Impact of People Management Practices on Business Performance*. London: CIPD.

Payne, S. L. and Wayland, R. F. (1999). 'Ethical Obligation and Diverse Values Assumptions in HRM', *International Journal of Manpower*, 20(5): 297–308.

Peccei, R. and Guest, D. (2002). 'Trust, Exchange and Virtuous Circles of Cooperation: A Theoretical and Empirical Analysis of Partnership at Work', Management Centre Research Papers No 11. London: King's College.

Pedler, M., Burgoyne, J., and Boydell, T. (1991). *The Learning Company: A Strategy for Sustainable Development*. Maidenhead, UK: McGraw-Hill.

Peetz, D. (2004). 'The Decline in the Collectivist Model', Centre for Work, Leisure and Community Research and Griffith Business School—Department of Industrial Relations Griffith University, April 2004, Report prepared for Queensland Department of Industrial Relations, Brisbane.

Penrose, E. (1959). *The Theory of the Growth of the Firm*. Oxford: Blackwell.

Perkin, H. (1989). *The Rise of Professional Society*. London: Routledge.

Peteraf, M. and Shanley, M. (1997). 'Getting to Know You: A Theory of Strategic Group Identity', *Strategic Management Journal*, 18(S): 165–86.

Petersen, T., Saporta, I., and Seidel, M. (2000). 'Offering a Job: Meritocracy and Social Networks', *The American Journal of Sociology*, 106(3): 763–816.

Pfeffer, J. (1992). 'Understanding Power in Organizations', *California Management Review*, 34(2): 29.

_____ and Salancik, G. R. (1978). *The External Control of Organizations: A Resource Dependence Perspective*. New York: Harper & Row.

Pfeiffer, R. S. (1992). 'Owing Loyalty to One's Employer', *Journal of Business Ethics*, 11(7): 535–43.

Phillips, J. and Tooma, M. (2004). *Law of Unfair Contracts in NSW*. Sydney, NSW: Lawbook.

Phillips, R. (1999). 'On Stakeholder Delimitation', *Business and Society*, 38(1) March: 32–4.

_____ (2003). *Stakeholder Theory and Organizational Ethics*. San Francisco, CA: Berrett-Koehler.

Phillips, R. A. (1997). 'Stakeholder Theory and a Principle of Fairness', *Business Ethics Quarterly*, 7(1) January: 51–66.

Pinnington, A. H. (1990). 'Leading Your Team', *National Interactive Video Centre Occasional Studies 2*. London: NIVC.

_____ (1991). 'The Formative Evaluation of Interactive Video', Ph.D. thesis, Uxbridge: Brunel University.

_____ (1992). *Using Video in Training and Education*. Maidenhead, UK: McGraw-Hill.

_____ (2002). 'Pierre Bourdieu's Theory of Practice: Potential for Management Research and its Sense of Reason in Practice', Developing Philosophy of Management Conference, St Anne's College, University of Oxford, 26th–29th June.

_____ (2003). 'Organizational Culture: Liberation or Entrapment?', in D. Tourish and O. Hargie (eds.), *Key Issues in Organizational Communication*. London: Routledge, pp. 205–19.

_____ (2004). Book review of: Paul Kearns (2003). *HR Strategy: Business focused, individually centred*. Oxford: Butterworth Heinemann, *Asia Pacific Journal of Human Resources*.

_____ (2005). 'Learning in a Competitive Field: MBA Students' Improvised Case Studies of IHRM', *International Journal of Human Resource Management*, 16(4) April: 619–35.

_____ and Bayraktaroglu, S. (1998). 'Management Agendas for Technology-Based Learning: Four Exempla', British Academy of Management Conference, working paper track, University of Nottingham, 14th–16th September.

_____ _____ (1999). 'Technologies for Employee Development: Corporate Culturalism or Communication Overload?', in C. Fraser, M. Barker, and A. Martin (eds.), *Organisations Looking Ahead: Challenges and Directions*. Conference Proceedings: 265–271, Griffith University Logan Campus, Queensland, Australia, 22nd–23rd November.

_____ and Edwards, T. E. (2000). *Introduction to Human Resource Management*. Oxford: Oxford University Press.

_____ and Hammersley, G. C. (1997). 'Quality Circles Under the New Deal at Land Rover', *Employee Relations*, 19(5): 415–29.

_____ and Lafferty, G. (2003). *Human Resource Management in Australia*. Melbourne: Oxford University Press.

_____ Morris, T. J., and Pinnington, C. A. (2003). 'The Relational Structure of Improvisation: A Case Illustration of Corporate Video Production', *International Studies in Management and Organization*, 33(1) Spring: 10–33.

Pittard, M. J. (1994). 'International Labour Standards in Australia: Wages, Equal Pay, Leave and Termination of Employment', *Australian Journal of Labour Law*, 7: 170.

_____ and Naughton, R. B. (2003). *Australian Labour Law: Cases and Materials*, 4th edn. Sydney, NSW: Butterworths.

Podsakoff, P., Ahearne, M., and MacKenzie, S. (1997). 'Organizational Citizenship Behaviour and the Quantity and Quality of Workgroup Performance', *Journal of Applied Psychology*, 82: 262–70.

Polanyi, M. (1967). *The Tacit Dimension*. London: Routledge & Kegan Paul.

Pollit, C. and Bouchaert, G. (2000). *Public Management Reform*. Oxford: Blackwell.

Porter, M. (1985). *Competitive Advantage: Creating and Sustaining Superior Performance*. New York: Free Press.

——— (1990). *The Competitive Advantage of Nations*. London: Macmillan.

——— (1991). 'Towards a Dynamic Theory of Strategy', *Strategic Management Journal*, 12(S): 95–117.

Portus, J. H. (1958). *Development of Australian Trade Union Law*. Melbourne: Melbourne University Press.

Power, M. (1997). *The Auditing Society: Rituals of Verification*. Oxford: Oxford University Press.

Prior, P. (1985). 'Enforcement: An Inspectorates' View', in W. B. Creighton and N. Gunningham (eds.), *The Industrial Relations of Occupational Health and Safety*. Sydney, NSW: Croom Helm, pp. 54–60.

Provis, C. (1996). 'Unitarism, Pluralism, Interests and Values', *British Journal of Industrial Relations*, 34(4): 473–95.

——— (2001). 'Ethics and Industrial Relations', paper presented at the Australian Association for Applied and Professional Ethics, University of South Australia, Adelaide.

Purcell, J. (1987). 'Mapping Management Styles in Employee Relations', *Journal of Management Studies*, 24(5) September: 533–48.

——— (1997). 'Pulling up the Drawbridge: High Commitment Management and the Exclusive Corporation', paper presented to the Cornell Conference, Research and Theory in Strategic HRM: An Agenda for the 21st Century, October.

——— (1999). 'Best Practice and Best Fit: Chimera or cul-de-sac', *Human Resource Management Journal*, 9(3): 26–41.

——— and Ahlstrand, B. (1994). *Human Resource Management in the Multidivisional Company*. Oxford: Oxford University Press.

——— Kinnie, N., Hutchinson, S., Swart, J., and Rayton, B. (2003). *Understanding the People and Performance Link: Unlocking the Black Box*. London: CIPD.

Quinlan, M. and Gardner, M. (1990). 'Researching Australian Industrial Relations in the Nineteenth Century', in G. Patmore (ed.), *History and Industrial Relations*. Sydney, NSW: ACIRRT (Australian Centre for Industrial Relations Research and Teaching) Monograph No.1, University of Sydney, pp. 55–87.

Radin, M. J. (1996). *Contested Commodities: The Trouble with Trade in Sex, Children, Body Parts and Other Things*. Cambridge, MA: Harvard University Press.

Rafaeli, A. and Sutton, R. I. (1987). 'Expression of Emotion as Part of the Work Role', *Academy of Management Review*, 12(1): 23–37.

Ramm, T. (1986). 'Laissez-Faire and State Protection of Workers,' in B. Hepple (ed.), *The Making of Labour Law in Europe: A Comparative Study of Nine Countries up to 1945*. London: Mansell Publishing, pp. 73–113.

Ramsay, H., Scholarios, D., and Harley, B. (2000). 'Employees and High-Performance Work Systems: Testing Inside The Black Box', *British Journal of Industrial Relations*, 38(4): 501–31.

Rawls, J. (1955). 'Two Concepts of Rules', *Philosophical Review*, 64: 3–32.

_____ (1971). *A Theory of Justice*. Oxford: Oxford University Press.

_____ (1993). *Political Liberalism*. New York, NY: Columbia University Press.

Ray, D. E. (1997). 'Title VII Retaliation Cases: Creating a New Protected Class', *University of Pittsburgh Law Review*, 58: 405–34.

Reed, M. (1996). 'Expert Power and Control in Late Modernity', *Organization Studies*, 17(4): 573–98.

_____ (1999). 'From the Cage to the Gaze?', in G. Morgan and L. Engwall (eds.), *Regulation and Organization*. London: Routledge, pp. 27–49.

_____ (2002). 'New Managerialism, Professional Power and Organisational Governance in UK Universities', in A. Amaral, G. Jones, and B. Karseth (eds.), *Governing Higher Education: National Perspectives on Institutional Governance*. Dordrecht, The Netherlands: Kluwer, pp. 181–203.

_____ (2004). 'Engineers of Human Souls, Faceless Technocrats or Merchants of Morality?: Changing Professional Forms and Identities in the Face of the Neo-Liberal Challenge,' 20th EGOS Colloquium, Lubljana, Slovenia, 1st–3rd July, Sub-Theme: *Professional Service Organizations and Knowledge Intensive Work*, Convener Celeste. P. M. Wilderom.

Reed, R. and DeFillippi, R. (1990). 'Causal Ambiguity, Barriers to Imitation, and Sustainable Competitive Advantage', *Academy of Management Review*, 15(1): 88–102.

Reich, R. B. (1991). *The Work of Nations*. New York: Knopf.

Reinhold, R. (2000). 'Union Membership in 2000: Numbers Decline During Record Economic Expansion', *Illinois Labor Market Review*, 6.

Riley, J. (2003). 'Mutual Trust and Good Faith: Can Private Contract Law Guarantee Fair Dealing in the Workplace?', *Australian Journal Labour Law*, 16: 1.

_____ (2005). *Employee Protection at Common Law*. Sydney: Federation Press.

Robens, A. (1972). *Report of the Committee on Safety and Health at Work 1970–72*. London: HMSO.

Robinson, S., Kraatz, M., and Rousseau, D. (1994). 'Changing Obligations and the Psychological Contract: A Longitudinal Study', *Academy of Management Journal*, 47: 137–52.

Rose, N. (1990). *Governing the Soul: The Shaping of the Private Self*. London: Routledge.

_____ (1991). 'Governing by Numbers: Figuring Out Democracy', *Accounting, Organizations and Society*, 16(7): 673–92.

_____ (1996). *Inventing Our Selves: Psychology, Power and Personhood*. New York: Cambridge University Press.

_____ (1999). *Powers of Freedom: Reframing Political Thought*. Cambridge: Cambridge University Press.

Rothschild, J. (2000). 'Creating a Just and Democratic Workplace: More Engagement, Less Hierarchy', *Contemporary Sociology*, 29, January: 195–213.

Rousseau, D. (1995). *Psychological Contracts in Organizations: Understanding Written and Unwritten Agreements*. Thousand Oaks, CA: Sage.

Rowan, J. R. (2000). 'The Moral Foundation of Employee Rights', *Journal of Business Ethics*, 24(2): 355–61.

Roy, D. (1958). 'Banana Time: Job Satisfaction and Informal Interaction', *Human Organization*, 18(1): 156–68.

Sartre, J. P. (1948). *Existentialism and Humanism* (trans. P. Mairet). London: Methuen.

Savage, M., Barlow, J., Dickens, P., and Fielding, T. (1992). *Property, Bureaucracy and Culture: Middle Class Formation in Contemporary Britain*. London: Routledge.

Scarbrough, H. (1996). 'Understanding and Managing Expertise', in H. Scarbrough (ed.), *The Management of Expertise*. London: Macmillan, pp. 23–47.

—— and Burrell, G. (1996). 'The Axeman Cometh: The Changing Roles and Knowledge of Middle Managers', in S. R. Clegg and G. Palmer (eds.), *The Politics of Management Knowledge*. London: Sage, pp. 173–89.

Schachter, S. and Singer, J. E. (1962). 'Cognitive, Social and Physiological Determinants of Emotional State', *Psychological Review*, 69: 379–99.

Schneider, B., Hanges, P., Smith, D., and Salvaggio, A. (2003). 'Which Comes First: Employee Attitudes or Organizational Financial and Market Performance?', *Journal of Applied Psychology*, 88: 836–51.

Schoenberger, E. (1994). 'Corporate Strategy and Corporate Strategists: Power, Identity and Knowledge Within the Firm', *Environment and Planning A*, 26: 435–51.

Schramm, J. (2003). 'A Return to Ethics?', *HR Magazine*, 48(7): 144.

Schuler, R. S. (1995). *Managing Human Resources*, 5th edn. Minneapolis/St Paul, MN: West Publishing Company.

—— (2001). 'Human Resource Issues and Activities in International Joint Venture', *International Journal of Human Resource Management*, 12(1) February: 1–52.

Schulz, M. and Jobe, L. A. (2001). 'Codification and Tacitness as Knowledge Management Strategies: An Empirical Exploration', *Journal of International Management*, 12: 139–65.

Shultz, T. and Brender-Ilan, Y. (2004). 'Beyond Justice: Introducing Personal Moral Philosophies to Ethical Evaluations of Human Resource Practices', *Business Ethics: A European Review*, 13(4): 302–16.

Schultze, U. and Stabell, C. (2004). 'Knowing What You Don't Know? Discourses and Contradictions in Knowledge Management Research', *Journal of Management Studies*, 41: 549–73.

Schumann, P. L. (2001). 'A Moral Principles Framework for Human Resource Management Ethics', *Human Resource Management Review*, 11(1/2): 93.

Schumpeter, J. A. (1950). *Capitalism, Socialism & Democracy*. New York: Harper & Row.

Scott, A. (1994). *Willing Slaves? British Workers Under Human Resource Management*. Cambridge: Cambridge University Press.

Scott, J. (1997). *Corporate Business and Capitalist Classes*. London: Routledge.

Seabright, M. A. and Schminke, M. (2002). 'Immoral Imagination and Revenge in Organizations', *Journal of Business Ethics*, 38(1/2): 19–31.

Selznick, P. (1969). *Law, Society, and Industrial Justice*. New York: Russell Sage Foundation.

Sen, A. (1992). *Inequality Re-Examined*. Cambridge, MA: Harvard University Press.

—— (1995). 'Capability and Well-Being', in M. Nussbaum and A. Sen (eds.), *The Quality of Life*. Oxford: Clarendon Press, pp. 30–53.

—— (1999 [1985]). *Commodities and Capabilities*. Delhi: Oxford University Press.

Senge, P. (1990). *The Fifth Discipline: The Art and Practice of the Learning Organization*. New York: Doubleday/Currency.

Sennett, R. (1998). *The Corrosion of Character: The Personal Consequences of Work in the New Capitalism*. London: W. W. Norton.

—— (1999). 'How Work Destroys Social Inclusion', *New Statesman*: 25–7.

Shaw, W. and Barry, V. (2001). *Moral Issues in Business*, 8th edn. Belmont, CA: Wadsworth.

Sheppard, B. H., Lewicki, R. J., and Minton, J. W. (1992). *Organizational Justice*. New York: Macmillan.

Sher, G. (1987). *Desert*. New Jersey: Princeton University Press.

SHRM (2004). Code of Ethics. Available at: http://www.shrm.org/ethics/code-of-ethics.asp

Shusterman, R. (1999) (ed.). *Bourdieu: A Critical Reader*. Oxford: Blackwell.

Simon, D. (1954). 'Master and Servant', in J. Saville (ed.), *Democracy and the Labour Movement*. London: Lawrence & Wishart, pp. 160–200.

Sinclair, A. (2000). 'Women Within Diversity: Risks and Possibilities', *Women in Management Review*, 15(5/6): 237–45.

Sisson, K. (1993). 'In Search of HRM', *British Journal of Industrial Relations*, 31(2): 201–10.

_____ (1994). 'Personnel Management: Paradigms, Practice and Prospects', in K. Sisson (ed.), *Personnel Management*, 2nd edn. Oxford: Blackwell, pp. 3–50.

Skinner, W. (1981). 'Big Hat, No Cattle: Managing Human Resources', *Harvard Business Review*, September–October: 106–14.

Sklair, L. (2001), *The Transnational Capitalist Class*. Oxford: Blackwell.

Slinger, G. (2000). *Essays on Stakeholders and Takeovers*. Ph.D. thesis, Cambridge: University of Cambridge.

Smith, A. (1776; 1999). *The Wealth of Nations* (The Glasgow edition of the works and correspondence of Adam Smith). Oxford: Oxford University Press.

Smith, N. H. (1997). *Strong Hermeneutics: Contingency and Moral Identity*. London: Routledge.

Smith, T. (2003). 'Everyday Indignities: Race, Retaliation and the Promise of Title VII', *Columbia Human Rights Law Review*, 34(3): 529–74.

Snell, R. S. (1993). *Developing Skills for Ethical Management*. London: Chapman & Hall.

_____ (1996). 'Complementing Kohlberg: Mapping the Ethical Reasoning Used by Managers for Their Own Dilemma Cases', *Human Relations*, 49(1): 23–49.

Solomon, R. C. (1993). *Ethics and Excellence*. Oxford: Oxford University Press.

_____ (1997). *It's Good Business: Ethics and Free Enterprise for the New Millenium*. Lanham, MD: Rowman and Littlefield.

Sorell, T. (2002). 'Morality and Emergency', Proceedings of the Aristotelian Society.

Spry, M. (1997). 'Damages for Mental Distress and the Implied Contractual Term of Confidence and Trust', *Australian Journal Labour Law*, 10: 292.

Standing, G. (1999). *Global Labour Flexibility, Seeking Distributive Justice*. Basingstoke, UK: Macmillan.

Starbuck, W. H. (1992). 'Learning by Knowledge Intensive Firms', *Journal of Management Studies*, 29(6): 713–51.

Steedman, H. and Wagner, K. (1989). 'Productivity, Machinery and Skills: Clothing Manufacture in Britain and Germany', *National Institute Economic Review*, May: 40–57.

Stehr, N. (1994). *Knowledge Societies*. London: Sage.

Sternberg, E. (1997). 'The Defects of Stakeholder Theory', *Corporate Governance: An International Review*, 5(1): 3–10.

Stewart, A. (1995). 'And (Industrial) Justice for All? Protecting Workers Against Unfair Dismissal', *Flinders Journal of Law Reform*, 1: 85.

_____ (1999). 'The Legal Framework for Individual Employment Agreements in Australia', in S. Deery and R. Mitchell (eds.), *Employment Relations: Individualisation and Union Exclusion*. Annandale, NSW: The Federation Press, pp. 18–47.

Stiles, P., Gratton, L., Truss, C., Hope-Hailey, V., and McGovern, P. (1997). 'Performance Management and the Psychological Contract', *Human Resource Management Journal*, 7(1): 57–66.

Stoney, C. and Winstanley, D. (2001). 'Stakeholding: Confusion or Utopia? Mapping the Conceptual Terrain', *Journal of Management Studies*, 38(5) July: 603–26.

Storey, D. J. (1985). 'The Problems Facing New Firms', *Journal of Management Studies*, 22(3): 327–45.

Storey, J. (1987). 'Developments in the Management of Human Resources: An Interim Report', Warwick Papers in Industrial Relations, No 17. Coventry: University of Warwick.

_____ (1992). *Developments in the Management of Human Resources*. Oxford: Blackwell.

_____ (1995). *Human Resource Management: A Critical Text*, 1st edn. London: Routledge.

_____ (2001). *Human Resource Management: A Critical Text*, 2nd edn. London: Thomson Learning.

Strauss, G. (2001). 'HRM in the US: Correcting Some British Impressions', *International Journal of Human Resource Management*, 12(6): 873–97.

Streeck, W. (1987). 'The Uncertainties of Management in the Management of Uncertainty: Employers, Labour Relations and Industrial Adjustment in the 1980s', *Work, Employment & Society*, 1(3): 281–308.

Strong, T. (ed.) (1992). *The Self and the Political Order*. Oxford: Blackwell.

Sturdy, A. and Fineman, S. (2001). 'Struggles for the Control of Affect—Resistance as Politics *and* Emotion', in A. Sturdy, I. Grugelis, and H. Willmott (eds.), *Customer Service, Empowerment and Entrapment*. Basingstoke, UK: Palgrave, pp. 135–56.

_____ Grugelis, I., and Willmott, H. (eds.) (2001). *Customer Service, Empowerment and Entrapment*. Basingstoke, UK: Palgrave.

Sykes, E. I. (1982). *Strike Law in Australia*, 2nd edn. Sydney, NSW: Lawbook.

Taylor, P. and Bain, P. (1999). 'An Assembly Line in the Head: The Call Centre Labour Process', *Industrial Relations Journal*, 30(2): 101–17.

Terry, M. (1999). 'Systems of Collective Employee Representation in Non-Union Firms in the UK', *Industrial Relations Journal*, 30(1): 16–30.

Tesser, A. and Rosen, S. (1975). 'The Reluctance to Transmit Bad News', in L. Berkowitz (ed.), *Advances in Experimental Social Psychology*, Vol. 8. New York: Academic Press, pp. 193–222.

_____ _____ and Tesser, M. (1971). 'On the Reluctance to Communicate Undesirable Messages (the Mum Effect): A Field Study', *Psychological Reports*, 29: 651–4.

The Kingsmill Report (2003). *Accounting for People: Report of the Task Force on Human Capital Management*. London: DTI.

Thomas, M. W. (1948). *The Early Factory Legislation: A Study in Legislative and Administrative Evolution*. London: Thames Bank Publishing.

Thompson, G. (2003a). *Between Hierarchies and Markets: The Logic and Limits of Network Forms of Organization*. Oxford: Oxford University Press.

Thompson, P. (2003b). 'Disconnected Capitalism or Why Employers Cannot Keep Their Side of the Bargain', *Work, Employment and Society*, 17(2): 359–78.

Thrift, N. (1999). 'The Rise of Soft Capitalism', in A. Herod, G. Tuathail, and S. Roberts (eds.), *An Unruly World?: Globalization, Governance and Geography*. London: Routledge, pp. 27–71.

_____ (2002). 'Performing Cultures in the New Economy', in P. du Gay and M. Pryke (eds.), *Cultural Economy*. London: Sage, pp. 201–71.

Torrington, D. (1993). 'How Dangerous is Human Resource Management?: A reply to Tim Hart', *Employee Relations*, 15(5): 40–53.

_____ and Hall, L. (1996). 'Chasing the Rainbow: How Seeking Status Through Strategy Misses the Point for the Personnel Function', *Employee Relations*, 18(6): 81–97.

Tourish, D. and Pinnington, A. H. (2002). 'Transformational Leadership, Corporate Cultism and the Spirituality Paradigm: An Unholy Trinity in the Workplace?', *Human Relations*, 55(2): 147–72.

Townley, B. (1993). 'Foucault, Power/Knowledge, and its Relevance for Human Resource Management', *Academy of Management Review*, 18(3): 518–46.

_____ (1994). *Reframing Human Resource Management: Power, Ethics and The Subject at Work*. London: Sage.

_____ (2004). 'Managerial Technologies, Ethics and Managing', *Journal of Management Studies*, 41(3): 425–45.

Trevino, L. K., Weaver, G. R., Gibson, D. G., and Toffler, B. L. (1999). 'Managing Ethics and Legal Compliance: What Works and What Hurts', *California Management Review*, 41(2): 131–51.

Trice, H. M., Belasco, J., and Alutto, J. A. (1969). 'The Role of Ceremonials in Organizational Behavior', *Industrial and Labor Relations Review*, 23: 31–58.

Truss, C., Gratton, L., Hope-Hailey, V., McGovern, P., and Stiles, P. (1997). 'Soft and Hard Models of Human Resource Management: A Reappraisal', *Journal of Management Studies*, 34(1) January: 53–73.

Tsoukas, H. (1996). 'The Firm as a Distributed Knowledge System: A Constructionist Approach', *Strategic Management Journal*, 17 (special issue): 11–25.

TUC (Trade Union Congress) (1999). *Partners for Progress: New Unionism in the Workplace*. London: TUC.

Tversky, A. and Kahneman, D. (1992). 'Advances in Prospect Theory: Cumulative Representations of Uncertainty', *Journal of Risk and Uncertainty*, 5: 297–323.

Tyler, M. and Taylor, S. (2001). 'Juggling Justice and Care: Gendered Customer Service in the Contemporary Airline Industry', in A. Sturdy, I. Grugelis, and H. Willmott (eds.), *Customer Service, Empowerment and Entrapment*. Basingstoke, UK: Palgrave Macmillan, pp. 60–78.

Tyler, T. R. (1999). 'Why People Cooperate with Organizations: An Identity-Based Perspective', in B. M. Staw and R. I. Sutton (eds.), *Research in Organizational Behavior*. Greenwich, CT: JAI Press, pp. 201–46.

_____ and Lind, E. A. (1992). 'A Relational Model of Authority in Groups', in M. Zanna (ed.), *Advances in Experimental Social Psychology*, 25: 115–92.

UK Commission for Health Improvement (2003). Available at: http://www.healthcare-commission.org.uk/assetRoot/04/00/00/52/04000052.pdf

Ulrich, D. (1997). *Human Resource Champions*. Boston, MA: Harvard Business School Press.

_____ and Beatty, D. (2001). 'From Partners to Players: Extending the HR Playing Field', *Human Resource Management*, 40(4) Winter: 293–307.

Undy, R. (1999). 'New Labour's "Industrial Relations Settlement": The Third Way? Annual Review Article', *British Journal of Industrial Relations*, 37(2) June: 315–36.

Vallacher, R. R. and Wegner, D. M. (1987). 'What Do People Think They're Doing? Action Identification and Human Behavior', *Psychological Review*, 94: 3–15.

Vallance, E. (1995). *Business Ethics at Work*. Cambridge: Cambridge University Press.

Velasquez, M. G. (2006). *Business Ethics: Concepts and Cases*, 6th edn. New Jersey: Pearson Education.

Veliyath, R. and Srinavasan, T. (1995). 'Gestalt Approaches to Assessing Strategic Co-Alignment: A Conceptual Integration', *British Journal of Management*, 6(3): 205–19.

Von Hippel, E. (1994). 'Sticky Information and the Locus of Problem Solving: Implications for Innovation', *Management Science*, 40(4): 429–39.

Waddington, J. (2003). 'Heightening Tensions in Relations Between Trade Unions and the Labour Government in 2002', *British Journal of Industrial Relations*, 41(2): 335–58.

_____ and Whitston, C. (1997). 'Why Do People Join Unions in a Period of Membership Decline?', *British Journal of Industrial Relations*, 35(4): 515–46.

Wailes, N., Ramia, G., and Lansbury, R. D. (2003). 'Interests, Institutions and Industrial Relations', *British Journal of Industrial Relations*, 41(4): 617–37.

Walsh, A. J. (2001). 'Are Market Norms and Intrinsic Valuation Mutually Exclusive?', *Australiasian Journal of Philosophy*, 79(4): 523–43.

_____ and Lynch, T. (2002). 'The Very Idea of Justice in Pricing', *Business and Professional Ethics*, 21(3/4): 3–23.

Walton, R. (1985). 'From Control to Commitment in the Workplace', *Harvard Business Review*, 63(2): 77–84.

Walzer, M. (1994). *Thick and Thin: Moral Argument at Home and Abroad*. Notre Dame, IN: University Notre Dame Press.

Warnock, M. (1966). *Ethics Since 1900*, 2nd edn. Oxford: Oxford University Press.

Watson, I., Buchanan, J., Campbell, I., and Briggs, C. (2003). *Fragmented Futures: New Challenges in Working Life*. ACIRRT, University of Sydney, NSW: The Federation Press.

Watson, T. J. (1977). *The Personnel Managers: A Study in the Sociology of Work and Employment*. London: Routledge.

_____ (1986). *Management, Organisation and Employment Strategy: New Directions in Theory and Practice*. London: Routledge & Kegan Paul.

_____ (1996). 'How Do Managers Think?—Morality and Pragmatism in Theory and Practice', *Management Learning*, 27(3): 323–41.

_____ (2001). *In Search of Management* (rev. edn.). London: Thomson Learning (originally Routledge, 1994).

_____ (2002). 'Speaking Professionally—Occupational Anxiety and Discursive Ingenuity Among Human Resourcing Specialists', in S. Whitehead and M. Dent (eds.), *Managing Professional Identities*. London: Routledge, pp. 99–115.

_____ (2003). 'Ethical Choice in Managerial Work: The Scope for Managerial Choices in an Ethically Irrational World', *Human Relations*, 56(2): 167–85.

_____ (2004). 'Human Resource Management and Critical Social Science Analysis', *Journal of Management Studies*, 41(3): 447–67.

_____ (2006). *Organising and Managing Work: Organisational, Managerial and Strategic Behaviour in Theory and Practice*, 2nd edn. Harlow: FT Prentice-Hall.

Weatherspoon, F. D. (2000). 'Don't Kill the Messenger: Reprisal Discrimination in the Enforcement of Civil Rights Laws', *Michigan State University Law Review*, 367–406.

Weaver, G. (2001). 'The Role of Human Resources in Ethics/Compliance Management: A Fairness Perspective', *Human Resource Management Review*, 11(1/2): 113.

Webb, J. (1999). 'Work and the New Public Service Class?', *Sociology*, 33(4): 747–66.

Webb, S. and Webb, B. (1902). *Industrial Democracy*. London: Longman.

———— (1920 [1894]). *The History of Trade Unionism*. London: Longman Green.

Weber. M. (1949). *The Methodology of the Social Sciences*. Glencoe, IL: Free Press.

——— (1978). *Economy and Society*. Berkeley, CA: University of California Press.

Webster, F. (2002). *Theories of the Information Society*, 2nd edn. London: Routledge.

Weick, K. E., Sutcliffe, K. M., and Obstfeld, D. (1999). 'Organizing for High Reliability: Processes of Collective Mindfulness', in B. M. Staw and L. L. Cummings (eds.), *Research in Organizational Behavior*, vol. 21. Greenwich, CT: JAI Press, pp. 81–123.

Weiss, H. M., Suckow, K., and Cropanzano, R. (1999). 'Effects of Justice Conditions on Discrete Emotions', *Journal of Applied Psychology*, 84: 786–94.

Westpac (2002). *Social Accountability Report*. Melbourne: Westpac Banking Corporation.

Wever, K. (1995). *Negotiating Competitiveness: Employment Relations and Organizational Innovation in Germany and the United States*. Boston, MA: Harvard Business School Press.

Whitley, R. (1999). *Divergent Capitalism*. Oxford: Oxford University Press.

Whittington, R., McNulty, T., and Whipp, R. (1994). 'Market-Driven Change in Professional Services: Problems and Processes', *Journal of Management Studies*, 31: 829–45.

Wiley, C. (2000). 'Ethical Standards for Human Resource Management Professionals: A Comparative Analysis of Five Major Codes', *Journal of Business Ethics*, 25: 93–114.

Wilkinson, A. (1998). 'Empowerment: Theory and Practice,' *Personnel Review*, 27(1): 40–56.

Williams, S. (1997). 'The Nature of Some Recent Trade Union Modernization Policies in the UK', *British Journal of Industrial Relations*, 35(4): 495–546.

Williamson, O. E. (1985). *The Economic Institutions of Capitalism*. New York: Free Press.

Williamson-Noble, J. and Haynes, K. (2003). 'Corporate Governance in Australia', *International Financial Law Review*, October. Available at: http://www.iflr.com/

Willmott, H. (1998). 'Towards a New Ethics? The Contributions of Poststructuralism and Posthumanism', in M. Parker (ed.), *Ethics and Organizations*, London: Sage, pp. 76–121.

Windolf, P. (1986). 'Recruitment, Selection, and Internal Labour Markets in Britain and Germany', *Organization Studies*, 7(3): 235–54.

Winstanley, D. and Woodall, J. (2000a). 'The Ethical Dimension of Human Resource Management', *Human Resource Management Journal*, 10(2): 5–20.

———— (2000b). *Ethical Issues in Contemporary Human Resource Management*. Basingstoke, UK: Macmillan Business.

Wittgenstein, L. [1889–1951] (1978). *Lectures and Conversations on Aesthetics, Psychology and Religious Belief*. Oxford: Basil Blackwell.

Wolin, S. S. (2004 [1960]). *Politics and Vision: Continuity and Innovation in Western Political Thought*. Princeton, NJ: Princeton University Press (first published, London: Garnett and Evans).

Wood, S. and Albanese, M. (1995). 'Can We Speak of a High Commitment Management on the Shop Floor?', *Journal of Management Studies*, 32(2): 1–33.

Woodall, J. and Winstanley, D. (2001). 'The Place of Ethics in HRM', in J. Storey (ed.), *Human Resource Management: A Critical Text*, 2nd edn. London: Thomson Learning, pp. 37–56.

Woodd, M. (1997). 'Human Resource Specialists—Guardians of Ethical Conduct?', *Journal of European Industrial Training*, 21(3): 110–16.

Woolf, A. D. (1973). 'Robens Report—The Wrong Approach', *Industrial Law Journal*, 2: 88.

Wright, P. M. and Boswell, W. (2002). 'Desegregating HRM: A Review and Synthesis of Micro and Macro Human Resource Management Research', *Journal of Management*, 28(3): 247–76.

———— Dunford, B. B., and Snell, S. A. (2001*a*). 'Human Resources and the Resource-Based View of the Firm', *Journal of Management*, 27(6): 701–21.

———— Gardner, T. M., and Moynihan, L. M. (2003). 'The Impact of HR Practices on the Performance of Business Units', *Human Resource Management Journal*, 13(3): 21–36.

———— McMahan, G. C., Snell, S. A., and Gerhart, B. (2001*b*). 'Comparing Line and HR Executives' Perceptions of HR Effectiveness: Services, Roles, and Contributions', *Human Resource Management*, 40(2): 111–23.

Yelnosky, M. J. (1999). 'Title VII, Mediation, and Collective Action', *University of Illinois Law Review*, 2: 583–629.

Young, I. M. (1990). *Justice and the Politics of Difference*. New Jersey: Princeton University Press.

Zajonc, R. B. (1965). 'Social Facilitation', *Science*, 149: 269–74.

Zipparo, L. (1999). 'Encouraging Public Sector Employees to Report Workplace Corruption', *Australian Journal of Public Administration*, 58(2): 275–8.

Zoffer, H. J. and Fram, E. H. (2005). 'Are American Corporate Directors Still Ignoring the Signals?', *Corporate Governance: International Journal of Business in Society*, 5(1): 31–8.

☐ INDEX